AUSTRALIANS **IN BRITAIN**

THE TWENTIETH-CENTURY EXPERIENCE

EDITED BY **CARL BRIDGE, ROBERT CRAWFORD** AND **DAVID DUNSTAN**

MONASH University
ePress

Published by Monash University ePress

Matheson Library
Building 4, Monash University
Clayton, Victoria 3800, Australia

www.epress.monash.edu.au

First published 2009

Copyright © 2009

All rights reserved. Apart from any uses permitted by Australia's Copyright Act 1968, no part of this book may be reproduced by any process without prior written permission from the copyright owners. Inquiries should be directed to the publisher.

DESIGN

AKDesign (*www.akdesign.com.au*)

COVER IMAGE

Australian nurses outside Australia House in London during the Second World War.

Courtesy of the Australian War Memorial Collection: Australian War Memorial Negative Number 002811.

PRINTER

Sydney University Publishing Service

This book is available online at:
www.epress.monash.edu/ab

ISBN 978-0-9804648-6-3 (pb)
ISBN 978-0-9804648-7-0 (web)

Pages: 256

AUSTRALIANS IN BRITAIN

THE TWENTIETH-CENTURY EXPERIENCE

CONTENTS

Chapter 1	More than just Barry, Clive and Germaine: An overview of Australians in Britain — *Carl Bridge, Robert Crawford and David Dunstan*	
Chapter 2	Australians and Britain in 2001: A demographic perspective — *Graeme Hugo*	
Chapter 3	Australian women in London: Surveying the twentieth century — *Angela Woollacott*	
Chapter 4	Australians in the England and Wales census of 1901: A demographic survey — *Carl Bridge*	
Chapter 5	Tom Roberts' London years — *John Rickard*	
Chapter 6	The Australian soldier in Britain, 1914–1918 — *Roger Beckett*	
Chapter 7	Reading the *British Australasian* community in London, 1884–1924 — *Simon Sleight*	
Chapter 8	'The crumbs are better than a feast elsewhere': Australian journalists on Fleet Street — *Bridget Griffen-Foley*	
Chapter 9	'Home' becomes away: Melburnians in Oxford in the 1920s — *Jim Davidson*	
Chapter 10	Australian books, publishers and writers in England, 1900–1940 — *John Arnold*	
Chapter 11	Australian tourists in Britain, 1900–2000 — *Richard White*	
Chapter 12	Part of the pageant: Australian tourists in postwar London — *Mathew Trinca*	
Chapter 13	Australian artists in London: The early 1960s — *Simon Pierse*	
Chapter 14	Tourists, expats and invisible immigrants: Being Australian in England in the 1960s and 70s — *Graeme Davison*	
Chapter 15	'We came on a holiday like you': The Australian community press in London in the 1970s and 80s — *David Dunstan*	
Chapter 16	Going 'OS' for the 'OE': Aussies, Kiwis, and Saffas in contemporary London — *Robert Crawford*	

A note about pagination and chapter identification

Page numbers in this book do not run consecutively across chapters. Instead, the page numbering restarts on the first page of each chapter and is prefaced by the chapter number. Thus 01.1 is chapter 1, page 1; 01.2 is chapter 1, page 2; 02.1 is chapter 2, page 1; 02.2 is chapter 2, page 2; and so on.

This system, in which page numbering is self-contained within each chapter, allows the publisher, Monash University ePress, to publish individual chapters online.

CHAPTER 1

MORE THAN JUST BARRY, CLIVE AND GERMAINE
AN OVERVIEW OF AUSTRALIANS IN BRITAIN

Carl Bridge, King's College, London
Robert Crawford, University of Technology, Sydney
David Dunstan, Monash University

Much is known about British migration to Australia[1] but little about the reverse phenomenon. To date, the handful of studies investigating this movement have tended to focus on the artistic rite-of-passage travels and exploits of well-known Australians. These range from the singer Nellie Melba and the poet Henry Lawson at the turn of last century to those equally notable Australians of more recent times who have followed in their footsteps, perhaps most famously represented by the larrikin intellectual storming of London in the 1960s by that cultural 'gang of four' Barry Humphries, Germaine Greer, Rolf Harris and Clive James.[2] Whilst it is difficult to overlook articulate and prominent individuals who may flaunt and, dare it be said, even make a profession out of their expatriate Australian 'identity', the focus on them leaves the vast bulk of Australians in Britain under-examined. These almost forgotten Australians include the middle-class tourists and soldiers of the first half of the century, and lesser and greater artists, writers, the people and public figures for whom Britain was a chapter in their life and a stage in their development. Perhaps more importantly, we should include those ubiquitous and often little known professionals, dentists, nurses and teachers, the backpacker bar workers and labourers, and today's merchant bankers, IT consultants and accountants.

This gap in the existing scholarship raises some interesting questions that so far have been ignored or glossed over. What relative weights should we put on each of these categories or social phenomena? Was the diaspora gendered? Was it class biased? How long did Australians stay and where? How much, if at all, did these things change over time? How have overseas experiences affected the lives and imaginings of these Australians? We might also ask whether the sequence of comings and goings has been a regenerative one, building further links over time. Indeed, to what extent have Australians seen Britain as a foreign country? Did the returning or just travelling community of Australians in Britain have a more intimate and dynamic relationship with the host society than other national groups? It is important to answer these bigger and wider questions and this book begins to do so. Demographic analysis must come first and the numbers are most revealing.

Table 1.1 tells us that there has always been a substantial Australian community in England and Wales (and other figures confirm that the same is the case for Scotland and Ireland). The numbers increased gradually from 1901 to 1961, almost doubled in the 1960s, flattened out in the 1970s, picked up again in the 1980s and leapt up by a third in the 1990s. As the cover illustration of this book and Angela Woollacott's chapter suggest, female Australians have long outnumbered their male compatriots. Bazza McKenzie's adventures in Pommieland have therefore been those of a distinct, if highly visible, minority. Age-wise, the average Australian in Britain has been consistently in her or his high twenties, which shows that most had made a conscious decision to leave Australia.[3]

Year	Male to Female ratio	Total
1901	3 to 4	21221
1911	3 to 4	23162
1921	3 to 4	26348
1931	4 to 5	28319
1951	NA	30718
1961	5 to 6	33120
1966	4 to 5	62040
1971	5 to 7	57000
1981	5 to 6	57141
1991	3 to 4	73217
2001	4 to 5	107871

Table 1.1 Australia-born in the England and Wales Census, 1901–2001
Source: UK Census data, 1901–2001

In addition to the numbers shown in Table 1.1 there have always been significant numbers of people born in Britain yet with substantial Australian experience. Of the 100,000 Britons who migrated to Australia between the world wars about a quarter came back and there was a similar return rate for the nearly half million who migrated in the 1950s and 60s. The extent to which these individuals continued to see themselves as Australian is, of course, a different matter. The number of Australians in the UK at any one time is further boosted by the presence of Australian tourists. Tourist numbers from Australia to the UK were between 5,000 and 6,000 p.a. between the wars. By 1950 the numbers had increased some five-fold to 30,000 and by 1968 they had skyrocketed to more than 250,000. Today there are some 800,000 short-term visitors each year.[4]

The pattern of settlement in the UK has generally been consistent, although there have been some changes in recent times. Census data shows that Australians have tended to live all over Britain with only a distinct minority concentrating in London, though the London concentration is gradually increasing. This pattern contrasts with almost all other migrant groups, but conforms to that for people from the old 'white' dominions. Calculated as a percentage of the population of the nation from which they came, Australians are, and have always been, second only to New Zealanders in the relative size of their migration to Britain. Much more work might be done in the area of comparative diasporas in the UK. This also invites the question of whether the Australians living in the UK can be viewed as a diaspora. During the first half of the twentieth century Australians popularly referred to Britain as 'Home', yet by the century's close, this notion had long since disappeared. Regardless of this conceptual shift, it is clear that across the century Australians in the UK consistently shared various defining features of diaspora as identified by the leading scholar in the field, sociologist Robin Cohen. They were dispersed from their 'original homeland'. They shared and nurtured a collective memory of Australia; and commonly had decided to leave Australia for employment purposes. These characteristics confirm their status as a diaspora.[5] For these reasons we and our contributors use the shorthand term 'Australian diaspora', alongside 'Australian expatriates' and 'the Australian community in Britain'.

The occupational profile of Britain's Australians over time provides further insights into who was arriving and for what reasons. In 1901, as Carl Bridge's chapter shows, the primary male occupations were retail, armed forces, clerical, the professions and living on their own means; while the main female occupations were housewife, domestic service, nursing and teaching. Fifty years later, the census reveals that Australia-born males were concentrated mainly in professional and technical work (including teaching), manufacturing, commerce and finance, defence and clerical, and that the women were on private means, in professional and technical work (including teachers and nurses), clothing manufacture, clerical, and personal service. Today two-thirds of both men and women are employed in professional and technical positions or in the City. Britain's Australians have been, for the most part, a skilled and talented slice of the energetic Australian middle classes and are increasingly so. Britain's long-term resident Australians, on the whole, men and women alike, were not free of duties, nor were they merely thrill seekers after liberation and fulfilment, and clearly they worked much more than they holidayed.[6]

The census data periodically offers insights into other aspects of the lives of Australians living in the UK, such as where they were living in London. In 1901 the top three concentrations were in Kensington, Lambeth and Wandsworth. In 1921 and 1931 they were in Battersea, Lambeth and Woolwich, and still in significant numbers in Kensington. By 1951 Earl's Court was known as 'Kangaroo Valley' and the Royal Borough of Kensington and Chelsea as 'New South Kensington'. Today, the top concentrations are in Westminster, Hammersmith and Kensington, with an emerging area in Wandsworth. Australians have always tended, then, to congregate in the relatively prosperous west and south-west. 'The Australian' pub in Chelsea was so-named as it was the favourite haunt of the Australian cricket team in 1882. The Australian High Commissioner's residence, 'Stoke Lodge', purchased just after the Second World War, is in Kensington, near the Royal Albert Hall. A 'Kangaroo Club' nightclub was operating in Earl's Court in the 1950s, and that famous drinking institution, 'The Church', was established in Fulham in 1979. The first of the Walkabout chain of bars started up in 1994 in Covent Garden, whilst the branch in Shepherds Bush, better known as the 'She Bu Walkie', is currently one of the largest venues in the city catering for an Australian clientele.

Our book begins, as we have in this introduction, with the numbers. In their respective demographic surveys Carl Bridge and Graeme Hugo interrogate the official statistics for what they reveal about the type of Australian who has decided to head to the Old Dart. Bridge and Hugo provide an overview of patterns that have occurred over the course of the twentieth century. While the two chapters reveal various changes, they are perhaps more revealing for the consistencies that they share. Both reveal that females continue to outnumber males; that their average age remains in the late twenties; and that a greater proportion of these Australians are employed in a skilled or professional capacity. These consistent trends suggest that the attractions of living in Britain speak to a select group of Australians. Each of the subsequent chapters explores different aspects of this appeal.

Most of the chapters in this collection highlight the ways in which the cultural heritage shared by Australia and Britain prompted so many Australians to move to Britain. Before the 1950s Australians popularly referred to Britain as 'Home' – even though few would ever make it there. For Simon Sleight's community of *British Australasian* readers, Britain *was* a 'home away from home'. From its beginnings as a financial and political digest of weekly affairs, the *British Aus-*

tralasian broadened its remit to include society news, travel and accommodation advice, sports reports, as well as listings of 'Australasians' sojourning in Europe. Long before the advent of such mass-market publications as *TNT Magazine* (discussed in David Dunstan's chapter 14), the *British Australasian* catered to the needs and preoccupations of the forebears of today's globalised young professionals.

Jim Davidson's Melburnians in Oxford in the 1920s went one step further. 'I'm thoroughly at home here now', declared a new expatriate, 'I fell in love with Oxford – indeed I lost my heart to all England'. This experience was not a uniform one. Going to Britain may have been an adventure but it did not require these Australians to immerse themselves in an altogether alien culture, let alone learn another language. Oxford was both a logical destination and a necessary rite of passage for an educated colonial elite. But as Davidson reveals the outcomes were not all the same. They were disappointing for some and seen even as academically unnecessary. Far from casting them in some new Imperial mould, the experience tended to help them to better define themselves as Australians. As this and other chapters reveal, learning the subtleties and nuances of life in Britain rather than the fundamentals proved to be the largest obstacle confronted by these Australians.

A common theme is the familiarity that these travelling Australians discovered they had with Britain. Despite living on the other side of the world, Australians were only too aware of Britain's geography. 'Arriving in London it was as if every reference point was familiar' observed Ruth Cracknell, quoted in Angela Woollacott's chapter. Cracknell goes on to describe the city as 'A monopoly board come to life, all the reading of the preceding twenty or so years making virtually every street and square and garden familiar'. Australia-born women outnumbered men in every available decennial year, as we have seen (Table 1.1). Sex discrimination was a common reason why Australian women left Australia, according to Woollacott, but colonialism, too, facilitated their move by 'both creating and validating their attraction to the imperial metropolis'. Richard White's tourists were similarly drawn by an overwhelming familiarity that stemmed from a lifetime of 'schools, newspapers, books, plays, cinema, radio, [and] political oratory'. It was, he writes, 'a validation of the known'. The excitement of finally seeing these famous places was equalled by the thrill of actually being there too. This buzz is conveyed by Graeme Davison's correspondents upon their arrival in London: 'We're very happy here: today we went into town – on a 97 horsepower scarlet painted London omnibus – and watched fascinated – like being in a book'. Even if it was only fleeting, the sense of being in a book or a postcard certainly captured the imagination of countless Australians.

Britain's status as centre of the empire proved to be another major magnet, particularly for the earlier generations of Australians who proudly regarded themselves as British. John Rickard's chapter on the painter Tom Roberts explores this relationship. Although Roberts was in fact an English expatriate, his movement 'to and fro between the centre and periphery' nevertheless illustrates the ways in which the Imperial capital occupied a prominent position in the hearts and minds of those living in the outer reaches of the empire. Through his painting he created more than one iconic image of Australian national identity and in so doing became one himself. But Roberts' Englishness was evident to his associates of the Heidelberg school who nicknamed him 'Bulldog'.

While the Second World War marked the beginning of the decline of the British Empire, Mathew Trinca's chapter nevertheless reveals that Australian visitors to Britain in the immediate postwar era remained loyal to the empire. 'As Australians reflected upon London's wartime valour they often accented the notion of a shared British nationality, rather than a subordinate position in an Imperial world order' concludes Trinca, revealing the way in which Australians accommodated their dual identities. An equally important aspect of the empire's centre was its geographic proximity to the Continent. Having travelled half way across the world, Australians recognised that for them Britain provided a convenient base for launching forays into the rest of Europe. Globalisation, mobility, communication technologies and the democratisation of tourism, Richard White points out, all contributed to a situation in which more Australians knew more people in Britain (other Australian visitors as well as British residents) than ever before.

Family and friendship networks within Britain further enhanced the arrivals' sense of familiarity with their new home. Many would spend their first nights in Britain with their formerly remote relatives, including, as Bridget Griffen-Foley reveals, the future media mogul Keith Murdoch. But Murdoch's first sojourn in London in the early years of the twentieth century was lonely and seemingly unfulfilled as he struggled to gain preferment in his chosen profession of journalism and to overcome a career-threatening stammer. Only later on his return did he find a place and rise to a position of eminence. Griffen-Foley's study of journalists covers a similar time span to Woollacott's of women. A tension emerges between work and leisure, between the exigencies of play and the dictates of career and personal self-fulfilment that were simply not possible in Australia. Griffen-Foley quotes the well-known Australian writer and journalist, Alan Moorehead, upon arriving in London in 1936, claiming the feeling 'that at last I was in the centre of the world instead of being on the periphery'. An almost unique version of the rite of passage were the 'ten bob a day tourists' of the Great War of 1914–18 outlined by Roger Beckett. Few of these soldiers were in Britain to advance their careers. However, the exploits of this 'workforce' both in Britain and on the battlefields across the Channel nevertheless reaffirmed the national rite of passage on the international stage. The Australian military, mostly airmen this time, would return to Britain a generation later during the Second World War. The concept of the tourist is in any case a problematic one, but doubly so as Richard White reminds us: Australians whose culture was 'British by default' could never claim to discover anything new. 'Travel to Britain was the necessary validation of the known rather than the discovery of the unknown'.

Some sojourners, of course, became a little too comfortable with their hosts' homes. 'Aware of the reputation of Australians for "botting" on their English relatives', Graeme Davison's well-mannered Australian subjects instead 'waited politely to be asked'. While kith and kin provided a solid support base, the chapters in this book imply that friendship networks had a greater impact on the individual's experience of London. Reflecting briefly on her own experience in London in the early 1980s, Angela Woollacott recalls that she, like the subjects of her chapter, also benefited from her network of friends: 'I had actually forgotten the density of this network until, in cleaning out my parents' house last year, I discovered letters I wrote home'. In addition to providing a place to 'doss' for those Australians lacking an accommodating relative, friends also provided a handy introduction to living in Britain – from buying a cheap meal to navigating the Tube. Unlike family, friendship networks were often dynamic. Living in a large city like London, for example, was a liberating experience. The anonymity and pace of life of the metropolis enabled individuals to escape their past, reinvent themselves, and to develop new careers and friendships. While some thrived on these opportunities, others suffered terribly from their own enforced anonymity.

Significantly, many of these friendship networks were also used to find the all-important job in Britain's familiar yet foreign work market. Britain offered enormous career opportunities to young Australians – using London to advance one's career was a central part of the rite of passage. For some, such as doctors, a stint in Britain was integral to their career, whilst others, particularly in the arts, hoped that the global city would be more accepting of their talents than their country of birth. Simon Pierse thus notes how Australians artists socialised 'at parties, in favourite pubs or … at the regular exhibition openings at London galleries' where 'contacts could be made and introductions given'. His focus is the 1950s and 60s when patronage, talent and a toleration of antipodean hubris resulted in sympathy and a vogue for Australian art in connoisseur circles. Similarly, Griffen-Foley notes how Australian journalists viewed a stint in London as both a necessity and an opportunity. Flocking to Fleet Street with their letters of introduction (and perhaps a couple of helpful tips from their journalist mates), they all hoped that their career would receive an enormous boost by snaring the next big exclusive. Only a few of them would realise this dream. A constant stream of writers and artists similarly headed for London in the hope that their British peers would recognise their talent but a small number were more interested in the size of the British market. As John Arnold's chapter reveals, a significant number of Australian authors in the pre-war era were able to reach a larger and more lucrative market through publication in Britain than they could possibly have hoped to reach in Australia. Arnold unearths the murky but commercially successful entrepreneurial publishing activities of some less than well-known figures in the British literary pantheon whose *metier* was exploitative pulp fiction and describes the associated cluster of Australian expatriate *litterateurs* and publishers.

The relationship was not, of course, all one-way. During the post-1945 decades, Australia's relationship with Britain underwent significant change. Britain was no longer 'Home' and was increasingly becoming a foreign destination. However, the end of the empire, Britain's entry into the European Economic Community, and the increasing republican sentiment in Australia did not halt the flow of Australians into Britain. The growing numbers of Australians entering the UK over the course of the second half of the twentieth century reveal that, despite ever tighter immigration laws, Britain had not lost its magnetic pull. The appeal though had changed. Australians were given the opportunity by cheap air travel to have in unprecedented numbers extended work and travel experiences in Europe in the 1970s and 80s. Mobile and wealthy through casual and temporary labour (both skilled and unskilled), the Australian immigrant community became well defined as part of a geographic enclave within the city's extensive cultural mosaic. As David Dunstan observes in his chapter, the Australian community press in London was reborn in the 1970s through catering to the needs of the new postwar generation of 'baby boom' backpackers. The duration of stay was in many instances dampened by the host community's increasing restrictions but with international travel experience now the norm, enhanced mobility became the defining experience. The Australian community press in these years especially was witness to new expressions of travel and tourism, popular culture, work, entertainment and leisure. This phenomenon was sustained by London's booming appetite for temporary labour and the attraction of cheap holidays in Europe.

During the latter decades of the twentieth century, fewer Australians were compelled to work abroad. Australian institutions now provided the necessary training for healthcare professionals whilst the government and audiences increasingly provided support for local artists and writers. However, the lure of Britain, or more specifically, London, continued to attract young Australians.

The dream of hopping on to 'escalator London' to advance one's career remains very much alive, thanks in no small part to the added incentive of earning a large wage in pounds. The effect, as Robert Crawford's chapter reveals, saw this generation become 'more professional, more likely to stay longer than the period of a two-year working-visa, and more integrated into the British community'. Young middle-class Australians were fortunate in having the skills required by burgeoning finance capital and the business skills markets. Such work has also stimulated further travel because these new age guest workers were also well-heeled experiential travellers. Cheap flights from the airports surrounding London meant that weekends were spent not only on the Continent but also in more exotic locations across Africa, the Middle East, and even North America. Tell-tale signs of this expanding Australian community were also becoming apparent in other ways, such as the setting up of the British Australian Rules Football League in 1990 and the creation of the *gumtree.com* community advertising website in 2000. More broadly, the recent emergence of the online lobbyist Southern Cross Group and of the Advance Global Professionals network has achieved wide penetration in Britain. The new generation of Australian immigrants, sojourners, expatriate workers or experiential travellers – the terms are interchangeable – lives in an increasingly 'wired' world. As testified by Ryan Heath, a card-carrying Australian echo-Boomer Generation Y iconoclast living and working in London. Heath argues that communities can exist without any physical anchor and in any number of changing locations, and that the internet is 'incredibly useful' as a resource for maintaining all-important friendship networks, which, if anything, are now more extensive, global and instantaneous.[7] Thus some verities remain. E-networks are networks nonetheless.

The chapters in this book move beyond the well-documented experiences of eminent 'baby boomer' public intellectuals and entertainers and function as an entry point to the wider Australian experience of living in Britain. Nevertheless, many Australian stories remain absent or are mentioned only in passing. Australia's sporting rivalry with the 'Poms', for example, has created a long history of Australian sportspeople arriving in Britain to represent their nation. The stories of those who were recruited to work for various Australian government agencies have similarly not found their way into this collection. And much more detail could be offered about the lives of the masses of Australian teachers, nurses and backpackers in Britain, which would emerge from a more sustained assault on the census data, a large scale oral history project and in-depth analysis of the records of the employment agencies. We have identified some dramatic changes in recent years but these require further work before they can be fully explained. More work of a comparative nature, looking at other immigrant and traveller groups, could be undertaken. A separate question perhaps beyond the scope of this study is what impact the Australian diasporic community has had on Australians' understanding of themselves. Unfortunately, the limitations of time and space have meant that we have been unable to address all of these issues – to this end, we encourage our readers to take up from where we have left off. Yet despite these gaps, we believe a cohesive story emerges throughout these chapters, revealing the nature of Australia's relationship with Britain as well as those changes that have taken place within Australia and Britain. Moreover, they reveal that this exchange of people, skills, and ideas has long been to the advantage of both countries. While the imperial connection is a thing of the past, this large and dynamic exchange confirms that the special relationship between Australia and the UK continues to thrive and is as much alive at the beginning of the twenty-first century as it was in 1901.

ACKNOWLEDGEMENTS

Many of the chapters in this volume are revised versions of papers given at the Research Workshop 'The Australian Diaspora in Britain since 1901: An Exploration', 29–30 September 2005, Australia House, London. This symposium was convened jointly by the Menzies Centre for Australian Studies, King's College London and the National Centre for Australian Studies at Monash University with assistance from the Monash Institute for Global Movements. The editors would like to thank Professor John Nieuwenhuysen, Director of the Monash Institute for Global Movements, and his staff for their support and Jean Dunn for her editorial contribution.

ENDNOTES

1. For some recent surveys see Jupp, 2004 and Prentis, 2008.
2. Prior studies include: Alomes, 1999; Bridge and Henderson, 2004; Britain, 1997; Fullilove and Flutter, 2004; Hassam, 2000; Nichols, 2007; Pesman, 1996; O'Reilly, 2007; Schultz, 2004; Woollacott, 2001.
3. UK Census data, 1901–2001.
4. Serle, 1950; Hammerton and Thomson, 2005; Jupp, 2004, 143; Alomes, 1999,167; L'Estrange, 2004; UK Census data, 1901–2001.
5. Cohen, 2008, 17.
6. UK Census data, 1901–2001.
7. Heath, 2006, 56.

PRIMARY SOURCES

UK Census data, 1901–2001.

REFERENCES

Alomes, Stephen. 1999. *When London Calls: The Expatriation of Australian Creative Artists to Britain*. Melbourne: Cambridge University Press.
Bridge, Carl; Henderson, Ian, editors. 2004. *Australia's Britain, Meanjin* 63 (3).
Britain, Ian. 1997. *Once an Australian: Journeys with Barry Humphries, Clive James, Germaine Greer and Robert Hughes*. Melbourne: Oxford University Press.
Cohen, Robin. 2008. *Global Diasporas: An Introduction*. Second Edition. London, New York: Routledge.
Fullilove, Michael; Flutter, Chloe. 2004. *Diaspora: The World Wide Web of Australians*. Lowy Institute Paper. No. 4. Sydney: Lowy Institute for International Policy.
Hammerton, A. James; Thomson, Alistair. 2005. *Ten Pound Poms: Australia's Invisible Immigrants*. Manchester: Manchester University Press.
Heath, Ryan. 2006. *Please Just F* Off It's Our Turn Now*. Melbourne: Pluto Press Australia.
Hassam, Andrew. 2000. *Through Australian Eyes: Colonial Perceptions of Imperial Britain*. Melbourne: Melbourne University Press.
Jupp, James. 2004. *The English in Australia*. Melbourne: Cambridge University Press.

L'Estrange, Michael. 2004. *The Australia-Britain Relationship Today: Patterns of History, Dynamics of Change, the Menzies Lecture 2004*. London: Menzies Centre for Australian Studies Kings College London.

Nichols, Dylan. 2007. *What Are You Doing Here? The Question of Australians in London*. Brighton, UK: Pen Press Publishers Ltd.

O'Reilly, David. 2007. *Britain's Global Australians: Sixteen Profiles*. London: Menzies Centre for Australian Studies KCL and Monash Institute for the Study of Global Movements.

Pesman, Ros. 1996. *Duty Free: Australian Women Abroad*. Melbourne: Oxford University Press.

Prentis, Malcolm. 2008. *The Scots in Australia*, Sydney: UNSW Press.

Schultz, Julianne, editor. 2004. 'Our global face: Inside the Australian diaspora', *Griffith Review* (6) (Summer 2004–2005). Meadowbank, Qld: Griffith University.

Serle, A.G. 1950. 'Great Britain and Australia, 1919–1939'. D.Phil. thesis. Oxford: University of Oxford.

Woollacott, Angela. 2001. *To Try Her Fortune in London: Australian Women, Colonialism, and Modernity*. New York, Oxford: Oxford University Press.

Cite this chapter as: Bridge, Carl; Crawford, Robert; Dunstan, David. 2009. 'More than just Barry, Clive and Germaine: An overview of Australians in Britain'. *Australians in Britain: The Twentieth-Century Experience*, edited by Bridge, Carl; Crawford, Robert; Dunstan, David. Melbourne: Monash University ePress. pp. 1.1 to 1.9. DOI: 10.2104/ab090001.

AUSTRALIANS AND BRITAIN IN 2001
A DEMOGRAPHIC PERSPECTIVE

Graeme Hugo, University of Adelaide
> Graeme Hugo is Professorial Research Fellow, Professor of the Department of Geographical and Environmental Studies and Director of the National Centre for Social Applications of GIS at the University of Adelaide.

> While there has been a strong gradient in UK-Australia migration from the former to the latter the counter-flow has long been significant. This paper traces the size and nature of the contemporary migration from Australia to the UK from a demographic perspective. It is shown that it has grown substantially in recent years including both permanent and long term moves. The size and composition of the Australian expatriate community in the UK is analysed using survey data. The diasporas connections with Australia are examined and some of its implications are explored.

While Australia is seen overwhelmingly as an immigrant nation it is also an important nation of emigration. More than a century ago, Ravenstein[1] put forward a series of 'migration laws', including one that 'each main current of migration produces a compensating counter current'. Although this observation has been consistently replicated, counter-currents remain under-researched. In the UK-Australia case there has been a pattern of circularity in migration for more than two centuries. One consistent component in this was the return of former settlers, both anticipated and unanticipated at the time of original migration. An insight into another element, however, is given by the novelist Miles Franklin in *My Brilliant Career* (1901) where her character, Robert Miller, moves to London to escape 'the prison of isolation' that was Sydney.[2] For much of the post-European settlement period of Australia's history a trip to the 'home country' was *de rigeur* for elite groups such as the intelligentsia and artists on the one hand, and the better-off on the other. Such movement was facilitated by the British Empire and Commonwealth linkages of the pre European Union period that made it possible for Australians to enter the UK easily and settle. Ian Britain and Storry Walton quote well-known Australians leaving in the early post-war years:

> Clive James left Australia because he had 'exhausted what challenges and comforts it could offer him'.

> Germaine Greer left because 'the outward bourgeois decencies, the "even tenor" of suburban life, became an offence when unmatched, unrelieved by any stimuli for the life of the mind'.

> Sidney Nolan felt he had no option but to leave Australia to escape the stultifying artistic and critical environment.[3]

However, overall emigration has reached unprecedented levels in recent years. This is apparent in Figure 2.1, which shows the increase in the permanent departures from Australia over the last few decades. The increase in recent years is apparent with the number of permanent departures between 2004 and 2005 being 17.1 per cent and the number doubling over the last decade. It is important to note the difference in trends between the overseas-born 'former settler' component of the exodus and the Australia-born element.

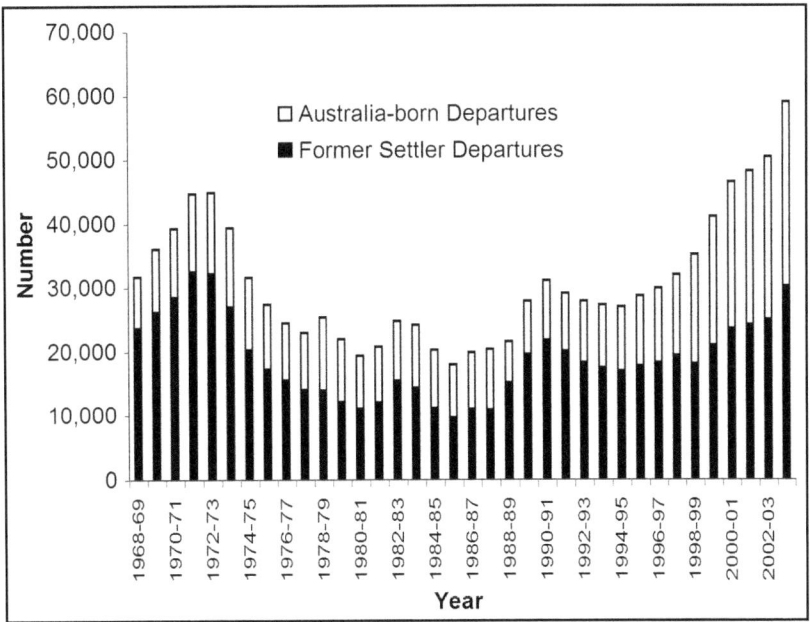

Figure 2.1 Australia: Permanent departures of former settlers and Australia-born persons, 1968-69 to 2003-04
Source: Department of Immigration and Multicultural and Indigenous Affairs [DIMIA] *Australian immigration consolidated statistics* and *Immigration update*, various issues; Commonwealth Bureau of Census and Statistics [CBCS] Demography Bulletins, various issues

Clearly, the Australia-born group has increased substantially in recent years. The distribution of destinations of the Australia-born and overseas-born groups leaving Australia between 1993 and 2003 are shown in Figure 2.2a and 2.2b.

In considering emigration from Australia it is important also to consider long-term migration. Figure 2.3 shows that this type of out-movement also has increased dramatically over the last decade or so, doubling since 1989. It will be noted that the Australian resident component of this emigration has particularly increased.

Turning to the UK, the pattern of permanent migration from Australia to the UK in recent years is depicted in Figure 2.4. For much of the early postwar years migration of former settlers has been the dominant element in emigration from Australia. Moreover, it should be noted that a part of the Australia-born emigration involves the Australia-born children of UK-born former settlers. It will be noticed in Figure 2.2 that the UK is an important destination both of returning settlers and of the Australia-born.

Looking first of all at the UK-born settler loss component of emigration to the UK, Figure 2.5 shows the permanent flows of the UK-born outside of Australia, and the largest flows were in the 1960s and early 1970s. This is the echo effect of the large UK immigration of the late 50s and early 60s. In the 1960s there was considerable concern in the Australian government about the issue of settler loss, especially as it related to British migrants. As a result there were a number of studies which investigated these issues[4] and the main findings were as follows:

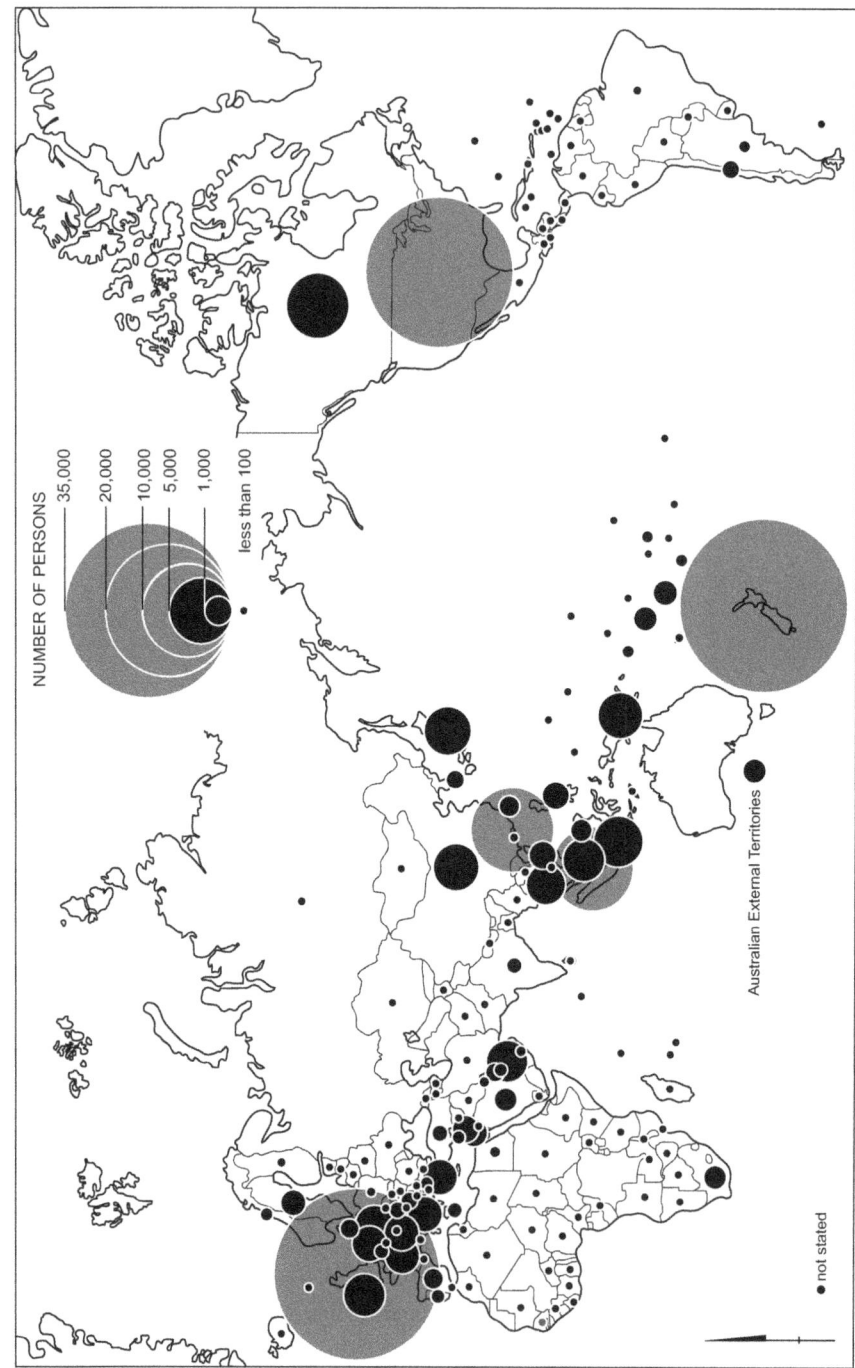

Figure 2.2a Country of destination of departures from Australia, 1993–2003 – permanent departures, Australia-born
Source: DIMIA unpublished data

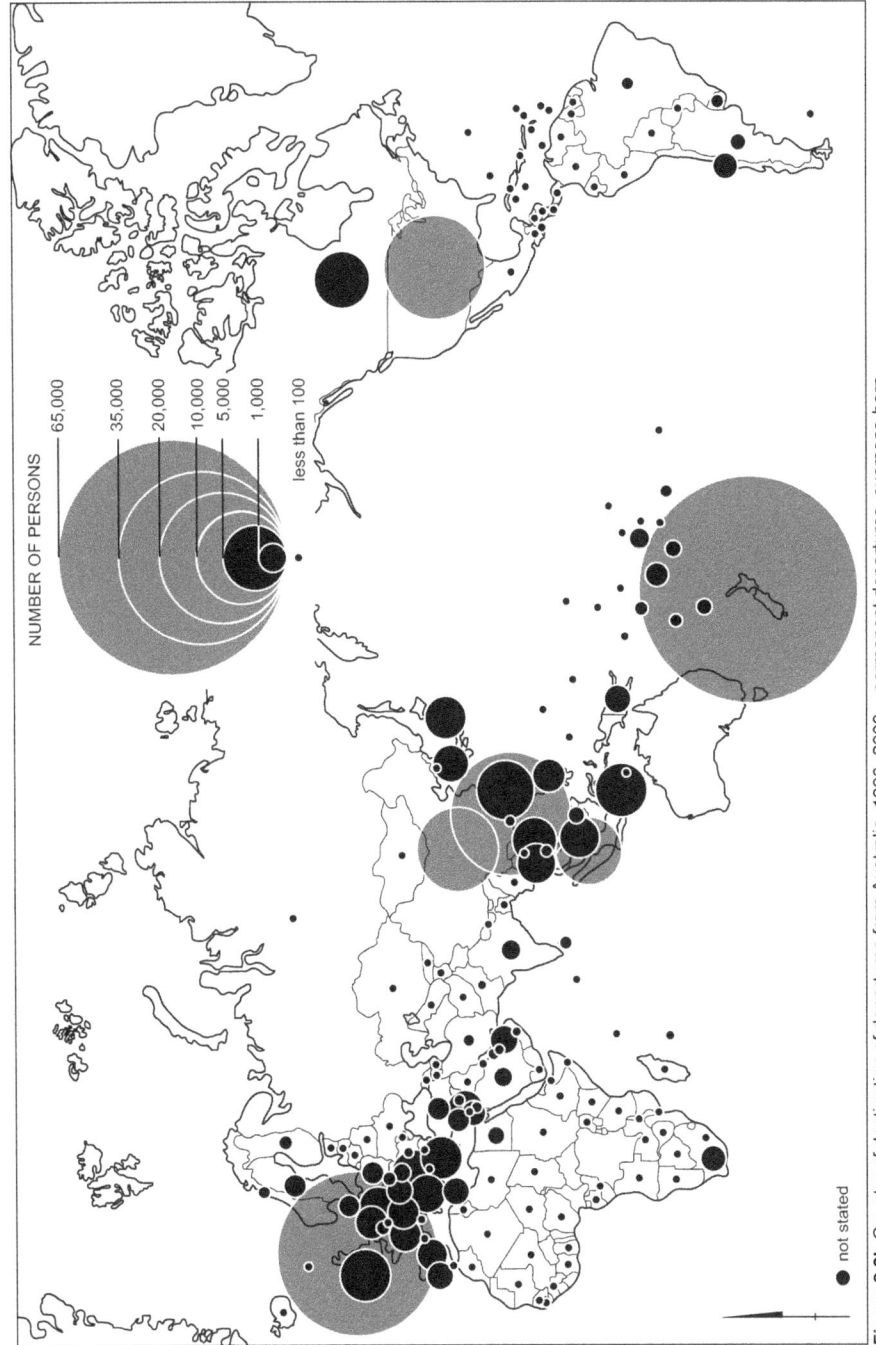

Figure 2.2b Country of destination of departures from Australia, 1993–2003 – permanent departures, overseas-born
Source: DIMIA unpublished data

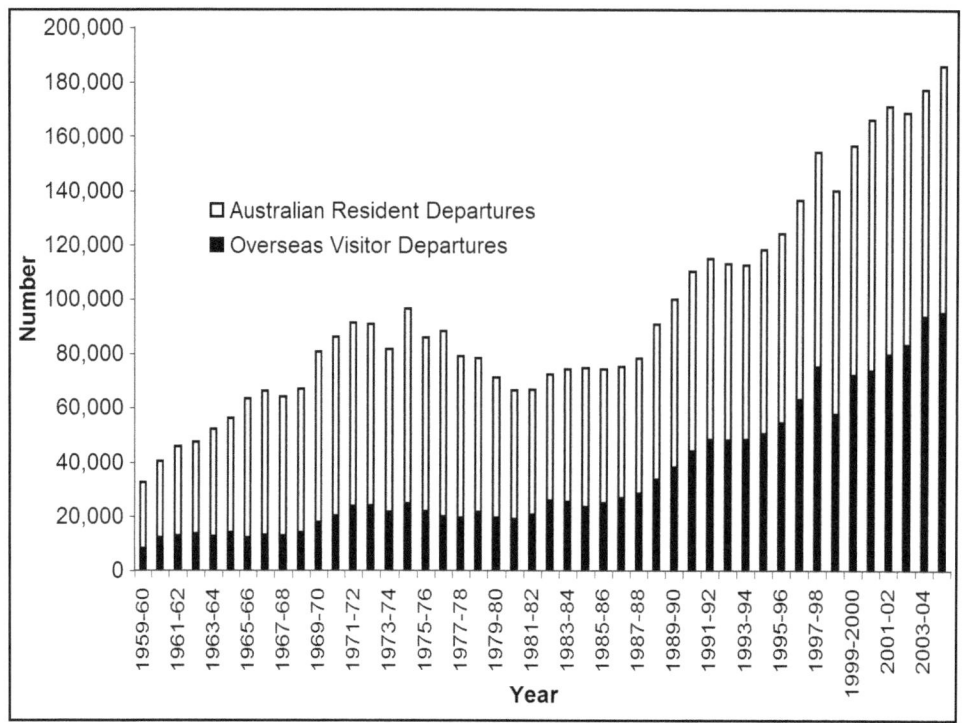

Figure 2.3 Australia: Long-term departures of Australian residents and overseas visitors, 1959–60 to 2003–04
Source: DIMIA *Australian Immigration Consolidated Statistics* and *Immigration Update*, various issues; CBCS Demography Bulletins, various issues

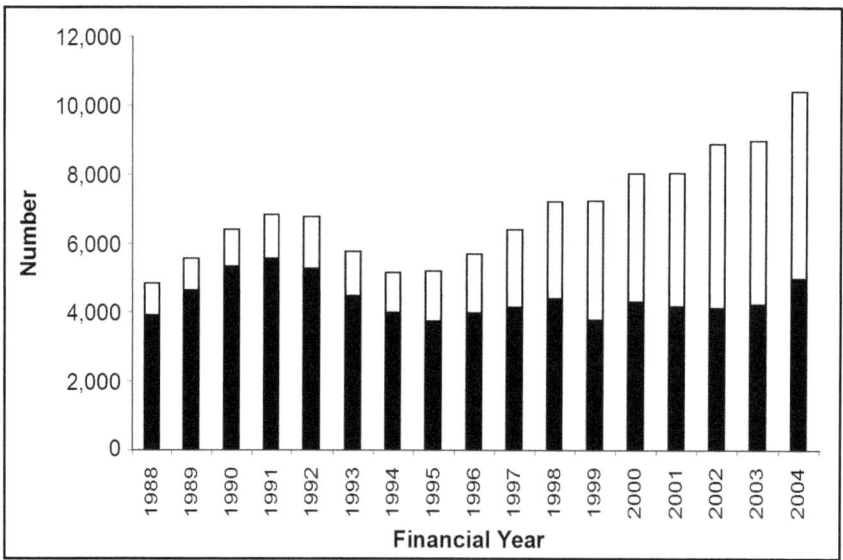

Figure 2.4 Australia: Permanent departures to the United Kingdom and Ireland by birthplace, 1988 to 2004
Source: DIMIA *Immigration update*, various issues

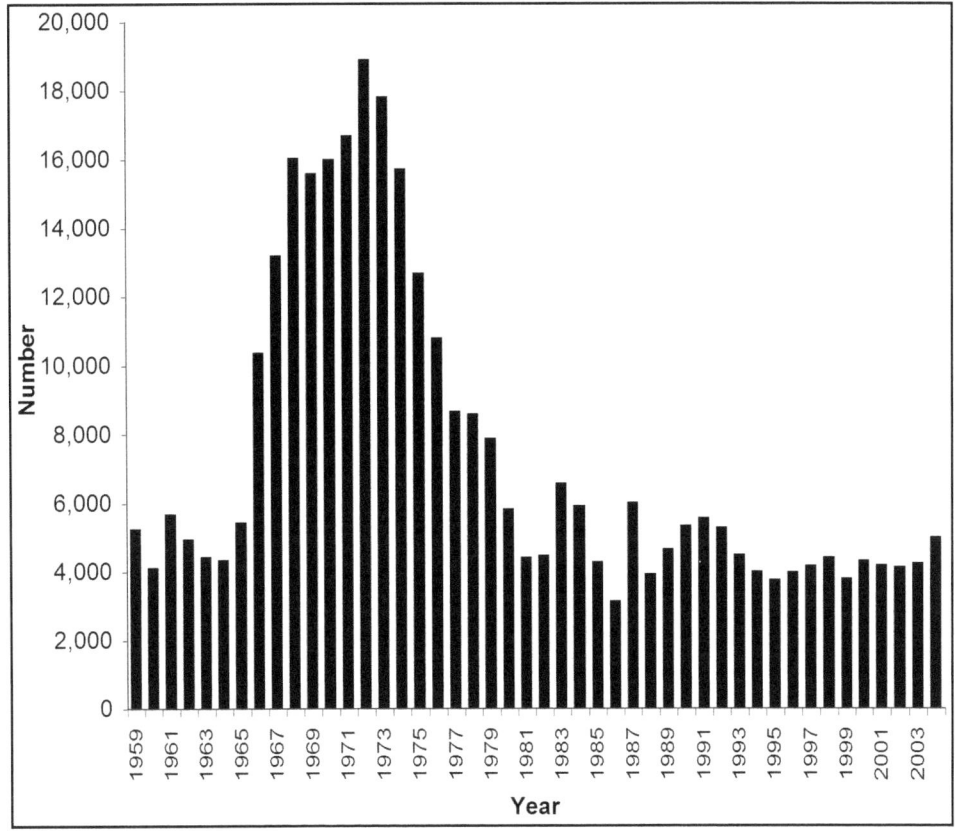

Figure 2.5 Australia: Permanent departures of the United Kingdom and Ireland-born, 1959 to 2004
Source: DIMIA *Australian Immigration Consolidated Statistics* and *Immigration Update*, various issues; CBCS Demography Bulletins, various issues

- In a study of immigrants arriving in 1959, some 15.3 per cent had returned to the UK by 1966–7.[5]
- Most decided to return within the first three years and quoted family reasons rather than economic factors.
- Another study found return rates of 22–24 per cent in the late 1960s (Immigration Advisory Council Committee on Social Patterns 1973).
- Highest rates of return were singles, males, professionals and skilled persons.
- There is a clear pattern of settler loss emigration reflecting the immigration patterns three to five years earlier.

A more recent set of data relating to settler loss is the Longitudinal Survey of Immigrants to Australia [LSIA], which interviewed a cohort of visaed immigrants arriving in Australia in 1993–95, and then a year later and again a further two years ahead.[6] Of the 5,192 proposed applicants in the initial survey 8.2 per cent (428) were from the UK. By the time of the third wave of interviews some 113 of the latter or 26.4 per cent were not contactable. Interviewers sought to categorise the non-contactable respondents and Table 2.1 shows that some 6.8 per cent of the original sample were found to have left Australia permanently and 5.8 per cent temporarily. An analysis of these data[7] had the following findings:

- The immigrants most likely to leave were those who entered Australia under the skilled business section of the migration programme.
- Immigrants from the UK had the second highest return rate to those from the USA.
- Those most likely to leave were highly educated with professional occupations.
- Most who left were in their 20s and 30s with a slightly higher representation of females.

Reasons	Number	Per cent
Unable to Track	26	6.1
Refused	8	1.9
Overseas Temporarily	25	5.8
Overseas Permanently	29	6.8
Other	25	5.9

Table 2.1 Reasons why principal applicants from the United Kingdom in Wave 1 were not interviewed in Wave 3
Source: LSIA

Figure 2.6 shows the age structure of the UK-born returning to the UK, and it is interesting that while the young adults identified in the LSIA study are apparent, there is also a strong representation of people aged 65 years and over. This is indicative of a significant retirement migration component in the settler loss. This is discussed in greater detail elsewhere,[8] but there are two components to this movement:

- People who migrated at an older age often to join their extended family but after the death of a spouse or a failure to adapt to Australia decide to return to their home country after a brief stay.
- People who migrated in the 1950s and 1960s as young, economically active individuals, reach retirement age and decide to return to their home country.

However, the majority of those leaving are in the workforce and, as Table 2.2 shows, they are concentrated in the higher skill areas. Nevertheless, it is important to point out that, as the Table shows, there is a substantial net migration gain of UK-born in all occupational groups especially the skilled areas.

Turning to the Australia-born component of the migration from Australia to the UK, it is apparent from Figure 2.7 that this has increased over the last decade or so. However, it is important to consider these data in conjunction with the long-term emigration of Australian residents. Figure 2.8 shows that the numbers of long-term departures of Australian residents increased rapidly between 1994 and 2002 and have since stabilised. Hence, overall there has been a substantial increase in the numbers of Australians of longstanding moving on a long-term or permanent basis to the UK. This is shown in Table 2.3 which shows the Australia-born permanent and Australian resident long-term departures from Australia to the UK in recent years. This upswing in movement is a function of two main developments:

- The *rite of passage* and elite migration of the past continues, but this type of movement has become more extensive and involves a wider range of groups than ever before, with a period working overseas becoming part of growing up for many young Australians.
- A new element, however, is career and work related migration. One important element of globalisation has been the internationalisation of labour markets, which has meant that whereas Australians previously restricted their search for work to within their state of residence or at most within Australia, many now operate in international labour markets.

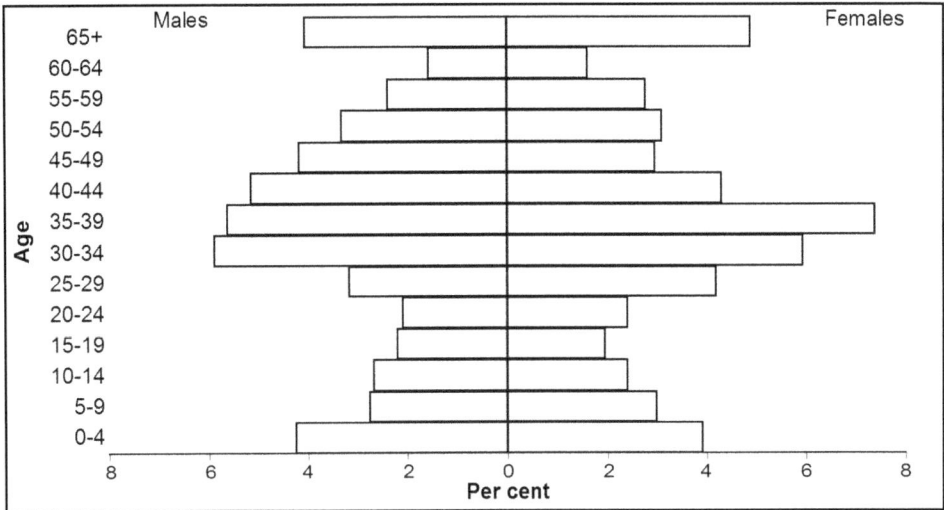

Figure 2.6 Australia: Age-sex structure of UK-Born settlers returning to the United Kingdom, 2003–04
Source: DIMIA Unpublished data

Occupation	Arrivals No.	Arrivals %	Departures No.	Departures %	Net Migration	Migration Effectiveness Ratio
Managers-Administrators	1,123	9.8	581	18.0	542	48.3
Professionals	5,010	43.6	1,377	42.6	3,633	72.5
Assoc. Professionals	1,058	9.2	258	8.0	800	75.6
Tradespersons & Related Workers	2,629	22.9	306	9.5	2,323	88.4
Advanced Clerks & Service Workers	319	2.8	124	3.8	195	61.1
Intermediate Clerical, Sales & Service Workers	912	7.9	400	12.4	512	56.1
Intermediate Production & Transport Workers	147	1.3	57	1.8	90	61.2
Elementary Clerical, Sales & Service Workers	215	1.9	104	3.2	111	51.6
Labourers & Related Workers	68	0.6	28	0.9	40	58.8
Total	11,481	100.0	3,235	100.0	8,246	71.8
Per cent in Workforce		61.1		66.8		

Table 2.2 Australia: Permanent arrivals and departures of United Kingdom-Ireland-born persons by occupation, 2003–04
Source: DIMIA Movements Data Base

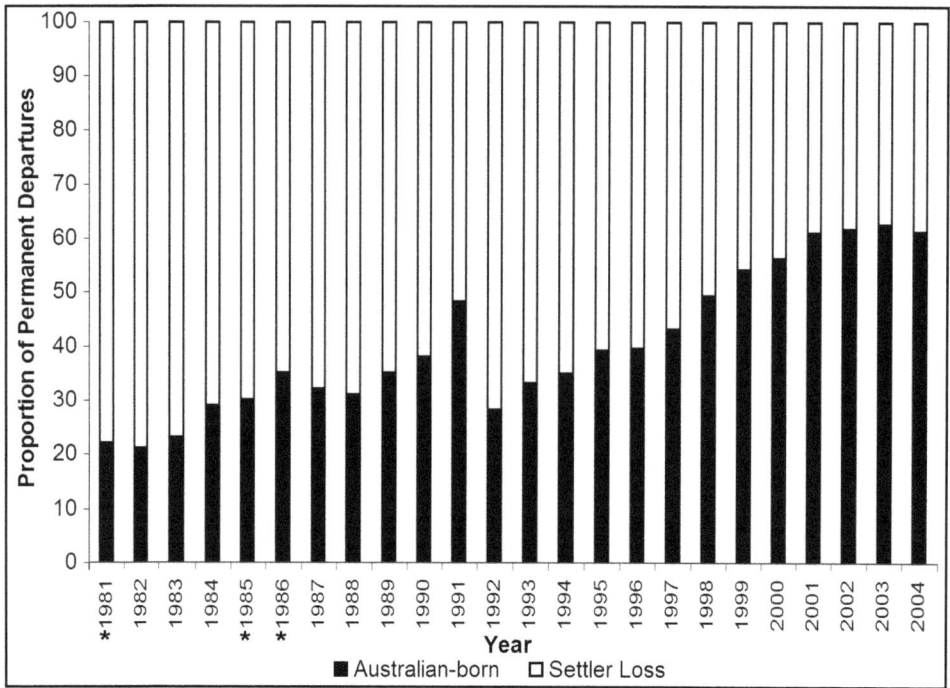

Figure 2.7 Permanent migration from Australia to the UK, 1981 to 2004
* Data incomplete
Source: Bureau of Immigration, Multicultural and Population Research Movements Data Base; DIMIA 2002 and Unpublished data

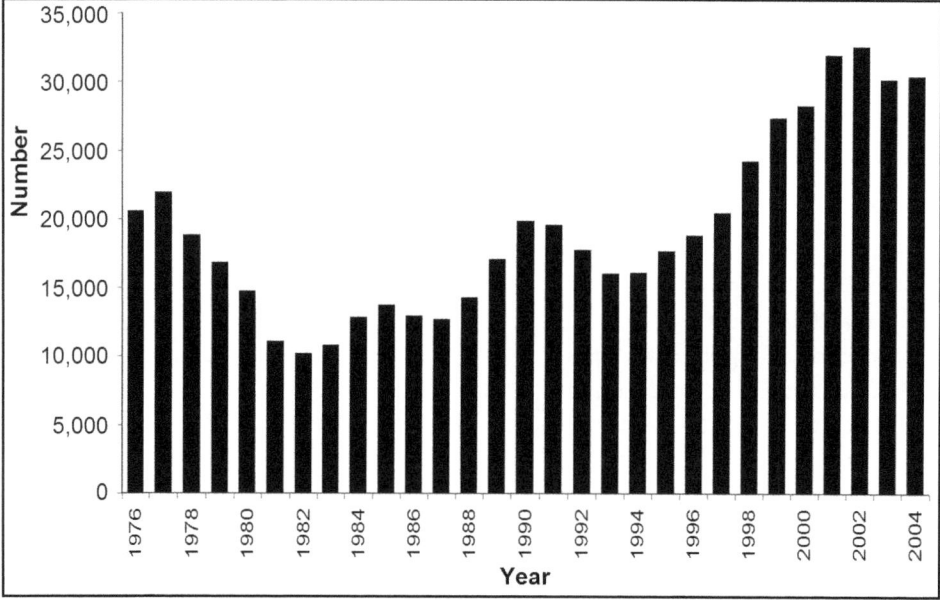

Figure 2.8 Australia: Long-term resident departures to the United Kingdom, 1976 to 2004
Source: Australian Bureau of Statistics (ABS) *Migration Australia*, various issues; DIMIA unpublished data

Year	Australian-born Permanent Departures	Australian Resident Long-Term Departures	Total
1991–92	1,759	17,732	19,491
1992–93	1,785	16,022	17,807
1993–94	1,681	16,074	17,755
1994–95	1,839	17,656	19,495
1995–96	2,039	18,773	20,812
1996–97	2,420	20,409	22,829
1997–98	2,961	24,188	27,149
1998–99	3,809	27,353	31,162
1999–2000	4,190	28,256	32,446
2000–01	4,776	31,931	36,707
2001–02	5,098	32,532	37,630
2002–03	5,244	30,131	35,375
2003–04	5,961	30,398	36,359

Table 2.3 Australian-born permanent departures and Australian resident long-term departures to the UK, 1991–92 to 2003–04
Source: DIMIA unpublished data

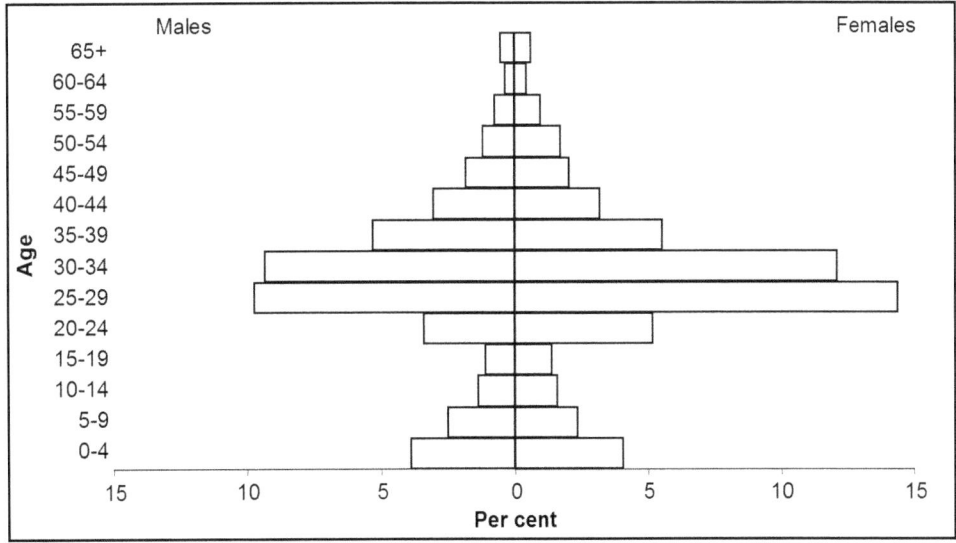

Figure 2.9 Australia: Age/sex structure of Australia-born emigrants to the United Kingdom, 1994–95 to 2003–04
Source: DIMIA unpublished data

The result has been an exponential increase in the numbers of Australians going overseas on a permanent or long-term basis. The most recent figures from DIMIA show that the overall number of Australia-born emigrants and Australian resident long-term departures has increased by 44.6 per cent in the last decade. It is apparent that the UK is their main destination.

Australian emigrants to the UK have a number of distinctive characteristics. Taking first of all the Australia-born permanent emigrants, Figure 2.9 shows the dominance of young adults in their 20s and 30s in the flow. The significant number of dependent children indicates that some move as families, but it also reflects the Australia-born children of returning UK-born former settlers. Another key feature is that there is a predominance of females, with the sex ratio among Australia-born permanent departures to the UK over the last decade being 80 males for every 100 females. This is an unusual pattern since males slightly outnumber females among all Australia-born emigration from Australia. It may be that this is a function of the greater involvement of *rite of passage* migration in the migration to the UK. Figure 2.10 demonstrates the difference in age structure between the returning settlers and the Australia-born departures to the UK showing that the former are more widely distributed across age groups while the Australia-born are overwhelmingly in their 20s.

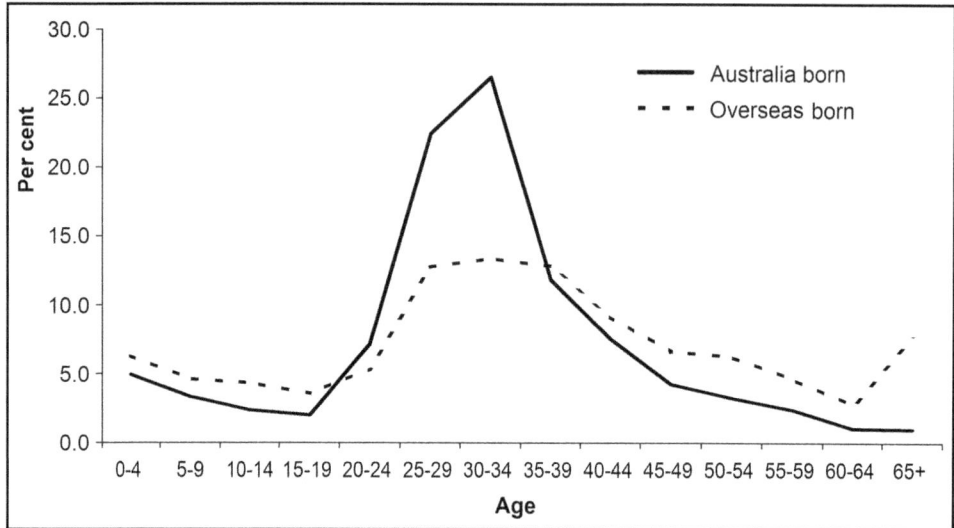

Figure 2.10 Age Distribution of Australia-born and overseas-born emigrants to the United Kingdom, 2003–04
Source: DIMIA unpublished data

Turning to the long-term departures to the UK, Figure 2.11 shows that this is absolutely dominated by those aged in their 20s, who account for 69 per cent of all movers. Clearly the *rite of passage* factor is dominant here. Moreover, there is a predominance of women with the sex ratio being 78.6 which also underlines this element. If we put together the age/sex information on all departures from Australia to the UK Table 2.4 shows a pattern somewhat different than that for all departures from Australia, particularly in two respects:

- There is an overwhelming emphasis on the 20–29 age group, which accounts for almost two-thirds of all permanent and long term migrants – twice the proportion for all departures. This is a factor assisted by the large number of *rite of passage* movers who go to the UK – often as the first stage to travelling to other countries.
- It is also noticeable that females substantially outnumber males, especially in the key 20–29 age group, again a reflection that Australian young women are more likely to engage in the *rite of passage* migration.

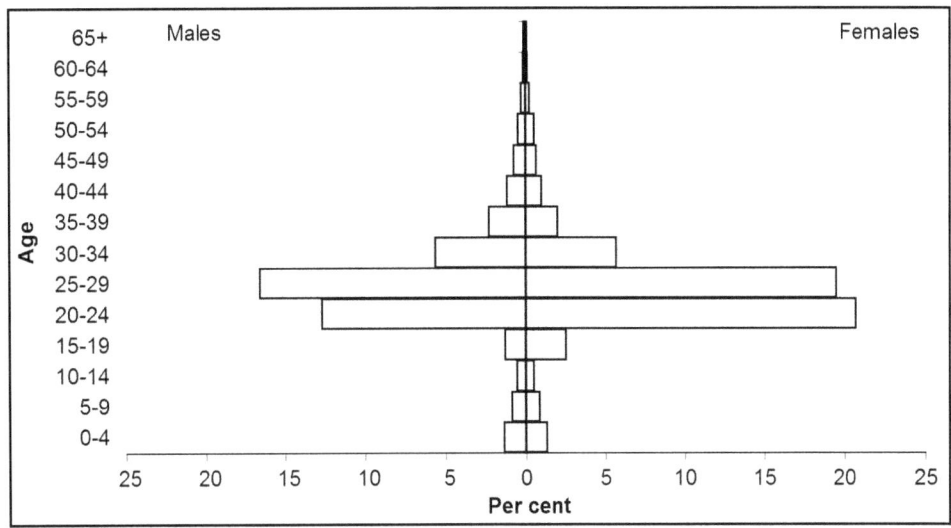

Figure 2.11 Australia: Age/sex structure of Australia-born long term resident departures to the United Kingdom, 1994–95 to 2003–04
Source: DIMIA unpublished data

Age	Males	Females	Total	Per cent
0–9	7,094	7,148	14,242	5.9
10–19	4,657	7,416	12,073	5.0
20–29	64,303	88,899	153,202	63.2
30–39	21,690	22,488	44,178	18.2
40–49	5,730	5,590	11,320	4.7
50–59	2,344	2,915	5,259	2.2
60+	912	1,075	1,987	0.8
Total	106,730	135,531	242,261	100.0

Table 2.4 Age/Sex Structure of Permanent and Long-Term Departures of Australia-Born to the United Kingdom, 1994–95 to 2003–04
Source: DIMIA Movements Data Base

It is apparent too that the Australian emigrants have a high skill profile. This is clear from the occupational structure shown in Table 2.5 which indicates that almost two-thirds of both permanent and long-term movers are in two categories. Firstly some 46 per cent were professionals. This group is especially important among the labour-market related migrants. The second largest group are in lower skill, clerical, sales, service and transport work, and largely reflect the *rite of passage* migrants. Managers and administrators are an important group and are clearly associated with labour market migration.

There is then a clear differentiation between the 'settler loss' and the Australian origin component of the migration from Australia to the United Kingdom. They are not only demographically different, but it is clear that their motives for migration are quite different as well. Hence, Table 2.6 shows that whereas family and life cycle factors dominate among the former settlers, it is the labour market and search for experience that are most significant among the Australia-born migrants.

Major Occupational Group	Australia-born Permanent Departures	Per cent	Long Term Resident Departures	Per cent
Managers-Administrators	759	16.0	2,652	10.2
Professionals	2,155	45.5	12,300	47.4
Assoc. Professionals	447	9.4	2,256	8.7
Tradespersons & Related Workers	234	4.9	1,959	7.6
Advanced Clerks & Service Workers	228	4.8	918	3.5
Intermediate Clerical, Sales & Service Workers	735	15.5	4,478	17.3
Intermediate Production & Transport Workers	31	0.7	310	1.2
Elementary Clerical, Sales & Service Workers	122	2.6	789	3.0
Labourers & Related Workers	25	0.5	267	1.0
Total	4,736	100.0	25,929	100.0

Table 2.5 Australia: Australia-born permanent and long term resident departures to United Kingdom by occupation, 2003–04
Source: DIMIA unpublished data

A.	**Emigration Involving Loss of Former Settlers**
	Retirement
	Other lifecycle events
	Failure to adjust economically
	Failure to adjust socially
	Changes in the origin country
	Changes in the Australian economy
B.	**Emigration of Other Australians**
	Employment transfer
	Other employment
	Extended working holiday
	Marriage migration
	Student migration
	Rite of passage
	Search for experience

Table 2.6 A typology of causes of emigration from Australia to the United Kingdom

While the main focus here is on people who have settled on a permanent or long-term basis in the UK, it is important also to examine briefly trends in short-term movement, for at least two reasons. Firstly, at any one time, a substantial proportion of the Australians in the UK are there on a short-term basis and it must be recalled that this group includes people who intend to stay away from Australia for up to a year, many of whom are *rite of passage* movers. Secondly, and importantly, it is clear from research that there are strong linkages between short-term, longer-term and permanent migration. It is apparent that a significant number of Australians in the UK come originally as short-term visitors. Figure 2.12 shows the increase in Australian resident short-term movement to the UK. In fact almost one in ten short-term departures out of Australia is directed to the UK. The growth in this movement has increased substantially in the last decade, with a lull due to the 9/11 and Bali Bombing incidents in the early part of this decade. The reasons given for travelling are presented in Table 2.7 and demonstrate strong family linkages between Australia and the UK, in that more than a third of trips are to visit relatives.

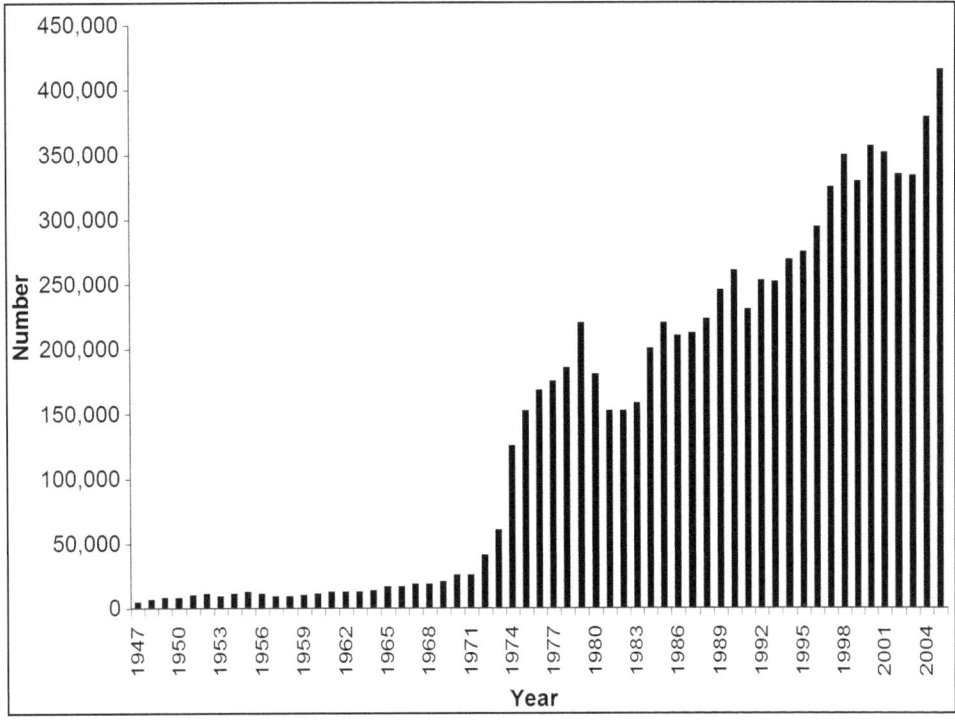

Figure 2.12 Australia: Short-term resident departures to the United Kingdom and Ireland, 1947 to 2005
Source: CBCS Demography Bulletins and ABS Overseas Arrivals and Departures Bulletins

	United Kingdom		Total		% to UK	Net Flow to Australia from UK
	No.	%	No.	%		
Transit/Student Vacation	424	0.1	5,345	0.2	7.9	-65
Convention	6,694	2.2	123,129	3.7	5.4	-422
Business	32,929	10.7	531,931	16.2	6.2	4,671
Visiting Friends/Relatives	108,899	35.3	860,589	26.1	12.7	99,413
Holiday	121,270	39.3	1,385,127	42.1	8.8	192,746
Employment	12,928	4.2	99,277	3.0	13.0	4,071
Education	4,012	1.3	42,804	1.3	9.4	1,031
Not Stated	6,365	2.1	66,880	2.0	9.5	5,414
Other	15,357	5.0	178,255	5.4	8.6	28,501
Total	308,876	100.0	3,293,336	100.0	9.4	335,361

Table 2.7 Australia: Short-term departures of Australian Residents to the United Kingdom and elsewhere by purpose of journey, 2002–03
Source: DIMIA unpublished data

THE AUSTRALIAN COMMUNITY IN THE UK

The immigrant population of the UK has increased from 2.98 million in 1971 (5.3 per cent of the total population) to 4.87 million (8.3 per cent). However, of the 1971 figure more than a quarter of the overseas-born, 0.71 million of them, were from Ireland and another 0.51 million were overseas-born but had UK-born parents and were mostly born in colonies. Hence in 2001 the overseas-born of the UK were a much more multicultural and diverse group. The Oceania-born population over that period increased by 119.8 per cent (compared with 64 per cent for the total overseas-born), from 78,200 to 171,900 persons.[9] The birthplace breakdown of the UK overseas-born population at the 2001 census is shown in Table 2.8. and this indicates that the Australia-born are the tenth largest group with only those born in Ireland, India, Pakistan, Germany, USA, Bangladesh, Jamaica, South Africa and Kenya being greater. At the 1991 census there were 73,336 Australia-born counted in the UK – a growth rate of 45.1 per cent over the decade of the 1990s.

However, it is clear that the UK census figures significantly understate the number of Australians in the UK, for the following reasons:

- The census includes only the Australia-born and many UK residents identifying with Australia and even having Australian citizenship were born elsewhere.
- Many of the Australians in the UK still identify with Australia and do not consider that they should be counted in the census.
- Some expatriates deliberately avoid being counted in the census.
- It excludes second, third and later generations.
- Hence, there are quite different estimates of the number of Australians in the UK and several commentators put it at 300,000.[10]

Country	Number of migrants
Ireland	537,108
India	467,634
Pakistan	321,167
Germany	266,136
United States	158,434
Bangladesh	154,362
Jamaica	146,401
South Africa	141,405
Kenya	129,633
Australia	107,871

Table 2.8 Top 10 countries of birth of migrants resident in the United Kingdom, 2001
Source: OECD database on immigrants and expatriates

Some insights into Australians in the UK can be gained from the results of a survey of 661 Australian expatriates.[11] Of those interviewed, some 21.2 per cent were born outside of Australia and 72.9 per cent have retained Australian citizenship, but 14.8 per cent intended to take up UK citizenship. The majority (92 per cent) are currently employed, most of them as professionals

(83.5 per cent). They are a relatively high income group as is evident in Table 2.9. The sample was selectively drawn from graduates of Australian universities so it is not surprising that 90.2 per cent had degrees. A third of the respondents were single reflecting the young age of the group with a quarter being aged less than 30 and 41.3 per cent in their 30s. Of the group 72.5 per cent left Australia at an age less than 30 years.

Annual Income (A$)	Per cent
Less than 50,000	18.8
50,000 – 99,999	33.1
100,000 – 149,999	18.5
150,000 – 199,999	12.2
200,000 +	17.4

Table 2.9 Australians in the UK: Current annual income in $A, 2002 (n=661)
Source: Australian Emigration Survey

One of the interesting features of the group is that of the almost two-thirds who were married, only one-third had a partner who was Australian and half had a partner who was born in the UK. Clearly one of the factors leading to more Australians living overseas on a long-term or permanent basis is the fact that more Australians are travelling overseas as a *rite of passage* as young adults and so many more meet and partner with a non-Australian. Hence, the proportion of Australians marrying non-Australians is increasing and the proportion of Australians with family loyalties and commitments extending trans-nationally is also increasing. A quarter of the total sample had married since they left Australia and 4.2 per cent had taken a partner outside marriage, while 39 had divorced and remarried while overseas. The family situation of the sample is depicted in Table 2.10 and again the young age of the group is evident, with almost one in five living in a group household and one in eight living alone. Only a quarter have children. This reflects the fact that a major part of the Australian community in the UK do not see themselves as staying permanently. However, more than a half either own (39.3 per cent) or are purchasing (12.6) their current place of residence in the UK.

Living Situation	Per cent
Single person household	13.9
Couple only household	39.5
Couple with children	24.9
Single parent	0.8
Other Group of related person	2.1
Unrelated group	18.7

Table 2.10 Australians in the UK: Current family status, 2002 (n=661)
Source: Australian Emigration Survey 2002

It is interesting to examine the reasons given by respondents for leaving Australia. Table 2.11 shows that overwhelmingly the motivations for going to the UK are work-related, with respondents stressing better employment opportunities, professional development, higher income, promotion, job transfer and partner's employment as the main causes for them going to the UK. However, the *rite of passage* factor is also evident in such responses as 'to travel the world', gain international experience, working holiday and lifestyle. Very clearly the expansion of the Australian community in the UK is strongly related to globalisation, the internationalisation of labour markets and the growth of London as one of the world's global cities.

Reasons	Per cent of Responses
Better employment opportunities	41.0
Professional development	40.2
Lifestyle	30.9
Higher income	29.5
Promotion/career advancement	24.5
Marriage/partnership	16.3
Overseas job transfer	11.6
Education/study	13.3
Partner's employment	10.4
To travel the world	15.4
Close family/friends	9.1
Gain international experience	4.5
Separation/divorce	1.7
Working holiday	1.2
To establish, relocate or expand business	1.5
Total (number)	661

Table 2.11 Australians in the UK: Reasons given by respondents for leaving Australia to live in the UK, 2002
Source: Australian Emigration Survey 2002

THE RELATIONSHIP OF THE DIASPORA WITH AUSTRALIA

With the increase in global international migration there has been a new interest in the formation of diaspora communities in destination countries. Much of the interest has been focussed on the rapid growth of communities from south countries in north countries and how they can be harnessed to facilitate development in their homeland.[12] Less attention has been focused on north-north migrations and the role of diaspora.[13] However, at least two points can be made with respect to this:

- Migrant communities from north countries living in OECD nations are increasing in size.
- The new information and communication technology facilitates them maintaining close and intimate contact with their homelands.

Let us now examine the relationship maintained by Australians in the UK with their homeland.

One of the most striking responses to both the survey being used here, and also in the in-depth interviews with Australians in the UK, was the strong level of identification with Australia, even among those with no intention of returning to live in Australia. Some 81.1 per cent in the survey indicated that they 'still called Australia home' and only 15.6 per cent did not. This was reflected in the strong reaction among expatriates about the dual nationality issue. Prior to 2002,

Australians had to give up their Australian nationality if they were to take on the citizenship of another country. Many expatriates, especially those who had partnered a non-Australian and whose children were born, and grew up, in other countries needed to gain the citizenship of their new country for their work. They expressed real anguish at having to give up their Australian citizenship. Two responses from UK respondents express this:

> I am not sure what you hope to determine in this study but I hope part of the results reflect the overwhelming expatriate anger at being disenfranchised by our government just because we chose to live in another country.

> The nature of what it is to be a citizen is changing as our world evolves. In my mind it makes little sense to penalise your citizens for taking advantage of global opportunities in a world where the market places of the globe are your customers. For countries to remain vibrant they need to allow their citizens the opportunities to live and work overseas and return home with ease. Allow dual citizenship or tri or quadruple citizenship. The reality is that more people are leaving than ever before, they will continue to leave. I know people that have taken up citizenship even knowing that they would lose their Aussie one. It didn't stop them although it did make them sad. Some were even angry that the government of Australia has the nerve to demand that you forgo your citizenship if you want to take that of another country.

Hence, Australian expatriates were at the forefront of the campaign which saw the Australian government eventually allow dual citizenship in 2002.[14]

The identities of Australian expatriates in the UK are complex. There are some who fiercely retain their Australian identity.

> I regularly struggle with the issue of national identity.

> It is important that people understand that you don't stop being Australian just because you don't live in Australia.

Others have been able to develop a trans-national or multiple identity involving both Australia and the UK.

> Being born, raised and educated in Australia set the values by which I live today. Had my wife and I had children we would have returned to Australia for their education.

For others there is a more complex pattern of identity. To some extent there may be a distinct identity as an expatriate as expressed by the novelists Nikki Gemmell and Caroline Brothers.

> Perhaps my husband and I are slipping towards some expatriate no man's land outsiders not only in the country we have chosen to live in but our own country as well. We wonder if we will ever settle contentedly into Australia again, and fear we won't. Perhaps we have entered, without even realising it, that strange state of exile where a memory of home is all we have left.

> Becoming an expatriate has also opened my eyes about the world in ways not available to me had I stayed at home. I am aware this life has a price – missing defining experiences, both public and private at home. But I characterise myself as an Australian member of an internationally minded community, who just happens to live her Australianism abroad.[15]

Others see themselves as a global citizen, albeit with a strong Australian streak.

> As the son of Irish immigrants, "home" was always Ireland. I am now told by my mother and my wife that Australia is now my "home". Cliché or not I regard myself as a citizen of the world but first and foremost – a Collingwood supporter.

What is clear is that Australians in the UK are able to maintain strong linkages with their homeland. Undoubtedly modern developments in information and communication technology such as email, cheap international phone calls, etc. allow people to maintain regular and intimate contact.

> When I open emails from loved ones, I hear the words read to me in their voices, their unique body gestures.

> My heart aches because it is pulled and stretched across seas, across lands, to encompass births, deaths, marriages, first homes, losing a job, gaining a job, major successes, major setbacks. When the phone receiver is replaced I smile in a distant land.[16]

Moreover, they can keep abreast of news, events and other developments in Australia. For example, the Australian Football League's website received 2.5 million hits each week during the 2004 season and of these a quarter were from outside Australia – 620,000 from the United Kingdom. In addition, the cheapening of air travel has seen visiting Australia, even from as great a distance as the UK, as being much more possible than ever before. Hence, only 15.1 per cent of respondents had not visited Australia since coming to the UK, and all of those are recent arrivals. Some 30 per cent have visited Australia more than five times. Ninety per cent of visits were to visit family in Australia.

Some 55.2 per cent of respondents indicated that they had intentions of returning to live in Australia and 30.1 per cent were undecided as to whether they would return or not. It is interesting to observe the reasons given in Table 2.12. It is notable here that job and economic factors are of little significance and the whole emphasis is on lifestyle and family. Indeed, some intending to return realised that they would need to make sacrifices in terms of salary and career. Others are torn between staying or returning because of career factors.

> I love Australia and want to return and hopefully make a contribution although I will need to compromise my career to do so.

> I'd just like to say that I wrote undecided (to the intentions to return question) even though I know I'll move back to Australia. But at present we don't know when or how as it depends on employment plus in order for my husband to get

a visa I will have to go there before my husband does and perhaps live and work there for more than six months.

We left Australia because in 1980–81, two PhDs in Physics in Adelaide had very little chance of getting reasonably equivalent jobs. We are still here because it is difficult to judge at a distance the costs and benefits of the return… I guess pragmatically we have emigrated but emotionally it feels more like an extended visit.

Reasons for Returning	Number
Lifestyle	90.4
Family	76.2
Work	15.6
Education	8.8
Other	2.5
Total (number)	365

Table 2.12 Australians in the UK: Main reasons for planning to return to Australia, 2002 (n= 661)
Source: Australian Emigration Survey 2002

It is interesting, too, that there has been an emergence of an increasing number of formal expatriate organisations of which some are international and others focus on a single country. These are becoming significant lobby groups in Australia, especially on issues influencing expatriates such as citizenship and voting rights.

One of the elements, which came through strongly in the survey among many respondents, was an ambivalence toward Australia. This is reflected by the head of one of the leading expatriate organisations:

> Many expatriates are bitterly disappointed at how Australians at home, and Australian governments, treat them – perhaps subconsciously – as traitors for having left. At the very least it's usually out of sight, out of mind. The 'tall poppy' syndrome may play a role, which we will never be able to measure. Expats are also punished – inadvertently perhaps – by the failure of Australian governments to properly consider the impact of laws and policies – in some cases the lack thereof – on Australians living abroad.[17]

It is partly a feeling that expatriates are not included in the mainstream of Australian society despite their size:

> I feel expat Australians tend to be forgotten once they leave the country. Only through my own efforts was I able to receive any information via the Embassy here about current events at home. The embassies don't ever give one the feeling they are particularly interested in us.

Another dimension of this is the 'tall poppy syndrome', which was mentioned by several respondents and a feeling that Australia was too inward looking:

> My return to Australia in 1997 was a real eye opener. I realised how inward looking it is… If your business is not property development or selling imported products then Australia is a career cul de sac.
>
> It is difficult for people who haven't lived overseas to view the very unentrepreneurial attitude of the Australian government and tax regime.
>
> I was very disappointed with the inward focus of Australia.
>
> Only family draws me back to Australia. The current Australian political situation is entirely unattractive and reinforces how parochial Australia is.
>
> It has been my personal experience that many Australians feel somehow that leaving Australia for long periods is somehow unnatural.
>
> I feel that London is where I "grew up": I arrived here when I was 22 years and found independence and confidence in myself and my abilities here.
>
> Every day I read with growing dismay the growing intolerance of political parties and followers towards refugees and asylum seekers and there have been times when I have felt ashamed of Australia and its treatment and attitudes towards human beings fleeing desperate situations, leading me to question my own citizenship.
>
> My brother, myself and two of his best friends were all high achievers and may be a bit more academically adventurous than average Adelaide people. We all separately came to UK and have never returned, finding the scope to grow much greater in UK.
>
> I'm sad about this because Aus is great but nothing I did when working was allowed or valued there… In Aus we were regarded as misfits and odd, in the wider world we have been regarded as entrepreneurial genius types. Unfortunately we have felt Aus has an ethos of "no tall poppies".

Others who have returned have found that their experience overseas is not only not recognised but seen as a negative when they apply for jobs.

> Australia pays a lot of lip service to gaining experience overseas but many employers cannot think outside the square when you've done it and returned.
>
> The brain drain will continue until Australia becomes more open-minded and more forward thinking.

CONCLUSION

Globalisation has seen an exponential increase in the flow across national borders of money, goods, people and ideas, and trans-national networks of all kinds have proliferated. These developments have threatened to undermine several aspects of the nation state as the dominant entity for organising policies, economic development, culture and identity.[18] This has led to a significant shift in thinking among many social scientists in the way in which they approach and study political, social and economic phenomena and processes and also of the 'spatial envelope' in which they study them. For example, Portes[19] has said that it is impossible to understand the sociology of many nations without considering their diaspora. Reis in a similar vein has written:

> The emphasis or adherence to the state centric model in the realm of international relations has contributed to the sidelining of entities known as diaspora as a valuable unit of analysis. In this sense, the nation state cannot account for certain features in the emerging global political economy, which can be better explained by using diaspora.[20]

It could be argued that in a globalising world, a national population should not be defined only as those living within the national boundaries but include the increasing number of citizens living in foreign countries. This represents a challenge across many areas. Dade argues that the most serious challenge posed by globalisation:

> ... is the massive migration and concomitant rise of transnational communities that obscure national borders and blur the distinction between foreign and local. Economic and social development in these new transnational communities presents an unanswered challenge to traditional development strategies that view communities only as being domestic or foreign.[21]

The Australian community in the UK is almost as large as the population of Canberra and the total Australian diaspora is around the size of Adelaide. Most expatriates still see themselves as Australians and many feel disenfranchised from the mainstream of Australian life. They are selective of the young, the bright, the innovative and Australians with the highest levels of human capital. If Australia engages them in the social, economic and political life of the country it can benefit considerably as a recent Senate Committee found.[22] However, achieving such an engagement will not be easy and will involve divesting ourselves of traditional and deeply entrenched views of the nation state.

ENDNOTES

1. Ravenstein, 1885, 199.
2. Gemmell, 2003, 9.
3. Britain, 1997, 148, 9; Walton, 2005, 5.
4. Summarised in Hugo, 1994, 29–31.
5. Appleyard and Segal, 1998.
6. Hugo, 2006b.
7. Hugo, Rudd and Harris, 2001, Chapter 3.
8. Hugo, 1994, 87–103.
9. Rendall and Ball, 2004.
10. MacGregor, 2003, 19–20.
11. Hugo, Rudd and Harris, 2003.

[12] Ellerman, 2003; Lucas, 2003; Asian Development Bank 2004; Martin, 2004; Johnson and Sedaca, 2004; House of Commons 2004; IOM 2005.
[13] Hugo, 2005b.
[14] Hugo, 2006a.
[15] Gemmell, 2003; Brothers, 2003, 48.
[16] Azure, 2003, 30.
[17] MacGregor, 2003, 19–20.
[18] Castles, 2003.
[19] Presentation to Conference on African Migration and Urbanisation in Comparative Perspective, Johannesburg, South Africa, 4–7 June 2003.
[20] Reis, 2004.
[21] Dade, 2004, 1.
[22] Australian Senate Legal and Constitutional References Committee 2005.

PRIMARY SOURCES

Asian Development Bank, 2004. 'Developing the diaspora'. Paper presented at Third Co-ordination Meeting on International Migration, Population Division, Department of Economic and Social Affairs, United Nations Secretariat, New York, 27–28 October.

Australian Bureau of Statistics. *Migration Australia*. Various issues. Canberra: ABS.

Australian Bureau of Statistics. *Overseas Arrivals and Departures, Australia*. Catalogue No. 3402.0. Canberra: ABS.

Australian Bureau of Statistics, 2005. *Migration Australia 2003–04*. Catalogue No. 3412.0. Canberra: ABS.

Australian Senate Legal and Constitutional References Committee, 2005. *They Still Call Australia Home: Inquiry into Australian Expatriates*. Department of the Senate, Parliament House: Canberra.

Azure A. 2003. 'Leaving and belonging'. In *Australian Expats: Stories from Abroad*, edited by Havenhand B.; MacGregor A. Newcastle, Australia: Global Exchange.

Brothers C. 2003. 'Hearts lie bleeding'. In *Australian Expats: Stories from Abroad*, edited by Havenhand,B; MacGregor A. Newcastle, Australia: Global Exchange.

Commonwealth Bureau of Census and Statistics. *Demography*. Various issues. Canberra: CBCS.

Department of Immigration and Multicultural and Indigenous Affairs, 2005a. *Immigration Update 2003–2004*. January. Canberra: AGPS.

Department of Immigration and Multicultural and Indigenous Affairs, 2005b. *Population Flows, Immigration Aspects, 2003–04 Edition*. Canberra: AGPS.

Department of Immigration and Multicultural and Indigenous Affairs. *Australian Immigration: Consolidated Statistics*. Various issues. Canberra: AGPS.

Department of Immigration and Multicultural and Indigenous Affairs. *Immigration Update*. Various issues. Canberra: AGPS.

Department of Immigration and Multicultural and Indigenous Affairs, 2002. *Immigration Update 2001–2002*. Canberra: AGPS.

Gemmell, N. 2003. 'Foreword'. In *Australian Expats: Stories from Abroad*, edited by Havenhand B.; MacGregor A. Newcastle, Australia: Global Exchange.

House of Commons United Kingdom. 2004. *Migration and Development: How to Make Migration Work for Poverty Reduction*. United Kingdom: The Stationery Office.

Immigration Advisory Council. 1973. *Inquiry into the Departure of Settlers from Australia: Final Report*. Canberra: AGPS.

International Organisation for Migration (IOM), 2005. 'Engaging diasporas as development partners' for Home and Destination Countries: A Policy Roadmap – Paper of the IOM.

MacGregor A. 2003. 'Australia remains part of us'. In *Australian expats: Stories from abroad*, edited by Havenhand B.; MacGregor A. Newcastle, Australia: Global Exchange.

United Nations. 2004. *World Economic and Social Survey 2004: International Migration*. New York: United Nations.

REFERENCES

Appleyard, R.T. 1964. *British Emigration to Australia*, Canberra: Australian National University.

Appleyard, Ray, A.; Segal, A. 1988. *The Ten pound Immigrants*, London: Boxtree.

Britain, I., 1997. *Once an Australian: Journeys with Barry Humphries, Clive James, Germaine Greer and Robert Hughes*. Melbourne: Oxford University Press.

Castles, S. 2003. 'Migrant settlement, transnational communities and state region'. In *Migration in the Asia Pacific: Population, Settlement and Citizenship issues*, edited by Iredale, R.; Hawksley, C.; Castles, S. Cheltenham, UK: Edward Elgar.

Crowley, F.K. 1954. 'The British Contribution to the Australian Population, 1860–1919'. *University Studies in History and Economics* 2(2): 55–88.

Dade, C. 2004. 'Transnationalism, foreign assistance, domestic communities: New opportunities and new challenges for Canada and the United States'. *Focal Point*, Special Edition (March): 1–3.

Eggleston, F.W., editor. 1933. *The Peopling of Australia*. Parkville, Vic.: Melbourne University Press.

Ellerman, D. 2003. 'Policy research on migration and development'. [Internet]. Available from: http://econ.worldbank.org/view.php?type=5&id-29100.

Hugo, G.J. 1994. *The Economic Implications of Emigration from Australia*. Canberra: AGPS.

Hugo, G.J. 1999. 'A new paradigm of international migration in Australia'. *New Zealand Population Review* 25(1-2): 1–39.

Hugo, G.J. 2005a. 'Migration from the United Kingdom to Australia: A new paradigm'. Mimeo.

Hugo, G.J. 2005b. 'The longitudinal survey of immigrants to Australia'. In *Immigration Research and Statistics Service Workshop on Longitudinal Surveys and Cross Cultural Survey Design: Workshop Proceedings*, edited by Morgan B.; Nicholson B. Jurys Inn, Croydon, 11–12 May 2004, Crown Copyright, London.

Hugo, G.J. 2005c. 'Diaspora and emigration in developed countries'. Report for IOM (January).

Hugo, G.J. 2006a. 'An Australian diaspora?' *International Migration*. 44(1): 105–133.

Hugo, G.J. 2006b. 'Temporary migration and the labour market in Australia'. *Australian Geographer* 37(2): 211–231.

Hugo, G. J.; Rudd, D.; Harris, K. 2001. *Emigration from Australia: Economic Implications*. Committee for Economic Development of Australia (CEDA) Information Paper No. 77. Melbourne: CEDA.

Hugo, G. J.; Rudd, D.; Harris, K. 2003. *Australia's Diaspora: Its Size, Nature and Policy Implications*, CEDA Information Paper No. 80. Melbourne: CEDA.

Johnson, B.; Sedaca, S. 2004. *Diasporas, Emigrés and Development, Economic Linkages and Programmatic Responses*. A Special Study of the U.S. Agency for International Development, Carana Corporation (March).

Jupp, J. 2004. *The English in Australia*. Melbourne: Cambridge University Press.

Lucas, R.E.B. 2003. 'The economic well-being of movers and stayers: Assimilation, impacts, links and proximity'. Paper prepared for Conference on African Migration in Comparative Perspective. Johannesburg, South Africa, 4–7 June.

Martin, P. 2004. 'Migration and development: Toward sustainable solutions'. International Institute for Labour Studies Discussion Paper DP153/2004. Geneva.

Office of National Statistics. 2004. *International Migration: Migrants Entering or Leaving the United Kingdom and England and Wales, 2002*. Series MN No. 29, Crown Copyright, London.

Price, C.A., editor. 1984. 'Birthplaces of Australian Population 1861–1981'. Working Papers in Demography, No. 13. Canberra: Australian National University.

Price, C.A. 1999. 'Australian population: Ethnic origins'. *People and Place* 7(4): 12–16.

Ravenstein, E.G. 1885. 'The laws of migration'. *Journal of the Royal Statistical Society* 48(2): 167–235.

Reis, M. 2004. 'Theorizing diaspora: Perspectives on "classical" and "contemporary" diaspora'. *International Migration* 42(2): 41–60.

Rendall, M.S; Ball, D.J. 2004. 'Immigration, emigration and the ageing of the overseas-born population in the United Kingdom'. *Population Trends* 116 (Summer): 18–27.

Walton, S. 2005. 'Shooting through: Australian film and the brain drain'. *Platform Papers* No. 5. Sydney: Currency House (July).

Cite this chapter as: Hugo, Graeme. 2009. 'Australians and Britain in 2001: A demographic perspective'. *Australians in Britain: The Twentieth-Century Experience*, edited by Bridge, Carl; Crawford, Robert; Dunstan, David. Melbourne: Monash University ePress. pp. 2.1 to 2.25. DOI: 10.2104/ab090002.

CHAPTER 3

AUSTRALIAN WOMEN IN LONDON
SURVEYING THE TWENTIETH CENTURY

Angela Woollacott, Macquarie University
  Angela Woollacott is Professor of Modern History at Macquarie University, Sydney. Her books include On Her Their Lives Depend: Munitions Workers in the Great War *(1994);* To Try Her Fortune in London: Australian Women, Colonialism and Modernity *(2001); and* Gender and Empire *(2006).*

The many thousands of Australian women who travelled to and sojourned in England across the twentieth century did so largely for reasons that were consistent. Despite one critic's notion that most were 'ordinary women', this essay contends that Australian women were drawn to the imperial metropole precisely because of its opportunities for growth, adventure and careers – whether they were single or married, arrived alone, with friends or family. Women could arrive in London both with particular goals in mind and also to be a tourist in the great new and yet familiar city. While there were several notable factors of continuity, there are ways in which we can see historical change. The factors of continuity include the dramatic response on first arrival, evoking at once the familiarity and the magic of London. They also include patterns of sharing housing and establishing networks with other Australians. The changes that have occurred include the attenuation of colonials' rights to stay and work in the UK, the presence in the late twentieth century of a few Aboriginal women, Australians' increased awareness of ethnic diversity in London despite their resistance to recognising their own diversity, and their new preparedness to mock the long-existent condescension towards them as colonials.

When novelist Kate Grenville was asked why she left Australia for London in the mid-1970s, for what would become four years based there and a total of six years overseas, she replied:

> For a lot of reasons. I'd always meant to do 'the tour' – you know how people do, in Australia, and I kept postponing it. I knew that there was a larger life than mine in Australia. I knew that there was more. I knew that there would be somewhere that was totally baffling all the time, and I wanted that experience, of not knowing where I was, or how things worked. It wasn't just a series of things I wanted to see, or know about, or have done; it was suddenly a whole lot of parts of myself that I wanted to allow to happen.[1]

Grenville reveals the intimate connection for so many Australian women between the pilgrimage to London, Australia's historical metropole, and self-development. With a marked consistency across the twentieth century, Australian women went to Britain in greater numbers than Australian men, because it represented opportunities larger than those they could see in Australia. The importance of self-development as a motive helps to explain the higher numbers of women who went. While some women were return migrants and others went with husbands or other family members, many saw London as offering possibilities precluded by gender expectations in Australia and by the constraints of home and family.

In this chapter I extrapolate from my book *To Try Her Fortune in London: Australian Women, Colonialism, and Modernity*, which looks at the period from 1870 to 1940, to consider Australian women's attraction to London across the twentieth century. I follow two lines of argument. One reviewer of my book, who was mostly kind towards it, suggested that I had misrepresented the historical picture somewhat by focusing on the extraordinary women who had gone to London for professional, educational or creative reasons. In so doing I had obscured the mass of 'ordinary women' who did not undertake such exciting adventures – those who were tourists, and who travelled with their parents and husbands.[2] I contend here that this notion of a majority of 'ordinary' uninteresting women is itself misleading. Looking at the middle and later decades of the twentieth century supports my argument that London (and England more generally) drew substantial numbers of Australian women precisely because of its opportunities for growth, adventure and careers – whether they were single or married. And I hope I showed in my book that one could arrive in London both with particular goals in mind and also to be a tourist in the great new and yet familiar city.

My second overarching theme is how to balance continuities with change over time. I will suggest that, while there were several notable factors of continuity, there are ways in which we can see historical change.

TO TRY HER FORTUNE IN LONDON

Let me start with recapping the main arguments of my book. Tens of thousands of Australian women were drawn to and resided in their imperial metropolis between 1870 and 1940. Australians were drawn to London as the largest city in the world at the turn of the century. But it was also the imperial metropolis, the centre of the place that many who never left Australia's shores referred to as 'Home.' Singers, musicians, writers, artists, and others all believed that to succeed they needed 'laurels in the wider world,' but specifically 'the hall mark of London approval.'[3] Some colonials were drawn to London for 'the season' or for shopping. In an era when tourism was becoming an industry, London was a global tourist destination, both in its own right and as a base for visiting the British provinces and the continent. For most white Australians, London – and the rest of the British Isles – was the locus of inherited cultural memory, the site of ancestral connections and the setting of major historical episodes. Some were drawn by the desire to visit relatives – including those who had left Australia and settled in England. Other components of London's centripetal pull included its primacy in the publishing, art, educational, reform, theatrical, musical, scientific, medical, legal, and political worlds. In September 1902, the successful Australian soprano Amy Castles was asked by a journalist from the *New Idea* whether she came across many Australian 'girls' in England and Paris. 'Yes, quite a lot,' she replied. 'In fact, I think that far too many Australians are going home to try their fortunes. Competition is very keen.'[4]

In October 1913 Alice Grant Rosman informed the readers of *Everylady's Journal*:

> [I]t is safe to say the average Australian girl cherishes an ambition to come to London some time or other, whether it be in search of fame, experience, or mere frivolous adventure. That a large percentage realise that ambition in these days of cheap travelling may be seen from the fact – or perhaps I should say the rumour – that there are no fewer than 25,000 Australians either temporarily o[r] permanently residing in London to-day.[5]

Rosman's figures were more fact than rumour. Starting with a trickle of a couple of thousand per year in the 1870s, the flow of Australians and New Zealanders to England rose to around an annual 10,000 from the late 1880s beyond the turn of the century, and then doubled in the interwar period.[6] By 1911 there were 23,000 Australian-born residents of England and Wales, of whom 13,000 were female.[7] In 1930 an Australian journalist noted: 'We meet ourselves everywhere; London is full of us, rushing about sightseeing, attending functions, or inscribing our names at Australia House, our national "foyer".'[8]

Communities of Antipodeans have been part of London since at least 1884, when the community newspaper the *British Australasian* was founded. After a short hiatus in the later stages of the Second World War, the numbers in London surged from the 1950s. One source suggests that in 1991 there were 42,000 Australians and New Zealanders in London.[9] One of my aims in the book was to present a kind of prehistory to what was already well-known – the postwar attraction of Australians to London – to show that it was a phenomenon with longer historical roots than often assumed. Stephen Alomes' book *When London Calls* (Alomes, 1999) is a richly detailed evocation of the expatriate Australian cultural elite in London from the late 1940s to the 1980s, showing the density of the cultural connections between Australia and London in that period – although he perhaps wasn't fully aware of the extent to which this was a continuation of the pre-war situation.[10] But there is less available work on the thousands and thousands of Australians who did not become famous, who went to London for an adventure, to get away from home, to see the world, to pursue education, jobs and careers.

The sources available to the historian privilege the professional and the prominent. But from the turn of the twentieth century large numbers of less visible women also went, taking jobs in music hall or choruses, the food service industry, teaching, nursing and other less glamorous areas. For such women, the romance, the distance, and the promise of adventure were what mattered. England – and London – held such appeal that visits there were often measured in years or could extend indefinitely. White colonial women's flight to London was culturally intelligible to their families and friends. Because departing for London was a recognized cultural ritual, women could undertake this huge step without being condemned for transgressing femininity through being overly ambitious, at a time when women's claims to the public domain were limited culturally.

The common formulation of the decision by a woman artist, professional or performer to embark was that she had decided 'to try her fortune in London',[11] which endorsed women's rights to compete for success, fame and, indeed, financial rewards. Going to London was therefore a way for an Australian woman to express and act on her ambition: to advance her education or skills, to absorb the latest styles, genres, research or techniques, to study under the most renowned practitioners, to gain access to the most respected publishing houses – or simply to get a job. It was also commonly accepted in many fields that opportunities in Australia were small and confined compared to those in England; therefore, displaying strong abilities was widely regarded as a sign that you should go to the metropole, to a larger arena.

While Australian men were drawn to London too, the statistics and contemporary observations show consistently over time that, except the years of the First World War when Australian troops were in Britain, there were more women than men making this pilgrimage 'home'. A 1907 commentator, when asked about the principal exports from Australia to Britain, replied that they were 'frozen sheep and pretty-voiced girls'.[12] In 1910 newspaper columnist 'Peggy' said of an Australian singer: 'She was just a unit in the large army of girls with voices – spelled with a big V – who come over yearly with ever so little capital and ever so many aspirations and dreams of conquering the world of music.'[13] While sex discrimination in Australia was a common reason that women left for London, colonialism facilitated their move by both creating and validating their attraction to the imperial metropolis. In the racialised and gendered cultural logic of the empire, white women's desire for London was evidence of refinement and feminine respectability.

WERE THEY 'PRIVILEGED' OR 'ORDINARY'?

Andrew Hassam comments that 'there is a danger in grouping feminism, modernity and colonialism as transgressive forces when this excludes the experience of the majority of Australian women who came to Britain with parents or husbands'.[14] I do not think it's quite accurate to characterize either colonialism or modernity as a transgressive force; rather, they have been large structuring historical dynamics. Moreover, Australian travellers to Britain have been influenced by both colonialism and modernity, whether they were young single women or older married men. But the point I really want to counter here is the suggestion that the majority of Australian women travelling to London arrived with parents and husbands and without personal ambitions. And indeed, I would argue that the two categories were not exclusive: many women arrived with family members *and* ambitions.

Familial relationships are complex, and belie assumptions of normalcy or straightforwardness. In 1930 a music critic pilloried the Australian mother who used her talented offspring as an excuse for the trip to Europe she so badly wanted:

> If Rosey happens to be one of those whose destinies seem to the public or her immediate circle of admirers to lie in the direction of a career overseas, when Mother insists on coming with her the upshot is almost invariably a disastrous handicap on Rosey … The mothers sigh that they must make a sacrifice for Rosey; what is really happening is that they are making a sacrifice of Rosey.[15]

Another contraversion of the idea that travelling with parents was a protected or ordinary experience comes from Penelope Nelson's account of her trip to London with her mother in 1959, when she was sixteen. Her mother, Micky McNicoll, who had been women's editor of the *Sunday Telegraph* and *Daily Telegraph* in Sydney, was given a round-the-world ticket as a retirement gift, and took her daughter with her. Nelson was taken aback to discover how cosmopolitan and well-known her mother was. Among other experiences, they went to lunch at the Notting Hill house of an Australian woman artist friend of her mother, an experience that Nelson describes as 'a preview of what would be known as the Swinging Sixties'. Not only was lunch accompanied by claret and port, their hostess offered her a pill she called a 'purple heart'. Nelson described her trip back to their flat on the top deck of a bus as being 'bathed by waves of exhilaration', some interesting colours and a pulsing rhythm.[16] A sixteen-year-old having a psychedelic experience when accompanying her mother to lunch in 1959 confounds the assumption that travel with family is necessarily 'ordinary' or boring.

In relation to the question of women travelling with their husbands, examples abound of dual career couples. An early example was Amy Mack and her husband Launcelot Harrison who arrived in England in 1914, where Harrison had hoped to take up a postgraduate research scholarship. While he served in the army, including in Mesopotamia, Mack worked in London as a publicity officer for the Ministry of Munitions and the Ministry of Food. A mid-century example, showing how complex and competitive marriages could be, is the writers George Johnston and Charmian Clift who moved to London in 1951 when Johnston became head of the *Sun* newspapers bureau. While the two continued to write both together and separately, and were celebrated members of the expatriate Australian community, the tensions in their literary careers were interlinked with the tensions in their marriage. Clift illustrates well the point that a married woman could have ambitions for herself.[17]

It is particularly important to recognise that the Australian women who travelled to London in the twentieth century were not predominantly from the social or economic elite. As I noted in my book, focusing on white Australian women's recourse to and exploitation of London forces us to see the connections stretching not only to Australian cities, but extending to small country towns, farms, and stations. In 1910 music critic Thorold Waters noted patronisingly that some of the hundreds of Australian women singers recently in London 'came directly from their little towns of Tantanoola, Bunyip, Gerang-Gerang, or wherever they might be.'[18]

While affluence and social connections helped, by no means were all Australian women in London well off. Grace Jennings Carmichael, a poet and nurse from Ballarat, died a pauper in a workhouse near London in 1904.[19] Others went on scholarships or scraped together a living; accounts of trips to London abound with stories of not having enough to eat, and not having cash to keep feeding the gas meter. Some were from the poorer classes, and some who were not left with only their fare, facing the necessity to work as soon as they landed. Painter of miniatures Bess Norriss left Australia in 1905 having saved thirty pounds for the trip.[20] Not only were these women from across Australia and up and down the socio-economic ladder, they were diverse in other ways too, including age and marital status – and these factors of diversity continued across the century.

CONTINUITIES OVER THE TWENTIETH CENTURY

Australian women arriving in London at very different moments in the twentieth century reacted in strikingly similar ways, evoking at once the familiarity and the magic of arrival. In 1901, journalist and novelist Louise Mack reacted this way: 'Oh London, London! how did I ever live without you? … I no longer say to myself, "*You're in London*." I accept it at last, and surrender to the spell of the City of Mists'.[21] Actress Ruth Cracknell's first reactions on her arrival in 1953 were only a little less romantic: 'Arriving in London it was as if every reference point was familiar. A monopoly board come to life, all the reading of the preceding twenty or so years making virtually every street and square and garden familiar, but so much more vivid now that one was a part'.[22] Romance and fantasy also colour the description, in a recent memoir by television comedian Noeline Brown, of her arrival in March 1965: 'As soon as I recovered from my shocking jetlag I started exploring the city. I walked everywhere and loved every minute of it. I was actually Overseas. The little girl who used to hang around the docks and dream about travel was actually doing it.'[23] Across the century Australian women recorded their journeys to and sojourns in Britain in diaries, letters, interviews and memoirs. Fictionalised accounts also span the century from Louise Mack's novel *An Australian Girl in London* (Mack, 1902) to Nikki Gemmell's novel *Love Song* (Gemmell, 2001).[24]

Another notable continuity was the custom of sharing housing and establishing networks. This was true in the boarding houses of the early century, and remained true. When Adelaide printmaker and writer-to-be Barbara Hanrahan arrived in London in February 1963 to attend the Central School of Art, like so many other Australian young women she found housing with friends of a girl she'd met on the ship. The flat was on the ground floor of a house in West Kensington, and it involved sharing a bedroom with Carolyn and Val and Peggy, all from Sydney. Not only were shared conditions in the house already crowded, if any Australian girlfriends of any of the four turned up, they were permitted to sleep on the floor of the sitting room. Sometimes, Hanrahan recalled, the 'flat was full of strange girls,' but most of the tenants didn't mind because it meant more people sharing expenses.[25] That this is still a practice of young Australians in London is shown in Rosie Whittam's account of her own recent experience. Commenting on the continuing Australian custom of sharing housing together, Whittam reports:

> the archetypal London house share can be fraught with problems. I was totally unprepared for the endless stream of flatmates' travelling friends arriving at short notice to crash. I once discovered a half-naked man, reclining on an airbed, in the middle of my kitchen. The flat was supposed to accommodate four tenants, but at one stage there were twelve crammed inside. The bathroom got so dirty that I stayed cleaner if I didn't take a shower.[26]

Australian women created shared households beyond London. While London has consistently drawn the largest concentration of Antipodeans because of its size and opportunities, others have sojourned elsewhere in Britain, drawn by family connections or other motives. In late 1972 Susan Marsden, a recent graduate of the University of Adelaide, arrived in England with friends Jane Lockwood and Margaret Mary Farrell. At first they headed for Doncaster to stay with Jane's sister, uncle and grandmother. Soon the four young women moved to Cambridge, where they rented 'Wiles Cottage' in the nearby village of Waterbeach. They decided on Cambridge for their joint adventure because of connections the Lockwood sisters, whose father was an academic, had there. For historian-to-be Susan Marsden, Cambridge was in many ways an archetypal experience of a metropolitan sojourn. She found a day job working for the Leicester Permanent Building Society, and at least for a while also waitressed in the evening. Like so many other young Australians, she travelled around Britain (often hitchhiking, a mode of transport not considered feasible by later arrivals) and the continent. Yet in some ways her sojourn was shaped in singular ways by Cambridge itself. She and her housemates made friends with Cambridge undergraduates, and soaked up the historic architecture of the colleges and the ambience of 'the Backs' and the Cam. Marsden reacted to her new Cambridge friends in ways shaped both by gender and colonial resentment. Her new male friends, still themselves undergraduates, seemed unimpressed by her status as a recent graduate, perhaps because of a slight disregard for an Arts degree (as opposed to science or engineering), and perhaps because of an Oxbridge condescension towards a colonial university. Marsden recorded in her diary: 'You feel something of an imposter declaring that you're a University graduate, or even having been at university. Of course, the feeling is partly fostered by our own defensiveness; what's Adelaide University vs. Cambridge[?]'. Despite recognising their own colonial lack of confidence, Marsden admitted to herself that it would be nice to be accorded some intellectual respect, rather than 'being given no status whatsoever for the B.A., Adelaide'. Her feminist analysis of the interactions between the Cambridge undergraduate men and her group of Australian women prompted her wry note that: 'We are their lighter side'.[27]

Without wanting to indulge too much in autobiography, the topic of networks and shared housing touches closely on my own experience. During my own 'gap year' of sojourning in London and travelling on the continent in 1981–82, I too benefited from a network of Australian women friends in London. I had actually forgotten the density of this network until, in cleaning out my parents' house in 2005, I discovered letters I wrote home in October 1981. In them, I describe the shared houses in which I found accommodation in London. First, there was the house in Brixton – actually two adjoined terrace houses – in which the eight permanent residents were mostly Antipodean. The household was so willing to accommodate transient Antipodeans (friends of residents) that it had a spare bedroom for this purpose, and a detailed system such that a visitor paid a fixed amount into the weekly kitty and was immediately slotted into the cooking, shopping and cleaning roster. I could have stayed in that house as long as I wished, but the woman friend with whom I was travelling and I moved on to another house shared by Australians, this one in Herne Hill. In my letters, I commented that it was wonderful finding such a rich network of Australians, but at times one wished one could meet more real English people. The networks flourished, I told my parents, because all new arrivals have Australian friends whom they look up and immediately they meet others. One of the things that struck me and on which I reported was that the networks into which I fell were dominated by women, many of whom were professionals or were doing creative work. Among them were two doctors, a friend learning to teach English as a second language, another who had just landed a job setting up a community radio station on a public housing estate, and a radiographer working in Sussex.[28] Yet in terms of the historical record, these were anonymous Australians – the kind who complicate the notion of 'ordinary women.' This phenomenon of congregating with other Australians was partly due to the practical incentives of sharing rent and basic expenses; partly to established personal contacts; and perhaps partly to the difficulty of assimilating – factors that were fairly constant across the century.

CHANGE OVER TIME

But some things did change, most importantly from 1962 onwards the rights of Australians to stay and work in the UK. At the turn of the twentieth century a sojourn in London represented 'going home'. Today only some of that imperial attachment remains. Instead we have evidence that a trip to Britain can be more like visiting a foreign country, with the meanings of colonial attachment challenged in multiple ways. The recent experiences of Julie Hope highlight the ways in which Britain is no longer 'home'. In early August 2005, fifty-year-old Hope, from Melbourne, was refused entry to Britain by immigration officials at Stansted airport after visiting the continent. Hope had a current six-month UK visa. Nevertheless, the officials detained and interrogated her for five hours, impounded her possessions, read her diary, refused to allow her to phone a lawyer, and finally deported her back to France. Hope, a divorced former garden decorator, who had rented out her Melbourne house and planned to have a 'late gap year' in Britain, had arrived earlier in the year. She stayed with friends, whom she helped around the house and garden and for whom she did some unpaid babysitting, and went to Normandy with a group of schoolchildren including the daughter of one set of hosts. She had recorded all this in her diary. Seemingly, the immigration officials believed that she was working illegally in the UK in return for accommodation, board and cash. According to Valerie Lawson, who wrote an account of Hope's deportation for the *Sydney Morning Herald*, of the 819,000 Australians who travelled to Britain in 2003, 315 were refused entry.[29]

While that is a small percentage, both the statistic and Hope's story are a reminder of the attenuation of legal ties and cultural identification between metropole and colony.

Another noteworthy change has to do with 'race' or ethnicity. For the period 1870 to 1940, I could find no evidence of any Indigenous Australian woman in England. This absence contrasts both with the small number of Aboriginal men who went to England in that period, and also with the small number of Canadian Aboriginal or First Nations women who travelled to England in the same years, and whom historian Cecilia Morgan is currently studying.

In the latter part of the twentieth century, a few Aboriginal women did make the trip – something that was facilitated by the Whitlam Government's removal of legislative restrictions. Early in 1972, before that legislative change, activist and writer Roberta Sykes went to England at the invitation of a group of Australian expatriates who wanted to draw attention to Aborigines' subordination. For Sykes, the trip was a mixed experience: she knew none of the organisers, had no money, and found that they expected her to go around the country by herself to events they had arranged. Moreover, when she arrived back in London after speaking to some Labour Party delegates at their annual Blackpool conference, she found that police had been looking for her at the request of the Australian government. She was accused of having, a year earlier, assisted an Aboriginal escapee in Western Australia, but the charge was false and soon dropped.[30] In recent years, there has been more of an Aboriginal presence in London. Notable events have included the November 2002 visit by Doris Pilkington Garimara, author of *Follow the Rabbit-Proof Fence* (Pilkington, 1996), the book on which the film was based.[31] And in 2005 the first 'Sorry Day' event to be held outside Australia occurred at Lincoln's Inn Fields on 25 May.

Australian women visiting London have become more aware of its ethnic diversity, although comments on this were registered as early as the 1920s. In 1963 Barbara Hanrahan found the ethnic diversity something she had to get used to, noting of her trips around London that she was 'surrounded by a new lot of curious people with so many different colours of skin, so many ways of living. Black men who smelt of carnation powder, mad old women offering you sweeties wrapped in cellophane, drunken Irishmen clutching bottles of milk.'[32] She also noted virulent racism, both in one of her Australian women flatmates, and in an English electrician she met.[33] Most Australian women in Britain in the twentieth century were of British descent, but this is definitely not true of all. For instance, I am currently working on Rose Quong, the Chinese-Australian actor and writer who made a career in London from 1924 to 1939, specialising in the professional performance of Chineseness. In the earlier part of the century a few were of continental European descent, but usually they did not emphasise this. More recently, in 2001 a Maltese-Australian woman Simone Ancilleri posted a submission on the Australian website 'WogLife' headed 'A wog in London'. She complains of the difficulties she experienced there as a hybrid or hyphenated Australian. Growing up in Western Sydney, she was 'just a wog' and her Australian friends accepted that she looked Maltese but had a broad Australian accent, and she had friends 'from all different backgrounds'. When she went to London she had hoped that she would meet 'people of all different nationalities with perhaps an Aussie here or there and not the other way around.' Instead she found that her 'backpacker's house' was 'little Australia', and that her housemates introduced her to their friends thus: 'This is Simone and she is from

Malta.' Her indignant reaction was: 'What! I was born in Australia and lived there for twenty three years of my life [so] I felt that I deserved to be called an "Australian".' While going to London on a working holiday for a couple of years was 'the ultimate Australian cliché', Ancilleri's time there only confused her in terms of ethnic and national identities. She complained: 'I can't go to the Australian pub and drink VB or XXXX and holler "Aussie, Aussie, Aussie, Oi, Oi, Oi!" without feeling like a complete fool.'[34] Thus while Australian women in London were not wholly of British descent even early in the century, the question of ethnicity versus Australianness is now perhaps more open for discussion.

One last topic that I wish to touch on is how women have reacted to English condescension toward them as colonials. This has changed over the course of the twentieth century but perhaps only subtly. Certainly, complaints by Australian women about being treated as colonials recurred across the century; even before 1900 it was a theme in the accounts of visitors and longer-term residents. Australians have resisted and resented their categorisation as colonials, and refuted particular insults they have perceived have been levelled at them. Both the insults and the resentment, it seems, have been a continuing thread. When historian Ann Moyal left Sydney for London in 1949, it was partly because she had been 'reared at [her] mother's knee on plans for England'.[35] The specific context of her departure was her first-class honours degree in History from the University of Sydney and a scholarship to the Institute of Historical Research, University of London. She would go on to the singular and glamorous career of being Lord Beaverbrook's personal research assistant. Moyal and her Australian friends were 'amused and baffled' to find their new English associates consumed with the cultural dimensions of class. A current preoccupation was Nancy Mitford's distinction between those who were 'U' (upper-class) and 'Non-U'. Moyal was informed by an English friend that she need not worry about this subject, because all Australians were by definition 'Non-U'.[36] While she recounts the insults she received with humour as well as resentment, other reports of British condescension are more heated.

I would suggest, though, that Australians have become more irreverent in their response. This irreverence is perhaps best epitomised by Kathy Lette, the writer and comedian, in her novel *Foetal Attraction* (Lette, 1993). Lette's character, Maddy, is a six-foot tall, witty, Jill-of-all-trades who left school early and has had jobs ranging from first mate on a prawn fishing boat off Darwin, to a trapeze artist for Circus Oz, to a scuba-diving instructor in the Whitsunday Islands. In Sydney she falls in love with an English TV celebrity and follows him to London, where she has to mix with those she mockingly calls the 'glitterati.' At first, Maddy is stunned by the condescension she receives from the supposedly politically progressive cultural elite, but she comes to accept it as a fact of life for an Australian in London. At the first high-powered cocktail party she endures, the comments of the writers, agents and activists to whom she is introduced include: 'Oh, you're Australian. I've always found Australians to be so insensitive.' 'An Australian in London. Now there's an original concept.' And 'Australia …? … That's where we stash our upper-class English murderers, isn't it?' The most damning line is one that she overhears in a conversation between two women: 'Oh, yes. I do all my own housework. I can't possibly ask a working-class woman to scrub my lavatory bowl. Occasionally when I get really desperate I ring an agency … but I always get them to send me an Australian.'[37] What Lette's novel illustrates is a greater preparedness by Australians to name and to satirise such English attitudes. Australians have always noticed and resented them, but the attenuation of the imperial relationship has made it more acceptable to lambast them. Australians have moved beyond both cultural cringe and colonial cringe.

In the historiographical debates surrounding British national identity since the collapse of empire, the formation of a multi-ethnic Britain, and whether or not the empire has shaped Britain itself, the temporary and permanent immigration of subjects from the white-settler dominions has been almost completely overlooked. The thousands and thousands of Australian women who were drawn to Britain across the twentieth century came for diverse reasons including travel, adventure, personal growth, getting away from home and gendered constraints, and seeking education, training and careers. London has exercised a consistent pull for them, despite the growing significance of alternative destinations such as New York. Some factors have stayed the same in this particular component of modern, global mobility, and yet we can also identify factors of change – factors that speak to the attenuation of imperial ties and colonial rights, even as the legacies of colonialism are the fundamental reason for the continuation of an Australian community in London today.

ENDNOTES

[1] Ellison, 1986, 155–156.

[2] Hassam, 2003, 310–311.

[3] *British Australasian*, 6 October 1910, 19; *British Australian and New Zealander*, 21 September 1933, 11.

[4] *New Idea*, 1 September 1902, 115.

[5] Alice Grant Rosman, 'Girls who are going to London town', *Everylady's Journal*, 6 October 1913, 604.

[6] Inglis, 1992, 105–06. By 1930 Gilbert Mant could explain that the reason 'Australians Are Unpopular in London' was that 'Something like 20,000 trippers are allowed to leave Australia each year'. *The British Australian and New Zealander*, 23 October 1930, 18.

[7] Inglis, 1992, 105–06. Inglis' figures support the 'rumour' cited by Alice Grant Rosman and add important evidence that more than half of these thousands of Australians were female.

[8] Isabel Edgar, 'Is It Fair?' *British Australian and New Zealander*, 30 October 1930, 8. Some 4,410 visitors signed in to Australia House in the spring and summer months alone. *British Australasian*, 5 October 1922, 12.

[9] Bouwman, 1993, 80.

[10] Alomes, 1999.

[11] For example, *British Australian and New Zealander*, 11 September 1930, 12.

[12] 'Our song-birds in London', *Lone Hand*, vol.1., May 1907, 105.

[13] Peggy, 'In the looking-glass', *British Australasian*, 21 April 1910, 20.

[14] Hassam, 2003, 311.

[15] Waters, Thorold, 'Cruel hints to youthful artists: The place of mother in the musical career', *Australian Musical News*, 1 January 1930, 3.

[16] Nelson, 1995, 5–6.

[17] See, for example, Brown, 2004 and Wheatley, 2001.

[18] Waters, Thorold, 'Australian Singers and English Agents', *British Australasian*, 30 June 1910, 29.

[19] Gardiner, 1979, 564.
[20] Mills, 1988, 7.
[21] Mack, 1902.
[22] Cracknell, 1997, 88.
[23] Brown, 2005, 97.
[24] Gemmell, 2001.
[25] Hanrahan, 1992, 23–26.
[26] Rosie Whittam, 'Best – and worst – of British', 'Travel'. *Sydney Morning Herald*, 25–26 February 2006, 3.
[27] Susan Marsden's diary of her trip to England and Europe 1972–73.
[28] Woollacott, Angela, My letters home from London, 11 October and 21 October 1981.
[29] Lawson, Valerie, 'Banished by Britain', *Sydney Morning Herald*, 3–4 September 2005, 28.
[30] Sykes, 1989, 157–159.
[31] Pilkington, 1996.
[32] Hanrahan, 1992, 35.
[33] Hanrahan, 1992, 61–62.
[34] Ancilleri, Simone. 2001. 'A wog in London'. [Internet].
[35] Moyal, 1995, 38.
[36] Moyal, 1995, 47.
[37] Lette, 1993, 39–41.

PRIMARY SOURCES

Ancilleri, Simone. 2001. 'A wog in London'. [Internet]. Posted online 17 April, 2001. Available from: 'WogLife' website http://www.wog.com.au.
Australian Musical News, 1930.
British Australian and New Zealander, 1930.
British Australasian, 1910.
Everylady's Journal, 1913.
Lone Hand, 1907.
Woollacott, Angela, My letters home from London, 11 October and 21 October 1981.
New Idea, 1902.
Marsden, Susan, 1972–73, Diary of her trip to England and Europe, by kind loan and permission of the author.
Sydney Morning Herald, 2005.

REFERENCES

Alomes, Stephen. 1999. *When London Calls: The Expatriation of Australian Creative Artists to Britain*. Cambridge: Cambridge University Press.
Bouwman, Rick. 1993. 'Australians and New Zealanders in London'. In *The Peopling of London: Fifteen Thousand Years of Settlement From Overseas*, edited by Merriman, Nick. London: Museum of London.

Brown, Max. 2004. *Charmian and George: The Marriage of George Johnston and Charmian Clift*. Dural, NSW: Rosenberg Publishing.

Brown, Noeline. 2005. *Noeline Brown: Longterm Memoir*. Crows Nest, NSW: Allen & Unwin.

Cracknell, Ruth. 1997. *Ruth Cracknell: A Biased Memoir*. Ringwood, Vic.: Viking.

Ellison, Jennifer, editor. 1986. *Rooms of their Own*. Ringwood, Vic.: Penguin Books.

Gardiner, Lyndsay. 1979. 'Carmichael, Grace Elizabeth Jennings'. *Australian Dictionary of Biography*. Vol. 7 (1891–1939). Carlton, Vic: Melbourne University Press.

Gemmell, Nikki. 2001. *Love Song*. Sydney: Vintage.

Hanrahan, Barbara. 1992. *Michael and Me and the Sun*. St Lucia, Qld: University of Queensland Press.

Hassam, Andrew. 2003. 'Review of Woollacott, Angela, To Try Her Fortune in London, Oxford, New York: Oxford University Press'. *Urban History* 30 (2): 310–311.

Inglis, K.S. 1992. 'Going home: Australians in England, 1870–1900'. In *Home or Away?: Immigrants in Colonial Australia*, edited by Fitzpatrick, David. Canberra: Division of Historical Studies and Centre for Immigration and Multicultural Studies, Research School of Social Sciences, Australian National University.

Lette, Kathy. 1993. *Foetal Attraction*. Chippendale, NSW: Picador.

Mack, Louise. 1902. *An Australian Girl in London*. London: T. Fisher Unwin.

Mills, Carol. 1988. *Expatriate Australian Black and White Artists: Ruby and Will Dyson and Their Circle in London, 1909–1919*. Working Paper No. 33. University of London, London: Sir Robert Menzies Centre for Australian Studies.

Moyal, Ann. 1995. *Breakfast with Beaverbrook: Memoirs of an Independent Woman*. Sydney: Hale & Iremonger.

Nelson, Penelope. 1995. *Penny Dreadful*. Milson's Point, NSW: Random House.

Pilkington, Doris. (Nugi Garimara). 1996. *Follow the Rabbit-Proof Fence*. St Lucia, Qld.: University of Queensland Press.

Sykes, Roberta B. 1989. *Black Majority*. Hawthorn, Vic.: Hudson.

Wheatley, Nadia. 2001. *The Life and Myth of Charmian Clift*. Sydney: HarperCollins Publishers.

Woollacott, Angela. 2001. *To Try Her Fortune in London: Australian Women, Colonialism and Modernity*. New York, Oxford: Oxford University Press.

Cite this chapter as: Woollacott, Angela. 2009. 'Australian women in London: Surveying the twentieth century'. *Australians in Britain: The Twentieth-Century Experience*, edited by Bridge, Carl; Crawford, Robert; Dunstan, David. Melbourne: Monash University ePress. pp. 3.1 to 3.12. DOI: 10.2104/ab090003.

CHAPTER 4

AUSTRALIANS IN THE ENGLAND AND WALES CENSUS OF 1901
A DEMOGRAPHIC SURVEY

Carl Bridge, King's College London
> Carl Bridge is Professor and Head of the Menzies Centre for Australian Studies. He was one of the organisers of the 2005 Symposium on Australians in Britain jointly organised by the Menzies Centre and the National Centre for Australian Studies, Monash.

> This analysis of Australians enumerated in the England and Wales Census of 1901 establishes that their characteristics were more British than foreign. Unlike foreign immigrant groups they settled all over the two countries, were predominantly female, and mostly young, skilled and in nuclear families. They were also more likely to be from Victoria than New South Wales, and Queensland and Tasmania than Western Australia or South Australia. In 1901, then, the Australian diaspora in England and Wales showed itself to be very much part of the wider British world.

Historians of the British Empire have, over ten years or so, turned to the task of mapping and analysing what we now call the British world: that is, that complex ganglion of relationships – the cultural and demographic glue – which held the informal empire of people together.[1] We are interested not only in the shared assumptions and outlooks but also in the shared relationships and networks. A key aspect of the mapping is to trace the patterns of migration, not simply, as in the past, from the metropole to the periphery, but also between the other constituent parts, what we might call cross migration. Return migration – that is, the flow of migrants who went home to Britain – is also part of this phenomenon. However, so is what we might label reverse migration, in which people born in the wider empire completely buck the trend and migrate to Britain.[2]

This complex process of migration across the British world is reflected in the Census of the British Empire, 1901, which among many other things gives places of birth for those enumerated in the various imperial censuses of that year. Migration was certainly not just from the UK to the colonies. For instance, in Orange River Colony, 28 per cent of the population not born in the colony was born in parts of the empire other than the UK; in Trinidad and Tobago, it was 33 per cent; in NSW only 9 per cent; but, spectacularly, in Western Australia, 42 per cent. Thus there was considerable cross-migration between the various parts of the British world other than the UK.[3] Of course, England and Wales had considerable overseas-born populations generally in 1901, the biggest being 93,345 from the Russian Empire, 65,990 from Germany and 41,255 from the United States.[4] However, the Russians in England and Wales were 0.07 of the total Russian population, the Germans, 0.12 and the Americans, 0.05;[5] whereas for the West Indies the percentage was 0.63, for Australia it was 0.55, for New Zealand 0.58, for Canada 0.34, for the South African colonies and the Indian Empire 0.18 apiece. Thus, to varying but very significant degrees, as much as five and ten times more for Australia, New Zealand and the West Indies, there was a greater propensity to migrate to England and Wales from elsewhere in the British world than from foreign countries.[6] If there is a single index of belonging to the British world then this is it.

My study of the Australia-born in the England and Wales census of 1901[7] and after is intended to fill in part of the British world jigsaw and also to contribute to Australian and British migration history in a novel way.[8] Using the recently digitised transcript provided by QinetiQ,[9] the census records where in Australia these Australians were born, their age, gender, relationship to head of household, occupational status, disabilities, if any, and place of residence in England or Wales.

First, let us look at the basic numbers. There were, according to the enumerators, 21,221 Australia-born in England and Wales on the evening of 30 March 1901.[10] However, it seems there was a considerable amount of double counting and misattribution (there are Melbournes in Derbyshire and Cambridgeshire, for instance), and my analysis of the transcripts of the returns has identified definitely only 15,295. Many more people who had lived in Australia but had not been born there, and who might have thought of themselves as Australians, would have been resident in England and Wales in 1901, but we have no straightforward way of getting at their numbers. As the census constitutes a snapshot, there is no way of knowing from it how long these Australians had been in England and Wales and how long they stayed, but it can be inferred from their occupations and their relationship to head of family that relatively few, probably under 10 per cent, were sojourners or tourists.[11]

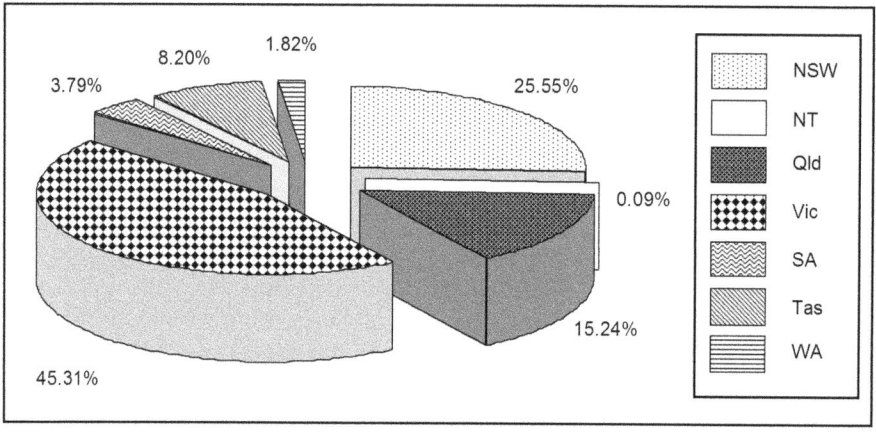

Figure 4.1 Australian population in England and Wales, 1901, where state of origin is known
Source: all graphs and tables are based on the QinetiQ transcription of the England and Wales census data for 1901 unless otherwise indicated.

Our 15,295 Australia-born came disproportionately from some states in Australia rather than others, as shown in Figure 4.1. New South Wales with 36 per cent of the population provided only 26 per cent of the Australians in England and Wales, whereas Victoria with 32 per cent provided 45 per cent. To lesser degrees, South Australia and Western Australia were under par and Tasmania and Queensland over. A third of those enumerated are simply recorded as having come from Australia. This was because the enumerators were instructed to record the birthplace of each person and, if that was in a British colony or dependency, the name of that colony or dependency.[12] Hence the large number whose place of birth is given as Australia but we can be most grateful that most ignored the instruction, which perhaps reveals a psychological assumption that other parts of the British Empire were not really abroad at all. Among those simply recorded as coming from Australia, there may be also some bias towards New South Wales, which at the time sometimes called itself Australia; though, as we shall see, the Victorian tendency is also much evident in other figures.[13]

These data demand some explanation, but without going into the details of the individuals' backgrounds in Australia this can only be highly speculative. (Recovering the Australian backgrounds would be a nigh impossible task for the vast majority of the people in question as the Australian census records for the individuals have not survived.) Before indulging in such speculation about the Australian background, let me add two other dimensions of data that we do have to hand; these are, average age and relationship to head of household.

The average age of all in England and Wales enumerated in the census and also for the Australia-born was 27 years, but there was considerable variation across the states. The average age for females in the 1901 census of Australia was 25 years, 27 years for males,[14] whereas the average for females in England and Wales was 28 years and 27 years for males.[15] New South Welshmen and Victorians were close to the Australian average age while Queenslanders were only 17 and, at the other end of the spectrum, Tasmanians were 35. To lesser degrees, South Australians were older than par and Western Australians were younger. Overall, Australia-born males in England and Wales were 25 years on average while females were 28. Thus Australian women in England and Wales were three years older on average than their sisters back in Australia and the men a year younger. Analysis of relation to head of household shows the overwhelming importance of the nuclear family unit in determining the location in family of these Australians. Fully 69 per cent were components of a nuclear family unit as head of household, wife, daughter or son.

How do we explain the state of origin, age and relationship to head of household data? And are there any relationships between them? There are several possible explanations for the preponderance of Victorians. Victoria was home to the largest numbers of migrants who had arrived in the period from the 1860s to the 1880s. Our Australia-born may be first generation Australians going 'Home' to school, or to an apprenticeship, or to a job obtained through family connections, or to care for family or take up family obligations. All of these reasons are apparent from perusing the census return columns for relation to head of household and also for profession or occupation. Some few Australia-born fitted the classic literary stereotype of people who had made their money in the colony and wanted a genteel retirement in the 'mother country'. Still others may have been fleeing the 1890s depression, which hit Victoria particularly hard.

What of New South Wales? It had been settled longer and had fewer in the first generation category. Queensland shadowed Victoria in that regard. And how do we explain the considerable average age variations for Queensland and Tasmania? Like Victoria, Queensland had a population surge in the 1880s.[16] Perhaps the Queenslanders in England and Wales are the children of migrants returning to British family connections and to education and job opportunities not available in less developed and – in the 1890s – economically depressed Queensland?

Why are the Tasmanians so much older? There is no obvious hypothesis. Perhaps for Tasmanians, and to a lesser extent South Australians too, Melbourne was metropole enough? According to the 1901 census of Australia, in 1900 over one-third of internal migration in Australia was out-migration from Victoria, principally to New South Wales, but Tasmanians were more than twice as likely to migrate to Victoria as New South Wales.[17] Australian immigration and emigration by sea in 1900 again shows the greatest number of emigrants as being from Victoria.[18] Further independent corroboration of the preponderance of Victorians may be found in Simon

Sleight's analysis of the list of Australasians in Europe published in the *British Australasian* on 5 July 1900.[19]

Let us now look more closely at gender. It is evident immediately from Figure 4.2 that, among the Australia-born adults, females considerably outnumbered males. Overall, the ratio is 4:3, and for adults higher still.[20] Most of these women are listed as housewives, but we have no ready means of knowing, for instance, whether the wives married in Australia or Britain or whether they married other Australians. If we examine the total population of England and Wales by age cohort and gender (see Figure 4.3) we see that the host population does not display the spikes in late childhood, teens and 30s and 40s that the data for the Australia-born does (see Figure 4.4). People with very young children held off from migrating, and it seems adults waited, as a rule, until they had acquired skills and means before making their move.

What do we know about occupations? Figures 4.5 and 4.6 give a broad indication of the position, though Figure 4.6 omits housewife as a category, as this was not considered an occupational category at the time.[21] For men I found occupational spikes for the military/naval, including the merchant marine (224), many of them officers and NCOs rather than privates, with the highest rank that of colonel; there are 71 in what I would like to call 'performing arts' (artists, singers, actors, musicians); and 43 ministers of religion, including three rabbis. The most common calling for women, other than housewife or living on own means, was domestic service (365), followed by nursing (163). When the data for females and males is combined to produce a top ten occupations (Figure 4.7), beyond living on own means (900), there is retail (415), domestic service (365), military/naval (including the merchant marine) (224), then clerks (211). Thus, these Australians tend to have skills and are economically active or dependants of the economically active. The figures for Australia-born with disabilities show no variation from the overall England and Wales norm.

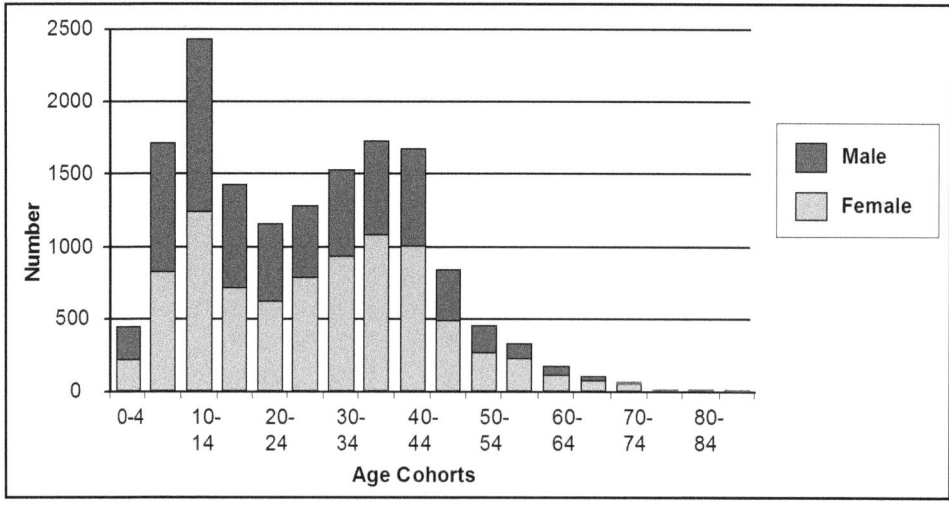

Figure 4.2 Gender of the Australians in England and Wales, 1901

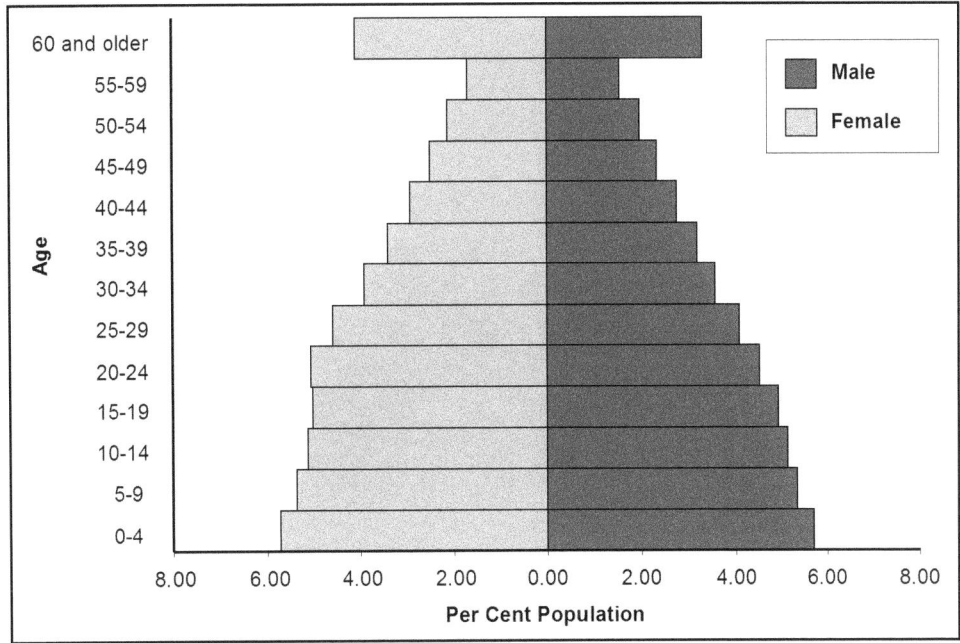

Figure 4.3 Age-Sex pyramid of the population of England and Wales, 1901
Source: Mitchell and Deane (1971, p.12).

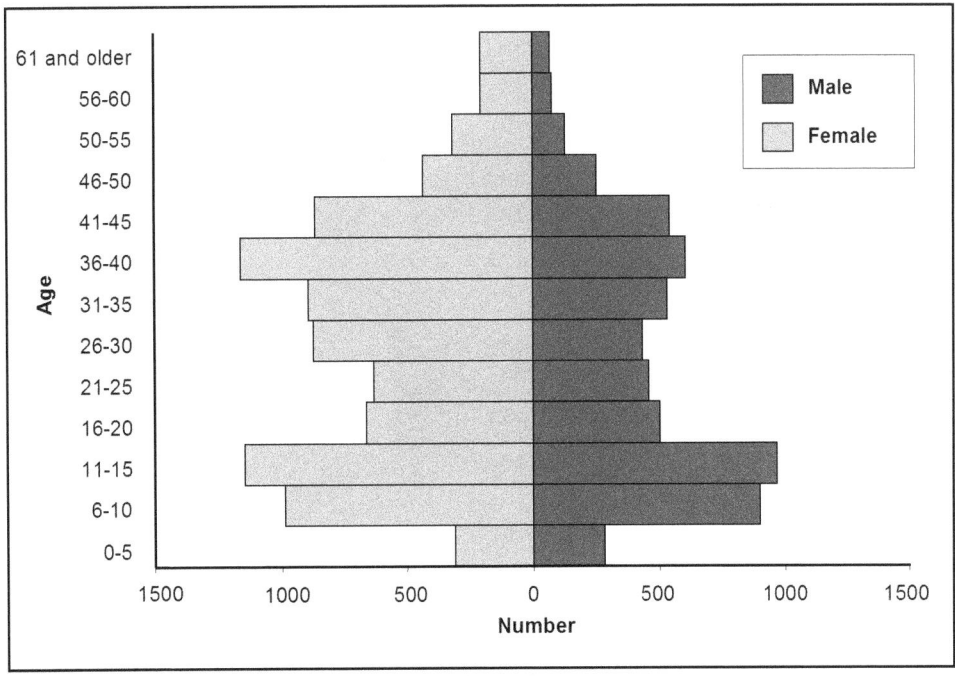

Figure 4.4 Age-Sex pyramid of the Australians in England and Wales, 1901

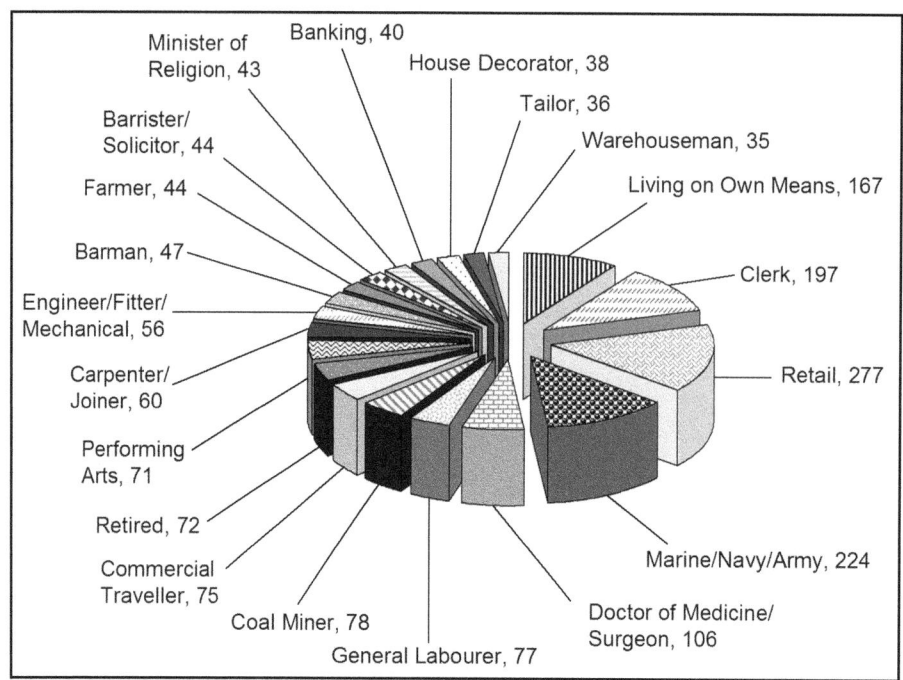

Figure 4.5 Top twenty male occupations for Australians in England and Wales, 1901

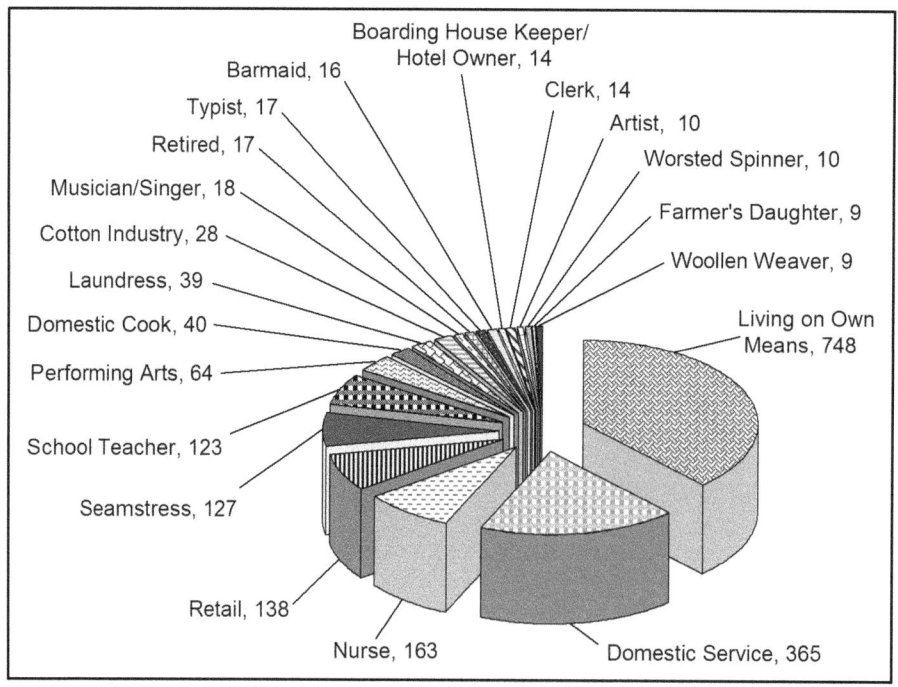

Figure 4.6 Top twenty female occupations for Australians in England and Wales, 1901

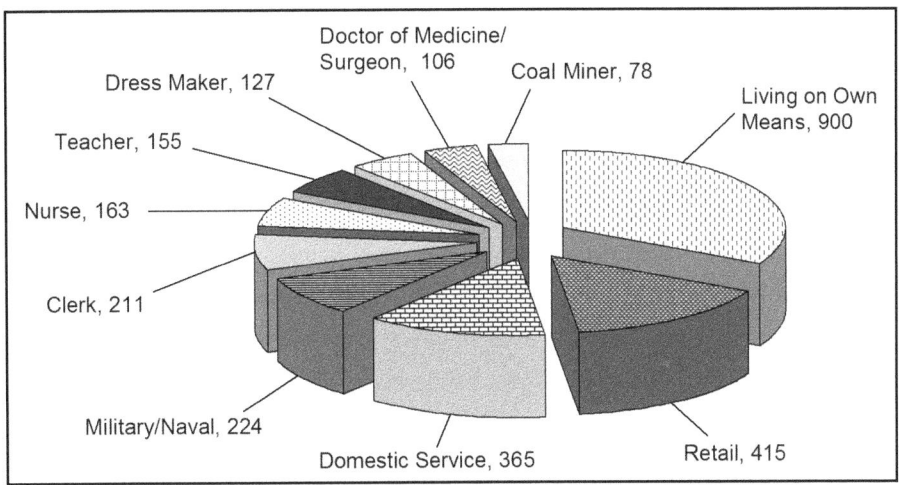

Figure 4.7 Top ten occupations for Australians in England and Wales, 1901

Where did the Australians settle in England and Wales? Figure 4.8 shows that there were concentrations of Australians in the main conurbations of London and Liverpool-Manchester, as one would expect, but also in south Wales, the north-east of England and along the southern coast. It is hardly surprising that these are the same areas from which British immigrants to Australia were principally drawn.[22] Unlike classical immigrant groups, however, which tend to stay in the large cities,[23] the Australians are found in considerable numbers virtually everywhere, which strongly suggests family and local connections before migrating, what might be called reverse chain-migration. The settlement distribution pattern is also somewhat gendered and age-related. For example, if we compare London and the rest of England and Wales, the average age of Australia-born women in London is 31, that of men 28, whereas the figure for women outside London is 27 and for men 24.[24] Australia-born Londoners were, thus, considerably older. The percentage of women in the total Australian population in London is 58 per cent, whereas for outside London it is 55. Australia-born children were on average aged seven across both England and Wales and in London. However, while children were 17 per cent of the total number of Australians in England and Wales in 1901, in London they were only 12 per cent, so Australian children were considerably more likely to be found outside London.

Let me now move on to two more detailed case studies. First, let us look at Wales. There were 506 Australia-born in Wales in 1901; their average age being 28. Of the 506, fully 295 were listed with no occupation, meaning that they were children or housewives. Of the rest, 29 were in collieries, in various posts from miner to surveyor. Others were scattered across a wide variety of occupations ranging from the professions (3 doctors, 1 clergyman, 6 engineers, 1 accountant) to trades of all sorts (2 bricklayers, 2 stonemasons, 1 carpenter, 1 plumber, 5 dressmakers and 1 milliner) to the unskilled (10 domestic servants, 5 labourers) and several were in relatively exotic jobs (an athletics coach, a music hall manager and a bath attendant). Thus most were skilled tradespeople of one kind or another with a smattering of professionals. The population distribution (Figure 4.9) shows a massive concentration in Glamorganshire, south Wales.

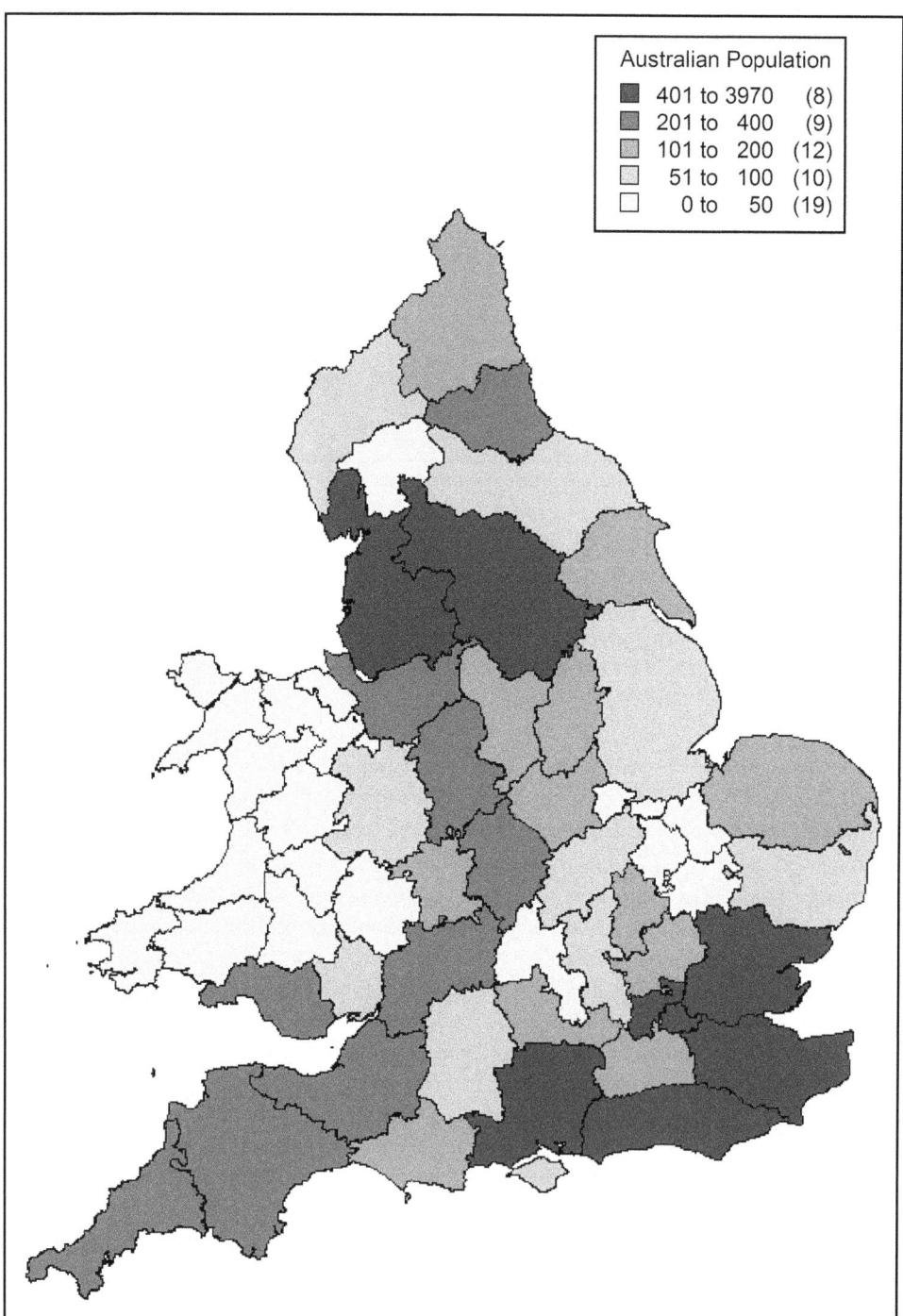

Figure 4.8 Distribution of the Australian population of England and Wales, 1901

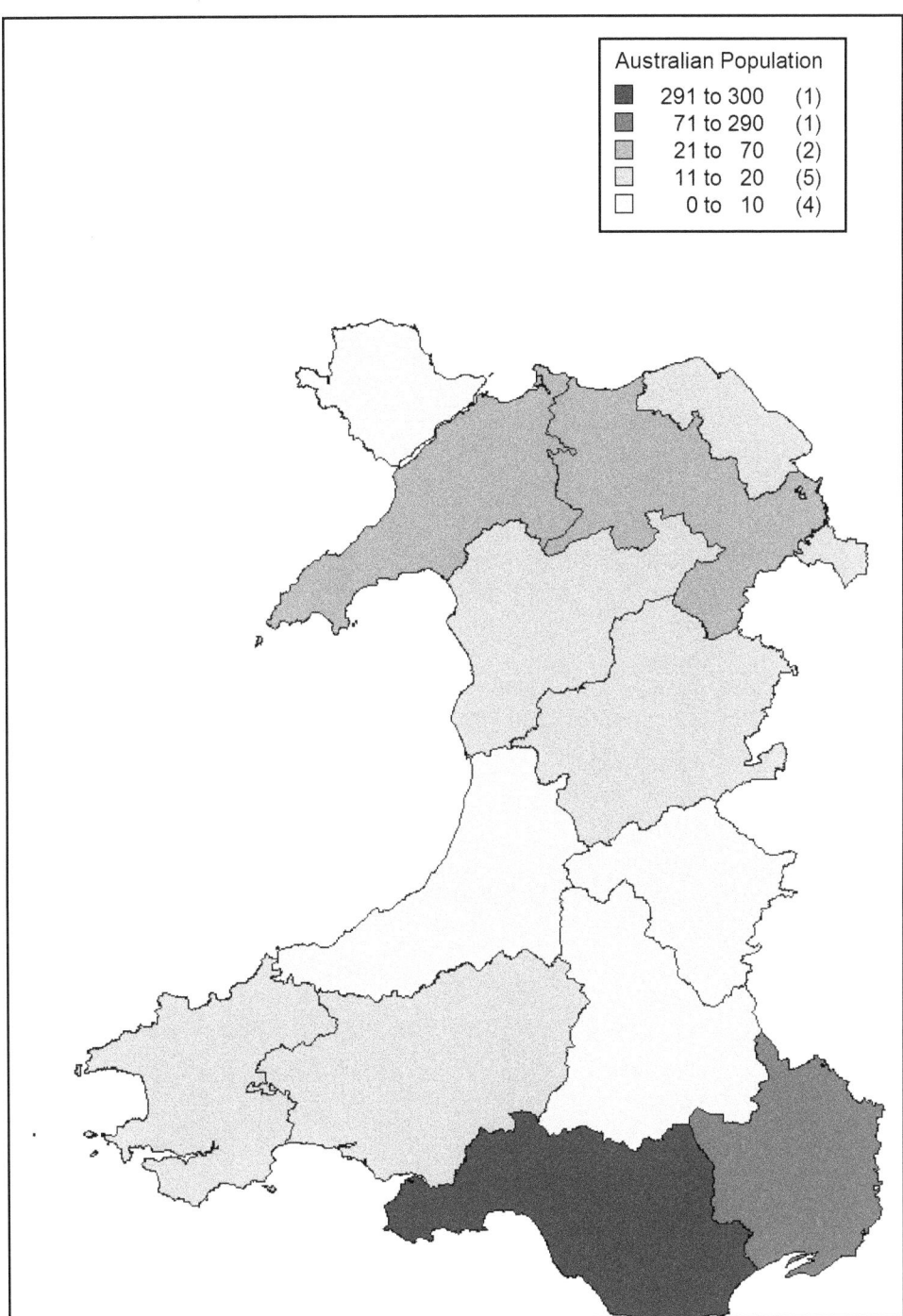

Figure 4.9 Distribution of the Australian population of Wales, 1901

Now, let me turn to a brief snapshot of London, here defined as the London County Council area plus the City of London. Table 4.1 shows a fairly even distribution across central London, but with a particular concentration in Kensington (Earl's Court, South and West Kensington), but also in Wandsworth, Paddington and Westminster. Kangaroo Valley seems to have a more venerable history than perhaps was thought.

London Borough	Number
Kensington	446
Lambeth	310
Wandsworth	253
Westminster	247
Paddington	241
St Pancras	172
Hampstead	166
St Marylebone	164
Camberwell	161
Islington	149
Fulham	148
Holborn	142
Stepney	141
Lewisham	134
Hackney	129
Hammersmith	118
Chelsea	104
Battersea	94
Southwark	79
Greenwich	78
Deptford	64
Poplar	58
Woolwich	56
Stoke Newington	40
Bethnal Green	29
Shoreditch	27
Bermondsey	26
City of London	16
Total	3792

Table 4.1 The Australians in London in 1901

London Borough	Average Age	Number of Females	Number of Males	Number of Australians
Kensington	33	309	137	446
Lambeth	26	174	136	310
Wandsworth	28	168	85	253
Westminster	32	138	109	247
Paddington	32	151	90	241
St Pancras	31	94	78	172
Hampstead	28	109	57	166
St Marylebone	31	109	55	164
Camberwell	29	85	76	161
Islington	33	82	67	149
Fulham	27	85	63	148
Holborn	30	78	64	142
Stepney	28	55	86	141
Lewisham	29	83	51	134
Hackney	25	64	65	129
Hammersmith	30	64	54	118
Chelsea	38	73	31	104
Battersea	30	59	35	94
Southwark	30	36	43	79
Greenwich	26	40	38	78
Deptford	27	37	27	64
Poplar	29	22	36	58
Woolwich	30	26	30	56
Stoke Newington	35	19	21	40
Bethnal Green	28	19	10	29
Shoreditch	26	16	11	27
Bermondsey	26	14	12	26
City of London	32	7	9	16
Total:	30*	2216	1576	3792

Table 4.2 The average age and female/male distribution of Australians across London, 1901
* Calculated by multiplying the average age for each borough by its number of inhabitants, then dividing the total of these figures by the total Australian population.

As mentioned above, Table 4.2 shows that the Australians in London had a higher average age (30 years) than was the case nationally (27 years). Is there any distinction between the genders in terms of where Australians lived in London? Tables 4.2 and 4.3 indicate a markedly greater propensity for female Australians to live in London's richer boroughs. Further, analysis of the occupational breakdown by borough shows that, for example in Kensington, these females are not, as one might surmise, in domestic service, but are housewives or 'living on own means' or schoolgirls. In poorer Stepney, the females are still housewives or at school. The 137 males in

Kensington include a preponderance of professionals, tradesmen and students, but also the Agent-General for Western Australia and a retired Chief Secretary; whereas in Stepney the 86 males are overwhelmingly tradesmen, skilled and unskilled labourers and schoolboys. An investigation of the distribution of Australia-born across London by borough and state of origin reveals no particular pattern in terms of state preferences for particular boroughs, other than confirming the tendency to live in the central west of the city. Again, the national trend for the greatest number to be from Victoria is reflected in London, and is evident whether the borough is rich or poor.

London Borough	Excess Females over Males (%)
Chelsea	40.38
Kensington	38.39
St Marylebone	32.93
Wandsworth	32.81
Hampstead	31.33
Bethnal Green	31.03
Battersea	25.53
Paddington	25.31
Lewisham	23.88
Shoreditch	18.52
All London	15.69
Deptford	15.63
Fulham	14.86
Lambeth	12.26
Westminster	11.74
Islington	10.07
Holborn	9.86
St Pancras	9.30
Hammersmith	8.47
Bermondsey	7.69
Camberwell	5.00
Greenwich	2.56
Hackney	-0.78
Stoke Newington	-5.00
Woolwich	-7.14
Southwark	-8.86
City of London	-12.50
Stepney	-21.99
Poplar	-24.14

Table 4.3 The excess of female over male Australians by borough, 1901

CONCLUSION

What, then, can we conclude overall from this analysis of the Australia-born in the 1901 census data for England and Wales?

- They were disproportionately from Victoria.
- The average age was 27, but Queenslanders were ten years younger on average and Tasmanians nine years older. Almost two-thirds of the adults were women.
- The population is relatively evenly spread across England and Wales suggesting reverse chain-migration.
- The adult males were overwhelmingly skilled people in trades and professions, with particular clusters for the military, performing artists, clergy and medical doctors.
- There were significant numbers of older children and teenagers.
- The Australia-born had an older average age (30) in London, and London's Australian women were more likely to live in the richer boroughs, and this in their own right and not as domestics.
- As a diasporic community the Australia-born were five times more significant as a proportion of population of their country of origin than were the major non-British world diasporas, such as the Russian and German, and ten times more than the American.

This Australian study suggests a complex web of relatively unrestricted migration flows and counter-flows such as one would expect from a fully interconnected British world rather than two separate countries.

Finally, we might ask whether this pattern also fitted for the other Dominions and the United States, whether those for the Russians and Germans were different, and for how long the pattern persisted. I am still working on the published census data for the period 1911 to 1971, but some characteristics are already clear. First, the strength of the pull of the British world varied from Dominion to Dominion and from time to time, stronger for New Zealand, Australia and South Africa than for Canada, but for all of them it was still much more significant per capita than for Germany, Russia, Poland and the United States. Second, the pattern of women predominating over men is common throughout the twentieth century for all of the former Dominions and persists to the present, whereas the Russian and Polish pattern is overwhelmingly male, and those for the United States and Germany vary over time. Third, though London acts as a magnet for all, those coming from the Dominions are less likely to respond to its attraction consistently across the century and still can be found all over the country. They also have a wider age and occupational distribution which equates more with that of the host community. In other words, the England and Wales census data shows that while we no longer have a British Empire, we still have a British world.

ENDNOTES

1. Bridge and Fedorowich, 2003,1–15. See also: Buckner and Bridge, 2003, 77–88; Buckner and Francis, 2005, 2006; Proudfoot and Roche, 2005.

2. Much of the data in this chapter is based on the *Census of England and Wales, 1901*, 1904, which provides a snapshot of the population on one night. There is, therefore, no way of telling how permanent or long-term the residency of the Australia-born was, but for the purposes of this chapter they will be described as immigrants.

3. *Census of the British Empire. 1901*, 1904, xl.

4. *Census of the British Empire. 1901*, 1904, 54.

5. In the census of 1900 the population of the Russian Empire was 126,367 that of Germany was 56,367 and that of the United States was 75,995. Mitchell, 1998, 4, 7, 50.

6. *Census of the British Empire, 1901*, 1904, 1.

7. *Census of England and Wales, 1901*, 1904.

8. The only previous works are a very evocative but largely impressionistic chapters in Inglis, 1992 and Woollacott, 2001. See also Richards, 2004a , 2004b.

9. Further details are available at: http://www.1901censusonline.com/.

10. *Census of the British Empire*, 54. There were also 18,829 Canadians and Newfoundlanders, 4,778 New Zealanders, 11,717 from the South African colonies, 10,198, from the British West Indies, and 52,848 from the Indian Empire.

11. The England and Wales Census for 1921 did make this distinction and the ratio of visitors to residents among the Australian-born enumerated then was one to nine.

12. Higgs, 2005, 89.

13. For the verification of place of birth, much of this analysis on a state basis, I am grateful to Australian Government: Geoscience 'Australia: Place Name Search'. [Internet]. available from: http://www.ga.gov.au/map/names.

14. Vamplew, 1987, 40. POP 275-285 Age structure, sex ratio and urban and rural distribution, Australia 1861-1981.

15. I am grateful to Kevin Tibbetts of QinetiQ for providing the average ages for England and Wales.

16. Woolcock, 1986, fig. 2.1, 30.

17. *Census of the British Empire. 1901*, 1904, xliv.

18. *The year-book of Australia*, 1902?, 73.

19. See Chapter 6 in this volume.

20. Interestingly, Graeme Hugo in Chapter 2 of this volume, shows that women still predominate 5:4 and that most Australia-born migrants are still in their 20s and 30s. Cf Fullilove and Flutter, 2004, 13, figure 2.2. Comparison between people departing Australia and the resident population by age, draws on a DIMIA unpublished tabulation for the financial year 2002–2003.

21. *Census of England and Wales, 1901*, 52–53 lists these.

22. See Jupp, 2004.

23. Panayi, 1994, 51.

24. The calculation excludes one male, whose age is indecipherable.

PRIMARY SOURCES

Australian Government, 'Geoscience Australia: Place name search'. [Internet]. Accessed 18 August 2008. Available from: http://www.ga.gov.au/map/names.

Census of England and Wales, 1901, General Report with Appendices. 1904. Cd. 2174. London: HMSO.

Census of the British Empire. 1901: Report with summary and detailed tables for the several colonies, &c., area, houses, and population; also population classified by ages, condition as to marriage, occupations, birthplaces, religions, degrees of education, and infirmities. 1906. Cd. 2660. London: HMSO, by Darling & Son, Ltd.

Genes Reunited Records Ltd. '1901 census online'. [Internet]. Accessed 18 August 2008. Available from:http://www.1901censusonline.com/.

The year-book of Australia. 1902? Sydney: The Year-Book of Australia & Publishing Company Ltd.

REFERENCES

Bridge, Carl; Fedorowich, K. 2003. 'Mapping the British world'. In *The British world: Diaspora, culture and identity*, edited by Bridge, Carl; Fedorowich, Kent. London: Frank Cass.

Buckner, P.A; Bridge, Carl. 2003. 'Reinventing the British world'. Round Table 92 (368) (January): 77–88. DOI: 10.1080/750456741.

Buckner, P.A.; Douglas, F., editors. 2005. *Rediscovering the British world*. Calgary: University of Calgary Press.

Buckner, P.A.; Douglas, F. 2006. *Canada and the British world*. Vancouver: UBC Press.

Fullilove, Michael; Flutter, Chloë. 2004. *Diaspora: The world wide web of Australians*. Double Bay, NSW: Lowy Institute.

Higgs, Edward. 2005. *Making sense of the census revisited: Census records for England and Wales 1801–1901. A handbook for historical researchers*. London: Institute of Historical Research and the National Archives of the UK.

Inglis, K.S. 1992. 'Going home: Australians in England, 1870–1900'. In *Home or away? Immigrants in colonial Australia*, edited by Fitzpatrick, David. Canberra: Division of Historical Studies and Centre for Immigration and Multicultural Studies, Research School of Social Sciences, Australian National University.

Jupp, James. 2004. *The English in Australia*. Melbourne: Cambridge University Press.

Mitchell, B.R. 1998. *International historical statistics: Europe 1750–1993*. 4th edn. London: Macmillan Reference.

Mitchell, B.R.; Deane, Phyllis. *Abstract of British Historical Statistics*. Cambridge: Cambridge University Press.

Panayi, Panikos. 1994. *Immigration, ethnicity and racism in Britain, 1815–1945*. Manchester: Manchester University Press.

Proudfoot, Lindsay J.; Roche, Michael M., editors. 2005. *(Dis)Placing empire: Renegotiating British colonial geographies*. Aldershot: Ashgate.

Richards, Eric. 2004a. 'Running home from Australia: Intercolonial mobility and migrant expectations in the nineteenth century'. In *Emigrant homecomings: The return movement of emigrants 1600–2000*, edited by Harper, Marjory. Manchester: Manchester University Press.

Richards, Eric. 2004b. *Britannia's children: Emigration from England, Scotland, Wales and Ireland since 1600*. London: Hambledon.

Vamplew, Wray, editor. 1987. *Australians: Historical statistics*. Broadway, NSW: Fairfax, Syme & Weldon Associates.

Woolcock, Helen R. 1986. *Rights of passage. Emigration to Australia in the nineteenth century*. London: Tavistock.

Woollacott, Angela. 2001. *To try her fortune in London: Australian women, colonialism, and modernity*. New York, Oxford: Oxford University Press.

Cite this chapter as: Bridge, Carl. 2009. 'Australians in the England and Wales census of 1901: A demographic survey'. *Australians in Britain: The Twentieth-Century Experience*, edited by Bridge, Carl; Crawford, Robert; Dunstan, David. Melbourne: Monash University ePress. pp. 4.1 to 4.16. DOI: 10.2104/ab090004.

TOM ROBERTS' LONDON YEARS

John Rickard, Monash University
> John Rickard is honorary professor at Monash University. His publications include Australia: A Cultural History *(1988, 1996) and* A Family Romance: The Deakins at Home *(1996)*.

> In examining Tom Roberts' London years (1903–1923) this article focuses on the painter's triangle of loyalties – Australian, English and British imperial – and questions the relevance of considering him an expatriate. New evidence is presented about the house Tom and Lillie built in Hampstead Garden Suburb, which served as a refuge from the difficulties and disappointments of Tom's career, as well as from the tiring drudgery of war work.

In the years he spent in England Tom Roberts would never have considered himself an expatriate. And, indeed, why should he have? He was born in England in 1856, migrating to Australia with his mother and younger sister and brother at the age of thirteen; spent the years 1881–1885 pursuing his art studies at the Royal Academy Schools in London; and was domiciled in England from 1903 to 1923. In so far as an expatriate is defined as a person who has withdrawn from residence in his native country, it would technically be more correct to describe Roberts as an expatriate Englishman in Australia.[1]

Humphrey McQueen begins his biography of Roberts by pointing out that the painter spent thirty-five of his seventy-five years in England and posits that 'understanding Roberts' ambitions and achievements requires an appreciation of the codes and assumptions that determined advancement and shaped prospects for a white man throughout the British Empire'. But while the imperial dimension of Roberts' career is important, McQueen shows less interest in the painter's Englishness, as distinct from Britishness, and his continuing relationship with the land of his birth. In her *Catalogue Raisonée* Helen Topliss describes Roberts in his London years as an expatriate, and in her contribution to the 1996 Tom Roberts exhibition she sees him as 'characteristic of that immigrant generation of artists, writers and craftworkers who had arrived in Australia at a sufficiently early age to adapt to the needs of a new country', but also describes him as having 'split loyalties'. Virginia Spate, however, identifies the Britishness and Australianness of immigrant painters from England and Scotland as 'one and the same thing', which is an odd way of putting it, but goes further in asserting that these painters 'contributed as much, if not more, to the development of an Australian style and iconography than did the native-born'. In this chapter I look at Roberts' London years with a view to teasing out his own sense of identity, and exploring what the trinity of Britishness, Englishness and Australianness meant to him.[2]

As early as 1899 Roberts had expressed his intention of making the move to England. In 1900, writing from New Zealand, he told his friend S.W. Pring that 'I may happen to see you in England – if I can clear enough by a sale I think of having – it's ho for the old country – there's nothing for a painter here'. But it was his extended work on 'The Big Picture', the commissioned painting of the opening of the first federal parliament in 1901, which finally served to justify the journey. Some of Roberts' friends commiserated with him about the time and effort the 'big picture' demanded. 'I hope the big machine is a success', wrote Charles Conder, 'but it must be an awful job to do'. But Roberts himself was totally committed to the project. He had been there in the Royal Exhibition Building in Melbourne, watching from a gallery, and described the occasion as 'very solemn and great': 'the heads on the floor looked like a landscape stretching away'. To Pring he confided:

> Friends pity me but they needn't. I know what a chance there is to produce something & am going for it for all it's worth. Machine? no. a document? – yes? & something more. The Royalty & and its suite of Governors of states and – the members, democracy – with the people – that's the Empire & and this all meets under one roof. And that's what I'm painting.

Roberts took for granted that this was a national occasion, but the 'big picture' was ultimately a portrait of the empire, captured in this one moment in the cathedral-like space of the Exhibition Building.[3]

Roberts persuaded the Australian Art Association, which had originally commissioned the painting, that he needed to travel to England to complete the portraits of the members of the royal party. The association agreed to meet the cost of freight for the painting and rental of a studio in London, but Roberts had to pay the fare for himself and his family. The painter was accorded an official farewell dinner, presided over by the Lord Mayor of Melbourne. Tom, his wife Lillie and their five-year-old son Caleb arrived in England in April 1903. They took lodgings in Manchester Square, later in the year moving to a flat in Putney. Although he had rented a studio in Warwick Square, the Imperial Institute also gave him the use of its South Africa Room, a big space for the painting with high north-facing windows, 'a room to dream in' as he described it.[4] There were still some fifty dignitaries to paint, and his 'brush' with royalty included lunch with the Duke and Duchess of York, now Prince and Princess of Wales, which was the kind of recognition Roberts always enjoyed. Late in the piece, it seems, it was decided that the painting, which the association had formally given to the Commonwealth, should in turn be presented to King Edward. So the long, laborious process culminated in a ceremony on 4 July 1904 at the Royal Academy, where the painting was put on display. The 'big picture' had come to rest, along with its painter, at the heart of empire.[5]

Roberts might well have felt satisfaction at the completion of a project which had meant so much to him. But his hope that mixing with the rich and famous would result in portrait commissions was largely disappointed. And the 'big picture' itself received only condescending notice from the critics. He was beginning to realise that at the age of forty-eight establishing a new career in London was not going to be easy. The heart of empire could seem a heartless place. As he put it in a much-quoted interview in 1906:

> England doesn't really *want* anybody. She has everybody and everything. The supply is in excess of the demand. She has the whole world to draw upon, and everyone comes here sooner or later. The only thing is to make her want you, and that is difficult, for she really only wants the exceptional in any line.

One can sense the self-doubt in his voice: was what he had to offer exceptional? Nor did Lillie warm to London. When Frederick McCubbin – the 'Prof' as Roberts always called him – wrote in 1904 expressing the hope that he and Lillie were liking London better, it was probably Lillie he had in mind, as her only experience of England had been in the course of a grand tour with friends in 1886. A year later we find Roberts telling the 'Prof' that 'the Missus' was beginning to think London was an interesting place. Lillie had taken up wood carving, learning to gild, and was soon making frames, with a view not only to saving money with Tom's paintings, but also contributing to the family income.[6]

With his three-year preoccupation with the 'Big Picture' at an end, it seemed as if Roberts suddenly had an empty canvas before him, and the sight was somehow unnerving. 'I'm beginning work here', he told Alfred Deakin in 1904, 'and have a very uphill fight before me. The mere quantity and variety of styles and efforts of different men is likely to affect one's own outlook – and you have to stand very firm and be sure'. The riches of the European art scene seemed constricting rather than liberating. To make matters worse he started having problems with his eyes: it was almost as if his loss of confidence was affecting what the painter was able to see. There was, however, no question of going back to Australia. The career commitment had been made. But the problems he was encountering did diminish the sense of having come 'home'.[7]

McCubbin's career offers an interesting contrast. Native-born, he had, at this time, never travelled outside Australia. While Roberts was finishing the 'big picture' in London, McCubbin was working on his own magnus opus: 'I am pegging on at the Pioneer and I feel like the poor devels [sic] I am painting in the picture rather sad about it however I am doing my best'. He was also canvassing the possibility of making a trip to Europe, which Roberts was encouraging, offering 'a truckle bed' in their flat to put him up for a couple of months. In 1904 McCubbin dismally reported on his one-man show at the Athenaeum, which he thought represented his 'best ever' work (it included his 'big picture') but for which receipts were only a few pounds over expenses: 'the indifference that is allied to contempt underlies all that Melbourne cares for Art'. Responding to Roberts' longstanding invitation, he remarked on his own 'unfortunate want of the initiative'. 'I sometimes think that it's all a dream & that there is no Europe, that it's a huge joke'. With so many of his fellow artists in London he was feeling lonely in the colonial outpost: 'Smike and You and the boys will look upon me as an Old Provincial I am afraid when I get to Europe'. But when at last he made the trip in 1907 he did have the satisfaction of knowing that the National Gallery of Victoria had recently used the Felton Bequest to acquire 'The Pioneer' for £350. That gallery did not buy a Roberts until 1920.[8]

From time to time Roberts would feel some cause for optimism – a short trip to Holland in 1905 resulted in 'the best painting work I've done so far' he told the 'Prof' – but in 1907 there was huge disappointment when a painting he had been working on for two years, 'The Sleeper Awakened', was rejected by the Royal Academy. This painting was inspired by the *Arabian Nights* and seemed an unlikely subject for Roberts, but was clearly meant to mark a new departure in his work. 'I got the "gem" biffed last night', he told Pring; 'So far, it seems a rum climax to two years work'. He was not prepared to give away too much about his feelings. His sense of failure was heightened by the knowledge that nine Australians had had paintings accepted by the academy. Caleb recalled his father lamenting that he had gone to England 'ten years too late' to achieve recognition.[9]

In the face of this and similar knockbacks, it was a sign of his grim determination that Tom and Lillie decided to build a house in the newly opened up Hampstead Garden Suburb. Lillie's father had died in 1905, a cause for considerable grief given the separation of distance, but a modestly sizeable inheritance made the move into property possible. There was also a saving involved, as the idea was for the house to have its own studio, which meant there would be no need to keep up the studio in Kensington he had rented since 1905.

Hampstead Garden Suburb, an extension of Golders Green, was an interesting choice. It was, of course, a move to the suburban periphery; the trust which established the garden suburb had only acquired the 240 acres in 1907. Its proximity to Hampstead Heath was a plus, but there were other reasons why this new development would have appealed to Tom and Lillie. The suburb was the lifework of Henrietta Barnett, wife of the Reverend Samuel Barnett, a man who has been described as, physically, 'peculiarly unattractive'. Both were very much committed to 'good works' and had got to know each other through the Charity Organisation Society. During a twenty-one-year stint at St Jude's Whitechapel they had built Toynbee Hall. Beatrice Webb described Henrietta as 'an active-minded, true and warm-hearted woman. She is conceited; she would be objectionably conceited if it were not for her genuine belief in her husband's superiority not only to the rest of the world but to herself'. In 1879 the Barnetts had acquired a house in Hampstead which served both as a 'cottage home' for girls, training them for domestic service, and as a retreat for themselves; ten years later they moved the cottage to Heath End. As the expanding metropolis began to encroach on the area around Hampstead Heath plans were made for an extension to the Heath reserve. It was in this context that Henrietta Barnett became enthused of the idea of ensuring appropriate suburban development in the vicinity of the Heath extension.[10]

Adopting the ideal of the garden suburb, Henrietta harnessed it to her social agenda. The architect Raymond Unwin, whose firm was already involved with Letchworth Garden Suburb, was enlisted. In 1911 Unwin, writing in the *Garden Cities & Town Planning Magazine*, explained the philosophy underpinning the Hampstead project:

> I ... felt it to be very important to secure some good centre to the estate, which it was intended should be developed as a community having a certain unity of social character. It was regarded by Mrs Barnett as one of the most important parts of the scheme, from the social point of view, that all classes should be housed within the area of the estate. Thoughtful people who have had experience of large towns in the neighbourhood of which there have been growing up vast suburbs often peopled by one class or another of the community, have realised the very grave evils resulting from this aggregation of people having such a one-sided and limited outlook on life. And while it is obviously not possible to mix together indiscriminately the dwellings of people of all classes, the promoters of the suburb felt that a great effort should be made to prove that it is not only possible, but as it is in every way most desirable, so by proper planning it may be arranged that all classes of the community should live together in such close relationship that even the smaller units of social life, such as the parish, should contain a sufficiently wide variety of types and classes of people to produce a healthy, interesting and open-minded society.

This obsession with the intractability of the class order might have seemed peculiarly English, but Henrietta Barnett's social agenda would have appealed to Roberts, with his experience of colonial democracy (and this was a time when Australasia was regarded as a social laboratory for the world). The aesthetic of the garden suburb would also have pleased him: the emphasis on architectural harmony, the use of local materials, the arts-and-crafts dimension. The suburb early on acquired something of an arty reputation, which rather irritated Henrietta. 'People often assume that the inhabitants of the Garden Suburb are all eccentric, sandalled, corsetless "cranks". That', she insisted, 'is not the case'. But the elderly author of the history of the suburb recalls that as a small child in the 1920s he 'certainly had the impression that women living north of Meadway were likely to wear bandeaux and shapeless homespun and probably had bare feet!'. If Roberts missed having easy access to the society of his brother artists in Chelsea, he could nevertheless feel that Hampstead Garden Suburb provided a congenial environment for an artist.[11]

* * *

Quite a few years ago – more than I care to remember in fact – I went in search of the house that Tom and Lillie had built. Although the house had been described by their contemporaries, many quoted by R.H. Croll, it did not seem that any of the more recent writers on Roberts had sighted it. Similarly, McQueen in his biography records in a footnote a 'personal visit' to Putney, where Tom and Lillie rented their flat, but no such visit to Hampstead Garden Suburb is noted. As will emerge, there is a reason why the house is difficult to locate.

As I walked from Golders Green tube station, going down Hoop Lane and into Meadway and the leafy quietness of Hampstead Garden Suburb, I was struck by the imposing uniformity of style – steep pitched roofs, big chimneys, casement windows, hedges but no garden walls. Everything seemed intact: why shouldn't the Roberts house have survived? I knew that it had originally been no.1 Bigwood Road, and that later it had been renumbered no. 27. I had also copied a primitive sketch of the house – no more than four or five lines – that Roberts had included in a letter to T.R. Bavin, in which he had described the house as 'a small one tacked on [to] a good studio'.[12] When, with the aid of my *London A to Z*, I found Bigwood Road my hopes rose. But on reaching no. 17, a house on the corner of Southway, I next encountered a block of institutional buildings labelled Hampstead Garden Suburb Institute. And then, on the other side of the institute, where I figured no. 27 should have been, was a school. Well, I thought, that explains the lack of reference to the house: it had made way for the school.

Rather disconsolate, I walked up Northway to the top of the hill and Central Square, which is dominated by two handsome brick churches designed by Edwin Lutyens: the parish church, St Jude-on-the-Hill, and the Free Church (a Roman Catholic church apparently being considered unnecessary). Both were closed to visitors on a week day. The square itself was a rather empty, desolate space, except for a couple of lads kicking a football.[13] I was beginning to lose interest in this highly planned, self-contained garden suburb. Until, that is, strolling down Southway I noticed no. 10, which bore a remarkable resemblance to Roberts' little sketch, with a room at the front, with studio-like windows, facing north. I considered knocking on the door there and then, but thought better of it. That afternoon I penned a letter to the owner/occupier with my enquiry. Within twenty-four hours I was rung by the owner, a Mr Robert Walker: and yes, in the course of his own research into the origins of his house, he had acquired copies of the architect's drawings from the Suburb Archive.

Figure 5.1 Tom and Lillie Roberts' house in Hampstead Garden Suburb
Source: Hampstead Garden Suburb Archive

The house had been built for a Mr Tom Roberts, a painter, and while Mr Walker was aware that the front room had been designed as a studio he had no idea of Roberts' status in the pantheon of Australian art. Invited to afternoon tea, I was able to inspect the house, only superficially altered since Tom and Lillie lived here, and was then able to pursue the research trail to the Suburb Archive. It had been one of the first houses built in that locality, which helps explain its originally been no. 1 Bigwood Avenue. It was actually used in advertisements for the Hampstead Garden Suburb development. Later, when Bigwood Avenue was extended to the north, the section where the Roberts house was located was renamed Southway, though looking at the overall plan, one assumes this must always have been the intention. The 1971 Conservation Study describes no. 10 Southway as 'a gem of small scale dignity by Geoffrey Lucas, a square block with a canted window to the ground floor and a big central chimney'. Mr Walker reported that in the late 1950s Tom Roberts' son materialised on the doorstep (he couldn't remember his name) with a woman he assumed to be his wife, taxi waiting, chiefly concerned, it seemed, to ascertain whether a gun had been left in the loft: it seemed an unlikely mission, given the time lapse, and they departed gunless. More recently Caleb's son Noel had been in touch, exchanging information with the Walkers. But no historian or biographer had set foot in the house that Tom and Lillie built.[14]

*   *   *

The house, built at a cost of about £670,[15] was a success. Tom and Lillie approved what the architect Lucas had designed for them:

> We've been lucky enough to have chosen a site that overlooks Hampstead Heath from which we are only a few minutes walk – The house is a small one tacked on a good studio – The Mrs has cupboards all over the place – (all nearly full!) & no passages – We are fit and well the Mrs enjoying things.

It was, however, out on the edge and there was difficulty getting a maid – 'we are too much in the wilderness!' As for the studio, it was 'a privilege to work in it'. Jessie Traill described it as 'a charming home', and an English friend remarked 'its great ingenuity in convenience of arrangement and economy of space', and saw both house and garden as bearing 'the impress of artistic design'. One might guess that Lillie had some influence on the house plan, but the garden was very much Tom's preserve: he planted sycamore trees, hawthorn, fruit trees (there were still eight pear trees when the Walkers bought the house), raspberry, currant and gooseberry bushes. For him 'a bit of gardening with the smell of the fresh earth' was 'like a tonic'. On Sundays Tom and Lillie presided over a kind of afternoon tea salon, sometimes in an arbour in the garden, otherwise in the studio in the midst of Tom's paintings.[16]

Tom and Lillie found themselves part of a lively community, its pioneers, attracted by the garden suburb ideal, expecting to have a say in its affairs. By 1910 a Club House had been built, with a hall, billiard room, smoking room and a women's meeting room. In 1911 King George and Queen Mary visited the Club House and took a two-hour look at the garden suburb, which was clearly the subject of public interest: was Tom there to renew his acquaintance with the Royals? Within a few years Henrietta Barnett was boasting that there was an art school, a music school, provision for adult classes and societies, a residential club house for working ladies, an eventide home and a rest home for tired working girls. She saw the residents of the suburb as being 'relieved of the oppression of wealth, and able to meet each other on the simpler and deeper grounds of common interests and shared aspirations'. Tom and Lillie may have been living on the suburban fringe, but they could feel themselves to be participants in an important social experiment.[17]

The move to Hampstead Garden Suburb coincided with an improvement in Roberts' artistic morale. In early 1909 he told Pring of 'a kind of dawning in … my work after four or five years of doubt and uncertainty' and later in the year he confirmed that 'after a long spell I've found some light, & things are clearer for me'.[18] In 1910 he could breathe a sigh of relief when the Royal Academy hung two of his paintings.

Although now living on the suburban fringe Roberts did not lose touch with the social life associated with the London art scene. He still dropped in on the Chelsea Arts Club, which had a significant Australian membership. Indeed, Bernard Smith, commenting on the exodus of Australian painters at this time, tartly observes that 'it was in the Chelsea Arts Club that the Heidelberg School established its last and least distinguished camp'. Nor is it a surprise to find Roberts, along with George Lambert, organising a reception and entertainment for Australian representatives and delegates attending the Imperial Conference in 1911. It was held at the Imperial Institute, but Roberts and Lambert enlisted many of their friends from the Chelsea Arts Club to take part. The *British Australasian* described the event as 'most brilliant and successful'. Boy Scouts formed a kind of guard of honour at the door and the band of the Grenadier Guards provided 'beautiful selections'. The popular Peter Dawson was on hand to sing 'Kangaroo and Dingo' and, less appropriately, 'Rolling down to Rio'.[19]

But the climax of the evening was a series of acted tableaux telling the story of 'Australian development and awakening'. 'Watched only by scanty packs of blackfellows', sleeping Australia is first visited by the adventurers of Spain who, 'careless of their own as for others' lives [are] uninterested in any new land that could not give them riches and slaves. Not for them will Australia awake'. Next on the scene are Dutch traders: they are keen, money-conscious observers, but, used to tropical islands, they do not respond to 'Australia's more subtle beauties'. Australia stirs but 'cannot yield herself to such sordid wooers – and she sinks to sleep again'. Now, at last:

> Enter the British, masterful but kindly wooers. As the natives, suspecting these strange newcomers, prepare to resent their intrusion, the Commander soothes their fears and restrains the impetuosity of his own men, at the same time claiming the land for Britain. At last Australia knows her own. It is for them she has waited so long, and at their touch she lives.

The fourth episode, in praise of the explorer, was performed by the 'Hon Walter James and a black', the latter the only unnamed actor in the entertainment. Then comes the discovery of gold: 'Australia rejoices, eager to shower all her wealth upon the men who love her'. Finally, the apotheosis: 'The sister States, occupied with local rivalry, disturb Australia by their lack of harmony. She uses all the means of entreaty and persuasion at her command to urge Federation'. In this episode it was noted that 'the part of a little black girl was taken by Miss Konody' – the daughter, it would appear, of Mrs Konody who was playing one of the States. Little Miss Konody was presumably 'blacked up' for the occasion, as must have been the case with the 'blackfellows' in earlier scenes, but from where had Roberts and Lambert recruited the explorer's black?[20]

Throughout this story of Australian awakening, the Aborigines are little more than background figures, unnoticed by the sleeping Australia. One is tempted to pursue the metaphor through to its logical conclusion – that, with the arrival of the British, Australia would get no sleep at all, and might well hanker for the peace and quiet of the Aboriginal centuries. Of course the entertainment was a light-hearted affair intended to please and amuse its imperial audience, but its celebration of British superiority has the ring of sincerity. The omissions are also telling: while explorers and gold-diggers are held up for esteem, convicts are tidily swept under the imperial carpet. On the other hand, one wonders whether Roberts, who had an interest in Aboriginal culture, was responsible for including the 'little black girl' in the Federation scene. Was it meant to suggest that in the great national and imperial moment that he had portrayed in 'the big picture' the Aboriginal presence could not be entirely ignored?

More confident in his painting, Roberts had a modestly successful solo exhibition in February 1914, and perhaps boosted by this was intending to pay a visit to Australia when the Great War intervened. He was on his way to Italy on a painting trip when, as he put it, 'the thing began to happen … I could not paint. I saw the boys in the trenches between me and the canvas', and he returned to England: 'It was no use. I had to join up, I simply couldn't keep out of it. I had planned my trip to Australia before the war, but I just had to postpone it, make a slight mistake about my age, and do my little bit'. On his return he joined the volunteers, 'the last ditchers' he called them, going on long route marches every Saturday. Sometime in mid-1915 an officer walked into the Chelsea Arts Club seeking volunteers for the military hospitals. Roberts was among a number of artists who answered the call. He found himself at the Third London General Hospital where he was to spend the rest of the war, by which time he had, as Caleb put it, reached 'the exalted rank of Sergeant'. 'I'm very proud to be a Tommy', he told Pring in 1915. But the work was often exhausting: he records one day when he was on duty from 6 a.m. until after 10 p.m. with only one half-hour break. According to Caleb 'he would come home to Golders Green on week-end leave and rest with little energy left for other interests'. For the rest of the war he hardly painted at all. He was either overlooked in the appointment of war artists or preferred the penance of the hospital work.[21]

In late 1919 Roberts at last set out on the journey to Australia, the trip justified partly in terms of restoring his health, which seemed to have been knocked by the years of war work (he was now in his sixties), and partly with a view to selling some paintings there. And Lillie had hopes that 'the voyage and visit to the old land will set him up to come back for a happy old age'.[22] That it did – and in 1923 he and Lillie finally returned to Australia and to something resembling retirement. By this time Caleb had married and was settled in England.

Tom's comments in press interviews during his 1919–1920 visit and on his and Lillie's arrival in 1923 point up the complexity of loyalties at play. He was proud to be a Tommy and to be doing his bit for Britain and empire, but he was also 'proud of the Australians' whose 'unconsciously fine bearing made people think they were officers instead of privates'. He was seeing 'the Australians' in London, and it was in that sense an English perspective, echoing the celebrated image that the poet John Masefield had offered in Gallipoli, when he praised the Anzacs for their 'physical beauty and nobility of bearing'. Sensitive, perhaps, because of his long absence in

England, Roberts seemed hesitant about his own Australianness: 'When people tell me I am not an Australian ... I reply that there are many people not Australians who do Australian things'. In 1923 he told the *Adelaide Evening Journal* that he hoped to stay in Australia, 'Mrs Roberts permitting':

> Mrs Roberts burst out laughing. 'My husband is a goose,' she said with whimsical tenderness. 'Also he will never really grow up. As a matter of fact he is just teasing me. He knows perfectly well that I share his partiality for Australia – the more so that he finds such sure inspiration here'.

The 'partiality for Australia' suggests not so much a sense of the expatriate coming home as the making of a difficult choice. And, of course, Lillie would in particular regret the separation from their only son and child, Caleb.[23]

There was never any doubt about Roberts' imperial loyalty and it seemed that his having been born in England strengthened that attachment. There is a nice symbolism to his making the journey to the heart of empire in 1903 with the 'big picture', so to speak, in his luggage. Both painter and painting would eventually return to Australia, though the latter technically only on permanent loan. But the historical tableaux he helped stage in 1911 had a significance for those involved simply because the entertainment took place in London: the tableaux represent a kind of Australian performance in honour of the empire. 'Australia' is the continent: the people in the tableaux are not 'Australians' but the 'masterful but kindly' British.

Many of Roberts' contemporaries saw him as being English. His nickname, Bulldog, loudly proclaimed it. His accent was perceived as being English. The native-born Norman Lindsay, who admired Roberts' work, was in no doubt that he was an Englishman. And I don't think Roberts would have disputed the fact: though he might well have seen himself as an Englishman who did Australian things. On returning to live in Australia in 1923 he was eager not to be seen as forsaking England. 'Don't run away with the idea that we didn't appreciate dear old England', he told the Adelaide journalist, adding nostalgically, 'We had a jolly little home at Golders Green, where many of the fraternity would congregate'. Hampstead Garden Suburb, and the values it represented, had been an important part of Tom and Lillie's English experience. Unlike the flat in Putney, it was a place where they could feel rooted in the soil.[24]

James Quinn, whom Roberts acknowledged as an important influence in reviving and renewing his powers, writing to Roberts from England told him that now he was 'back home I am sure you will see the character of the Australian bush as no Australian, who has not been away from home can see it'. This was very close to Lindsay's view: 'The mind from abroad, when it has vision, possesses a wider perspective. It sees virtues and advantages that escape the native-born, whose sense of them is blunted by familiarity'. It was important in Roberts' role in helping create the Heidelberg School that he had just returned from England, but 'it was in Australia that I gained my first impressions of the beauty of the world, and the bush taught me'. And it is this perspective from abroad that Spate is pointing to when paying tribute to the contribution of 'immigrant painters' to 'Australian style and iconography'.[25]

It is not germane to my argument here whether this interpretation of the contribution of Roberts and other 'immigrant painters' is valid or not, though I think it is patronising of McQueen to conclude, with respect to Roberts' first decade in England, that 'in courting respectability he had achieved irrelevance'.[26] In seeking to make a living in England, was Roberts 'courting respectability'? (Roberts, whether in Melbourne or London, clearly thought there was nothing wrong with a bit of 'respectability' which, as far as he was concerned, could co-exist with a whiff of bohemia.) And it is relevant to note here that art historians are not so ready as they once were to dismiss out of hand Roberts' English and later Australian works.[27]

At the outset I suggested that strictly speaking Tom Roberts was an English rather than an Australian expatriate. But perhaps the real point is that for someone like Roberts it is not rewarding to apply the label 'expatriate' at all. For him perhaps more than for anyone, W.K. Hancock's classic formulation, 'independent Australian Briton', is appropriate.[28] Within the bounds of the empire, Tom Roberts moved to and fro between centre and periphery. There were choices involved relating to career and family, but from his point of view it was not a choice between being English or Australian. If some of his contemporaries saw him as an Englishman, so be it: but he knew that, for him as a painter, the Australian bush, much more than the Royal Academy Schools, had been his teacher.

ENDNOTES

1. The *Macquarie Dictionary* defines 'to expatriate' as 'to withdraw (oneself) from residence in one's native country' or 'from allegiance to one's country', and 'an expatriate' as 'an expatriated person'. 'Native country' implies the country of one's birth. http://www.macquariedictionary.com.au, accessed 16 October 2008.
2. McQueen, 1996, 3–4; Topliss, 1985, 25; Topliss and Spate, 1996, 160, 166, 68.
3. Conder to Roberts, n.d., Roberts Papers, Mitchell Library, State Library of New South Wales, MSS A2479/39; Roberts to Pring, 25 April 1900, 21 June (no year given, but written from the Exhibition Building where Roberts was working on the 'big picture' 1901–1903), S.W. Pring Papers, Mitchell Library, State Library of New South Wales, MSS 1367/2.
4. McQueen, 1996, 481.
5. Rickard, 1996, 271; McQueen, 1996, 479–481. There had also been a visit to Paris to see to the engraving of the painting, which the Art Association was going to market.
6. *British Australian*, 30 August 1906, quoted Topliss, 1985, 25; McCubbin to Roberts, 4 November 1904, Roberts Papers, Mitchell Library, State Library of New South Wales, MSS A2479; Roberts to McCubbin, 23 October 1905, Photocopy, Mitchell Library, State Library of New South Wales, MSS 8188, Box 596/5.
7. Roberts to Deakin, 4 August 1904, Quoted in Crawford, 1964, 155.
8. McCubbin to Roberts, 14 June 1904, 25 August 1905, Roberts Papers, Mitchell Library, State Library of New South Wales, MSS A2479. 'Smike' was the nickname for Arthur Streeton.
9. Roberts to Pring, 27 April 1907, Pring Papers; McQueen, 1996, 520; Caleb quoted in Croll, 1935, 96.
10. Ikin and Green, 1990, 7, 9.
11. Ikin and Green, 1990, 25, 39.
12. Roberts to Bavin, 16 October 1909, Bavin Papers. National Library of Australia, MS 560.
13. As Nikolaus Pevsner had observed in 1951, 'The Central Square in spite of its public buildings has never become a real social centre, because not only shops, but also cinemas, pubs, cafés have been refused admission'. (Quoted in Ikin and Green, 1990, 43).

14 Shanklin Cox and Associates, 1971, 127. Author's journal, 3 September 1992.
15 This is noted on the Abstract Specification Form for the house, Hampstead Garden Suburb Archive.
16 Roberts to Bavin, 16 October 1909, Bavin Papers, National Library of Australia, MS 560; Traill and E.R. Garnsey. Quoted in Croll, 1935, 90–93; Roberts to McCubbin, 14 November 1909, Photocopy, Mitchell Library, State Library of New South Wales, MS 8188, Box 596/5. The pear trees were still there when the Walkers acquired the house in 1956, but subsequently died one by one. The garden was, he said, 'deeply shaded by hawthorn and sycamore trees' and 'nothing would flourish in the flowerbeds!' Subsequently the garden was re-landscaped with very little of the original garden surviving. (Copy, Walker to Noel Roberts, 24 October 1910, Author's possession.)
17 Ikin and Green, 1990, 42; Barnett, 1917, 205.
18 Roberts to Pring, 11 February 1909, Pring Papers, Mitchell Library, State Library of New South Wales; Roberts to Bavin, 16 October 1909, Bavin Papers, National Library of Australia, MS 560. McQueen assumes that 'the Robertses would not have presumed on their previous acquaintance' with the King and Queen. In Tom's case, I am not so sure!
19 Smith, 1962, 152; *British Australasian*, 1 June 1911 quoted in Croll, 1935, 99–101.
20 Croll, 1935, 99–101.
21 Newscutting, n.d. but c.1920, in large book, Roberts Papers, Mitchell Library, State Library of New South Wales, MSS 4586, Box 1X(2); Caleb quoted in Croll, 1935, 96–97; Roberts to Pring, 18 July 1915. Pring Papers, Mitchell Library, State Library of New South Wales; re war artists, McQueen, 1996, 592.
22 McQueen, 1996, 606.
23 Newscutting, *Evening Journal* (Adelaide), 16 May 1923, Book 114, Roberts Papers, MSS 4586, Box 1X(2); Masefield, 1916, 25.
24 Newscutting, *Evening Journal* (Adelaide), 16 May 1923, Book 114, Roberts Papers, MSS 4586, Box 1X(2).
25 Quinn to Roberts, 12 January 1924, Mitchell Library, State Library of New South Wales, MSS A2480, Vol. 3; Lindsay, quoted in McQueen, 1996, 638; newscutting, *Herald* (Melbourne), 20 March 1920, Roberts Papers, Mitchell Library, State Library of New South Wales, MSS, 4586/1X(2), 105; Topliss and Spate, 1996, 68.
26 McQueen, 1996, 559.
27 See, for example, Pearce, 1996, 168–178.
28 Hancock, 1930.

PRIMARY SOURCES

Author's Journal, 1992.
Bavin Papers, National Library of Australia.
British Australian, 1906.
Hampstead Garden Suburb Archive.
Tom Roberts Papers, Mitchell Library, State Library of New South Wales.
S.W. Pring Papers, Mitchell Library, State Library of New South Wales.
Walker to Noel Roberts, 24 October 1910, copy in author's possession.

REFERENCES

Barnett, Henrietta. 1917. In *Problems of Reconstruction: Lectures and Addresses at the Summer Meeting at the Hampstead Garden Suburb, August, 1917*. London: T. Fisher Unwin Ltd.

Crawford, R.M. 1964. 'Tom Roberts and Alfred Deakin'. In *In Honour of Daryl Lindsay: Essays and Studies*, edited by Philipp, Franz; Stewart, June. Melbourne: Oxford University Press.

Croll, R.H. 1935.*Tom Roberts: Father of Australian Landscape Painting*. Melbourne: Robertson & Mullens.

Ikin, C.W.; with Green, Brigid Grafton. 1990. *Hampstead Garden Suburb: Dreams and Realities*, London: New Hampstead Garden Suburb Trust.

Hancock, W.K. 1930. *Australia*. London: Ernest Benn.

Masefield, John. 1916. *Gallipoli*. London: Heinemann.

McQueen, Humphrey. 1996. *Tom Roberts*. Sydney, Macmillan.

Pearce, Barry. 1996. 'Reflections on the Late Work'. In *Tom Roberts*, edited by Radford, Ron. Adelaide: Art Gallery of South Australia.

Rickard, John. 1996. 'The Big Picture'. In *Victorian Icon: The Royal Exhibition Building Melbourne*, edited by Dunstan, David. Melbourne: The Exhibition Trustees.

Shanklin, Cox and Associates. 1971. 'Hampstead garden suburb: A conservation Study'. Hampstead Garden Suburb Archive.

Smith, Bernard. 1962. *Australian Painting 1788–1970*. Melbourne: Oxford University Press.

Topliss, Helen. 1985. *Tom Roberts, 1856–1931: A Catalogue Raisonnée*. Melbourne: Oxford University Press.

Topliss, Helen and Spate, Virginia. 1996. In *Tom Roberts*, edited by Radford, Ron. Adelaide: Art Gallery of South Australia.

Cite this chapter as: Rickard, John. 2009. 'Tom Roberts' London years'. *Australians in Britain: The Twentieth-Century Experience*, edited by Bridge, Carl; Crawford, Robert; Dunstan, David. Melbourne: Monash University ePress. pp. 5.1 to 5.13. DOI: 10.2104/ab090005.

THE AUSTRALIAN SOLDIER IN BRITAIN, 1914–1918

Roger Beckett, King's College London
    Roger Beckett was granted his University of London doctorate in 2008 for his thesis: 'The AIF in Britain 1914–1918' pursued at the Menzies Centre for Australian Studies.

The First World War was the occasion of a major influx of Australians into Britain. From summer 1916 to the end of the war there were never fewer than 50,000 Australian troops in Britain. Britain was the base for the training of Australian reinforcements and technical specialists. The sick and wounded from the BEF were evacuated from France for treatment in British hospitals and Australian auxiliary hospitals. Control of Australian military activity in Britain was divided between Administrative Headquarters at Horseferry Road in London and UK Depots on Salisbury Plain. London provided the administrative, disciplinary and medical back-up for all of the AIF overseas and their new preparedness to mock the long-existent condescension towards them as colonials.

Britain experienced what was probably the largest and most sudden influx of Australians in the twentieth century when members of the Australian Imperial Force (AIF) arrived during the First World War. Little has been written about their experience and their effect upon the British. Historians Michael McKernan and Eric M. Andrews take a generally negative view of the experience of the AIF in Britain.[1] The chapter title 'From Hero to Villain' in McKernan's The Australian People and the Great War summarises the argument. Andrews's conclusions are almost as bleak: 'the Australians had been transformed from heroes to criminals in the eyes of the British authorities'.[2] Both rely upon anecdotal evidence to support their conclusion that the meeting of the British with large numbers of young Australians led to mutual disillusionment. But no firm statistical evidence can be offered that this was the case. The experience of the majority of individual Australian soldiers was likely to have been very different from the 'over here and oversexed' caricature of some press reports and the rather lurid episodes in some memoirs.

A total of 331,781 Australian soldiers embarked for overseas service with the AIF, as did 3011 members of the Australian Army Nursing Service.[3] The majority of the AIF served with the British Expeditionary Force on the Western Front. Almost without exception AIF members serving in France would have visited Britain. From mid-summer 1916 until mid-1919 there were never fewer than 50,000 Australian troops in Britain, excluding men on furlough.

Soldiers in such numbers would have many different experiences, and often conflicting opinions about those experiences. A similar range of experience and opinion would be found in the attitudes of their hosts. At the Australian Engineers Training Depot (AETD) at Brightlingsea in Essex, activities organised by the AIF in the summer and autumn of 1917 included a circus, gymkhana and sports, together with weekly plays and concerts. A Literary and Debating Society was formed in November 1917 and met weekly. A 'khaki choir' sang at the Wesleyan church and the AIF provided a harpist, Driver Francesco Pisania, to play at New Church.[4] A chronicler of the experience of the AIF in Brightlingsea comments:

> All these respectable, conventional, and 'small town' Australian activities were reported in the Brightlingsea column of the three local newspapers exactly as if their participants were Essex shopkeepers and their families and not soldiers

in the bloodiest year of the bloodiest war so far in history. Psychologically this cosy routine was perhaps essential for all involved.⁵

In contrast, the activities of the Australian troops in the vicinity of the Salisbury Plain camps in the months after the Armistice were described thus:

> For discipline and regulations they cared not a jot. They fought the military police. Some of the worst characters deserted their regiments and lived rough in the adjacent woods in far worse than Robin Hood fashion. While the main body remaining in camp jeered at their officers, insisted on lifts to Salisbury in every passing car, and made themselves a general nuisance to the world around them.⁶

The experience of most of the troops, of course, fell in between these extremes, embracing the routines of camp or hospital and the occasional leave in London or elsewhere. To understand some of the reasons for these variations it is vital to recognise both the varied nature of the AIF experience in Britain and the context within which they occurred.

The experience of the AIF divides into two distinct periods. At first the troops were largely the responsibility of the High Commission and of the ad hoc organisation created to discharge that responsibility. Thereafter, from the summer of 1916 onwards the main force of the AIF was serving as a part of the British Expeditionary Force, and an AIF military command structure existed in Britain. The initial AIF contingent left Australia in November 1914, with Britain as its intended destination. Concern that the camps on Salisbury Plain would not be ready in time, plus the need to stiffen the defences of the Suez Canal against a possible Turkish attack, meant that the troops disembarked in Egypt to complete their training.

The small number of Australian troops in Britain in early 1915 placed few demands upon the High Commission in London. This situation changed when sick and wounded from Gallipoli began to be evacuated direct from the peninsula. During 1915 a total of 12,140 Australians and 3983 New Zealanders arrived after being evacuated as casualties from the Mediterranean theatre of war or from Mediterranean garrisons.⁷ It had been the original intention of the AIF to establish a records office in London, and it was upon this small organisation that responsibility fell for Australian troops arriving in Britain. The lack of an effective AIF organisation in Britain and, in particular, the absence of effective Australian Army Medical Service direction, resulted in confusion due to lack of knowledge and well meaning but ill informed interference. The High Commission was faced with the need to create from scratch a medical service to deal with Australian casualties and a base depot to which recovered sick and wounded could be drafted. British hospitals would provide the initial treatment, but the task of following the progress of casualties through the system and of providing convalescent care and rehabilitation was accepted as an Australian responsibility.

The limited resources available to the High Commission meant that volunteer groups and individuals undertook much of the contact and liaison with the Australian wounded in British hospitals. As early as July 1915 there were notices in the press proposing support for the arriving Australians. Surgeon General R.H. Fetherston spoke of the 'number of semi-official visitors at hospitals who were giving orders and instructions regarding Australians'.⁸ After Fetherston's report, in the autumn of 1915, the High Commission put in place a scheme whereby regular visits to hospitals were made by non-commissioned officers, who then reported back to medical officers at the High Commission. This improved the situation, but critical comments from the 'amateur' visitors now began to appear in the press in Australia and caused problems for the Defence Department. The High Commission was asked by the Department of External Affairs in Melbourne to investigate the allegation that Australian soldiers discharged from hospital were 'sleeping rough' on the Embankment in London. A letter was obtained from the Metropolitan Police confirming that there had been no reports of Australians on the Embankment.[9] In November 1915 the High Commission forwarded to Melbourne a letter from seven Australian soldiers in the 1st Southern General Hospital at Edgbaston, Birmingham, which stated that 'they have heard some Australians have been neglected but speaking for themselves they are receiving every comfort and are exceptionally well attended to'.[10] This appears to have been an attempt to counter the adverse comments appearing in the home press.

Captain J.A. Smeal AAMS, who was Registrar at Harefield Hospital, inspected Imperial Hospitals and reported in December 1915:

> The idea that Australians are discontented in English hospitals owing to their lack of freedom by the rules and regulations which suit the English 'Tommy' is, in my opinion completely false. In fact one Australian doctor who is now [a Royal Australian Medical Corps] officer in one of these hospitals expressed his belief that they were more contented and better behaved in an English hospital than in an Australian one.[11]

Some of the confusion surrounding the hospitalisation of AIF members and their subsequent treatment as convalescents arose from a lack of clear leadership by the Australian Army Medical Service. In April 1916 Professor Grafton Elliot Smith of Manchester University, Chairman of the Manchester and District Committee of the Australian War Contingent Association, reported:

> Some member of the Committee visited every Australian soldier every week and attended to his material wants and ministered to his social welfare. When it is realised that at one time there were as many as seven hundred wounded Australians in this district scattered over an area bigger than London you will have some idea of the Committee's task.[12]

The committee report complained that their work was delayed as they had been told that all Australian wounded were going to Harefield Hospital. In the event 730 men were found in 87 different hospitals.

Australians arriving in Britain after April 1915 came with both the advantage and the disadvantage of the reputation won by the AIF at Anzac Cove. Michael McKernan highlights the significant point that after Gallipoli the Australians, even those reinforcements who had not served at Anzac Cove, arrived as heroes. The Canadians, in comparison, 'slipped quietly into the trenches in France beside the British and French, creating no separate identity for themselves'.[13] Such a reputation was not necessarily an aid to maintaining discipline. Surgeon General W.D.C. Williams instituted an enquiry into problems at Harefield Hospital, and the response from the commanding officer blamed a system that kept fit men in hospital:

> Out of the 500 patients 400 are strong lusty men with very little wrong with them and these men have been spoiled by the attention that they have received and the eulogies of the public press ... If Harefield was used more as a hospital and less as a Dumping ground it would be more easily managed.[14]

Surgeon General Williams had already written to Fetherston in Melbourne criticising the arrangements at Harefield: 'They are in a bad way at Harefield Park ... In fact so bad have things become that they have begun, or are about to begin to erect cells to confine convalescent prisoners. God knows what it will be like when they get to a couple of thousand'.[15] The hospital registrar attributed much of the problem to the nearby inn: 'Before the hospital was opened the inn had a very small business ... being supplied with beer only by an old one-horsed vehicle which called occasionally. Now a two-horse van supplies it daily'.[16]

The problems at Harefield highlighted a key issue in the process of rehabilitation of casualties, the decision as to when a soldier should pass from medical to military control. It was to address this point that the command depot was introduced. In April 1915 the War Office had created this new form of convalescent establishment.[17] The command depots were intended to provide an additional stage of treatment between the hospital and the regimental depots. Previously, British policy had been to provide convalescent units for men leaving hospital who were not fit to proceed directly to their regimental depots. Accommodation had been provided for Australians at one of these convalescent hospitals, Woodcote Park in Epsom, Surrey, where 10 huts, each containing 48 beds, were handed over for the use of the AIF. Control of the hospital remained with the Imperial authorities but Australian doctors and orderlies were appointed to deal with Australian patients. Accommodation was increased to 1000 beds by the end of 1915.[18]

The introduction of the new depots, which were to be placed under the command of military rather than medical personnel, replaced the system of military convalescent hospitals. The function of the command depot was 'To ensure by suitable medical treatment that the increasing number of infantry soldiers invalided from the Expeditionary Forces may become fit as quickly as possible'.[19] Command depots were military units, and to conform with the new policy a depot at Bostal Heath, near Woolwich in southeast London, was placed within Lt Col. Sir Newton J. Moore's command. Moore had been appointed Commandant of the Australian and New Zealand Depot on 29 May 1915. The Anzac depot at Weymouth in Dorset was similarly reclassified and became Command Depot No. 2. The purpose of the command depots was to progressively improve the health of the sick or wounded man after his discharge from hospital, with the aim of returning him to active service.

With the transfer of the main body of the AIF to France there was brief consideration of the idea of setting up an exclusively Australian medical system, which would have involved establishing Australian general hospitals in the south of France to which Australian casualties could have been evacuated. Such a scheme was quickly recognised as impracticable and Australian treatment of casualties conformed totally to the Imperial system. Australian general hospitals in France treated any casualties, not simply Australian ones. Any British Expeditionary Force casualties not expected to return to duty within a month were evacuated to Britain. Table 6.1 shows the numbers of AIF casualties arriving in Britain in 1916, 1917 and 1918.

Year	1916				1917				1918			
Quarter	1st	2nd	3rd	4th	1st	2nd	3rd	4th	1st	2nd	3rd	4th
Battle casualties	11	1189	14780	3357	4025	12056	5759	11651	3531	11728	14980	1434
Non battle casualties	9	1491	3720	8783	9814	4838	6888	9249	4937	5897	5620	4051
Total casualties	20	2680	18500	12140	13839	16894	12647	20900	8468	17625	20600	5485

Table 6.1 AIF casualties evacuated from France, 1916-18
Source: A.G. Butler, *Official History Australian Army Medical Corps*, Australian War Memorial, Canberra, 1945, vol. 3, p. 919.

No Australian general hospitals were established in Britain to treat Australian casualties arriving from France. All casualties went, on arrival, to British hospitals. Once fit enough to be moved, they were transferred to the Australian auxiliary hospitals. Harefield in Middlesex was the first and the largest of these, but growing numbers of casualties from the Somme offensive led to the opening of additional auxiliary hospitals at Dartford in Kent and at Southall in West London in the autumn of 1916. After treatment patients were discharged to various command depots and those not expected to be fit within six months were sent to Weymouth, whence they were repatriated to Australia.

Sick and wounded Australians arrived in Britain for treatment; new reinforcements arrived in Britain for training. By the end of 1916 the policy was that all new recruits would receive only limited basic training in Australia. On arrival in Britain they would undergo the full 14 weeks standard British infantry training, after which further specialist training would be given where appropriate. In Egypt the training of new recruits had been under the command of British officers. In Britain it became an Australian responsibility, but a shortage of instructors meant that the force was dependent upon the British army for much of it. In April 1917 Sergeant Eric Evans, who had been repatriated to Australia after service in Gallipoli and who had subsequently re-enlisted, included in his diary a description of a typical British sergeant major serving as his drill instructor:

> One of the Tommy sergeant majors, by the name of Jabson, gave us a right drill-bashing yesterday. He is some guy – an old Imperial soldier and looks it, roars like a bull and is a typical British warrant officer. He gives orders on parade as only an Imperial can but he is a real decent chap off parade.[20]

A shortage of instructors was not the only problem. The bulk of the new recruits arrived in Britain during the winter of 1916–17, which was one of the coldest on record. The combination of the weather and poor organisation took its toll. The memoirs of F.V. Culverhouse, who arrived as reinforcement in early 1917, describe the training:

> Alternating periods of violent exercise followed by standing still as we gradually freeze. Alternately giving exercises that caused you to get overheated and then such drills as would let you freeze. That made sure that only the fittest could survive it.[21]

In March 1917 former Sydney journalist George Goddard commented that 'About half our company are at present in hospital. This climate has played havoc with them and three of them are not expected to get over their illnesses – pneumonia'.[22] As late as April, Eric Evans noted in his diary, 'Yesterday we were to be inspected by General Sir Newton Moore but he did not turn up. Another guy did the inspection and took the salute at the march past. I suppose it was too cold for "Salutin" Moore as he is known'.[23]

The numbers affected by illness in the early months of 1917 were highest of the war because the depots at that time were full of newly arrived reinforcements. There had been no problems in the summer months. Unlike the Canadians in 1914, the Australian troops were in huts not tents but they were still unprepared for the levels of sickness experienced. A.G. Butler comments:

> Some camps were ill-sited – exposed and bleak – in particular Larkhill, Rollestone and Perham Downs. But most important there had not been time to build up a staff capable of rising to the occasion; living, messing, training, sick parades were mechanical – there was no vision.[24]

A soldier's eye view of the situation was given by Private G.V. Rose, 30th Battalion, who arrived at No. 9 Camp Hurdcott on 30 January 1917:

> After breakfast we were taken out on the icy parade ground and were roared at by Col. Steele (known afterwards as the 'Food King' but at the time as that B— B—) His speech was something like this:
>
> You men are not in Australia now. You've come here to work hard, d— hard. You are going to France to fight very soon (sensation in the ranks). Got to fight b— hard, fight like hell. I don't want you sick – sick man no bloody good, worse than a dead man – it takes two men to look after him. When you get leave come back on time. If you don't you get twenty-eight days.

There appeared to be little realisation by those in authority of the dangers posed by the very cold weather to those unaccustomed to it, and there appeared to Private Rose to be a lack of medical care:

> These colds to my mind were mostly caused by the hardening process to which we were subjected. No overcoats were allowed on parade and mufflers had to be worn under tunics if worn at all.
>
> The Tommies (Notts. & Derby Regt.) on the other hand used to wear their greatcoats every day on parade and also on route marches.
>
> Men parading sick, many of them fit to be in hospital were given a dose of Mist Expect. or Mist Tussi and told by the doctor (— of the north coast NSW) that they were malingering. He has more than one life to answer for.
>
> One man, Price of our platoon, was told that if he paraded next day sick he would be brought up before the orderly room for malingering. Next day he did not parade he was brought to the [Army Medical Corps] on a stretcher and sent straight to Fovant Hospital. During the week a Fovant Hospital Doctor

sent our quack a note saying it was no use sending up dead men to be cured. They preferred to have them earlier.[25]

Stuart Braga suggests that the problems in the training camps during the winter of 1916–17 were the result of British policy, but it is clear from the accounts above that much of it was the fault of the AIF. The level of sickness in the AIF UK depots reached 10 per cent by the end of February 1917 and this level would not be exceeded even at the peak of the influenza pandemic of the following year, when it reached only 8 per cent.[26]

Infantry training was not without other hazards. All men were required to throw three live grenades before being allowed to go on a draft. Evans, in a letter home, records an accident which caused the death of a soldier,[27] Private Stephens, and describes his own experience of bombing training:

> This bombing is not the game it is cracked up to be especially with some of the roosters we have here, they lose their block when they know it is a live one they have a hold on. A few days ago one got half his head blown off and several had bad wounds, they looked awful, poor devils, it made us feel a bit skew whiff for a while, then the Sgt.-Major came along and said, 'come on lads it's all in the game get to it', and we got to it and soon forgot it.[28]

While the training period for infantry was laid down as 14 weeks, this was not adhered to during periods of high demand for reinforcements. In his report upon handing over command of UK Depots in April 1917, Newton Moore reported that:

> Orders have constantly been received from the War Office directing that partially trained men shall be sent if trained men are not available, and there is now a standing order that men who have reached a standard equivalent to nine weeks or over are deemed to be available if the demand for trained men cannot be met.
>
> At the end of October [1916] the demands for Infantry were so urgent that all men in the eighth week were hurriedly put through a course of musketry and sent Overseas. It has been observed that although rolls are sent with drafts, showing the standard of training the men have received, this has not always been taken into consideration in commenting on this efficiency.[29]

It is clear from these comments that the decision to draft to France men who had not completed the full period of training was made by the War Office. The AIF was, in this matter, treated as if it were a British training unit.

The number of Australian troops in Britain, and the resulting need for support services, led to the creation of a large Australian military organisation in Britain. Command of Australian troops was divided throughout the war. The Administrative HQ in Horseferry Road in London was responsible for the administration of all of the AIF overseas, for medical services and for liaison with the War Office. AIF UK Depots at Tidworth Camp on Salisbury Plain was responsible for training, for the command depots and for discipline. The majority of the personnel of the training depots were men on six-month secondment from frontline units in France, but there were a substantial number of Australian personnel permanently based in Britain.

Despite regular announcements of the 'combing out' of fit men from the permanent establishment, the AIF in Britain, and in particular Administrative HQ, was suspected both by the men serving in France and by the Australian press of providing a safe haven for those wishing to avoid active service. The pejorative term 'Horseferry Dragoons' was used in this description by a correspondent to the Melbourne *Age*, calling himself 'Old Anzac', of 'Hundreds of men who wear soldiers' uniforms, all tailor made and look like tailor's models':

> their chief occupation seems to be parading the streets of London casting condescending glances at the poorer Anzac from the trenches … They are known to the ordinary fighting man as the 'shiny legging, tailor made and gold tooth brigade'.[30]

Criticism of Administrative HQ ranged from the scurrilous soldiers' song 'Horseferry Road' to speeches in the Australian parliament.[31] On 12 June 1918, in the House of Representatives, the Member for Ballarat, David C. McGrath, who had recently returned from serving in the AIF, made a speech in which he was extremely critical of the staff of Horseferry Road and voiced the widely held conviction of many soldiers that some men got favoured treatment:

> Do not let it be possible for a man to go from here, as a late reinforcement, and be immediately claimed by somebody in Horseferry Road as a private only to emerge two months later with two stars. Immediately such a man gets promotion he is no longer eligible to serve in the field. He is free. When a man becomes an officer at Headquarters and gets one star on his shoulder he will never hear the guns booming.[32]

The sensitivity of Horseferry Road to such criticism is demonstrated by the amount of effort put in to refuting the claims.[33] McGrath had himself served at Horseferry Road, and his transfer to service in France was the occasion of a typical attack by the *British Australasian*:

> Not long ago we had at Horseferry Road soldier politicians, or ex-politicians, one of whom has been returned to Australia and discharged as unfit after collisions with our military authorities, the rights and wrongs of which are hotly in dispute.
>
> Another, Sgt. McGrath, is now at his own request on service in France, much to the sorrow of numerous men on leave who found his ability and good will of much service to them in settling various little difficulties when he held a position on the Administrative HQ staff.[34]

Despite the best efforts of the headquarters staff to prove the contrary, the belief that ablebodied men were hiding from active service within Administrative HQ never disappeared. Even when reporting a 'comb-out' of fit men from Horseferry Road, the *British Australasian* could not resist the comment that this 'will afford some of them an opportunity to gratify their long cherished desire to see active service'.[35]

The London HQ was also criticised for its location in what was seen as a less than salubrious part of London. There was a general feeling that the Horseferry Road area was unsuitable as a base for the Australian troops. The *British Australasian* described it as 'A reeking slum with half a dozen second-rate public houses within a stone's throw and Delilah lurking up every murky passage about the place'.[36] The problem which most concerned many interested parties was not hotels and alcohol but the relations of the Australian troops with British women. For the military authorities the primary concern was the loss in manpower due to venereal disease. Infected soldiers were confined to isolation hospitals. The question of the Australians' relations with women is obviously important. The AIF was a force comprised of young men; 57 per cent were aged 25 or under and 81 per cent were unmarried.[37] For such a group, the need for female company was a major issue. The same situation would arise on an even greater scale during the Second World War with the United States servicemen in Britain. David Reynolds notes that 'the persistent advances of amorous GIs were notorious', but also comments that 'it was commonplace that many British females were as "over-sexed" as American males'.[38]

The popular view of the Australian soldiers in Britain between 1916 and 1919 is very similar to that taken of the Americans after 1942. The difference is only in the scale of the perceived problem. Concern about developing relationships between Australian soldiers and local women was not confined to Britain. Fear that Australians would 'fall prey' to the 'wiles' of British women prompted an attempt in Australia, reported by *The Times*, to introduce a law permitting proxy marriage by AIF members overseas:

> The bill was desired by several Australian women's organisations on the grounds that the duration of the war was greatly disturbing the normal course of engagements ... Very many hundreds of Australians have married English girls whilst in England.[39]

The first Australian arrivals in Britain were perceived by some as innocents needing protection from the wicked world rather than as potential troublemakers. An unnamed correspondent wrote in *The Times* on 9 July 1915:

> Two cases have recently come to my knowledge in which Australian soldiers from country districts, entirely ignorant not only of London but of any large town have been greeted by women whose hospitable demeanour and fashionable clothes greatly impressed them.
>
> Fortunately before accepting the women's invitations to tea they happened to mention the matter to a lady who is interested in the welfare of soldiers in London and she had no difficulty in learning that these women were well known to the police as possessing the worst possible reputation.
>
> It is cruel recompense to men who have come halfway round the globe to fight England's battles that they should be allowed, innocently and unforwarned [*sic*] to run the risk of being robbed by these birds of prey of all they possess. An obvious way of helping them would be to post warning notices in the carriages of the trains which bring them to London.[40]

AIF diaries and memoirs tend to separate women into two types, and images of the 'good' and the 'bad' girl arise frequently:

> In our drifting to and from London we came to learn that there were girls and girls. There were the parasites, the lounge lizards, ready to sell themselves to anyone who had the price, and the fine self sacrificing girls who did war work and formed many a clean and honest friendship that was an inspiration to men, jaded and embittered by two years of war.[41]

Accounts of individual experience almost invariably stress that the writer shunned involvement with the less suitable females. This may simply reflect the mores of the time and a disinclination to admit past sins, but somebody was certainly giving the 'good-time girls' a good time.

Australians feature prominently in press reports of immoral activities in the vicinity of the camps. The *Weymouth Telegram* of 20 April 1917 reported the prosecution of a local woman for keeping a disorderly house, in which the police described 'frequent visits by Australian soldiers'.[42] A Sergeant McNab of the AIF was said to have 'induced a girl to leave to stay with him'. She was charged with giving false information on a registration form; he was charged with aiding and abetting.[43] Despite the large numbers of Australians who passed through No. 2 Command Depot at Weymouth, the town seems to have maintained good relations with the force. When a young Australian soldier was accused of stealing from a local woman the magistrate dismissed the charge, telling the woman that 'we know rather more about you than we wish to express in public'.[44]

Some reports of the activities of Australian men with local women suggest more naivety than villainy. When Private Arnst of the AIF married a woman in London in May 1917 she gave her age as 28, but it transpired that she was 44 years old, and already married with six children.[45] The case was reported of a young Australian who, after drawing 15 pounds in back pay at Horseferry Road, was picked up by a woman and taken back to her room, where he was allegedly robbed: 'So that he should know the place again he smashed the doors and windows in the front of the house'. A police inspector reported that the area, Campbell Road, was notorious and the soldier was cautioned and bound over to be of good behaviour.[46]

When paternity claims were made against Australian troops it was the task of the 'OC Troops' at Administrative HQ to investigate them. Interviewing the complainant was sometimes an eye-opening experience:

> Some of the women interviewed were of a good type, perhaps the soldier was responsible for their downfall, others were the opposite and very little sympathy was due them.
>
> The interviews were very remarkable, and, to the OC troops, in some cases very embarrassing. In some cases the facts were laid out in a cold unashamed way, in others in a modest way. In some it was hard to believe that one was speaking to a specimen of the gentler sex.
>
> One girl of about seventeen summers obtained an order from a notorious absentee in respect of a pair of twins, and on his arrest some months later he asked

for permission to marry another damsel, whom he stated was about to become a mother.[47]

It would be incorrect to see the Australian troops only in the role of villain where relationships with local women were concerned. About 8000 met and married British women, and most returned with them to Australia. In October 1918 a driver in the 10th Field Company of Engineers married a girl, only to see her face a charge of bigamy when her first husband returned from the army.[48] He stood by his bride and applied to the Paymaster at AIF HQ for the £100 needed in bail and sureties to free her from Exeter gaol, where she awaited trial. Bigamous marriages of members of the AIF became a matter of serious concern, and in June 1918 an AIF Order required that any soldier marrying in church must produce a certificate showing his 'marital condition'. In the case of registry office weddings, the registrar would correspond directly with the OC Records at Administrative HQ.

If the vexed question of the relationships of Australian soldiers with British women can be considered a moral rather than a disciplinary issue, then the subject of greatest concern to the Australian authorities was absence without leave (AWL). This was true throughout the war, but the problem became much greater in 1918. Table 6.2 shows the comparative figures for District Courts Martial (DCM) in June to November 1916 and January to June 1918. At the end of June 1916 there were 20,522 AIF troops in the United Kingdom, and by the end of the year the number had increased to 60,378. If 40,000 is taken as the average number in the country for the six months to November, the rate is 2.87 courts martial for AWL per 1,000 men. In the first six months of 1918 there were on average 50,000 troops in Britain, which gives a rate for of 28.26 per 1000. This is a more than 10-fold increase. Summary awards of punishment for the six months ending 30 June 1918 totalled 13,662, of which 65 per cent were for AWL.[49]

Offence	June to November 1916		January to May 1918	
	No.	%	No.	%
Desertion	0	0	44	2
Absent without leave	115	57.5	1413	77
False papers	7	3.5	77	4
Escaping custody	19	9.5	118	7
Insubordination	17	8.5	62	3
Fraud (paybook)	7	3.5	76	4
Other	35	17.5	52	3
Total	200	100	1842	100

Table 6.2 AIF UK depots: Cases tried by District Courts Martial
Sources: National Archives of Australia, AIF 369 1 262; Deputy Assistant Judge Advocate General, 'Memorandum on courts martial statistics for six months to 30/6/18', copy in J.G. Latham papers, National Library of Australia, 1009/20/526

In 1917 the newly appointed commanding officer of UK Depots, Major General J.M. McCay, offered an amnesty. Routine Order no. 1272 of 9 August 1917 announced that all men serving detention for AWL or 'Out of Bounds' would have their sentences remitted and be released on 10 August. Absentees with less than 30 days absence who surrendered by 25 August would not be punished, and those absent for more than 30 days would have the fact of their surrendering taken into account when assessing their punishment. This carrot apparently failed, for on 24 September Special Order 1912 announced that 'In future all cases of AWL exceeding 14 days will be tried by DCM'. With both carrot and stick proving unsuccessful, McCay turned to exhortation, with a direct appeal to the troops:

> I speak as one soldier to others. We all know that our comrades in France want reinforcements urgently and are looking to us to join them. Yet there are still those among us who go Absent Without Leave.
>
> AWL is the best friend the Germans have in the AIF. Consequently he who goes AWL is betraying his mates in his own platoon, his own section. It is more than a question of duty to country or authority; besides that it is a desertion of our own mates of our own rank. Most of us do not go AWL and it is up to you and me to make it clear to those who are inclined to do so that they would be betraying us as well as our mates in France.[50]

The majority of cases coming before courts martial in London were for desertion or AWL. Up to 28 days AWL would, for privates, be punished on a sliding scale that ranged from loss of a day's pay to detention. Non-commissioned officers were likely to come before a District Court Martial for less than a 28-day absence.[51] The AIF provosts in London waged a constant campaign against absentees, as *The Times* reported on 1 March 1917:

> The Australian Military Police paid a surprise visit yesterday to the Commonwealth Bank near Broad Street. When a number of the AIF presented themselves at the Bank to make withdrawals they were asked to show their passes. Many had overstayed their leave and some had no passes. They were placed under arrest and brought before Mr Alderman Hanson at the Guildhall where they were ordered to be handed over to the authorities.[52]

In October the same year *The Times* carried an account of a raid by the Australian Military Police on a public house in London:

> Louis Henry Golding licensee of the Phoenix Hotel, Bishopsgate St., was charged with four summonses alleging aiding and abetting deserters.
>
> On Sept. 3 Warrant Officer Hawkins of the Australian Military Police visited the hotel and found a number of Australians drinking in the bar. During an examination of passes three of them disappeared. Other passes were found to be overdue. The three men were found upstairs behind a locked door. Eight men on the premises were deserters twenty-five to forty eight days overdue.

What was most worrying for the AIF by the beginning of 1918 was where the AWL was occurring. Almost three quarters of courts martial and nearly 70 per cent of summary punishments were awarded in the command depots and the Overseas Training Brigade, that is, among men of whom the majority were likely to have seen active service. The memorandum from the Deputy Assistant Judge Advocate General cited for Table 6.2 noted that the problem was greatest in the command depots, but the writer seemed unable to decide upon a single reason for the levels of absence. The memorandum noted an increasing number of men who had done no fighting and had been AWL and in custody for years: 'It seems clear that a class of habitual offenders is being created. In some cases the men are absolutely depraved'.[53] However, it suggested that 'others are simply men who have fought well but have decided that they have done enough'. This view is supported by the fact that the AWL problem was smallest in Command Depot No. 2, which was at Weymouth and through which the men marked for repatriation would pass. Once a man was listed for repatriation, there was little incentive to go AWL.

Men sentenced to detention in excess of 28 days were held in a military detention barracks. Before November 1917 the AIF did not have their own barracks and men were held in one of 15 such British barracks. Once convicted and sentenced, they were handed over to the Assistant Provost Marshal of the AIF depot at Tidworth, who would then make arrangements for them to be held in one of the British barracks. Where the men would be held depended upon where there were vacancies; on occasions prisoners had to be taken a considerable distance under the escort of a non-commissioned officer and two Other Ranks. Apart from the administrative inconvenience of this arrangement it also proved to be expensive. In January 1917 AIF prisoners were delivered to nine different detention barracks at a total cost in excess of £200.[54] A further problem was that prisoners suffering from VD were held in No. 1 Australian Dermatological Hospital at Bulford on Salisbury Plain. This required a guard of an officer and 78 men, and the lack of security made it relatively easy for prisoners to escape:

> Venereal patients in detention were difficult to deal with in the venereal hospital in Bulford. There were no means of keeping separate good and bad characters. Discipline was hard to maintain, adequate exercise could not be given, and treatment was difficult as the man had to be paraded for treatment singly, or even be handcuffed.[55]

The AIF requested a prison large enough to accommodate 600 prisoners. The offer of Dorchester and Cambridge prisons provided a combined capacity of only 270; the average number of AIF detainees was 320. The AIF asked for Wandsworth prison but this request was refused and an offer was made of Gloucester and Devizes. These two units would still not have provided sufficient accommodation and the AIF asked for Lewes prison in Sussex. The Lewes Detention Barracks, which had been used to accommodate members of Sinn Fein brought over from Ireland, was taken over by the AIF on 1 November 1917, except for one wing of 24 cells retained for civilian use. The Detention Barracks were used to hold soldiers serving sentences ranging from 14 days to two years.

An important factor in the discipline of the AIF appears to have been the extent of opportunity for a social life outside a purely military sphere. In the major camps, numbers were so great that local civilian facilities were overwhelmed and civilians were less likely to welcome individuals into their homes. The negative stereotype of the soldier would be reinforced by lack of personal contact. Organisations such as the YMCA made efforts to provide social and leisure activities, but these could not replace genuine social interaction outside the camps. The higher levels of crime, disorder and venereal disease attributed to the soldiers in the large encampments support the view that these conditions contributed to bad behaviour. Accounts of the Australian Flying

Corps in Gloucester and the Field Engineers in Essex reveal a much better integration of the Australians into the local community.[56] In both cases, while there were instances of high spirits and minor hooliganism, there is no evidence of the large-scale bad behaviour reported in the vicinity of the large training camps or in the metropolis.

Relations between the men (and women) of the AIF and the British remained generally good to the end. There is little evidence of the disillusionment described by some writers, other than the inevitable war-weariness that was general by 1918. There were problems with the discipline, particularly around the larger camps, but where opportunities existed for social integration with the locals these were seized with enthusiasm by the Australians. The 'habitual offenders' and the poor imposition of discipline that had existed in 1916 were still there two years later, but these alone do not account for the situation in 1918.[57] The manpower shortage in the AIF resulted in widespread fatigue and there is no doubt that the increased AWL rates for 1918 reflect a profound weariness. The highest levels of AWL were occurring in those units that held men who had served in France. It is no exaggeration to suggest that AWL rates in 1918 indicate that a substantial proportion of the force had experienced enough of the war and wanted to serve no more. Australia, alone among the combatants, had not adopted conscription and no other national force was under the same pressures.

ENDNOTES

1. McKernan, 1980; Andrews, 1993.
2. Andrews, 1993, 186.
3. Butler, 1930–43, 3, 88, table 11.
4. Foynes, 2003, 46–49.
5. Foynes, 2003, 36.
6. Street, 1952, 173.
7. Macpherson, 1924, 377, table 3.
8. National Archives of Australia (NAA), AIF 239 8 88.
9. NAA, AIF 8 45.
10. NAA, AIF 239 8 40.
11. NAA, AIF 239 8 88.
12. Correspondence and report in AWM, 10 4332/8/87.
13. McKernan, 1980, 5.
14. Letter, 12 August 1915, in AWM, 32 123.
15. Cited in Tyquin, 2003, 222. Williams sailed with the First Contingent as Director of Medical Services AIF, but had been effectively sidelined, and was employed in Britain only in connection with repatriation.
16. AWM, 25 265/3.
17. Butler, 1930–43, 1, 496.
18. Butler, 1930–43, 1, 496.
19. Butler, 1943–45, 504.
20. Evans, 2002, 40–41.

21. John Oxley Library, State Library of Queensland, OM64-31/7.
22. Letter home, John Oxley Library, State Library of Queensland, 2885/24.
23. Evans, 2002, 41.
24. Butler, 1930–43, vol. 2, 561.
25. G.V. Rose, 30th Bn AIF, Memoir.
26. Braga, 2000, 231; Macpherson, 1924, 3, 202.
27. Evans, 2002, 55.
28. Letters, Private 19th Reinforcement Draft, 11 April 1917, Imperial War Museum, London, P443.
29. AWM, 2 DRL 0868.
30. *Age* (Melbourne), 19 January 1917.
31. The first verse of 'Horseferry Road' gives a good feeling for the tone of the song:

    He was stranded in London and strode
    To Army Headquarters in Horseferry Road
    And there he met a poofter lance corporal who said
    You've got blood on your tunic and mud on your head
    You look so disgraceful that people will laugh
    Said the cold-footed bastard from Horseferry staff.

    A slightly different version of the full song can be found at: http://www.awm.gov.au/1918/soldier/superiors.htm, accessed 15 October 2008.
32. *Commonwealth Parliamentary Debates* (Australia), 12 June 1918.
33. See correspondence in AWM, 10 4301/14/17.
34. *British Australasian*, 6 September 1917, 5.
35. *British Australasian*, 1 March 1917.
36. *British Australasian*, 22 February 1917.
37. Beaumont, 2001, 116.
38. Reynolds, 1995, 201.
39. *The Times* (London), 18 December 1916.
40. *The Times* (London), 9 July 1915.
41. Maxwell, 1936, 82.
42. *Weymouth Telegram*, 20 April 1917.
43. *Weymouth Telegram*, 24 August 1917.
44. *Weymouth Telegram*, 15 October 1918.
45. *Weymouth Telegram*, 15 June 1917.
46. *The Times* (London), 2 July 1917.
47. History of 'OC Troops in London, AWM, 224 MSS 567.
48. Correspondence of the Rev. E.E. Haward, Imperial War Museum, London.
49. Deputy Assistant Judge Advocate General, Memorandum on courts-martial statistics for six months to 30/6/18, Copy in J.G. Latham papers, NLA, 1009/20/526.
50. AWM, 21 311/16 pt 5.

51 History of 'OC Troops in London, AWM, 224 MSS 567.
52 *The Times*, 1 March, 1917.
53 Latham papers, National Library of Australia, 1009/20/526.
54 Wilson, 2005, 15.
55 AWM, 2 DRL 0868.
56 Goodland and Vaughan, 1992; Foynes, 2003.
57 For a view on the problems arising from lax imposition of discipline, see Barr, 2005.

PRIMARY SOURCES

Age (Melbourne), 1917.
Australian War Memorial (AWM), 10 4332/8/87.
AWM, 2 DRL 0868.
AWM, 224 MSS 567.
Correspondence of the Rev. E.E. Haward, Imperial War Museum, London.
G.V. Rose, 30th Bn AIF, Memoir, Imperial War Museum, London.
Letters, Private 19th Reinforcement Draft, Imperial War Museum, London, P443.
Letter home, John Oxley Library, State Library of Queensland, 2885/24.
John Oxley Library, State Library of Queensland, OM64-31/7.
National Archives of Australia (NAA), AIF 8 45.
NAA, AIF 239 8 88.
Latham papers, National Library of Australia, 1009/20/526.
Commonwealth Parliamentary Debates (Australia), 12 June 1918.
British Australasian, 1917.
The Times (London), 1916; 1917.
Weymouth Telegram, 1917.

REFERENCES

Andrews, Eric M. 1993. *The Anzac Illusion*. Melbourne: Cambridge University Press.
Barr, Geoffrey. 2005. *Beyond the Myth*. Canberra: HJ Publications.
Beaumont J., editor. 2001. *Australian Defence Sources and Statistics*. Melbourne: Oxford University Press.
Braga, S. 2000. *Anzac Doctor: Life of Sir Neville Howse*. Sydney: Hale & Iremonger.
Butler, A.G. 1930–1943. *The Australian Army Medical Services in the War of 1914–1918*. Vols. 1–3. Canberra: Australian War Memorial.
Butler, A.G. 1943–1945. *The Australian Medical Services in the War of 1914–18*. Vols. 1–3. Canberra: Australian War Memorial.
Evans, E. 2002. *So Far from Home*, edited by Patrick Wilson. Sydney: Kangaroo Press.
Foynes, J.P. 2003. *The Australians at Brightlingsea*. Self-published.
Goodland, D.; Vaughan, A. 1992. *Anzacs over England*. Stroud: Alan Sutton Publishing.
McKernan, Michael. 1980. *The Australia People and the Great War*. Melbourne: Thomas Nelson.
Macpherson, W.G. 1924. *History of the Great War: Medical Services General History*. Vol. 3. London: HMSO.
Maxwell, J. 1936. *Hell's Bells & Mademoiselles*. Sydney: Angus and Robertson.
Street, A.G. 1952. *The Gentlemen of the Party*. London: Country Book Club.
Reynolds, David. 1995. *Rich Relations*. New York: Random House.

Tyquin, M. 2003. *Little by Little: A Centenary History of the RAAMC*, Canberra: Department of Defence.

Wilson, Graham. 2005. 'A prison of our own: The AIF detention barracks 1917–1919'. *Sabretache* 46(2): 13–30.

Cite this chapter as: Beckett, Roger. 2009. 'The Australian soldier in Britain, 1914–1918'. *Australians in Britain: The Twentieth-Century Experience*, edited by Bridge, Carl; Crawford, Robert; Dunstan, David. Melbourne: Monash University ePress. pp. 6.1 to 6.17. DOI: 10.2104/ab090006.

CHAPTER 7

READING THE *BRITISH AUSTRALASIAN* COMMUNITY IN LONDON, 1884–1924

Simon Sleight, Monash University
  Simon Sleight is a graduate of Warwick, University College London and Monash University. His work explores the processes of making place and the Australian presence in Britain.

Accessing the Australasian expatriate community in London through the pages of its newspaper, the *British Australasian*, this chapter charts the shifting composition and interests of each over a 40-year period. Established in 1884, the *British Australasian* operated initially as a markets paper yet gradually broadened its outlook to incorporate the more diverse tastes of an increasingly eclectic readership. Under the guiding hand of three principal editors the newspaper transformed its offices into a social centre and lobbied for greater recognition of its correspondents' needs. Competing national agendas ultimately prompted a minor crisis, however – a moment revealing much about the contingencies of life in one's 'home away from home'.

Continuing an established tradition, Australians still delight in 'falling towards England'.[1] Upon arrival, most newcomers head straight for London, where strategically placed newsstands dispense a number of community-focused magazines such as *In London*, the latest publication to target affluent young Aussies, Kiwis and South Africans. *In London* blends travel advice, shopping tips, sports reports and job listings with notices of forthcoming social events. As well as providing space for the articulation of nationalistic sentiment, the magazine suggests a shared Southern Hemispheric identity that Angela Woollacott observes as the *raison d'être* for one of its rivals, *TNT Magazine*.[2] Both publications seek – and simultaneously foster – a transnational market, a market whose patrons hail from multiple locations to experience (whether willingly or not) a new collective identity forged in the crucible of 'the Big Smoke'.

In 1884, long before the advent of the 'gap year', Walkabout pubs or Contiki's 'Grand Tour', another publication went on sale, claiming attention from and for a different yet familiar market-based and London-oriented group: British Australasians. Its pages reveal much about the place of Australians – and Australasians – in 'the British world'. Cast at its inception as 'A Newspaper for Merchants, Shareholders, Land Selectors, and Emigrants, And all interested in the Magnitude and Growth of British Interests in Australia, New Zealand, Tasmania, and the Western Pacific', the *British Australasian* came to represent a still broader coalition of interested parties. Leafing through the first 40 years of its archive we encounter the constituent individuals and institutions of an ever-shifting expatriate community during a period of sustained imperial power and emergent nationalism.

The mid 1880s proved a propitious time to start a newspaper in London for Australasians – so much so, in fact, that two such titles commenced publication in 1884. On 2 October the first issue of a new tabloid weekly, the *British Australasian*, rolled off the press. It was devised and financially supported by R.H. Inglis Palgrave (an eminent London banker and sometime editor of the *Economist*) and Robert Lucas Nash, a financial journalist, sub-editor of the *Economist* and the *British Australasian*'s inaugural editor. The *Anglo-New Zealander and Australian Times* (edited by a London-based *Argus* employee, Charles Short) had first appeared two months earlier. Revealingly, the terms of the latter title were soon reversed to *Australian Times and*

Anglo-New Zealander, 'reflecting the preponderance of Australian interests on this side'. In 1888 the two newspapers merged, an absorption that left a lasting imprint on the *British Australasian*.

Both newspapers began circulation during a period of massive capital transfer from Britain to the Antipodes. A high point in a boom decade occurred in 1884, when £20.8 million was invested in Australia.[3] A succession of good seasons in the colonies had increased pastoral wealth, and new developments in refrigerated shipping during the early 1880s allowed Australasian exporters to access hitherto untapped British markets with their fruit, frozen lamb and other perishable goods. The mining surge that was driven by the discovery of silver deposits at Broken Hill as well as the findings in Western Australia encouraged London investors to finance new ventures. The fragments of empire seemed to be drawing together: steamships criss-crossed the globe with ever-increasing speed and frequency, while Sydney and Melbourne were at last connected by rail in 1883.[4] The creation of the Imperial Federation League in Britain in 1884 further sought to cement the unity of the colonies and the Mother Country.[5] The *British Australasian* followed the League's progress, publishing its manifesto, supporting its campaigns and reporting on its push for both a Colonial and Indian Exhibition and a Colonial Conference (events that would later bring large numbers of overseas visitors to London during the summer months of 1886 and 1887). Even the high cost of the cable service – 6 shillings and 7 pence per word for press messages between Sydney and London in 1886 – tended to favour the utility of the newspaper, which functioned as a storehouse for information travelling along what might be termed (to alter Henry Parkes's famous phrase) 'the copper threads of kinship'.[6] Ashes cricket tests, the New Guinea crisis of 1883 and the Sudanese military intervention in 1885 are further examples of events that garnered increased attention – if not understanding – for colonial affairs and good copy for Nash's newspaper.

And Nash was clearly the right man for the job. At its inception the *British Australasian* was primarily a markets paper; Nash had cut his journalistic teeth on the *Economist* and in preparing an 1869 monograph, *Money Market Events*.[7] Although English by birth, Nash's interest in Australasian finance and economic development was clear – he would later publish books on the infrastructure of New South Wales and *The Banking Institutions of Australasia*.[8] The latter is doubly significant, as it details the histories of the 20 Australasian banks with branches in London in 1890 and was issued from the *British Australasian*'s own press. The air of confidence that pervades the work is also in evidence throughout Nash's newspaper editorship.

Early editions carry articles on 'Practical Federation' (which Nash eagerly advocated), 'The Great Land Companies' and the raising of £500,000 in London for the construction of Melbourne's tram network.[9] Room was also found for the occasional sports result or banquet report, but under Nash's eight-year guidance, and especially until 1888, the *British Australasian* was concerned principally with movements: movements of money, movements of share prices, movements of ships between ports and the great political transitions wished for: Australian federation and the super federation of empire. In his first pieces, Nash condemned the 'superficial knowledge possessed here' and 'the driblets of news doled out to English readers' regarding Australasian topics. Such criticism was not unusual. When Alfred Deakin visited the Colonial Conference in 1887 he famously attacked the 'absolute innocence' of the British in colonial matters, telling his British hosts that the paltry attention given by their newspapers to Australasia was 'a missing link in the unity of the Empire'.[10] Like Deakin, Nash clearly intended to foster mutual understanding and forge fresh bonds.

Who was reading Nash's newspaper? British investors and potential migrants may well have been interested, and so too those with access to Australia's great public libraries or overseas sales points. Passengers making the long voyage south aboard steamers also read the *British Australasian*, with the paper stating in 1906 that 2000 copies of each edition were reserved for this purpose. Undoubtedly though, the vast majority of Nash's readers were in Britain. Ros Pesman estimates that by the 1890s around 10,000 people were arriving in the United Kingdom from Australia annually; Andrew Hassam proposes that 200,000 arrived from Australia and New Zealand between 1876 and the century's end.[11] Accurate figures are difficult to obtain, although recent analysis reveals 15,295 individuals recorded as born in Australia in the 1901 Census of England and Wales. Travelling via the United States to Britain in the jubilee year of 1887, James Francis Hogan encountered a range of seafarers. Some were 'scions of noble and gentle houses' returning after a tour of the colonies; others were just setting out, graduates exchanging the learning of the university for the university of knowledge through travel. Others still had been 'doing the colonies' for manufacturing orders, and Hogan's party was completed by a youthful female artist and 'not a few young colonists' hoping to catch sight of the Queen on their first trip 'home'.[12] One wonders how representative this company was.

From 1888 until 1912 the *British Australasian* published its own list of 'Australasians in Europe', both settlers and sojourners. This information enlightens as well as omits, but a few suggestive trends emerge from a slice analysis based on a comparison of five different weeks across five different years (see Table 7.1). Note the increasing proportion of married and unmarried women (sufficient, perhaps, to prompt the initiation of a ladies' column in the newspaper in July 1905); the relative steadiness of numbers of dependants and percentage of New Zealanders in Britain; and the significant, though fluctuating, presence of Australasians in Scotland, the overwhelming majority of whom gave their postal address as the Australasian Club in Edinburgh. Established around 1877, some 21 years before its English namesake, Edinburgh's Australasian Club was one of the longest established Australasian societies in Britain yet probably the least mentioned by historians.

At best these figures represent a slim sample of those in Europe. Most likely these were individuals subscribing to the newspaper, which in any case reduced the column inches devoted to its Australian address book over time. Further clouding the picture, in 1911 Valerie Desmond even suggested that one's lack of material progress in the capital could affect one's chances of inclusion in the *British Australasian*'s list. 'When frequent changes of address', she stated, 'make it too plain that the C.Y.A. [Clever Young Australian] is bilking his landlady, and the change of locality is from humble to worse – well it discreetly draws the curtain. The "British Australasian" is a most genteel publication'.[13] Perhaps more insightful was the editor's admission that 'only a very small proportion' of 'the many thousands' of Australasians in Europe featured in the directory.[14] By March 1912 the list had gone, 'owing to the ever-increasing numbers of visitors'.[15] Further statistical analysis of census data is clearly needed to establish whether the broad trends deducible from these catalogues are typical. What can be said with greater surety is that the preponderance of names on the *British Australasian*'s lists are representatives of 'the travelling class', the privileged portion of society possessing the material wherewithal and time to make the long trip possible, and who closely associated first-hand experience of Britain with social prestige.[16]

	1888	1894	1900	1906	1912
Total persons listed	916	603	555	481	711
	(%)	(%)	(%)	(%)	(%)
Men	74.0	79.3	69.0	62.6	45.7
Married Women (Mrs.)	14.2	12.3	20.0	22.0	30.4
Unmarried Women (Miss)	4.4	3.1	5.9	10.2	15.2
Women (total)	18.6	15.4	25.9	32.2	45.6
Dependants	7.4	5.3	5.1	5.2	8.7
Total	100	100	100	100	100
From Australia	83.8	76.6	82.9	83.4	59.5
From New Zealand	15.9	22.7	16.2	16.0	6.2
From Fiji / New Guinea	0.1	0.2	0.4	0.2	0
Multiple regions specified	0.2	0.5	0	0.4	0.4
Origin not given	0	0	0.5	0	33.9
Total	100	100	100	100	100
In London	71.5	59.5	75.6	72.3	89.2
In Oxford / Cambridge	7.3	2.5	0.5	0	0.3
In Scotland	9.4	17.1	9.5	15.4	2.2
Elsewhere in Britain	9.6	19.2	11.2	10.6	5.8
Total in Britain	97.8	98.3	96.8	98.3	97.5
In Continental Europe	2.2	1.7	3.2	1.7	2.5
Total	100	100	100	100	100

Table 7.1 Residency patterns of the 'Australasians in Europe' listed in the *British Australasian*, 1888–1912
Note: The first list, published in the 4 July 1888 issue, forms the basis of the figures in the 1888 column. Thereafter the issue closest in date to 4 July was consulted, until the very last list, on 15 February 1912. Due to the fact that many respondents named their place of origin as 'Australia' or 'New Zealand', I have not calculated totals for individual states.

Responses to correspondents provide further insights into the *British Australasian*'s readership. In March 1901, for example, readers were informed that South Australian lamb could be purchased at the Smithfield Market, but that the editor was not aware of any restaurants in London specialising in colonial fare. The paper had earlier dispensed financial advice, reassuring 'T.G.' from Newcastle that the National Bank of Australasia was 'an admirably managed institution' and 'W.B.H.' that he was sure to find success with investments and employment in the Western Australian goldfields.[17] Correspondents were even advised about which Australian stocks to buy and sell.[18]

By the time that the queries from T.G. and W.B.H. were answered, Philip Mennell had become editor-proprietor. Nash had left, confidence intact, for the Sydney *Daily Telegraph* at the end of 1892, before the bank collapses of the following year. Mennell was the second of four editors to oversee the *British Australasian* during the period considered here. His British birth belies his Australian experience as a journalist, first on the *Bairnsdale Advertiser* and later with the Melbourne *Age*. His assurances about the promise of Western Australia should not surprise us: in the year before his appointment Mennell found time, aside from completing his *Dictionary of Australasian Bibliography* (one of the earliest works of its kind and noteworthy as a federalising project), to publish *The Coming Colony*, a panegyric to Western Australia, 'the Cinderella State' or, as he would later term it, 'an El Dorado in a Sahara'.[19] Perhaps buoyed by the success of his own investments there, Mennell tirelessly promoted in the pages of his newspaper the transfer of both people and capital to his favoured state.

Mennell reoriented the *British Australasian* to embrace a greater spread of subjects. The financial pages, shipping reports and federation comment remained, but space was now found for society news, concise book reviews, correspondence and a theatres column. Such developments arguably paralleled an increasing diversity of interests among Mennell's readers: the Australasian community in London could now be defined by more than finance alone. Following the absorption in 1888 of the *Australian Times and Anglo-New Zealander*, the new-look *British Australasian* retained some elements of its former rival, most particularly the 'Colonial Gossip' column and advertisements for Westminster tailors and city boarding houses. From its turn-of-the-century home in the London Wool Exchange (a testament to the continued importance of Australasian pastoral production on the stock market), the *British Australasian* was slowly transformed.[20] In 1884 the paper had declared that its interests were economic; under Mennell's hand, artists, sightseers and society ladies began to find their tastes catered for too.

A sign of the increased confidence and surety of ground of the *British Australasian* can be seen in its willingness to agitate for reforms on behalf of its readers. In 1893, for example, readers were asked to write in on the subject of 'The best method of increasing the efficiency of the Agent-Generals' Offices'. Competition winner, Arthur Clayden, received praise for his centralising arguments:

> A large central building should be erected, easy of access and known throughout the United Kingdom ... Here the inquirer should find every requisite particular to guide his steps. Passing through a pair of folding doors opening on to the street, he should find himself in a large hall, in which each of the seven colonies would be represented by its officials.

Such an establishment, the winning essayist concluded, would host 'descriptive and educational lectures' and come under the remit of a high commissioner.[21] A version of Clayden's vision would begin to take shape on the Strand 20 years later with the establishment of Australia House.[22] The *British Australasian* took up other causes, too: free trade between the Australian states; Imperial Preference 'as a kick towards the goal of Imperial Free Trade'; an end to the double income tax for Australasians in Britain; Australasian women's loss of political status under British suffrage laws; and emigration, with frequent demands for a parity of effort with Canada on the issue of attracting British migrants to Australia.[23]

Echoing the newspaper's heightened assertiveness, the late 1890s and early 1900s bore witness to a surge in the number of formal associations for Australasians in London. The Australasian Club, Australian League, Colonial Club, London branch of the Australian Chamber of Commerce, and other societies all date from this period, and the *British Australasian* assiduously reported their meetings, thus facilitating a process of cultural consolidation. Angela Woollacott identifies the Austral Club (founded in 1902) as of particular significance in this regard. Initiated by two feminists, it proved a boon to professional and creative women of independent means in the imperial capital, providing a place to meet or read papers and a stage on which to perform recitals.[24] Weekly 'At Home' events were a regular feature, and at its Dover Street venue, the *British Australasian* informs us, artists such as Melbourne's Elsie Berry made their first singing appearances in London.[25]

Moreover, in the early 1900s the newspaper's offices were themselves a thriving social centre. The *British Australasian* had long welcomed visitors to peruse its book collection and purchase overseas newspapers and during E.C. Buley's three-year stint at the editor's desk from 1905 the range of services offered at what became known as 'The Rendezvous' proliferated. By 1892, 31 newspaper titles could be purchased from the Fleet Street offices.[26] Initially located in Finsbury Circus (cable address 'Kangarooby') and later in High Holborn, The Rendezvous was a bookshop and information centre combined, with free advice dispensed on 'where to stay, where to shop, what to see and how to see it', personal mail stored and facilities provided for letter writing.[27] Described by one visitor as 'a little bit of our own country, set down in the middle of London', it also provided an opportunity for expatriate artists and authors such as Martin Boyd, Will Dyson, Will Ogilvie, Vance Palmer and Katharine Susannah Prichard to meet.[28] Luggage storage and ticketing facilities were added when Charles Chomley filled the editor's position in 1908. From 1918 onwards Australia House began to assume some of these roles, but a later description of the Australian High Commission building could have been applied with equal accuracy to The Rendezvous: it was indeed a 'national "foyer"'.[29] The *British Australasian*'s bookshop first moved into Australia House in 1922, and a newspaper stall later operated on the ground floor.[30] The newspaper itself followed by 1933.[31] The resources offered at the newspaper's offices before its move to Australia House are indicative of three trends: more visitors in London, a coalescence of the community there, and the rising proportion of tourists (further evidenced by a new motoring column).

Under Charles Chomley's editorship, the *British Australasian* took on a more artistic flavour. Special summer numbers featured illustrations, poetry, short stories and interviews with representatives of the Australasian arts community in London.[32] Chomley also arranged for artworks to be exhibited at The Rendezvous, where by January 1910 one could find 56 paintings, 26 drawings and 6 works of statuary by artists including Tom Roberts, Norman Lindsay and Harold Parker.[33] Chomley's prior engagement in Melbourne as editor of *Arena* highlighted his interest in the arts, society gossip, female suffrage and politics, themes he would infuse into the *British Australasian* after investing in the concern and assuming the role of editor-proprietor.[34]

Chomley's house in Ladbroke Gardens became, as Brenda Niall notes, another social centre for Antipodeans, with its owner's restless temper and radical ideas encouraging a climate there in which anything could be discussed.[35] Chomley could certainly debate: in 1905 he published *Australian Pros and Cons: A Guide to the Principal Questions of the Day, Giving the Best Argu-*

ments on Both Sides.³⁶ Socialism, protection, old-age pensions, vegetarianism: such were the topics carefully considered, with the author just about managing to restrain his passion for free trade in a chapter on the practicalities of protectionism.³⁷ Niall also notes that it was Frances Fitzgerald Elmes, a journalist and novelist, who 'supplied the professionalism' of the *British Australasian*. Her death from influenza in 1919 must surely have shaken Chomley, for Frances, so the gossipers whispered, had borne him two children.³⁸ Elmes's dedication contrasted sharply with the conditions under which the newspaper was often produced. At the Chomley residence family members took turns at the dining-room table with scissors and paste, and daughters Isla and Francie assisted with the social columns and the reviews of books, concerts and plays that were now so regular a feature.³⁹ Others who worked on the *British Australasian* during this period included writer Alice Grant Rosman, Spencer Brodney (an assistant-editor and probable theatre critic), Penleigh and Martin Boyd, and Margaret Agnese Baxter (an author of the ladies' column).⁴⁰ By the late summer of 1914 Chomley's newspaper was firmly established as a key component of the Australasian community in London, and Chomley would remain in the editor's chair until his death in October 1942.

The advent of war brought new readers and gave the paper added importance. Some aspects of the *British Australasian*'s role during the First World War had been foreshadowed during the Sudan intervention and then later the South African War at the turn of the century. In 1885 telegrams carried news of the Australian contingent to readers; 15 years later the newspaper followed in detail the progress of the New South Wales Lancers, printed casualty lists and advertised 'the Bushmen's fund'.⁴¹ A sense of greater immediacy and urgency is apparent in the case of the 1914–18 conflict. 'Phyllis', the writer of the ladies' column, described the flight across Europe of sojourning Australasians at the war's outset.⁴² The newspaper then charted the swift establishment of the Australian and New Zealand War Contingent Associations and the Australasian Women's War Club, an organisation that gathered at the *British Australasian*'s offices.⁴³ Time and again readers were reminded of their 'soft berths' in London and asked to make financial contributions.⁴⁴

Prior to the landings at Anzac Cove, Chomley and his staff followed the movements of the thousands of Australasian troops serving in British regiments. After the landings the casualty lists printed in the newspaper ran to many pages. Later in 1915, Chomley arranged for his paper to be sold to soldiers at half price, an offer greatly appreciated by among others Captain Charles Bean, who wrote in to say that the *British Australasian*'s arrival was eagerly anticipated at Gallipoli for it contained 'the only news we get of the wounded who go to England'.⁴⁵ The position of Anzacs in England, whether wounded or on leave, became a campaigning cause for the newspaper, which agitated for the establishment of separate Anzac hospitals and for greater allowances and more beds to be provided for soldiers on furlough in the capital.⁴⁶ It also sought Australian government allowances for wives of soldiers serving in Europe, a demand eventually met in August 1918.⁴⁷ Advice on the suitable use of time on leave was also issued, and in 1916 a handbook followed – *The Colonials' Guide to London: For Anzac, Canadian and other Overseas Visitors* – sponsored by the *British Australasian* and carrying its advertising.⁴⁸

The Colonials' Guide was, in part, a response to the perceived rowdiness of Australasian – now 'Anzac' – soldiers when in London. Established routines of the expatriate community had been radically challenged by the influx of tens of thousands of troops and accompanying family members into Britain. The *British Australasian* reflected the degree of anxiety. While Buley, scripting the 'Overlander' column during the war, chided Anzac soldiers for their rough treatment of female peace demonstrators in Trafalgar Square ('it is un-Australian and un-soldierly', he wrote, 'to pelt women with yellow ochre'), 'Phyllis' criticised antipodean women for their 'slap-dash, second-rate slanginess' in conversation with troops.[49] By mid-1916 Buley was insisting that new arrivals 'follow more closely the Anzac traditions': respect in one's appearance and wise selection of one's acquaintances.[50]

By and large, it seems the influx was welcomed: the pages of the newspaper record private acts of generosity, like the weekly tea parties arranged for wounded Australians by Mrs Rita Fiske and the welcome extended to strangers by Miss Dorothy Brunton and her mother at their London flat, the Digger's Rest, where an inscription over the door ran 'Abandon rank all ye that enter here'.[51] In the later war years and afterwards the newspaper regularly listed weddings between overseas troops and local civilians.[52] But class patterns underwent disruption nevertheless, and at least one reader fretted over the impact upon English perceptions of Australia. Identifying herself an Australian while revealing her own prejudices, Muriel Witmoth wrote in to the *British Australasian*:

> English people are inclined to think of them [the soldiers] merely as Australians, and forget that in Australia, as in every other country, there are various grades in the social scale, and as one should not expect the little delicate refinements of life from a Limehouse dock labourer, so one should not expect it from a Yarra bank labourer or an outback woodsman.[53]

Here in Brunton's letter the 'travelling class' senses its 'other'.

'Australasian', a term employed with caution in this chapter, had a long-since-forgotten meaning in Britain – and most especially London – of the nineteenth and early twentieth centuries. It is worth noting in this regard that a combined 'Australasian' team, featuring athletes from Australia and New Zealand, carried off the Davis Cup in 1907 at Wimbledon and competed at Wembley in the 1908 Olympic Games with a specially designed flag. In the minds of the British, 'Australasians' (a description which sometimes embraced, as our 'Australasians in Europe' list indicates, white colonists from Fiji and New Guinea) were commonly imagined as a unified mass. This possibly accounts for *British Australasian*'s own title. In a sense the word merely expressed the financial realities and federalising dreams of the period. The Bank of Australasia, for instance, was London based; the Bank of New Zealand, in 1890, had five branches in the Australian states, one in Great Britain and two in Fiji.[54] On a few fleeting occasions at the end of the nineteenth century the possibility of New Zealand joining the Australian states in Federation was also raised, and it should be remembered, too, that at the Inter-colonial Convention of 1883 both New Zealand and Fiji sent representatives to Sydney to discuss the New Guinea question.[55] As a self-description 'Australasian' appeared to present few problems to visiting colonists in late-nineteenth-century London. The 60 gentlemen, for instance, who enrolled in the Australasian Club at its inauguration in 1898, attended smoking concerts thereafter and dined at the Ship and Turtle Tavern in Leadenhall Street, certainly seemed happy with the term, and none was British.[56] Except, of course, that they all were, at least in terms of racial sentiment. There was not necessarily any contradiction in being both British and Australian or New Zealander, or even British and Australasian, at this time.

For its part the *British Australasian* managed to employ both the 'Australasian' of its title and 'Australian' in a thoroughly slipshod manner. 'Anglo-Australians', as a case in point, were told that the *British Australasian* was essential reading for them, and on one occasion a woman was described as both an Australian and a New Zealander in consecutive sentences.[57] As Andrew Hassam notes, 'Anglo-Australian' was one of a number of terms, including 'Anglo-Colonial', 'Australian Briton' and 'United Kingdom colonist', used to label Australians (and New Zealanders). He relates this plurality to difficulties in defining the degree of Britishness of those outside Britain.[58] The issue was confused further on 6 July 1905 when a hyphen was inserted in the newspaper's title: a coupling that created a new adjective and suggested a type, just at the instant in the paper's history when stirrings of Australian nationalism were in evidence, particularly in the summer specials.

Two of those specials present a revealing insight into the contradictions and complexities of Australasia in Britain. There are several possible readings of Will Dyson's front cover to the *British Australasian*'s summer numbers of 1910 and 1914 (see Figure 7.1).[59] Here we see a stockman – or perhaps a station owner – with stockwhip and cork hat, standing before London's St Paul's Cathedral. The posture suggests virility, insouciance, arrogance almost. The figure is master of all he surveys. Or is he? Is it rather that the subject is detached entirely from the scene in the background to which his back his turned, the grey lifeless London with its rolling fog? The flora in the top corners of the composition evokes abundance, the background sterility. Is the figure we see even located in London? Perhaps this image is the visual manifestation of lines from Henry Lawson's 1900 poem, 'The Rush to London':

> It may be carelessly you spoke
> Of never more returning,
> But sometimes in the London smoke,
> You'll smell the gum leaves burning;
> And think of how the grassy plain,
> Beyond the fog is flowing …[60]

Is Dyson's British Australasian homesick? Or could it be that the figure is entrapped within Paul Carter's 'mirror-logic of empire', able only to discover a true identity once authenticated overseas, and perceiving this identity as Dyson and the newspaper's Australasian readers would have: coming back to them, second hand?[61] How many readers, one wonders, might have glimpsed their reflections in this image?

The stirrings of nationalism, in this instance New Zealand nationalism, ultimately forced a name change upon the *British Australasian*. In February 1924, after complaints from the High Commissioner for New Zealand, Sir James Allen, the title was altered to the *British Australian and New Zealander*.[62] Allen felt that the New Zealand component was frequently forgotten in the word 'Australasia', a claim backed up by the New Zealand Chamber of Commerce, not to mention the *British Australasian* itself. Chomley bemoaned the lack of an adequate term to define his readership, but acquiesced with the request.[63] The 'Australasian' community had split semantically in two, though of course it had never really existed as a unified whole, a little like the British host society in which the newspaper was based.

Figure 7.1 The Stockman and St Paul's: Will Dyson's cover for the *British Australasian*, summer 1910
Source: *British Australasian*, 30 June 1910, summer supplement, p. 1. Courtesy of the Newspapers Collection, State Library of Victoria.

Yet the *British Australasian* reminds us of something essential: that to rediscover Australia in Britain we need sometimes to think of Australasia in Britain and remember the New Zealand contribution. Until quite recently, after all, it was not such a long walk from Australia House to New Zealand House down the road, a location possibly even within earshot of a fully voiced 'cooee'. In the offices of the *British Australasian*, a succession of industrious editors charted the rise and fall of the Australasian ideal, and captured the flavour of an increasingly diverse expatriate scene. For settlers and sojourners alike the newspaper functioned as social glue, aiding the establishment of new relationships and keeping readers up to date with developments across the seas. In their British 'home from home' many found the newspaper essential reading. Similarly, for the historian the *British Australasian* is an indispensable guide to the period: an access point into the expatriate community that the newspaper helped bond, and an overview of the key locations in which the community coalesced.

APPENDIX

NAME CHANGES TO THE *BRITISH AUSTRALASIAN*, 1884–1965

The British Australasian, 2 October 1884–27 June 1888.
British Australasian, Australian Times and Anglo-New Zealander, 4 July 1888–15 September 1892.
British Australasian, Australian Mail and Anglo-New Zealander, 22 September 1892–22 December 1892.
British Australasian and Australian Mail, 29 December 1892–6 July 1893.
British Australasian and New Zealand Mail, 13 July 1893–29 June 1905.
British-Australasian, 6 July 1905–14 February 1924.
British Australian and New Zealander, 21 February 1924–1947.
Australia and New Zealand Weekly, 1948–1965.

ENDNOTES

1. James, 1985.
2. Woollacott, 2001, 15.
3. Vamplew, 1987, 186.
4. See *The British Australian* (hereafter *BA*), 5 May 1887, 412; *BA*, 1 December 1892, 1370.
5. See Paul, 2004, 64–77.
6. Potter, 2003, 196.
7. Nash, 1869, *Money Market Events, and the Value of Securities Dealt in on the Stock Exchange in the Year 1868*.
8. Nash, 1890. *The Banking Institutions of Australasia: A Reprint of Articles Published in the British Australasian, Australian Times and Anglo-New-Zealander*.
9. *BA*, 2 October 1884, 1; 30 October 1884, 30.
10. *BA*, 12 May 1887, 433.
11. Pesman, 1996, 23; Hassam 2000, 3.
12. Hogan, 1889, 6, 7.

13. Desmond, 1911, *The Awful Australian*, 95.
14. *BA*, 3 November 1910, 34.
15. *BA*, 22 February 1912, 27.
16. See White, 2005, 89-90; White, 1986, 44; Pesman, 1996, 23.
17. *BA*, 30 November 1893, 1403; 7 December 1893, 1438.
18. *BA*, 13 June 1901, 977.
19. Mennell, 1892, *The Coming Colony, Practical Notes on Western Australia*; *BA*, 25 July 1901, 1253-1257.
20. From the Strand, the paper moved around the City to Fleet Street, the Wool Exchange in Coleman Street, Finsbury Circus and High Holborn.
21. *BA*, 7 December 1893, 1430.
22. See *BA*, 15 June 1911, 20; 22 June 1911, 19. See also Pryke, 2006.
23. See *BA*, 8 March 1888, 212; 6 July 1905, 6; 25 May 1911, 3; 6 July 1905, 12; 9 January 1908, 3. See also Chomley, 1904, *Protection in Canada and Australasia*.
24. Woollacott, 2001, 102–103.
25. *BA*, 6 January 1910, 16.
26. See *BA*, 7 January 1892, 5.
27. See *BA*, 18 June 1908, 27.
28. *BA*, 5 July 1906, 8; Niall, 1990, 93.
29. Quoted in Woollacott, 2001, 76.
30. Woollacott, 2001, 77; Australian High Commission, 1929, *The Australian's Guide Book to London*, 53.
31. Woollacott, 2001, 77.
32. *BA*, 24 July 1913, Summer special (includes poems by Barbara Baynton, Will Ogilvie, a short story by Katharine Susannah Prichard and illustrations by Ruby Lind); *BA*, 30 July 1914, Summer special (includes poems by Alice Grant Rosman and features on Australian art and theatre).
33. *BA*, 6 January 1910, 11.
34. See de Serville, 1979, 642–643.
35. Niall, 2002, 126.
36. Chomley, 1905, *Australian Pros and Cons: A Guide to the Principal Questions of the Day, Giving the Best Arguments on Both Sides*.
37. Chomley, 1904, *Protection in Canada and Australasia*.
38. Niall, 1990, 74–76.
39. Niall, 1990, 72.
40. Edgar, 1988, 454; *BA*, 11 March 1915; Niall, 1990, 72; Boyd, 1965, 116; Matters, 1913, *Australasians Who Count in London*, 11.
41. See *BA*, 14 May 1885, 465; *BA*, 12 October 1899, 1561–1563; 25 January 1900, 143; 1 February 1900, 259.
42. *BA*, 6 August 1914, 18.
43. See *BA*, 20 August 1914; *BA*, 7 January 1915, 16.
44. *BA*, 10 September 1914, 9.

45 *BA*, 28 October 1915, 3.
46 See *BA*, 1 July 1915, 3.
47 *BA*, 4 November 1915, 9; *BA*, 8 August 1918, 3.
48 Manders, 1916, *The Colonials' Guide to London: For Anzac, Canadian and Other Overseas Visitors*. See also *BA*, 4 November 1915, 14.
49 *BA*, 13 April 1916, 5; *BA*, 31 August 1916, 21.
50 *BA*, 27 July 1916, 5. See also White, 1987, 63–77.
51 See *BA*, November 1915, 26; 22 May 1919, 12.
52 See *BA*, 5 June 1919, 12 (192 such weddings in a week).
53 *BA*, 17 January 1918, 7.
54 Nash, Robert Lucas. 1890. *The Banking Institutions of Australasia: A Reprint of Articles Published in the British Australasian, Australian Times and Anglo-New-Zealander*, 6.
55 See Sinclair, 1987, 90–103.
56 See *BA*, 9 June 1898, 1176; *BA*, 16 June 1898, 1305; *BA*, 27 October 1898, 1944–1996.
57 *BA*, 6 July 1905, 12.
58 Hassam, 2000, 16.
59 *BA*, 30 June 1910, Summer Supplement, 1; *BA*, 30 July 1914, Summer Supplement, 1.
60 Lawson, 1967, 386.
61 Cited in Hassam, 2000, 42. See White, 2001, 109–127.
62 *BA*, 14 February 1924, 4.
63 *BA*, 14 February 1924, 4.

PRIMARY SOURCES

Australian High Commission. 1929. *The Australian's Guide Book to London*. London: Australian High Commission.

British Australasian.

Chomley, Charles. 1904. *Protection in Canada and Australasia*. London: P.S. King & Son.

Chomley, C.H. 1905. *Australian Pros and Cons: A Guide to the Principal Questions of the Day, Giving the Best Arguments on Both Sides*. Melbourne: Fraser & Jenkinson.

Desmond, Valerie. 1911. *The Awful Australian*. Sydney: John Andrew.

Manders, A. Staines. 1916. *The Colonials' Guide to London: For Anzac, Canadian and Other Overseas Visitors*. London: Fulton-Manders.

Matters, Mrs Leonard W. 1913. *Australasians Who Count in London*. London: James Truscott.

Mennell, Philip. 1892. *The Coming Colony. Practical Notes on Western Australia*. London: Hutchinson.

Nash, Robert Lucas. 1869. *Money Market Events, and the Value of Securities Dealt in on the Stock Exchange in the Year 1868*. London.

Nash, Robert Lucas. 1890. *The Banking Institutions of Australasia: A Reprint of Articles Published in the British Australasian, Australian Times and Anglo-New-Zealander*. London: British Australasian Co.

REFERENCES

Boyd, Martin. 1965. *Day of My Delight: An Anglo-Australian Memoir*. Melbourne: Lansdowne.

Edgar, Suzanne. 1988. 'Rosman, Alice Trevenen (1882–1961)'. Australian Dictionary of Biography. Volume 11. Carlton, Vic.: Melbourne University Press.

Hassam, Andrew. 2000. *Through Australian Eyes: Colonial Perceptions of Imperial Britain*. Carlton, Vic.: Melbourne University Press.

Hogan, James Francis. 1889. *The Australian in London and America*. London: Ward & Downey.

James, Clive. 1985. *Falling Towards England*. London: Jonathan Cape.

Lawson, Henry. 1967. 'The Rush to London' (1900). In *Henry Lawson: Collected Verse*, edited by Colin Roderick. Volume 1 1885–1900. Sydney: Angus & Robertson.

Niall, Brenda. 1990. *Martin Boyd: A Life*. Carlton, Vic.: Melbourne University Press.

Niall, Brenda. 2002. *The Boyds: A Family Biography*. Carlton, Vic.: Melbourne University Press.

Paul, Aron. 2004. 'One king to bind them all: The imperial federation movement, the imperial monarchy and the triumph of sentiment'. *Melbourne History Journal* 23: 64–77.

Pesman, Ros 1996. *Duty Free: Australian Women Abroad*. Melbourne: Oxford University Press.

Potter, Simon J. 2003. 'Communication and integration: The British and dominions Press and the British world, c.1876–1914'. In *The British World: Culture, Diaspora and Identity*, edited by Bridge, Carl; Fedorowich, Kent. Hoboken: Taylor & Francis.

Pryke, Olwen. 2006. 'Australia House: Representing Australia in London 1901–1939', PhD thesis, Sydney: University of Sydney.

de Serville, P.H. 1979. 'Chomley, Charles Henry (1868–1942)'. Australian Dictionary of Biography. Volume 7. Carlton, Vic.: Melbourne University Press.

Sinclair, Keith. 1987. 'Why New Zealanders are not Australians: New Zealand and the federal movement, 1881–1901'. In *Tasman Relations: New Zealand and Australia, 1788–1988*, edited by Sinclair, Keith. Auckland: Auckland University Press.

Vamplew, Wray. 1987. *Australians: Historical Statistics*. Sydney: Fairfax, Syme & Weldon.

White, Richard. 1986. 'Bluebells and fogtown: Australians' first impressions of England 1860–1940'. *Australian Cultural History* (5): 44–59.

White, Richard. 1987. 'The soldier as tourist: The Australian experience of the Great War'. *War & Society* 5 (1): 6377.

White, Richard. 2001. 'Cooees across the Strand: Australian travellers in London and the performance of national identity'. *Australian Historical Studies* (116): 109–27.

White, Richard. 2005. *On Holidays: A History of Getting Away in Australia*. Melbourne: Pluto, 2005.

Woollacott, Angela. 2001. *To Try Her Fortune in London: Australian Women, Colonialism and Modernity*. New York, Oxford: Oxford University Press.

Cite this chapter as: Sleight, Simon. 2009. 'Reading the *British Australasian* community in London, 1884–1924'. *Australians in Britain: The Twentieth-Century Experience*, edited by Bridge, Carl; Crawford, Robert; Dunstan, David. Melbourne: Monash University ePress. pp. 7.1 to 7.14. DOI: 10.2104/ab090007.

CHAPTER 8

'THE CRUMBS ARE BETTER THAN A FEAST ELSEWHERE'
AUSTRALIAN JOURNALISTS ON FLEET STREET

Bridget Griffen-Foley, Macquarie University
   Bridget Griffen-Foley is an Australian Research Council Queen Elizabeth II Fellow and the Director of the Centre for Media History at Macquarie University in Sydney.

This chapter explores the experiences of Australian journalists who worked on Fleet Street between 1900 and the outbreak of the Second World War. Concentrating on several individuals, it considers the powerful lure of Fleet Street, the reasons for departure from Australia, first impressions of London, the opportunities provided by being abroad, experiences of success and failure, working and social life, and the particular challenges and opportunities facing women journalists. It examines the theme of education in the public writings and private reflections of Australians who worked on Fleet Street, and reflects on the circularity and complexity of the imperial journalistic experience.

Long before the 'Dirty Digger', Rupert Murdoch, made his mark on the newspaper landscape of London, Australian journalists were working on Fleet Street.[1] In *When London Calls: The Expatriation of Australian Creative Artists to Britain*, Stephen Alomes notes that many Australians other than the high profile Germaine Greer, Barry Humphries, Clive James and John Pilger have been based in London.[2] Situating his study in the decades following the Second World War, Alomes makes an important contribution to our understanding of the factors that propelled Australian writers, journalists, artists and actors to live for a time, or permanently, in Britain.

This chapter addresses the experiences of Australian journalists on Fleet Street between 1900 and the outbreak of the Second World War. This is a particularly interesting period as in the late nineteenth century cable rates had fallen, making it possible for Australians to participate in British public life on a day-to-day basis; and, as we shall see, in the early twentieth century the Australian press was flourishing and Australian journalism was becoming increasingly professionalised.[3] While travel was both slower and more expensive than in the postwar period, so many Australian journalists made the journey to London in the first decades of the twentieth century that they could be said to constitute a 'tradition'. The chapter focuses on individual Australian journalists who worked on Fleet Street: Louise Mack and (later Sir) Keith Murdoch in the 1900s; Florence James and G.W. Warnecke in the interwar years; and Alan Moorehead, Noel Monks and Robert Raymond and his family in the 1930s. These journalists have been selected because they give a cross-section of male and female experiences in the decades before the Second World War, and because accounts of their activities in London are extant.

Under consideration are the 'imagined' Fleet Street, the reasons for departure, first impressions of London, experiences of success and failure on Fleet Street, working and social life, and the particular opportunities and challenges facing women journalists. The principal focus is on Australians who worked for the London press, although passing references will be made to some journalists who worked in the London bureaux of Australian newspapers. Wartime experiences are not considered at any length; Murdoch's activities in the First World War warrant a separate study, as do Australia's distinguished correspondents in the Second World War.

Journalism is a peripatetic profession. As Alomes points out, journalism is about 'journeys', a word that is itself linked etymologically to the French *journée* (the day) and *journal* (a newspaper as well as a diary of events).[4] The dreams of journalists often involved other newspapers, other towns, other editors and other stories. Elizabeth Morrison has compared Australian journalists to roving actors, performing before any audience that could 'understand the language and respond to the play'. Journalists worked their way around country towns and the six capital cities, in search of a more expansive canvas for their work.[5] In 1902 22-year-old R.C. Packer left the *Tasmanian Mail* for Sydney because it was 'the biggest place possible on this side of the world'. In 1920 17-year-old C.S. McNulty, who had been working in Perth, came to Sydney and joined *Truth*.[6] Some journalists spread their wings even further, to the sub-imperial South Pacific of New Guinea and Fiji. Numerous New Zealand journalists aspired to 'make it' in Australia, and there were also Australian journalists who took up positions in New Zealand.[7] This traffic was facilitated, in part, by links between the labour press in the two countries.

For some journalists, such as Packer, this internal or trans-Tasman migration was challenge enough. But many others regarded working in Sydney or Melbourne as a stepping-stone to something larger. In their daily work and in their inner city, nocturnal existences, journalists met 'everyone', from politicians to police, prostitutes to theatrical performers, and actors to artists. As they interviewed visiting celebrities and (male reporters, at least) yarned in pubs, journalists dreamed of escaping the daily grind and furthering their careers overseas. Curious and migratory, journalists were drawn towards the next big story – somewhere else.[8]

That 'somewhere else' was usually London. In recent years both Ros Pesman and Alomes have explored the place of 'Home' and the 'Mother Country' in the Australian psyche. Ever since convicts had been transported to Australia, and soldiers and free settlers had crossed the seas, the return to Britain had been culturally important. The 'overseas trip' was a ritual event, a rite of passage and, it was generally believed, a once-in-a-lifetime experience. The colonial tradition associated Britain, especially London, with the mind and 'culture', and Australians were pulled to London by career possibilities in journalism, writing and theatre.[9]

By the end of the nineteenth century Australians were literate and wealthy enough to buy newspapers on a per capita basis far in excess of their British contemporaries. A prolific and diverse press flourished, with an enormous range of titles published, until the emergence of publishing chains in the 1920s. Alomes's assertion, then, that the culture of Australian journalists was 'predominantly that of suburban career values' fails to acknowledge the diversity and the challenges of journalistic culture and career paths in Australia.[10] Australian newspapers were either metropolitan or provincial, and city newsrooms were bohemian rather than suburban.[11]

Journalism remained the mainstay of colonial literary production because publishing books locally was expensive and the market was small. Novelists, poets and playwrights sought from journalism their basic source of income and, as we shall see, many Australian journalists went to England intent on developing their craft as creative writers.[12] Alomes *is* right to point out that Australian journalists felt constrained by the essential parochialism of their metropolitan newspapers, which were produced for capital city markets. The fact that London's newspapers, by contrast, had a national audience was a powerful drawcard for Australians such as Robert Raymond, who joined the *Daily Sketch* in 1940. He recalls his excitement at 9 p.m. when the presses would start running so that the early edition could 'catch the trains ... for the dash through the night to the remotest corners of the kingdom'.[13] Journalists who remained in Australia did not have the opportunity to write for a national daily newspaper until the *Australian Financial Review* and the *Australian* in the early 1960s.

Just as London was 'Home' for Australians, Fleet Street was the 'home' of the Fourth Estate. Fleet Street extends eastwards from Temple Bar as far as Ludgate Circus. Taking its name from the Fleet River, Fleet Street was sandwiched between the cities of London and Westminster and occupied a strategic importance in the Middle Ages. It was the chief western artery into London and connected the king's palace and the courts at Westminster. Even before William Caxton set up the first printing press in 1477 in Westminster, Fleet Street was the centre of literacy in Britain as a result of the activities of the Order of the Knights Templar and the Carmelites of Fleet Street and nearby Whitefriars.[14]

Fleet Street became the home of booksellers and printers, and papers were stamped at Somerset House before despatch. By the mid-eighteenth century Fleet Street had emerged as the main distribution centre for most of London's newspapers and a Mecca for tourists. The proliferating coffee houses provided a sort of 'club' and 'press room' for some of the best-informed men in Europe. For most visitors, especially those from overseas, Fleet Street represented Dr Johnson's London and a chance to see the literati at their leisure. The term 'Fleet Street' refers in part to the many lanes and alleyways leading off it, and the street itself was in an almost constant state of realignment. Between 1880 and 1914, its south side east of Temple Bar was set back. This geographical realignment coincided with important changes in the role of the newspaper. In the late nineteenth century the mass production methods of the American newspaper industry thoroughly altered the small family business concerns of Fleet Street. W.T. Stead and Alfred Harmsworth (later Lord Northcliffe) transformed English journalism.[15]

For Australian journalists, Fleet Street was the spiritual and physical home of the old journalism – papers of record and opinion – and the 'New Journalism',[16] designed to appeal to the newly literate lower and lower-middle classes. Australian journalists embarked on the voyage for a number of reasons. The Melbourne *Herald*'s Alan Moorehead 'yearned to go abroad, to get to the centre of things and events that I had been hearing about all my life'. He put every penny he could aside to 'escape – at first to London' and then, perhaps, 'the whole world'. Arriving in London in 1936, he had the feeling 'that at last I was in the centre of the world instead of being on the periphery'. His compatriot Noel Monks, who had gone to London a little earlier, entitled his autobiography *Eyewitness*, suggesting that from the vantage point of Fleet Street he was an eyewitness to 'real' history.[17]

Other Australian journalists, particularly women, were escaping from or delaying marriage. Louise Mack, author of the popular books *Teens* (1897) and *Girls Together* (1898), wrote the 'Woman's Letter' for the hugely popular and irreverent weekly newspaper, the *Bulletin*. By 1900 her marriage to a barrister was floundering as a result of his drinking binges and bankruptcy, and she decided to flee to London. To avoid awkward questions, the 30-year-old let her family and friends think that she was going away for a short time because of work.[18]

Florence James, who was born in New Zealand in 1902, came to Sydney with her family in 1920. As a result of her father's engineering career the family had lived a migratory existence, but James seems to have been particularly influenced by her time at St Cuthbert's College in Auckland. Here she had been encouraged to write for the school magazine by her female English teacher, who had a degree in political science and mathematics. In Sydney James was sent to the Conservatorium of Music and then moved on to the University of Sydney, where she was awarded the University Medal for Philosophy in 1926. On graduating James immediately started work in her father's office to earn her fare to Europe for her 'Grand Tour'. She also became involved with the Theosophical Society, through which she met her fiancé William John ('Pym') Heyting, a young Dutch lawyer reared in Indonesia. In September 1927 James left for London, ostensibly to further her writing career, on the understanding that she would return and the couple would be married by the end of 1928.[19]

At farewell parties, journalists usually contributed a sovereign to a purse for their departing colleague. By the time Mack boarded her ship in April 1901 she was physically and emotionally exhausted, as she was also leaving behind her marriage. Journalists watched with some trepidation as their 'Not Wanted on Voyage' bags – often containing a typewriter – disappeared into the ship's hold. As streamers stretched and parted and the hooter gave its throbbing blast, James stood on the deck of the *Balranald* and 'waved vigorously to the dear figures' beside Mrs Macquarie's Chair, a historic landmark on Sydney's harbour foreshore.[20]

Using ship stationery, journalists wrote long letters to their families and friends during the 12,000-mile voyage, which lasted about two months. James wrote effusively to her younger sister about the tennis, concerts and dances she and her female companion were enjoying. Tall and strikingly attractive, James became particularly friendly with a young South African science student travelling to Cambridge, 'so you can imagine the interesting talks'.[21] The extroverted and temperamental Mack, however, was disappointed with her fellow passengers. She had hoped to meet 'all kinds of delightful charming cultivated people … and we would talk about Shelley and Rossetti and Chopin and Italy and Greece and Paris, or they would talk and I would listen'. Mack felt let down; her classical education was not getting off to a good start, as she was surrounded by more 'plain, homely uninteresting BODS' than she had ever seen in her life.[22]

By April 1908 22-year-old Keith Murdoch, a reporter on the Melbourne *Age*, had saved enough money for his fare and invested £500 in bonds to keep him for at least a year. He had three goals: to expand his newspaper experience, study at the London School of Economics and seek advice for a humiliating stammer.[23] Murdoch, travelling steerage, was seasick and nervous about socialising because of his speech impediment. This was the first time that he had been away from his large family and his long letters to his father, a Presbyterian minister, were a mixture of anxiety and grim determination:

> I am dreading these first weeks in London. My stammering has not [been] improved by the trials of the voyage and I hardly feel fit. But I am determined to make a name here before I leave the place, and I'm sure I won't leave even should it cost me every penny I possess until I'm better qualified for good journalistic work.[24]

During the voyage, journalists stopped at ports such as Colombo, travelled through the Mediterranean and had their first taste of the 'Continent'. Despite her misgivings about her companions, Mack was enthralled by what she saw as the exoticism of the Orient and the sophistication and antiquity of Europe. A thrill went through 'this raw Australian breast – Age, age, antiquity, romance. *Coffee!*' As Pesman observes, the objective of travel was the past as much as the present. White Australia was young; it was above all the past, and a romanticised past, that most Australian travellers sought.[25]

Mack arrived in Tilbury in 1901 expecting an overwhelming throng of ships in a dull yellow fog with the city of London rising from the very bank. Instead, hers was the only ship berthed, the sky was blue and the sun was shining. As she walked down a dirty wooden wharf, only a few houses and a couple of hotels were visible. But it did not take her long to warm to London. Australians studied British history and literature at school, and the city Mack had heard and read so much about was no longer an abstraction. She walked and walked around Bloomsbury, Tavistock and Russell Square, feeling that she was walking with the ghosts of poets and artists who had starved and suffered and written and died in the gigantic metropolis.[26]

When Moorehead arrived in 1936, he felt liberated at being in the first real crowds he had ever known:

> I loved the march of faceless strangers in the street. To be known by no one, watched by no one, to join the ant-like anonymous procession – this was a new and exhilarating kind of privacy … one was entirely free, one could go anywhere and do anything.[27]

James sent memorabilia to her family – a map of the underground to illustrate the vastness of the city, a postcard of buses at Piccadilly Circus, a leaf from Kew Gardens – and wrote capacious letters recounting her visits to London's landmarks. She felt that she had a sort of privileged knowledge she was behoved to share with relatives and friends in Australia: 'No one can realise the peculiar beauties of England until they have been here, & that is quite certain'.[28] James's close friend Dymphna Cusack, who had taken up a teaching position in outback Australia, addressed James as 'Dear and envied Globe-Trotter'.[29]

Most journalists were armed with references and letters of introduction. Mack had a letter to a fiction editor who paid well for newspaper serials. An Australian magazine reported that she had 'struck a payable lead with a prominent magazine a few days after sighting the white cliffs' and was 'beginning with the best prospects'. But now that she was in London, Mack was determined to shed her old life and write only what pleased her. She moved into an attic and began writing a novel, *An Australian Girl in London*, often going for days without seeing a soul. As the months passed, Mack struggled to pay her rent, went without heating and lost weight. As her time, energy and money waned, she did not waste precious money on stamps and simply stopped writing to her worried relatives.[30]

When Mack delivered her manuscript to the publisher of her first novel, she was virtually penniless. She made an appointment with the fiction editor of the Harmsworth Press, which she had heard paid well for serials. At the interview, the editor explained what he wanted: stories had to have a domestic interest, a love interest and an allusion to mystery; they must gain 'the sympathy of the reader'; each instalment had to be left up in the air so that readers would keep buying the paper. Presented with an example of a popular plot, Mack was horrified that anyone could print such rubbish. However, she was desperate, so she went home and started to write. While struggling to master the formula, she learned that her novel was to be published in the spring of 1902. Meanwhile, she wrote a serial for a Harmsworth publication that proved popular with readers, and the editor commissioned more.[31]

An Australian Girl in London tells the story of a young woman who goes to England, has adventures among the English, marries an Englishman, but remains passionately devoted to Australia. For all its exclamatory style and girlish archness, the book was well received by critics and W.T. Stead engaged Mack to write for *The Review of Reviews*. He had started a new feature, a sort of endless serial based on well-known people and current events. Set in Australia, Mack's chapters had bronzed Australians coping with fire and drought in the outback, garden parties at Government House for the visiting Japanese fleet, and so on. Royalties from the novel were not enough to keep her, so Mack concentrated on writing serials for Stead and other publishing houses. She had a vivid imagination and could write quickly so, after a hesitant beginning, she became a prolific freelancer. She made a great deal of money, which she spent on moving into a comfortable flat, buying new clothes and attending concerts and the theatre. Mack became a regular at Stead's Friday 'at homes' at Mowbray House, where the magazine's contributors mixed with writers, artists, socialites, politicians and visitors from abroad. She resumed writing letters to her family and Australian publications such as the *Bulletin*, filling them with descriptions of her gay social outings and her journalistic successes.[32] She was no longer satisfied by the romantic ideal of starving for her art, and she was so caught up in the excitements and busyness of her new life that the literary aspirations she had carried with her to London simply faded away.

Unlike Mack, Keith Murdoch was intent on getting work on Fleet Street as soon as his ship berthed in May 1908. Geoffrey Syme of the *Age* had expressed his appreciation of the 'soundness and general excellence' of Murdoch's work. Murdoch also had a brief, formal letter from Prime Minister Alfred Deakin commending him as 'a worthy young reporter seeking experience abroad'.[33] There were introductions to Presbyterian church leaders in London and Scotland and to the editors of church journals. The most important of these was to William Robertson Nicoll, a Scottish non-conformist and editor of the *British Weekly*. Murdoch lost no time making an appointment to see Nicoll in June 1908. Nicoll gave the young Australian letters of introduction to other papers and said that he wanted to learn how Murdoch got on. One of these papers, the *Church Family Newspaper*, paid Murdoch £2 10s for three days' work covering the Pan-Anglican Congress. When Murdoch sent an article to Nicoll to peruse, he was advised to read the London papers carefully and write more succinctly. Murdoch was disappointed that Nicoll only intended to help him 'indirectly'. Murdoch's letters to his father were rather contradictory. In one, he referred to Nicoll's 'cold, stern slaughter of some hopes'; in another, Murdoch indicated that he had told Nicoll that he did not consider himself at present fit for a London appointment.[34]

Mack had been very conscious of an audience – journalistic and familial – back in Australia. She had conveyed tales of success to the 'stay-at-homes' waiting for the adventurer to fail, and concealed her hunger and despair.[35] Murdoch, however, wrote deeply personal and agonisingly self-critical letters to his father while staying with an aunt and her husband, a doctor, in north London. The doctor put Murdoch in touch with speech experts and Murdoch decided to stay with his aunt for three months while undertaking speaking exercises.[36]

Murdoch claimed that Robert Donald, editor of the *Daily Chronicle*, informed him that 'colonial experience was of little use' on Fleet Street. Murdoch's reports of how he was received by London editors varied according to his moods. In one letter to his father, he claimed that Donald had offered him sub-editorial work, but that he (Murdoch) had turned it down as he had no sub-editorial experience. Murdoch was encouraged, instead, to send in paragraphs to the *Daily Chronicle*.[37]

While it seems that Donald did have some time for Australians, they were, of course, competing with journalists from other parts of Britain. London broadsheets like *The Times* and the *Daily Telegraph* recruited a few graduates each year from Oxford and Cambridge. Most journalists from the British Isles – from Manchester and Yorkshire, Scotland and Ireland – served apprenticeships with provincial newspapers before chancing their luck on the national papers published from Fleet Street.[38] In 1910 an Australian journalist, Reginald Carrington, hungrily accepted a sub-editorial position with the *North Mail* in Newcastle. The former Melbourne *Argus* journalist had spent four years calling on the senior staff of each office in Fleet Street and attempting to sell articles, interest editors in his suggestions on how to improve their newspapers, and write a novel. On one particularly grim day, he had left 10 articles at different newspaper offices, and all had been rejected. He had done other bits of work – drafting pamphlets for advertising agencies and filling in at a wire service – but by 1910 he was in debt. Returning to Australia, Carrington wrote 'The Quest: A True Story of an Australian Journalist's Five Years' Search for Fame in Fleet Street'.[39]

Electing to remain in London, Murdoch placed a few articles with the *British Weekly* and the *Daily Chronicle*, but he still felt overwhelmed by both personal and professional challenges. He came to realise that there would be no quick improvement to his speech and decided to move between distant relatives in London. In August 1908 he wrote:

> No doubt this city frightens the stranger who comes to teach it something. I think it is the determined will power of the city that shatters the knees of the stranger when he knocks against it. Tremendous strength of mind is needed to force one's way along.[40]

By December he was spending one hour daily doing speaking exercises, and two hours writing paragraphs for newspapers. For eight or nine hours a day he would read and attend the London School of Economics, where he sat in on lectures in sociology, economics and logic. He felt inadequate – a 'baby in thought and knowledge' – because he had not been to university, and he became particularly interested in the theories of L.T. Hobhouse.[41]

There were occasional bursts of optimism as Murdoch studied voraciously and thought he detected a slight improvement in his speech. In late 1908 he told his father, 'Real hard study here will be useful, and I'm going to become a moving force yet'; 'Journalism certainly is precarious. But I'm young and strong and sh[oul]d not fear'.[42] Mostly, however, he was worried – about his talents, about money, even about his Christian faith. In January 1909 he lamented, very simply, that the newspapers 'don't want my stuff'. But he was determined to stay and get at least six months' good experience.[43]

There was a pervasive Australian view that success lay in first being acclaimed in Britain. Many Australian newspapers imported their editors from Britain; the broadsheet *Sydney Morning Herald* recruited few Australian editors until as late at the 1960s.[44] As Simon Potter points out, the proprietors of large dominion newspapers could afford to send their sons back 'Home' for training. Lauchlan Mackinnon of the Melbourne *Argus* and David Syme of the *Age* both made sure that their sons had the chance to see the workings of top London and Scottish newspapers.[45]

In his letter to Murdoch in 1908, Geoffrey Syme had expressed the wish that the experience Murdoch gained on Fleet Street would be of great service to him and perhaps to the *Age*. Murdoch took this to be a half promise to re-employ him, and in February 1909 he asked his father to call on Syme and his wife. Patrick Murdoch was deputed to tell Syme that Keith was 'studying hard with a view to doing useful press work' and returning to the *Age* in late 1909 or 1910.[46]

In the meantime, Murdoch was '*going to get rid of my stammer*' and 'prepare myself for great work'. He visited Edinburgh for treatment from a Mrs Calwell at a cost of some £15. He was soon back in London, living in a dingy hostel for young Scotsmen and offering his services to newspaper offices.[47] He seems to have had some success and his confidence was growing, as he joined the Colonial Institute and the Press Club and followed imperial politics. Telling his father that Britain was concerned about the growth of the German fleet, Murdoch suggested that Australia should contribute a Dreadnought in return for three or four second-class cruisers. He attended a Navy League meeting and debates in the House of Commons, and joined a committee for sending out slum boys to Australia.[48]

Murdoch's spirits soared when he was interviewed about opening a new branch office for the *Pall Mall Gazette* at a salary of £104 a year, plus commission. But at the final interview with the editor in September, his speech 'collapsed and we both realised I would not do'. Shattered, Murdoch wrote to his father, 'London does not agree with me'. He was suffering from insomnia and indigestion, from a lack of good air and 'good solid work'. He asked his father to cable him £100 and sailed for Melbourne, via the United States.[49]

Murdoch's biographer C.E. Sayers entitled his chapter about Murdoch's activities in 1908–09 'London Failure'; a later biographer, Desmond Zwar, headed his chapter 'Defeat'.[50] There can be no doubt that Murdoch had often despaired during his 18 months on Fleet Street. But while he had confided his anxieties and disappointments to his father, it is doubtful whether he did so to Syme, who took him back onto the *Age*. Murdoch had obtained at least some journalistic experience on Fleet Street, his interest in public affairs had deepened, and he had attained an understanding of how the worlds of journalism and politics operated in London.

With rigid self-discipline and constant exercising Murdoch brought his stammer under reasonable control. In 1911 he became a founding member of the Australian Journalists' Association (AJA), evidence of Australian journalism's improved professional status and organisation. By now he was reporting on federal parliament, which sat in Melbourne, for the *Age*. This position gave the complex young man the opportunity to mix with leading Australian politicians, including Prime Minister Andrew Fisher, a friend of his father. Having observed the way in which political and journalistic networks operated in London, he began using an aunt's guesthouse to entertain Fisher and other government ministers. Murdoch was enticed to represent the Sydney *Sun* in Melbourne.[51]

In September 1914 he lost narrowly to C.E.W. Bean in the AJA's ballot to appoint an official Australian war correspondent. However, a few months later Murdoch's employer transferred him to London as managing editor of the United Cable Service, which serviced both the *Sun* and the Melbourne *Herald*. A sensational letter he wrote condemning the disastrous Allied landing at Gallipoli and celebrating the 'magnificent manhood' of Australian troops brought him to the attention of Lord Northcliffe. Murdoch made the most of his notoriety and began to hobnob with Cabinet ministers and act as an intermediary between Australian and British politicians.

Meanwhile, Bean's determination to document the experiences of ordinary Australian soldiers became a central component of the triumphalist Anzac tradition. The men from Australia and New Zealand who had been at Gallipoli became iconic figures, and Australia as a nation was seen to have stepped onto the world stage.[52]

The AJA's monthly publication, the *Australasian Journalist*, was now routinely running paragraphs about the 'exodus' of Australians and New Zealanders to Fleet Street.[53] Articles with headings such as 'Fleet-Street Customs: Status of London Editors and Sub-editors' and 'The Inky Way in Britain: Ex-Maorilander's Experience' became staple fare. The *Journalist* published memoirs suggesting that the best way to survive in Fleet Street was by working for a news agency or churning out serials. It also recounted the difficulties faced by Australasian journalists, particularly when some London newspapers succumbed to the soaring price of newsprint during the war and ceased publication.[54] But what the *Journalist* liked most was the Australian journalist who flourished on Fleet Street. In 1919 it reported that Murdoch had 'obtained a good position in London journalistic circles' and was 'on terms of friendship with many of the Cabinet Ministers'. Murdoch's rise to fame had been 'meteoric', he was always to be seen at *The Times* office, and bureaucrats never succeeded in preventing his access to important personages.[55]

Murdoch himself had not forgotten the struggles of his first term on Fleet Street. In an article for the *Journalist* in June 1920, on his way back to Australia to cover the tour of the Prince of Wales, he asserted that the Empire Press Union (EPU) should establish a formal exchange scheme for Australian journalists:

> London being the world centre of journalism, and an important factor in Australian affairs, it is the aim of the ambitious Australian journalist to spend some time there ... Whilst this can be won only by taking on the hard struggle of free-lance work in London, it will remain a singularly difficult, hazardous undertaking.

His article also suggested that the fact that he had blossomed in London only by working for an Australian cable service rankled. Northcliffe supported the idea of an exchange during his visit to Australia in 1921, by which time Murdoch had returned to Melbourne to edit the *Herald*. Murdoch's proposal was also discussed at various EPU conferences, but nothing came of it.[56] Nevertheless, some ties between journalists in Australia and Britain were formalised. In 1921 the AJA and the National Union of Journalists agreed to accommodate members of either society going to work in the territory of the other.[57]

It was not until the bombing of Pearl Harbor that many Australian newspapers established offices in New York or Washington. This meant that Australian journalists often got their first chance to work overseas by joining their newspaper's Fleet Street bureau. An article published in an EPU circular in 1913 noted that dominion newspapers which sent staff on rotation to London ensured that 'constant intimacy is maintained with affairs in this country'.[58] One such journalist was G.W. Warnecke, a returned serviceman who was asked to open the London office of *Smith's Weekly* and its stablemate, the Sydney *Daily Guardian*, in 1923. Even though he was well paid, Warnecke was frustrated that he was unable to get interviews and stories in the 'offhand' way he had in Sydney. He was surprised that he had to write and make appointments to interview politicians and business executives, and frustrated by his inability to access Cabinet ministers at all. Lacking Murdoch's contacts, and not being a part of a network of public school graduates and exclusive clubs, he was unable to penetrate the coterie of journalists, editors and politicians in London. But despite the professional frustrations, he felt that, in a personal sense, 'my eyes were opening, and my ears were listening'. He had been on the fringes of the labour movement in Sydney, and he began to haunt Bloomsbury, mixing with writers such as the poet Anna Wickham and the Australian novelist Christina Stead, and the prominent British communists William Gallacher and Shapurji Saklatvala. An ardent Irish nationalist, Warnecke became secretary of the London branch of the Irish Workers' League and marched under its banner in the 1924 May Day procession. He met and married an Irish opera singer, Nora Hill, before returning to Australia later that year.[59]

If Warnecke was exasperated by the task of interviewing 'tenth rate Australian visitors & foreign diplomats',[60] Florence James was struggling just to make a living from her pen. In May 1928, seven months after arriving in London, James wrote to her fiancé saying that she would not allow her parents to pay for her return home. She would not 'leave this side of the world until I have earned the right to':

> You know that I want to make writing my life work, well Pym I'm going to be established in that work before I renounce the most favourable opportunity I shall ever have in my life for doing so …
>
> This letter leaves you entirely free of all obligation to me, and I take my freedom in my own hands. What the future holds I cannot say, but should our lives lie together it will be a new woman you must win and a new man who must woo her.[61]

James confided to her parents that Avril, the young scientist she had met on the voyage, was obviously in love with her and was about to move to London. However, she stressed that Avril was not the cause of her reservations about marrying Pym. James described herself and Pym before her departure as 'babes in arms, blundering about!' Explaining to her mother that she had had a 'splendid education' in London, she signed her letter 'Your big daughter Florence'.[62] When Pym implored her to return to Sydney and sent £50 for her return passage, she cabled the money back to his account.[63]

By July 1928 James had amicably parted from Avril when his South African fiancée arrived in Britain.[64] After a spell working at a guesthouse in Edinburgh, James returned to London and 'the writing game' determined to be 'a serious minded woman with no time for frivolities'. In October she declared to her mother: 'Oh it's good to be in London even if one can't see & do all one would like; the crumbs are better than a feast elsewhere'. James's attempts to write popular serials – which were amusing and entertaining but 'not art' – met with no success. In November she enrolled in a freelance course at the London School of Journalism. She found the course helpful and practical because she was not 'a journalist by temperament or inclination'.[65] She was oddly encouraged when a friend of a friend told her that she had had to bombard Fleet Street for two years before her work was accepted.[66]

James's efforts to write a novel and saleable serials were interspersed with writing copy for an advertising agency. In early 1931, with accounts drying up and the agency shedding employees, she complained to her mother, 'never has there been such depression'.[67] Fortunately, however, she was put onto the contract staff of a Fleet Street news agency. The agency decided on the topics of stories and sold the serial rights, while she conducted interviews and wrote the stories. James earned a good commission and was content to leave the business side of things to other people. Although she had lived in Sydney, she was deputed to write articles about the Northern Territory and on kangaroo hunting with Aborigines, posing as an experienced hunter.[68] James left the agency to ghost books for a Mr Siggins, who had lived in Africa for several years, but after some months he went broke.[69]

She had at least cleared her debts, and an interview with Dr Maria Montessori produced a profitable sideline. Happy with the first story, the Italian educationalist arranged for James to rewrite her articles and lectures for English consumption. This arrangement brought James to the attention of senior staff at the *Daily Express* and the *Evening Standard*, and proved that she was capable of writing features as well as serials.[70] She was pleased that she had managed to learn the 'craft side' of her work at other peoples' expense by freelancing, working in advertising and writing for Mr Siggins. She joined the Quill Club, persisted with work on her novel and remained determined to 'make a name for myself among modern writers'.[71]

James had continued to correspond with Pym Heyting, who moved to London and joined a legal practice. On their marriage in 1932, James told her family in Australia: 'Pym will never change very much, he is such a serious, sober old darling, but he has come out of his shell a lot since the old days'.[72] In 1928 James, fearful of being a young wife trapped by domesticity, had informed her parents that Pym had a fine brain and the will to succeed, 'but I'm going to do well too, & not just as Pym's wife, but as *me*'.[73] Heyting supported James' decision to keep on working after their marriage as they were saving for a home – something James yearned for because she had been moving from flat to flat since leaving Australia.

Heyting was concerned about the mental strain and loneliness of writing,[74] and his wife attempted to give her life structure by keeping a diary. She set financial and literary goals, recorded each effort to write and sell a story, and berated herself for getting out of bed late and eating sweets. James believed that she had to struggle with her weakness of character and could only 'write greatly if I am fighting to live honestly and sincerely'. She sold stories to the *Daily Dispatch*, the *Manchester Evening News* and the *Yorkshire Post*, and by 1934 was again concentrating on her novel. She also worked as a literary agent and tried to place the manuscripts of Australian novelists such as her friend Dymphna Cusack.[75] In 1935, the year James gave birth to her first child, she encouraged Cusack to come to London. Now a full-time mother and writer, James said of her early years in London:

> I had my Fleet Street experience in the depths of the depression when scraping a living was almost a 24 hours a day job … one cant [sic] come to London on the off chance that one will be able to earn enough by free lance journalism to keep one.[76]

As Alomes notes, the onset of the Great Depression made the journey from Australia to London less common until after the war.[77] By the early 1930s neither James nor her father was able to afford the cost of her return passage to Australia. But still the dream of many journalists was to work on Fleet Street. When the Australian trade journal *Newspaper News* was launched in 1928 it included a regular column, 'Notes from Fleet Street', and during the Depression some journalists managed to scrape together the fare to go to England.

In 1930 Moore Raymond left Brisbane to try his luck on Fleet Street. He secured a job on the *Daily Express* and became an established theatre and film critic. But Raymond's brother-in-law, Russell Hill, found the labour market no healthier than in Australia. After placing only a few paragraphs, he put his lifesaving skills to use and became a swimming instructor in London. When Raymond's father died in 1934, his widow decided that she and her youngest son, 12-year-old Robert, should make an extended visit to London and meet up with the family.[78]

A number of journalists from Australia and New Zealand secured work on the *Daily Express*, the *Sunday Express* and the *Evening Standard*. This was largely due to one of the newspaper group's executives, Frederick Doidge, whose career illustrates the complexity of the imperial journalistic experience. The Australian-born son of the proprietor of the *Cootamundra Liberal*, Doidge began his journalistic career in New Zealand and became founding president of the New Zealand Journalists' Association. Before his discharge from the New Zealand infantry in 1918, he was seconded to the British Ministry of Information under Lord Beaverbrook. Doidge went on to become an executive with the Express Newspapers group and play a key role in Beaverbrook's 1931 Empire Free Trade Crusade.[79] Doidge recruited an Australian, C.L. Hains, as circulation manager of the *Daily Express* and enticed the New Zealand-born cartoonist David Low to the staff of the *Evening Standard*.[80]

In 1935 Noel Monks, who had begun his career on the Hobart *Mercury* before joining the Melbourne *Sun News-Pictorial*, worked his passage to London. On his arrival in May, the burly 27-year-old dropped by the *Daily Express* in case it was 'short of a genius'. After two days of trying to get past the front hall, he discovered the password – 'Empire Trade'. When he mentioned that he knew Henry Gullett, leader of the Australian trade mission that had just arrived in London, Monks was told he could start work the following day. The fact that Doidge was about to return to New Zealand meant that Monks had arrived at the *Daily Express* at just the right time.[81]

Monks and Alan Moorehead were part of a network of Australasian journalists on Fleet Street who were holding weekly luncheons by 1920. The London Association of Empire Newspapers Overseas and the Overseas Committee of the Institute of Journalists served an industrial as well as a social purpose.[82] Male journalists congregated at the Surrey, the pub opposite Australia House in the Strand, and the famous old journalists' pub, the King Lud. Many Australian journalists, such as Florence James and Moore Raymond, had rooms in Chelsea, an artistic quarter that became very fashionable in the 1960s. They read and wrote at the Chelsea Public Library (which had, as a bonus, central heating) and joined the Chelsea Arts Club, the Press Club and the Savage Club.[83]

Australian journalists took to drinking coffee rather than tea, and wine rather than beer with their meals. They visited continental restaurants with menus featuring exotic items such as Vienna schnitzel and Hungarian goulash. Moorehead had an affair with a woman called Katharine who was engaged to an older man. He would later write that Katharine had been engaged in 'Pygmalionism':

> What fun to educate him, to be herself a teacher, just for a while, to take him to the theatres, the galleries and the restaurants ... Little by little under her

guidance I was beginning to change my spots and take on the camouflage and the colours of Europe.

Robert Raymond, who followed his older brother into London journalism in 1940, became involved with a German Jew who had been smuggled out of Germany. Through his girlfriend, the Anglo-Celtic Raymond began mixing with central Europeans for the first time in his life.[84]

War was an Australian and journalistic theme, the key to seeing the world.[85] The First World War had brought several Australian journalists closer to the centre of imperial affairs. It had advanced the careers of Murdoch, Doidge and, of course, C.E.W. Bean, who became official historian of Australia's part in the war and founder of the Australian War Memorial. Australian journalists spotted new opportunities in the 1930s. Throughout the summer of 1935 all Monks could think about was his 'first war'. As a colleague was despatched to Abyssinia for the *Daily Express*, Monks resigned from the newspaper and sailed for North Africa on the understanding that his work also would be used if possible. Much of Monk's copy was used, and he was welcomed back to his old desk at the *Daily Express* after a brief, unhappy spell on the Melbourne *Herald*.[86] By 1936 Monk's friend Alan Moorehead was looking for a way to escape his affair with Katharine, now a married woman. Monks knew that the *Daily Express* needed a correspondent in Gibraltar and told the foreign editor that he had a friend who by luck was just about to leave for Gibraltar. And so Moorehead, by volunteering to pay his own fare, went off to Spain to cover the civil war.[87] The Spanish Civil War and the theatres of the Second World War were covered comprehensively and with distinction by a generation of Australian journalists including Monks, Moorehead, Ronald Monson, Chester Wilmot, Godfrey Blunden and Osmar White.[88]

Australian journalists went to Fleet Street with a variety of ambitions: to prove their journalistic credentials and further their careers when they returned to Australia; to explore new opportunities writing fiction; to travel further in Europe and to military fronts; and to escape the expectations of parental eyes and marriage. Mostly, however, they sought to be educated, whether formally – by well-known journalists and editors, attending the London School of Journalism or the London School of Economics, and visiting galleries, museums and libraries – or informally, by mixing with continental Europeans and acquiring sophisticated lovers. The idea of furthering – or perhaps even beginning – one's education was a recurring motif in the public writings and the private correspondence of Australian journalists who, in Reginald Carrington's words, quested for fame on Fleet Street. The title of Moorehead's autobiography, *A Late Education*, referred not to his university studies, but to his travels and to his affair with the worldly Katharine.

Few Australian journalists found working on Fleet Street easy. Carrington, Mack, Murdoch and James had their work repeatedly rejected and lived, for a time at least, in poverty. Monks, who secured a post on the *Daily Express* within days of his arrival, was a lucky exception. The experiences of James and Frederick Doidge serve to remind us of the complexity and the circularity of the imperial experience. There was not a simple linear, one-way traffic between Australia and London. Journalists moved between the provinces and the metropolises of Australia and the British Isles, and between New Zealand, Australia and Britain, taking advantage of the mobility facilitated by their profession and the opportunities offered by war.

As the lives of the individuals addressed in this chapter show, some Australian journalists made their home in Britain, others returned to Australia or divided their time between different countries. Murdoch established a career at the helm of Australia's first publishing chain, becoming managing director and chairman of the Herald & Weekly Times Ltd and playing a leading organisational role in the Australian media industry and Melbourne art circles. 'Lord Southcliffe', as he was known, was knighted in 1933 and served as Director-General of Information in 1940.[89] Mack became editor of the *Italian Gazette* in 1904 before managing to get to Belgium in 1914 as an early woman war correspondent, reporting for the London *Evening News* and *Daily Mail*. She continued to write novels and toured the Pacific Islands, New Zealand and Australia with travel talks and films for schools until her death in Sydney in 1935.[90] James returned to Sydney in 1938, contributing to the women's supplements of the *Sydney Morning Herald* and the *Daily Telegraph* and writing popular novels including *Come in Spinner*. With her two daughters she went to London again in 1947, divorced Pym Heyting and worked as a literary agent before returning to live permanently in Australia in 1963.[91] Monks remained in Britain, working as foreign and war correspondent for the London *Daily Express* and then the *Daily Mail*; on his death in 1960 the *Sunday Dispatch* described him as 'one of the greatest reporters of our day'.[92] Moorehead's frank wartime despatches for the *Daily Express*, backed by three books and a biography of Field Marshal Montgomery, won him great fame. After the Second World War he lived in Italy and Britain and wrote many acclaimed works of military history, science and biography, visiting Australia several times for research.[93] Robert Raymond remained in London during the Second World War, reporting for the *Daily Sketch* and the Sydney *Daily Mirror*, before making films in Africa and returning to Australia. In 1961 he co-founded the seminal television current affairs program *Four Corners* and in the 1980s served on the board of the Australian Broadcasting Corporation.[94]

A sense of nostalgia has accompanied Fleet Street for at least a century; while each journalist or editor would recount his or her one great exclusive,[95] many would look back to the 'golden age' of journalism before the crassness of Northcliffe. Then, in 1988, a 'Farewell to Fleet Street' exhibition was held at the Museum of London. The diaspora from 'The Street', the dream of generations of journalists from Australia and other English-speaking countries, was born in 1986 with the removal of four national newspaper titles to Wapping.[96] Ironically, the exodus was led by an Australian – Sir Keith Murdoch's son, Rupert.

ACKNOWLEDGEMENTS

This chapter by Bridget Griffen-Foley was originally published as '"The crumbs are better than a feast elsewhere": Australian journalists on Fleet Street'. *Journalism History* 28 (1) (Spring 2002): 26–37. It is reproduced here with permission. *Journalism History* is published by the E.W. Scripps School of Journalism, Ohio University, Athens Ohio, USA.

ENDNOTES

1. In c.1971 the satirical magazine *Private Eye* labelled Murdoch the 'Dirty Digger' for his 'vandalising' of the British press. See Shawcross, 1993, 144, 156.
2. Alomes, 1999, xii.
3. See Walker, 1976, 204–5; Lloyd, c.1986, chs 1–2.
4. Alomes, 1999, 185.

5   Morrison, 1997, 74, 178, points out that a high proportion of the most influential metropolitan journalists of the 1880s and thereafter were previously contributors to, or editors of, country newspapers.
6   Griffen-Foley, 2000a, 12–13; Griffen-Foley, 2000b, 273.
7   Alomes, 1999, 40; Hamilton, 1999, 102.
8   Alomes, 1999, 39.
9   Pesman, 1996, 2–3; Alomes, 1999, 2, 6, 8.
10 Morrison, 1998, 468; Alomes, 1999, 39.
11 For the links between journalism and bohemia in Australia, see Kirkpatrick, 1992, 3ff.
12 Stewart, 1988, 179.
13 Alomes 1999, 40; Raymond 1992, 188.
14 Bell, 1912, v; Boston, 1990, 14–16; Jenkins, 1986, 10.
15 Boston, 1990, 41, 42, 90–94.
16 See Wiener, 1988.
17 Moorehead, 1970, 39, 46; Monks, 1955.
18 Phelan, 1991, 99–102.
19 Anon., 1991, 42–44; North, 2001, 3, 9.
20 Phelan, 1991, 101–102, 106; James to family, 17 August 1928, James Papers, Mitchell Library, State Library of New South Wales, Box 9, MS 5877.
21 James to 'dear little chap', 17 September 1927; James to family, 14 October 1927, James Papers, Mitchell Library, State Library of New South Wales, Box 9, MS 5877.
22 Phelan, 1991, 107.
23 Serle, 1986, 622–627.
24 C.E. Sayers, 'A life of Keith Murdoch, Newspaper Reporter', 37, Murdoch Papers, National Library of Australia, Folder 9, Series 11, MS 2823. Murdoch's letters to his father were given to Sayers when he was researching his unpublished biography of Murdoch.
25 Phelan, 1991, 108–9. Also see Pesman, 1996, 156, 162–163.
26 Phelan, 1991, 110, 114–116.
27 Moorehead, 1970, 46, 47.
28 James to 'dearest little chap', 4 November 1927, James to mother, 22 May 1928, James Papers, Mitchell Library, State Library of New South Wales, Box 9, MS 5877.
29 North, 2001, 11.
30 Phelan, 1991, 114–117.
31 Phelan, 1991, 118–124.
32 Phelan, 1991, 124–130.
33 Sayers, 'A life of Keith Murdoch', 33. See also Zwar, 1980, 8.
34 Sayers, 'A life of Keith Murdoch', 37. Keith to Patrick Murdoch, 3 July 1908, Murdoch Papers, National Library of Australia, Folder 5, Series 11, MS 2823.
35 Phelan, 1991, 114.
36 Sayers, 'A life of Keith Murdoch', 40.
37 Ibid., 43–44.

38. Raymond, 1992, 117, 178, Milne, 1931, 1; Falk, 1933, 52–56, 61.
39. R.N. Carrington, 'The Quest: A True Story of an Australian Journalist's Five Years' Search for Fame in Fleet Street', MS, c.1910, Mitchell Library, State Library of New South Wales.
40. Keith to Patrick Murdoch, 3 July and 6 August 1908, Murdoch Papers, National Library of Australia, Folder 5, Series 11, MS 2823.
41. Sayers, 'A life of Keith Murdoch', 45–46, 49.
42. Keith to Patrick Murdoch, 6 August and December 1908, Murdoch Papers, National Library of Australia, Folder 5, Series 11, MS 2823.
43. Sayers, 'A life of Keith Murdoch', 46.
44. Alomes, 1999, 40, 53; Souter, 1981, 377.
45. Potter, 2000, 54.
46. Sayers, 'A life of Keith Murdoch', 33, 62.
47. Keith to Patrick Murdoch, 10 May 1909, Murdoch Papers, National Library of Australia, Folder 5, Series 11, MS 2823. Also see Zwar, 1980, 13.
48. Sayers, 'A life of Keith Murdoch', pp. 60–62. See also Keith to Patrick Murdoch, 10 May, 17 June and 14 October 1909, Murdoch Papers, National Library of Australia, Folder 5, Series 11, MS 2823.
49. Sayers, 'A life of Keith Murdoch', 54–55. Also see Zwar, 1980, 16.
50. Sayers, 'A life of Keith Murdoch'; Zwar, 1980.
51. Zwar, 1980, 16–17.
52. For Murdoch, see Serle, 1986, 10, 623. For a more general discussion of the Anzac tradition, see Carlyon, 2001.
53. *Australasian Journalist* was also known as *Australian Journalist* or simply the *Journalist*.
54. For example, *Australasian Journalist*, 25 June 1914, 26; 25 August 1914, 9; 25 November 1914, 11; 25 September 1915, 21; 15 September 1920, 216.
55. *Australasian Journalist*, 15 April 1919, 58; 23 June 1920, 126.
56. *Australasian Journalist*, 23 June 1920, 124; 15 November 1920, 251; 15 October 1921, 220, 235; 15 April 1922, 75.
57. Bundock, 1957, 87. See also *Australasian Journalist*, 31 March 1920, 66.
58. Cited in Potter, 2000, 55.
59. Warnecke to Voltaire Molesworth, 30 October 1923 and 9 January 1924, Molesworth Papers, Mitchell Library, State Library of New South Wales, Folder 4, Box 3, MS Set 71. See also Warnecke's unpublished memoirs, copy in possession of the author.
60. Warnecke to Voltaire Molesworth, 9 January 1924, Molesworth Papers, Mitchell Library, State Library of New South Wales, Folder 4, Box 3, MS Set 71.
61. James to Pym Heyting, 16 May 1928, Molesworth Papers, Mitchell Library, State Library of New South Wales, Folder 4, Box 3, MS Set 71.
62. James to parents, 17 May 1928, James to mother, 18 June 1928, Molesworth Papers, Mitchell Library, State Library of New South Wales, Box 9, James Papers, MS 5877.
63. James to mother, 2 July 1928, James Papers, Mitchell Library, State Library of New South Wales, Box 9, MS 5877.
64. James to mother, 2 July, 6 August 1928, James Papers, Mitchell Library, State Library of New South Wales, Box 9, MS 5877.

65. James to family, 22 July 1928, James to father, 3 October 1928, James to mother, 11 October, 27 November 1928, James Papers, Mitchell Library, State Library of New South Wales, Box 9, MS 5877.

66. James to father, 16 May 1929, James Papers, Mitchell Library, State Library of New South Wales, Box 9, MS 5877.

67. James to mother, 28 October 1930, 22 January 1931, James Papers, Mitchell Library, State Library of New South Wales, Box 9, MS 5877.

68. James to father, 11 February 1931, James to mother, 17 February, 4 March 1931, James to sister, n.d. (mid-January 1932), James Papers, Mitchell Library, State Library of New South Wales, Box 9, MS 5877.

69. James to family, 5 and 12 November 1931, James to father, 26 May 1932, James Papers, Mitchell Library, State Library of New South Wales, Box 9, MS 5877.

70. James to mother, 21 October, 10 December 1931, James to family, 19 October 1932, James to Christina Stead, 5 October, 23 and 29 November 1933, James Papers, Mitchell Library, State Library of New South Wales, Box 9, MS 5877.

71. James to father, 26 May 1932, James to mother, 8 June 1932, James Papers, Mitchell Library, State Library of New South Wales, Box 9, MS 5877.

72. James to family, 25 August 1932, James Papers, Mitchell Library, State Library of New South Wales, Box 9, MS 5877.

73. James to mother, 18 June 1928, James Papers, Mitchell Library, State Library of New South Wales, Box 9, MS 5877.

74. Pym Heyting to James's parents, 13 November 1932, Molesworth Papers, Mitchell Library, State Library of New South Wales, Box 10, James Papers, MS 5877.

75. See James's diaries, 1933–34, James Papers, Mitchell Library, State Library of New South Wales, Box 1, MS 5877.

76. James to Dymphna Cusack, 20 November 1935, James Papers, Mitchell Library, State Library of New South Wales, Box 13, MS 5877.

77. Alomes, 1999, 12.

78. Raymond, 1992, 99, 104–6, 117, 118, 178.

79. Waterson, 2000, 5, 148.

80. *Newspaper News*, 1 February 1929, 11; 1 February 1938, 15.

81. Monks, 1955, 26–7; *Australasian Journalist*, July 1960, 4. Also see Waterson, 2000, 5, 148–149.

82. *Australasian Journalist*, 30 April 1920, 75. Also see *Newspaper News*, 1 January 1938, 9; 1 September 1938, 6.

83. Alomes, 1999, 49; Raymond, 1992, 177, 212. Also see James to Cusack, 20 November 1935, James Papers, Mitchell Library, State Library of New South Wales, Box 13, MS 5877.

84. Raymond, 1992, 203, 216–218, 264–265; Moorehead, 1970, 58–61.

85. Alomes, 1999, 195.

86. Monks, 1955, 28–59.

87. Moorehead, 1970, 63–64.

88. See Torney-Parlicki, 2001, 671.

89. Zwar, 1980.

90. Phelan, 1991.

91 North, 2001.
92 *Sydney Morning Herald*, 20 June 1960.
93 Torney-Parlicki, 2001, 671; Serle, 2001, 438.
94 Raymond, 1992 and Raymond, 1999.
95 Raymond, 1992, 185.
96 Boston, 1990, 92, 116, 132.

PRIMARY SOURCES

Australasian Journalist, 1914–1922, 1960.
Carrington, R.N. 'The Quest: A True Story of an Australian Journalist's Five Years' Search for Fame in Fleet Street', MS, c.1910, Mitchell Library, State Library of New South Wales.
James Papers, Mitchell Library, State Library of New South Wales.
Molesworth Papers, Mitchell Library, State Library of New South Wales.
Newspaper News, 1929, 1938.
C.E. Sayers, 'A life of Keith Murdoch, newspaper reporter', Murdoch Papers, National Library of Australia.
Keith to Patrick Murdoch, 3 July, 6 August and December 1908, 10 May, 17 June and 14 October 1909, Murdoch Papers, National Library of Australia.
Sydney Morning Herald, 1960.
Warnecke, George unpublished memoirs. Copy in possession of the author.

REFERENCES

Alomes, Stephen. 1999. *When London Calls: The Expatriation of Australian Creative Artists to Britain*. Cambridge: Cambridge University Press.
Anon. 1991. 'Great Spinner of a True Tale'. *ABC Radio 24 Hours*. (October).
Bell, Walter George. 1912. *Fleet Street in Seven Centuries*. London: Sir Isaac Pitman & Sons.
Boston, Ray. 1990. *The Essential Fleet Street: Its History and Influence*. London: Blandford.
Bundock, Clement J. 1957. *The National Union of Journalists: A Jubilee History 1907–1957*. Oxford: Oxford University Press.
Carlyon, Les. 2001. *Gallipoli*. Sydney: Macmillan.
Falk, Bernard. 1933. *He Laughed in Fleet Street*. London: Hutchinson & Co.
Griffen-Foley, Bridget. 2000a. *Sir Frank Packer: The Young Master*. Sydney: HarperCollins.
Griffen-Foley, Bridget. 2000b. 'Packer, Sir Douglas Frank Hewson (1906–1974)', *Australian Dictionary of Biography*. Vol. 15. Carlton, Vic.: Melbourne University Press.
Hamilton, Paula. 1999. 'Journalists, gender and workplace culture, 1900–1940'. In *Journalism: Print, Politics and Popular Culture*, edited by Curthoys, Ann; Schultz Julianne. St Lucia, Qld: University of Queensland Press.
Jenkins, Simon. 1986. *The Market for Glory*. London/Boston: Faber & Faber.
Kirkpatrick, Peter. 1992. *The Sea Coast of Bohemia: Literary Life in Sydney's Roaring Twenties*. St Lucia, Qld: University of Queensland Press.
Lloyd, Clem. c.1986. *Profession: Journalist, a History of the Australian Journalists Association*. Sydney: Hale & Iremonger.
Milne, James. 1931. *A Window in Fleet Street*. London: John Murray.
Monks, Noel. 1955. *Eyewitness*. London: Frederick Muller.

Moorehead, Alan. 1970. *A Late Education*. Harmondsworth: Penguin.

Morrison, Elizabeth. 1997. 'Grub Street inventor: James Harrison's journalism, old and new, in Geelong, Melbourne and London'. In *Disreputable Profession: Journalists and Journalism in Colonial Australia*, edited by Cryle, Denis. Rockhampton: Central Queensland University Press.

Morrison, Elizabeth. 1998. 'Newspapers'. In *The Oxford Companion to Australian History*, edited by Davison, Graeme; Hirst, John; Macintyre, Stuart. Melbourne: Oxford University Press.

North, Marilla. 2001. *Yarn Spinners*. St Lucia, Qld: University of Queensland Press.

Pesman, Ros. 1996. *Duty Free: Australian Women Abroad*. Melbourne: Oxford University Press.

Phelan, Nancy. 1991. *The Romantic Lives of Louise Mack*. St Lucia, Qld: University of Queensland Press.

Potter, Simon. 2000. 'Nationalism, imperialism and the press in Britain and the dominions'. D.Phil. thesis, Oxford: Oxford University.

Raymond, Robert. 1992. *From Bees to Buzz-Bombs: Robert Raymond's Boyhood-to-Blitz Memoirs*. St Lucia, Qld: Queensland University Press.

Raymond, Robert. 1999. *Out of the Box*. Henley Beach: Seaview Press.

Serle, Geoffrey. 1986. 'Murdoch, Sir Keith Arthur (1885–1952)'. *Australian Dictionary of Biography*. Vol. 10. Carlton, Vic.: Melbourne University Press.

Serle, Geoffrey. 2001. 'Alan McCrae Moorehead'. In *The Oxford Companion to Australian History*, edited by Davison, Graeme; Hirst, John; Macintyre, Stuart. Melbourne: Oxford University Press.

Shawcross, William. 1993. *Murdoch*. London: Pan Macmillan.

Souter, Gavin. 1981. *Company of Heralds*. Carlton, Vic.: Melbourne University Press.

Stewart, Ken. 1988. 'Journalism and the world of the writer'. In *The Penguin New Literary History of Australia*, edited by Laurie Hergenhan. Melbourne: Penguin Books.

Torney-Parlicki, Prue. 2001. 'War Reporters and Reporting'. In *The Oxford Companion to Australian History*, edited by Davison, Graeme; Hirst, John; Macintyre, Stuart. Melbourne: Oxford University Press.

Walker, R.B. 1976. *The Newspaper Press in New South Wales, 1803–1920*. Sydney: Sydney University Press.

Waterson, D.B. 2000. 'Doidge, Frederick Widdowson 1884–1954'. *Dictionary of New Zealand Biography*. Wellington, N.Z.: Allen & Unwin; Dept. of Internal Affairs.

Wiener, Joel H. Editor. 1988. *Papers for the Millions*. New York: Greenwood.

Zwar, Desmond. 1980. *In Search of Keith Murdoch*. Melbourne: Macmillan.

Cite this chapter as: Griffen-Foley, Bridget. 2009. '"The crumbs are better than a feast elsewhere": Australian journalists on Fleet Street'. *Australians in Britain: The Twentieth-Century Experience*, edited by Bridge, Carl; Crawford, Robert; Dunstan, David. Melbourne: Monash University ePress. pp. 8.1 to 8.19. DOI: 10.2104/ab090008.

CHAPTER 9

'HOME' BECOMES AWAY
MELBURNIANS IN OXFORD IN THE 1920s

Jim Davidson, University of Melbourne
> Jim Davidson is an honorary fellow of the School of Historical Studies, University of Melbourne. His biography of W.K. Hancock is to appear early in 2010.

> While most Australians who went to Oxford in the 1920s came away fulfilled and schooled for success, there were usually tensions evident in their expatriate lives. This chapter examines the response of five Melburnians to Oxford, ranging from Sir Keith Hancock – completely at home in England as in Australia – through that of the anglophile S.C. Leslie to the critic A.A. Phillips, the educationist Esmonde Higgins, and the historian Kathleen Fitzpatrick, each of whom rejected it in varying degrees. Oxford was a defining moment in the lives of all of them, often in ways that had been unanticipated and unimagined.

Many knots and groups of Australians have, one way and another, found themselves meeting up and sometimes reconstituting themselves in England. Perhaps the most famous were those involved with the satirical magazine *OZ*, who in the late sixties ran away with it from Sydney to swinging London. Here I want to talk about another group altogether: five people from Melbourne University who went to Oxford for further study in the decade following 1918. Oxford had a profound effect on all of them, and each was transformed by it – not always in a manner that might have been anticipated.

The period immediately after the First World War saw the mechanics of academic expatriation first fully put in place. While Rhodes Scholarships had drawn young men to Oxford since 1904, a free passage scheme to take them there by ship had only just been implemented. At the same time, links with Britain were entering a period of unusual intensity. It had always been the case in Australia that more professors than not were British-born, and were so still; but in this period the influence of the Round Table, both high-class seminar and closed society promoting the imperial cause, was pervasive. Many key figures belonged to it; among the establishment, it was trendy. Both of Keith Hancock's mentors, Ernest Scott in Melbourne and E.O.G. Shann in Perth, were members.

The Oxford awaiting young Australian graduates in 1920 was going through one of its rare periods of transition. The war had shattered it: the dead were many – almost 3000 of them – students, recent graduates, younger fellows. Women, a presence at the university since the 1880s, had only just been admitted to degrees; Greek had just been dropped as an obligatory requirement for the BA. There were still, in the depths of All Souls, junior biblical scholars, and in some cases, even a financial disincentive to marriage, since the stipends attached to some fellowships would then be docked.[1]

Just as for many years it took 25 Australian shillings to make a British pound, so the expectation was that Australians would read for an undergraduate degree all over again. In fact, owing to Scott's emphasis on primary sources, a Melbourne graduate was more professionally trained in history than an Oxford one. He was, of course, less sophisticated. That, in fact, created another barrier. There was at least two or three years age difference between the arriving Australian and Englishmen fresh from a public school. Fortified by their class privileges, such people seemed to know more about the world, which they gazed upon disdainfully, and less about life. Sometimes they would proclaim an ability to detect an Australian accent – a talent that rarely extended to reproducing it correctly. For their part Australians could take consolation from the fact that one of Oxford's most notable figures, Gilbert Murray, classicist and League of Nations activist, was one of their own. More immediately they had the Colonial Club, figured prominently in sporting activities, and, although Rhodes House was going up at only the end of this period, occasional functions for Rhodes Scholars.

> One afternoon in the early nineteen-twenties [Keith Hancock wrote in his autobiography, *Country and Calling*] when six or seven Rhodes Scholars were gossiping with me in Balliol, I said something prim and another Australian jeered – 'Listen to the parson's son!' He was a parson's son himself … And when a Canadian chipped in I said at a venture, 'You're one too'. He was. Then the three of us turned inquisitor against all the others. Everybody in that room, so it turned out – Australian, New Zealander, Newfoundlander, Canadian, Rhodesian, South African – was a parson's son. The coincidence was not quite so unusual as might be thought, for the Rhodes Scholars of those days, despite their wide diversity of geographical background, had for the most part a closely similar background … And from their similar families they went to schools of pretty much the same stamp. Although I did not know it, the path that I was following between the ages of nine and nineteen was little different from the paths that my contemporaries were following in the widely different landscapes of Natal, Taranaki or British Columbia.

'For ten years or more', he concluded, 'I was being shaped for Oxford without ever imagining that this was my destiny'.[2]

It all sounds seamless. Certainly this passage is classic Hancock: the characteristic sense of congregation, the assimilative liberalism, the imperial spin on span. His own career looks seamless too: after graduating from Melbourne and a spell of lecturing in Perth, he won a special Rhodes scholarship for Australia at large. In Oxford, his expected good result was capped by an unusual distinction: he was the first Australian to win (in the annual special examinations) a fellowship at All Souls. Subsequently, even though Hancock wrote a *Survey of British Commonwealth Affairs* and edited the thirty-odd volumes recounting how Britain mobilised on the home front during the Second World War – and even though he was knighted by the British for this achievement – he returned to Australia to take up a post at the Australian National University in 1957. The most Hancock would state, in 1980 as in 1930, was that he was 'in love with two soils'.[3]

In fact Oxford had come as a jolt to him. He was wrong-footed at the beginning, by setting off at the end of the Australian academic year 1921 and arriving well into the English one. Although Balliol was relatively welcoming, his acute homesickness led him to discern in the high-vaulted college chapel an improbable similarity with his father's church at Moonee Ponds.[4] Concerned to achieve maximum effectiveness, he cut his losses. For social life, there was little need to venture beyond Balliol – or for intellectual life either, since he found admirable mentors in the Master, A.L. Smith, and two of the college tutors, Kenneth Bell and Humphrey Sumner. And, since he was dissuaded from undertaking a research degree, Hancock outlined his own program of systematic reading to be undertaken while doing his second BA. He was, as he put it later, 'a dreadfully purposeful young man', for he was intent on returning to Australia within three years.[5] Only when well into his fellowship at All Souls was he prepared to relax this timetable. Years later, even after he had gone to Adelaide and returned to England once more, he struck a future Oxford vice-chancellor as pining for home in a way that few Australians did.[6]

It was Australia, not England, that Hancock saw as his mother country; the opening of *Country and Calling* is partly an attempt to earth his family as fully as possible here, and not in Britain. (The Scotland of his mother's family was a complication that did not even count.) Europe attracted him far more, and for a long time it was in European history, not in British or Australian or Commonwealth history, that he wished to make his mark. Hancock permanently absorbed the forms of British high academic discourse. He adopted the custom of addressing people by their surnames only, and of clinching the point he was making with a humourless grin ('Gotcha!'). But he was never totally assimilated by Oxford. Often when the English claimed him as one of their own, he would play the Australian card – no doubt since it was the best way of asserting his independence or individuality. Indeed, for all his sense of achievement and feeling of acceptance, Hancock never quite got over the sense of being a foreigner in England. At a deep level he felt guilty about even being there: he did not wish to be seen as a 'deserter' (his rather military word) from Australia.[7]

*   *   *

When Hancock arrived at Balliol, he would soon have heard stories of Esmonde Higgins, who had faded away from the college the year before. Higgins was somebody he had known well at Melbourne, for he was treasurer of the Historical Society and on the board of *Melbourne University Magazine*, effectively the student newspaper of the day. Hancock was inclined to hero-worship him: 'he glows inwardly and has big gusts of clarity'.[8] He may have been almost as influential as Ernest Scott in inducing Hancock to trade in classics for history. Certainly history students were at the heart of radicalism at Melbourne during the First World War, and Higgins one of the leaders. He declared, in co-authored articles attacking Empire, that 'Australia is a nation, not a continent', and that members of the Round Table were 'absentees in sentiment'.[9] For all that – and no less attractive to Hancock – Higgins himself was well-born, the nephew of the advanced liberal Henry Bournes Higgins.

However, Higgins combined a strong sense of principle with emotional instability – a disastrous combination. He lacked confidence, even self-esteem; it was as though he could not trust the advantages of his own background, ratified though they had been by his intellectual precocity. Even before he reached university he was attacking the capitalist order, and at one point, since he believed it to be less capitalist, was pro-German – at least in his schoolboy diary.[10] But it is entirely characteristic that he would not only come to enlist, but would turn up to his graduation ceremony in military uniform.[11] After a short period of service in France, and while wondering quite what to do next, he accepted the offer by H.B. Higgins to pay for him to study at Oxford.

Hancock, now editor of *Melbourne University Magazine*, published an account of Oxford written by Higgins shortly after his arrival there. 'You seem in a remote, pre-modern world', he wrote; 'everything looks quiet, ivied, beautiful, studious and secluded'.[12] But gradually the charms wore thin, and increasingly, as an Australian, Higgins felt 'not exactly an intruder, but a waif'. He told them at home that 'I love being here, think it one of the finest places in the world', but

'I can't feel settled where there aren't people to yarn with about the things I'm most closely interested in'.[13] To his disgust, many Australians 'ape the ruling class atmosphere', taking *The Times* and trying 'to booze in a gentlemanly way'.[14] He spoke of starting an Australian Club, but Uncle Henry advised that that had been tried at Cambridge, and had been found to be a mistake: the effect had been to separate the Australians even more from the English.[15] Repeatedly he advised his nephew that it would be best to conform in small matters, since the English placed great store on such things. Higgins now realised how Australian Melbourne University had been; and on going to Ireland with Vance Palmer, he discovered that he was really Irish-Australian.[16]

Meanwhile, he began to have serious doubts about the craft of history. Marxism had begun to appeal to him, not least because it offered a schematic view of history which he could both follow and propound, particularly as it was forward-looking. 'But at Oxford', he noted derisively, 'historians, members of a ruling class, themselves at rest above the tumult, feel that the world is at rest. They cannot think of change, of struggle, except [as] a struggle against those who are *not* content with the present system'. Rather than seeking to establish what has created present day conditions, they seek 'to invest the present with the sanctity of the past'. Hence the great concern with constitutional history. There was a sense of the state, and even of society, having been constructed as a delicate mechanism, as if by myriad disinterested acts.[17]

Oxford quickened Higgins's socialism, which had never really been abandoned, into something like Bolshevism. At last he approved of a tutor, the Guild Socialist G.D.H. Cole, and this probably helped steady him to the point where he completed the requirements for his degree. In Balliol, too, he had found 'I'm quite in love with a little chap called Rothstein' – pre-Freudian talk for being entranced by someone and their ideas. Rothstein was a Bolshevik: his father had been Lenin's chief agent in Britain before the revolution, and both father and son would be founders of the British Communist Party. Soon Higgins was writing of the need 'these days … to smash, without worrying too much what is to be smashed'. Once he joined the Party, as he did in 1921, he likened (to his puzzled parents) being a Communist to being a Jesuit. There had to be the same submission to authority in order to advance a higher cause.[18]

Leaving Oxford for London, Higgins worked for the Labour Research Department, an unaffiliated left-wing think tank. His world was now very different from that of Hancock, who had tried to secure him a job in Perth, and, once arrived in England, wanted to go on a walking tour with him.[19] Higgins though had been to Russia, in 1920, when it was a red-hot thing to do: by that stage Balliol had read him the riot act, and ordered him to settle down and apply himself to his studies. But the trajectory of his life would be entwined with Communism for some time yet. Paradoxically, a Communist takeover meant that the Labour Research Department was losing influence. By 1924 he had returned to Australia, although well aware that it was 'too young, lazy, cheerful and smug' for socialism.[20]

Less academically motivated than Hancock, Higgins found himself in Oxford on a journey of self-discovery. It exposed the contradictions in his personality, more urgently than had been the case in Melbourne, rendering more attractive the authoritarian solution it also proffered. He yearned for the decisiveness that his temperament repeatedly resisted. Wishing to burn his boats, or at least to put the indulgent liberalism of his uncle to the test, Esmonde wrote a hostile review of H.B. Higgins's latest book for *Labour Monthly*: permitting himself a tart reply, his uncle nonetheless took it in his stride.[21] Similarly, Esmonde walked away from Oxford, not even bothering to take out the degree he was entitled to.[22] 'Between you & me', he wrote to his parents at the end of 1921, 'I'm *very* glad to be away from that place'. In spite of a few good friends, 'it tasted nasty now'.[23]

* * *

Also at Oxford at this time was A.A. Phillips, later to become famous as a literary critic. He had known Hancock well in the Public Questions Society at Melbourne; but he did not share his admiration for Scott, whose lectures he found wanting in ideas. Phillips went to Oxford to do a B.Litt. and then a Diploma of Education. The B.Litt. he found a disappointment, both in its subject matter and in its failure to teach research skills; but he admired the Oxford tutorial method, once he had devised his own way of accessing it. What is most striking, though, is how little impression Oxford made on him: towards the end of his life I saw a good deal of him, and it was a long time before I became aware he had even been there. The televised version of *Brideshead Revisited*, he remarked, got the feel of the place very well; but Oxford appears to have been an anticlimax. Melbourne had been much more stimulating: discussions between radical and conservative students about Freudianism was one of the things recalled. The ineffable assumption of English superiority clearly got to him. For Phillips, being an Australian in the broader imperial culture was rather like being Jewish in everyday gentile society; essentially an inflection. After all, he had an aunt, Marion Phillips, who had a seat in the House of Commons and had written a monograph on Macquarie. Indeed, it was a cultivated family: while mainly engaged in the law, there was also a pronounced literary bent. His grandfather had written for the Victorian reviews, and was president of the Shakespeare society, as was Phillips's father (who was also chief president of the Australian Natives' Association). His mother had published short stories and a novel. So A.A. Phillips resisted being dismissed as a 'colonial oddity'; instead he virtually expunged Oxford from his writings and conversation.[24]

* * *

If Arthur Phillips was prompted, after Oxford, to seek new personal definition, another Jewish member of the group in practice sought to evade or postpone it. Clem or Sam, Lazarus or Leslie; the variation of both first name and surname is striking. In Melbourne 'Sam' Lazarus had been friendly with Hancock, a fellow resident of Trinity College, and was his assistant editor with *Melbourne University Magazine*. From Balliol they would go together to Germany in 1922. He was friendly too with Higgins, probably closer, and like him he enlisted. (It was characteristic of his charmed life that the war was over before he got to France.) But while he had, at Melbourne, forecast the downfall of capitalism, Lazarus saw the internationalism of Wilsonianism as the compromise position which might save the world from Bolshevism.[25] In Oxford, he told Higgins that the state, and the rightful obligations it could demand from its citizens, was a proper concern for study. That was the necessary preliminary to reform.[26]

Meanwhile Lazarus told Higgins's mother (who must have wished it was her son writing) that 'I'm thoroughly at home here now: I fell in love with Oxford – indeed I lost my heart to all England'.[27] Completing a DPhil, he took up a lectureship at the University College of North Wales. But Bangor was not Oxford, or even Melbourne; and, having said that the time would come when he would return, Lazarus took up a senior lectureship in philosophy at the University of Melbourne in 1924. While there he helped to start the Labour Club, which was founded paradoxically in Trinity College.[28] After Oxford it all seemed terribly impacted; he began to want to go back to Britain. This was achieved in 1926, when he went to the imperial conference as an adviser to S.M. Bruce. It seems that Hancock may have had a hand in this: Casey, Bruce's acolyte, was a good friend of Hancock's, the historian becoming godfather to his son. Lazarus stayed on in London and joined the civil service.

In Britain, Lazarus, or S.C. Leslie as he became, found that he could combine a conservative lifestyle with socially progressive politics, in a way that would not be easily done in Australia. He also oscillated between business and government, concerned as he became with advertising, public relations, and propaganda. Early in the Second World War, as part of the general mobilisation of the civilian population, he anonymously wrote the well-known publication *Front Line 1940*. Later, he wrote important speeches for his Minister, Herbert Morrison, on nationalisation. Later still, having worked for a long time as head of the Economic Information Division of the Treasury, he became on his retirement a consultant.[29]

Yet it was not a clear path to comfortable conservatism. Rather, as with his name, the focus of his career, and even his politics, there was a flux, a persistent change in valency. Indeed, while retaining a life-long interest in Jewish questions, and Israel, he became a Christian Scientist. Given his qualifications and personal style, Leslie's mutability could be accommodated more readily in England. As Hancock wrote of his old friend to Higgins, in 1936:

> His ideas are Marxian again: his income is very much higher: his wife rather more shrewish … He himself is still very, very nice – just as sharp and witty in speech, and with the same quick grin across his (alas definitely fatter) face. I like talking with him, though our old relationship tends oddly to perpetuate itself: he the resourceful doctrinaire, and I the un-ready, protesting, more realistic, more muddled brat of an Archdeacon.[30]

*   *   *

When all these men had left Oxford, the young Kathleen Pitt, later Fitzpatrick, arrived in England with her family in 1926. She had hoped for a scholarship to Cambridge; a severe, donnish woman soon put paid to that when she remarked, 'Here in Cambridge, you know, we don't think much of the degrees of these American universities'. Stung by the unshakeable assumption of superiority, Miss Pitt withdrew her application, and gained admittance to Oxford instead. She was not yet clear what she wanted to do, apart from gaining a further, more rounded education – but she was fortunate in having a family who would, and could, support her.[31] But then, as she later recollected, she had not known a single woman at Melbourne University who was from the working class.[32]

At Somerville College she responded to the warmth and concern of a kindly principal, but Oxford was an uphill battle for Kathleen. For a start, the riverine vapours of the place did not agree with her, and she succumbed to bronchitis and a perpetual cold, abetted by the severity of her first English winter. She also had to cope with the coldness of the English: for her first ten days in Somerville, Kathleen later recalled, at the meal table no-one spoke to her. Whatever notions Australians then had of a broader British kinship, the English seemed to share none of them.

Later she did make friends, but Kathleen was acutely aware of her isolation as an Australian woman. Her male counterparts were more numerous, and linked up with each other in a variety of ways.

To make matters worse, the presence of women at Oxford was still problematic. It still felt like a concession: there were subtle forms of discrimination practiced by lecturers, while the women's colleges, edgy about their status, imposed strict discipline. The male students were indifferent, if not hostile; Oxford would accept only one woman for every four men, so of necessity they were earnest and scholarly rather than frivolous upper class types. The men responded by asking London debs to their balls, or professional actresses to take part in student theatre productions – anything but college girls. This was a shock to Kathleen, who remembered that in Melbourne 'the men students had quite liked the women students and mixed freely with them'. But she was up against the strong homosocial mores of the English public school and, indeed, of English public life – even if they were probably less homosexual than she imagined.[33]

Having been persuaded to abandon all thoughts of a research degree, Kathleen was to find that the second BA she now undertook was but a drudge and a disappointment. She felt, as Arthur Phillips did, that after Melbourne it added surprisingly little to her intellectual development.[34] Nevertheless she applied herself, indeed too much so: Kathleen was debilitated and defeated from overwork as she sat in the examination hall reading her final papers. She knew her material, but could not martial her facts and arguments. She slunk home with a second. But, as Kathleen put it, 'I had been "Home" and now was coming home'.[35]

❊   ❊   ❊

In her autobiography, *Solid Bluestone Foundations*, Kathleen refers to male colleagues who 'looked back with evident nostalgia … to the Paradise Lost of Oxford'.[36] There is much truth in this remark, but as this chapter demonstrates, the response was often more complex and mixed. Hancock probably exemplifies this best, with his self-diagnosis of a basic tension between country and calling. He professed to have never cared much for the English countryside, and indeed the greater pull of the Australian bush (and what it represented) propelled him back to Australia. Ultimately it made an environmental historian of him. The opposite was his old friend 'Sam'/Clem Lazarus/Leslie, who did become an anglophile, with his CBE, and chairmanship of the editorial board of *Round Table*: but as suggested earlier, his wide range of interests, fluctuating valencies and eye for the main chance made this a sensible outcome. It must also be remembered that for a long time the public service in Australia would not recruit graduates, preferring to take people directly from school.

The other three coped with their Oxford legacy in various ways. A.A. Phillips bided his time, and then when Leavis produced *The Great Tradition*, Phillips responded by calling his book of 1958, centred on Lawson and Furphy, *The Australian Tradition*. 'I was deliberately flying a skull-and-crossbones', he later recalled.[37] For those more seriously damaged, such as Kathleen Fitzpatrick and Esmonde Higgins, the process was more protracted. While conceding that she gained certain things from Oxford, Kathleen was left with a scholarly inferiority complex. Nonetheless Oxford significantly crystallised her sense of being Australian, and made her active for women's causes – notably the University Women's College at Melbourne. Meanwhile her own progress, after a temporary reprieve at Sydney, was long and arduous: it took ten years, via the detour of business education and typing and shorthand, to get to the desired lectureship at Melbourne.[38] Similarly Esmonde Higgins turned to postgraduate study only at the end of his life, after a long period in adult education and a slow return to democratic socialism. It was as though he had finally got – after many defeats but by his own efforts – to the fast-forward position in which his Uncle Henry had placed him at Oxford all those years before.

There was once a terrible white South African joke describing a black man on a bicycle. However racist the description, it certainly fits Esmonde Higgins: an accident looking for a place to have it. But he, like the other Australians followed here, were all products of a small country, indeed community – for there was not much linkage then between the major Australian cities. For a long time Australians went to Oxford as much to be completed as to gain qualifications. Like people from the north of England, or later from working class backgrounds – with whom they found affinity – Australians came up against unshakeable patrician rigidities. The expectation was one of assimilation; the result more usually one of helping to define a distinctive sense of being Australian. In the process such people often found their personalities sharpened and their priorities reordered in ways they might never have imagined.

ENDNOTES

1. Information from S.J.D. Green, college historian, All Souls College, 2002.
2. Hancock, 1954, 55.
3. Hancock, 1930; Hancock, 1976, p.vi.
4. Hancock, MS 'Oxford Dinner 3 May 1969', Hancock Papers, P96/31/15.
5. Hancock, 1954, 79.
6. Sir John Habbakuk, interview, October 1999.
7. Hancock, 1954, 126.
8. Carr, 2001, 220.
9. These two phrases are from articles written for *Melbourne University Magazine* in 1917 by Higgins and Harry Minogue, quoted in Carr, 2001, 97.
10. Carr, 2001, 91.
11. Nettie Palmer, Diary, 13 April 1918, NLA 1174/16/3.
12. Higgins, 'Oxford to an Australian', *Melbourne University Magazine*, 13/3 (October 1919), 137.
13. Higgins to parents, 26 August 1919, ML MSS 740/5.
14. Higgins, 'Oxford', ML MSS 740/3/19.
15. H.B. Higgins to Esmonde Higgins, 26 February and 6 April 1919, ML MS 740/10.
16. Carr, 2001, 110.
17. Autobiographical Notes, 23 July 1920, ML MSS 740/3/19, pp. 53–55.
18. Carr, 2001, 109, 112–114, 122.
19. Hancock to Higgins, 21 December [1920] and letter from Paris [1921], ML MSS 740/7/144, 164.
20. Carr, 2001, 116.
21. Carr, 2001, 125–130.
22. Communication from Anna Sander, Archivist, Balliol College, 25 August 2005.
23. Higgins to parents, ML MSS 740/6/343.

24 Phillips, 1983b, esp. 28, 34; Davidson, 1983, esp. 34, 39; Kiernan, 1979, esp. 7–9.
25 Lazarus on capitalism, *Melbourne University Magazine* 11/3 (October 1917), 94, and Wilsonianism 13/2 (August 1919), 74.
26 Lazarus to Higgins, 5 May 1920, ML MSS 740/11/129.
27 Lazarus to Mrs Higgins, 2 November 1921, ML MSS 740/6/333.
28 Watson, 1979, 17.
29 S.C. Leslie obituary, *The Times*, 11 January 1980.
30 Hancock to Higgins, ML MSS 740/12/89-90.
31 Fitzpatrick, 1983a, 189.
32 Fitzpatrick, 1983b, 120.
33 Fitzpatrick, 1983b, 124–126; Fitzpatrick, 1983a, 199–206.
34 Fitzpatrick, 1983b, 122; Fitzpatrick, 1983a, 206–207.
35 Fitzpatrick, 1983a, 207–208, 210.
36 Fitzpatrick, 1983a, 203.
37 Phillips, 1983a, 34.
38 Fitzpatrick, 1983b, 126–130.

PRIMARY SOURCES

Esmonde Higgins, Autobiographical Notes, 23 July 1920, Mitchell Library [ML] MSS 740/3/19.
Hancock Papers, Noel Butlin Archives Centre, Australian National University, P96.
Sir John Habbakuk, interview with the author, October 1999.
Melbourne University Magazine [MUM], 1917, 1919.
Nettie Palmer, Diary, National Library of Australia [NLA], 1174/16/3.
S.C. Leslie obituary, *The Times*, 11 January 1980.

REFERENCES

Carr, Adam. 2001. 'Three generations of Melbourne radicals 1870–1988'. PhD thesis. Melbourne: University of Melbourne.
Davidson, Jim. 1983. *Sideways from the Page: The Meanjin Interviews*. Sydney: Fontana, Collins.
Fitzpatrick, Kathleen. 1983a. *Solid Bluestone Foundations*. Melbourne: Macmillan.
Fitzpatrick, Kathleen. 1983b. 'A Cloistered Life'. In *The Half-Open Door*, edited by Grimshaw, Patricia; Strahan, Lynne Sydney: Hale & Iremonger.
Hancock, W.K. 1930. *Australia*. London: Benn.
Hancock, W.K. 1954. *Country and Calling*. London: Faber and Faber.
Hancock, W.K. 1976. *Professing History*. Sydney: Sydney University Press.
Kiernan, Brian. 1979. 'Introduction' to *Responses: Selected Writings*, by Phillips, A.A. Melbourne: Australia International Press.
Phillips, A.A. 1983a. 'Interview'. In *Sideways from the Page*, Davidson, Jim. Sydney: Fontana, Collins.

Phillips, A.A. 1983b. In *Memories of Melbourne University*, edited by Hume Dow, Richmond, Vic.: Hutchinson.

Watson, Don. 1979. *Brian Fitzpatrick, a Radical Life*. Sydney: Hale & Iremonger.

Cite this chapter as: Davidson, Jim. 2009. '"Home" becomes away: Melburnians in Oxford in the 1920s'. *Australians in Britain: The Twentieth-Century Experience*, edited by Bridge, Carl; Crawford, Robert; Dunstan, David. Melbourne: Monash University ePress. pp. 9.1 to 9.10. DOI: 10.2104/ab090009.

CHAPTER 10

AUSTRALIAN BOOKS, PUBLISHERS AND WRITERS IN ENGLAND, 1900–1940

John Arnold, Monash University

John Arnold is a Senior Lecturer at the National Centre for Australian Studies at Monash University. He has published widely in the field of Australian publishing history and is co-general editor of the four-volume Bibliography of Australian Literature *(2001–08)*.

This essay examines Australian books, publishers and writers in England from the beginnings of the twentieth century to the outbreak of the Second World War. By a combination of general overview, individual profiles, case studies and statistical analysis, it aims to show that Australian writers and publishers had an impact on the London literary scene. This was particularly so with Jack Lindsay, P.R. Stephensen and Eric Partridge. Others included W.N. Willis, father and son, issuing pulp fiction under their Anglo-Eastern Publishing Company and Camden Publishing Company imprints. Australian expatriate writers were prolific contributors to the insatiable market for crime and romance novels. Over one hundred Australians had at least one book of creative writing published in London while they were in England at some time between 1900–1940. Australian writers who never left their home country had their novels published in London, the phenomenon of the circulating library providing a ready market for now neglected or forgotten writers. Despite the presence of Australians (and Australian originated books) in London, they were not necessary promoting their Australianness or Australia generally. Their contribution was as aspiring writers and journalists who happened to be Australians working alongside, and in competition with, hundreds of others.

There has been much written about the Australian market for English books and visits to Australia by distinguished and successful English writers.[1] But what about the trade and movement the other way? Little has been written on the circulation of Australian books in London and the impact of Australian writers and publishers on the English literary scene. This is understandable because there has been a long held assumption that the influence has been negligible or effectively non-existent. But it has not been entirely one-way traffic. This chapter attempts to redress the balance by outlining ways in which Australian books, publishers and Australian writers did have some impact in England, focussing on the period 1900–1940.

PUBLISHING AUSTRALIANS IN ENGLAND

In 1900 George Robertson published Henry Lawson's two books of verse – *Verses, Popular and Humorous* and *Humorous Verses* – under a joint Sydney (Angus and Robertson) and London (Australian Book Company) imprint. He had previously published Lawson's first separate book of verse, *In the Days When the World Was Wide and Other* Verses (1896), jointly with Young J. Pentland from the latter's London office. Robertson and Pentland had trained together in Glasgow and remained close friends. Further titles were issued jointly and the two publishers established the Australian Book Company during Robertson's visit to England in 1899–1900 for the London imprint of Angus and Robertson initiated titles. Robertson also sent copies of his books to Simpkin and Marshall, the London book distributor and publisher.[2] As this practice developed the books were sent with a Simpkin and Marshall title-page. In 1902 Angus and Robertson printed 4000 copies of their trade catalogue for inclusion in *Whitaker's Reference*

Guide of Current Literature. They also made several attempts to compile a list of Anglo-Australians living in London, for '[t]hese returned Australians are nearly always wealthy'.[3]

Two Australians who published their own writings in London in the first decades of the twentieth century were Arthur Maquarie and William Baylebridge. Maquarie, born Arthur Frank Macquarie Mullens in Dubbo, New South Wales, in 1874, changed his name by deed poll to Arthur Maquarie, leaving the 'c' out of Macquarie in doing so.[4] He graduated from the University of Sydney and then went overseas around 1895. In England he helped prepare Henry Lawson's London writings for publication and worked as a freelance journalist. He then moved to Florence in Italy and taught English there. He had nine books of verse and plays published by commercial and semi-commercial publishers in London between 1900 and 1915 and it is likely that he paid for or contributed to the production costs. Maquarie reissued some of his books from Florence in attractive bindings from his own Olive Press imprint using sheets printed by the Chiswick Press in London, either those used for the London editions or possibly especially printed for the Olive Press issues. The Olive Press also published some other books by him, the last in 1950. Maquarie died in 1955. William Baylebridge was born William Blocksidge in Brisbane in 1883.[5] Educated at Brisbane Grammar School and later by a private tutor, he went to England in 1908, travelled in Europe, and spent some time in the Middle East before returning to Australia in 1919. In London he had three books of verse published by David Nutt under his real name and self-published at least seven books of verse and one of essays either anonymously, as 'W.B'. or William Blocksidge. Back in Australia he continued to publish his writings privately, mainly as William Baylebridge, including in them revised versions of his earlier works. His published works refer to five other titles that have not been traced and some, if not all of these, may also have been self-published in London. Baylebridge died in 1942.

W.N. WILLIS: FATHER AND SON

Two of the more interesting Australians involved in publishing in the second and following decades of the twentieth century were W.N. Willis, father and son of the same name, through their Anglo-Eastern and Camden Publishing companies and 'their brilliant young author', 'Bree Narran'. William Nicholas Willis senior was what might be described as a self-made, knockabout man. Born in Mudgee, New South Wales, in 1858 he followed a variety of occupations, including storekeeper and newspaper proprietor, before winning the NSW Legislative Assembly seat of Bourke as a Protectionist in February 1889.[6] In Sydney he established himself as a land and financial agent, advertising that he needed no 'black-tracker to show him though the land laws'. Holding his seat in 1891, he represented Barwon from 1894–1904. In 1890 Willis cofounded the notorious *Truth* newspaper. To protect himself from litigation, he sold the paper to partners, including fellow MP, W.P. 'Paddy' Crick, and John Norton, although he remained a major shareholder. In 1896 Willis sold his interest to Norton, possibly as a result of blackmail. When his drinking mate and crony, Crick, was Secretary for Lands in 1901–04, Willis was involved in numerous shady land deals. A Royal Commission was appointed in 1905 to inquire into these and Willis promptly fled to South Africa, where he had visited and made money before. He returned to Sydney under police escort in 1906 to face criminal charges with Crick of fraud and conspiracy. But a jury twice failed to convict the pair. Willis left Australia for good around 1909.[7]

Figure 10.1 This postcard advertisement for one of author Bree Narran's popular titles stimulates the imagination with images of race, sex, class and a fateful decision about to be made. It was one of many published in Britain by the expatriate Australian father and son team of W.N. Willis and their Anglo-Eastern Publishing Company
Source: John Arnold collection

Cyril Pearl in *Wild Men of Sydney* summarises Willis's post-Australian career: He '… went to England and became a publisher of cheap pornography. As the "Anglo-Eastern Publishing Company," he decorated the bookstalls with a series of gaily-jacketed books on prostitution, and gilded vice'.[8] There is an implied assessment here based on a judgment of books by their covers and titles rather than one gained by actually reading them. Under his own name Willis was responsible for 15 or so books, most issued by either the Anglo-Eastern Publishing Company or the Camden Publishing Company, but also a few with mainstream publishers. His books campaigned against the evils of 'the white slave trade', that is prostitution, and include titles such as *Crime of Silence: About the Hidden Plague*, *The White Slaves of London*, *White Slaves in a Piccadilly Flat*, *Why Girls Go Wrong*, *Western Men with Eastern Morals*, and the co-authored *The White Slaves of Toil*. He also wrote a couple of sporting novels, including *Blue Grey: A Sport Abroad* and *The Lady Jockey*.

Willis's crusade against the evils of the white slave trade was supported, allegedly, by religious figures such as the Bishop of London. He and other dignitaries are quoted in the unsigned preface – headed 'The Importance of Mr W.N. Willis's Books' – to Willis's *Should Girls be Told?* The preface begins:

> When Mr Willis wrote the first of his several books on the social evil, the public at large was afraid to speak, even in whispers, on the distressing subject. Gradually, however, his untiring and persistent efforts to awaken the national conscience to the system of commercialised vice (with its attendant evil, venereal disease) which thrives in our midst, have succeeded in completely revolutionising public opinion.[9]

Using the name of Marion Lehane-Willis, Willis wrote a novel entitled *The Painted Women*. This was another warning against the evils of a sinful life. A young innocent girl, Peg, is taught how to use men by Margaret, a painted woman dying of tuberculosis. Peg must never love any man but must get them to love her so she can use and abuse them at her will: in short to become the ultimate painted woman. Needless to say, after initial success and a life of kept luxury, things go wrong. Peg ends up in the gutter and dies in her late twenties a wreck of a human being.

Although running a campaign to protect girls from the evils of prostitution, and publishing a sexual science series with such titles as *Wedded Love or Married Misery* and *Marriage and Birth Control* by 'Brenda Barwon', Willis was no supporter of women's rights. He wrote the following response to Marie Stopes' *Married Love* in which she gave a rational and factual account of satisfying sexual intercourse from a woman's viewpoint:

> Let's us ... in the name of true normal manhood and womanhood and indeed of the name of the British Empire endeavour to keep the imagination down at all costs – never purposely call it into play as suggested by Mrs Stopes ... the human imagination is the most deadly foe to the clean wholesome methods of Nature ...[10]

Defiance, by 'Wentworth Oliver' is one of Willis's more interesting novels.[11] Although melodramatic, *Defiance* does have an interesting modern theme. It is about a couple, both writers – he successful and established, she just starting out – who deliberately defy convention by deciding to go to Europe to live together. Initially, they have no choice as the man's estranged wife is still alive, but even after her death the lovers make the conscious decision not to get married despite having children and being snubbed by former acquaintances when they visit England.

The most interesting author in the Anglo Eastern/Camden stable was 'Bree Narran'.[12] He was the author of some 15 novels and numerous translations of *risqué* French novels such as those by Paul De Kock. The Bree Narran novels are fanciful melodramatic romances, sympathetic to women. They often revolve around an exploitive cad and bounder with a female accomplice who has been trapped into circumstances from which she cannot escape. The cad wins his way into women's hearts, or cultivates friendship with wealthy young men, and then cleverly relieves them of their money. Good, however, eventually prevails as the villains end up getting their just punishment: usually death, not from the law, but from misadventure when one of their schemes goes badly wrong.

Some have passing Australian references. *Six Nights on the Moon* involves travel across the world to the Pacific and Australia in an airship. In *Seven Nights*, set during the war, the heroine is nursing convalescing soldiers, one of whom is a bronzed ANZAC named, somewhat appropriately, Loughlan Macquarie – his Christian name spelt 'Loughlan' rather than the 'Lachlan' of Governor Macquarie. The nurse and the soldier end up marrying.

Both Cyril Pearl and Miller and Macartney indicate that the Bree Narran novels were written by Willis but his entry in the *Australian Dictionary of Biography* suggests they were written by his son, also William Nicholas Willis. A reading of books by Willis senior and those of Bree Narran gave initial support for this interpretation, but further research and correspondence with family members suggests that they were in fact the work of Willis senior.[13]

The Bree Narran novels appear to have been published from February 1919 to the early or mid-1920s, and possibly none thereafter, while most of the translations by Bree Narran appear to have been published in the early 1930s. It is hard to determine how many were first published before Willis's death in 1922 and how many after. They are all undated and not all of them are listed in the *English Catalogue of Books*. Neither are they all held in the British Library.

A further complication is that most of the books, in addition to always having been undated, were also issued at various times by both the Anglo-Eastern Publishing and Camden Publishing companies, although probably initially by the former. Both companies were either formed or owned by Willis senior, although it is possible he had an interest only in the Camden one. This is first listed in the volume of the *English Catalogue of Books* covering 1906–1910, while both companies appear in the list of publishers in the following volumes covering the years 1911–1935, and then only Camden which continues right up to 1955. At all times, Camden is at the same London address, 323 Upper St, Islington, while the Anglo-Eastern company moves about, but is never at 323 Upper St. Its 1930s and last listed address is in Cecil Court, off Charing Cross Road.

What likely happened was that William Nicholas Willis wrote the Bree Narran books but they were marketed by his entrepreneurial son, Willis Jr, known as Billy. He was born at Randwick, Sydney, in 1898 and enlisted in the 6th Light Horse Regiment of the AIF on March 1916 and as a private saw active service on the battlefields of France.[14] He spent a period in London with his father before sailing to Sydney in September 1919 after receiving his discharge. Returning to London a year or so later, he joined his father's publishing company, taking it over after Willis senior's death in 1922. As there appears to be little or no publishing activities in the mid to late 1920s, he may have been doing other things during these years, but he reactivated the company in the very early 1930s from the Cecil Court address. However, it was either wound up or went bankrupt in late 1932.[15] Willis then moved to Dublin and opened Billy's Snack Bar, followed by one of the city's first late night restaurants. In 1939 he opened the Green Rooster and ran it until shortly before his death in 1960. As the Bree Narran novels were still being issued under the Camden imprint in the late 1940s and even in the early 1950s, Willis Jr may have still had an interest, or possibly sold it and allowed the books to be published under license. There are no records so this is all speculation. Various obituaries refer to him as a 'man of much enterprise and ideas', 'a brilliant raconteur' with 'a fund of anecdote and reminiscence'.[16] Two mention his work in his father's publishing business but, tellingly, neither makes any reference to his being an author, let alone being 'Bree Narran'. A 1933 catalogue of the Anglo-Eastern Publishing Company[17] lists over sixty titles although it is unlikely that all were actually published. It is here that Bree Narran is described as 'the world-famous Author, whose sales exceed Three Million Copies' with *One Night* and *Three Nights* leading the way with print runs of over 200,000 each. One has to suspect (or assume) here that Billy Willis is displaying his entrepreneurial and raconteuring skills.

The books of the Anglo-Eastern Publishing Company are more interesting than just postwar cheap pornography, as suggested by Cyril Pearl. They may have had salacious covers, covered somewhat taboo topics, and, today, would be regarded as 'pulp fiction'. But in the Bree Narran novels and in *Defiance*, Willis showed that he could write. He certainly had an imagination and there was always a message, whether deliberate or not, in his books. The cad and bounder, in the long run, always got their just punishment. With regard to the novels of Bree Narran, if the company's sales figures are to be even half-believed, he is without doubt one of Australia's least known but most successful authors.

THREE BOYS FROM QUEENSLAND TAKE ON THE LONDON LITERARY ESTABLISHMENT

In the 1920s, it was three former students from the University of Queensland – Jack Lindsay, P.R. Stephensen and Eric Partridge – who had the most marked influence on the English publishing and literary scene. They were all publishers in the private press movement: Lindsay and Stephensen with the Fanfrolico Press, Partridge with his Scholartis Press and Stephensen with the Mandrake Press.

The Fanfrolico Press[18] was founded in Sydney in 1925 by Jack Lindsay and John Kirtley, a stock broker's clerk but also an aspiring printer. They had already produced a book of Lindsay's verse[19] together and, in 1925, a lavish edition of Jack's translation of Aristophanes' verse drama *Lysistrata*. With the encouragement of Norman Lindsay, they decided to take the press to London. They arrived in May 1926 and issued their first book, a revised edition of their Sydney *Lysistrata*, the following December. Two further titles followed, Kenneth Slessor's *Earth Visitors* and a translation by Lindsay of the complete works of the Roman satirist Gaius Petronius.

With the publication of the Petronius work, Kirtley decided to leave the press and return to Australia. His decision to hand over its operation to Jack Lindsay was due partly to homesickness and partly to scheming between Lindsay and his old University of Queensland friend, P.R. Stephensen, then at Oxford in the last year of his Rhodes Scholarship. Stephensen joined the press as business manager in mid-1927 and brought to it his effervescent energy and enthusiasm. In their 20 or so months together he and Lindsay produced or planned 19 books and launched and published a literary periodical, *The London Aphrodite*. Their reception and reputation was mixed. Aldous Huxley supposedly parodied the pair in his 1928 novel about postwar bohemian London, *Point Counter Point*,[20] while D.H. Lawrence, in a letter to P.R. Stephensen, was critical of what he saw as their apparent lack of discernment after Jack sent him copies of two Fanfrolico books: '[B]ut oh! if you Australians didn't do it all so easy! It's as if you could eat a thousand dinners without ever swallowing one of them or having anything in your stomachs: everything just tasty'.[21]

Stephensen left Fanfrolico to found the Mandrake Press in mid-1929. His place was taken by yet another Queenslander, Brian Penton, later a noted newspaper editor in Australia.[22] He joined the Press in September 1929 but only lasted six months or so, his place being taken in turn by Philip Lindsay, Jack's younger brother and soon to become a prolific historical novelist. By this time the Press was in financial difficulties and it would be declared bankrupt in August 1930. In its four or so years in England, the Fanfrolico Press published 39 books plus the 6 bi-monthly numbers of *The London Aphrodite* (August 1928–June 1929). In terms of overall sales, Fanfrolico was probably second only to the better known Nonesuch Press.[23] Looking back some 30 years after the Press folded, Jack Lindsay wrote:

> What had we achieved in the Fanfrolico Press? Nothing, if one is to judge by the total absence of any comment in the literary records. True, we played our part in the raising of book-production standards in general, which resulted from the expansion of fine-presses in the Twenties; and we did some useful books ... It was in *The London Aphrodite* that we made our wider impact, and this was too unconventional a product to meet any recognition from the critics, then or later ...
>
> It seems to me ... that we did have a valid place in the decade and that if we are left out of the picture the intelligibility of that world is lessened.[24]

In sales, reception, design and content, the Fanfrolico Press had both successes and failures, but the latter far outweighed the former, and in their resurrection of neglected authors and support for freedom of expression, Lindsay and Stephensen made a notable, if minor, contribution to English cultural life. The contemporary chronicler of the private press movement, Will Ransom, wrote that a 'personal quality ... joyful seriousness ... infuses the Fanfrolico Press'[25] while the historian of the private presses, Roderick Cave, wrote: 'In its brief life Fanfrolico had published some very interesting books, and the 1920s would have been poorer without its attempts to storm the battlements of the English literary establishment with a new critique'.[26]

New Zealand born Eric Partridge (1894–1979)[27] fought in the first war in the AIF and then returned to Australia to study at the University of Queensland. He was awarded the 1921 Queensland Travelling Scholarship over Jack Lindsay to study at Oxford. After completing his degree he taught at Manchester University and then, in September 1926, took up a Lectureship in English at the University of London. Early in 1927 he approached Jack Lindsay with a plan to invest money in, and become a partner in, the Fanfrolico Press. The idea came to nothing, partly because Jack wanted Stephensen as his partner. But Partridge did advance the press £200 to publish his biography of the nineteenth century English poet Robert Landor, along with a selection of his works. This appeared in June 1927. Partridge then formed his own private press, the Scholartis, a made-up word emphasising his aim of combining scholarship with the arts in terms of book production. The colophon on many of its titles was 'Liberality, Originality, Distinction' and it was notable for its support of young and emerging writers. The Press[28] published over ninety books, including titles by H.E. Bates, John Brophy, Jack Lindsay, R.H. Mottram, Norah Hoult and Osbert Burdett as well as numerous edited literary texts, and it also took over the remaining stock of Partridge's Fanfrolico Landor book. It gained notoriety when Partridge published Norah C. James' *Sleeveless Errand* (1929), a novel about dissolute London bohemian life, only to have to the book banned and withdrawn from circulation.

Like Fanfrolico, Scholartis also issued a periodical, *The Window: A Quarterly Magazine*. Edited by Partridge and Bertram Ratcliffe, the four numbers were published in 1930. Contributors to the magazine include H.E. Bates, John Brophy, John Drinkwater, T.F. and Lawrence Powys, Edmund Blunden and John Hadfield. Although it published its last book as late as 1935, the Depression, according to Partridge, 'killed the Scholartis Press' forcing its proprietor to give up being a publisher.[29] He became a full-time author and a noted lexicographer, famous for his dictionaries of soldiers' and underworld slang.

Stephensen's Mandrake Press was backed by the bookseller Edward Goldston, who in the early twenties had made a staggering £10,000 profit from buying a Gutenberg Bible from a monastery in Austria and selling it at auction in America. The first book from the press was *The Paintings of D.H. Lawrence*. It was published in June 1929 in two editions: 10 copies on vellum at £52/10/– and 500 copies at 10 guineas. There were 60 orders for the vellum edition alone and, although production costs would have run to over £2000, it would have provided the new press with around £1500 to £2000 profit.[30]

Thereafter, Mandrake Press books were more modest but still attractive publications. A further 31 books were produced[31] before the Press folded in 1930. In addition to reprints of classics, authors published included Stephensen himself (a collection of short stories entitled *The Bushwhackers*), fellow Australians Jack McLaren, W.J. Turner and Vernon Knowles, plus books by Liam O'Flaherty, Rhys Davies, Edgell Rickword and Aleister Crowley. Stephensen's involvement with occultist Crowley, once described as 'the most evil man in the world', probably contributed to the press's eventual bankruptcy.

While with Fanfrolico, Stephensen was active in the campaign against the banning of Radclyffe Hall's lesbian novel, *The Well of Loneliness* (1928). Published by Jonathan Cape, the novel was castigated as obscene by columnist James Douglas in the *Sunday Express* and suppressed at the instigation of the Home Secretary, Sir William Joynson-Hicks (known amongst his detractors as 'Jix'). Stephensen, with typical gusto, threw himself into the cause, editing and publishing a witty booklet critique of the censoring entitled *The Sink of Solitude*.[32] Published under the imprint of the Hermes Press, the booklet contained striking drawings by Beresford Egan and a lampoon against both Douglas and Joynson-Hicks that included the following stanza:

In JONATHAN'S office consternation spreads
And while THE MILLION READERS in their beds
Peruse JAMES' Sunday outburst, weep, and sigh;
Jo: CAPE sits down to write a long reply.

But all in vain – poor JO: is in a fix,
Among the Million Readers one is JIX.
From JIX to JIMMY deep calls unto deep
For moral sheep will follow moral sheep;
While rapidly the book sells out of stock,
Two great men quiver with a holy shock,
Two men now burst with holy indignation
To save the morals of the British nation.[33]

Stephensen was also involved in two other verse parodies against censorship. One was *Policeman of the Lord* published by the Sophistocles Press late in 1928 or early 1929, the other was *The Well of Sleevelessness*, published by the Scholartis Press in 1929. The title was a play on Radclyffe Hall's *Well of Loneliness* and Norah C. James' *Sleeveless Errand* (1929). After the Mandrake Press folded Stephensen worked in a variety of fringe publishing jobs before returning to Australia in 1933 to run the *Bulletin*-backed Endeavour Press.

BOOKS BY AUSTRALIAN AUTHORS PUBLISHED IN LONDON

The following table extracted from Miller and Macartney[34] shows the number of works of creative literature by Australian authors published in England over the period, 1900–1940. The figures in brackets represent the percentage in that genre for each decade of the total for the four decades covered.

Decade	Fiction		Poetry		Drama	
	No.	%	No.	%	No.	%
1900–10	429	24.71	31	20.81	11	28.95
1911–20	380	21.89	50	33.56	7	18.42
1921–30	452	26.04	46	30.87	14	36.84
1931–40	475	27.36	22	14.76	6	15.79
Total	1736	100.00	149	100.00	38	100.00

Table 10.1 Works of creative literature by Australian authors published in England, 1900–1940
Source: Miller with Macartney, 1956

The grand total is 1923. As one would expect, 90.3 per cent are novels or collections of short stories, while 7.7 per cent are books of verse and the balance (2 per cent) drama or plays. The numbers for the first two decades of the twentieth century are influenced by the prolific output of writers such as Louis Becke, Guy Boothby, B.L. Farjeon, A.G. Hales, E.W. Hornung, Fergus Hume and Morley Roberts.[35] The figures for the following two decades reflects both the demand for crime and romance fiction and the influence of the circulating library on fiction publishing in the inter-war period. John Lane, export manager for the Bodley Head, said during a visit to Australia in 1933:

> One of the most interesting features of bookselling in Great Britain today is the enormous number of cheap libraries which have been established throughout the country, in which, for a subscription of 2d a week and no deposit readers

can obtain a very good supply of first-class literature ... [they] will do much to improve the taste in literature of the industrial classes in England. Already they have mitigated against the sale of the 'trashy' penny magazine.[36]

The Australian writer and critic, Nettie Palmer, in England in 1935, was struck by what she described as the 'phenomenon of the year in London: the twopenny library'.[37]

Many writers, both English and Australian, were only published because of the guaranteed purchases by the myriad of circulating libraries.[38] Georgia Rivers[39] and Jean Campbell[40] are two classic Australian examples. Neither left Australian shores but both had several novels published in London by Hutchinson and its subsidiaries Long and Skeffington in the 1930s when the two women were aged in their thirties. But neither, despite their continuing writing, was published in London after the war. Their novels are now not only forgotten but also very hard to obtain. They are neglected writers whose better work is worth reading.[41]

It is unclear how these Australia-based writers made contact with their English publisher. They possibly worked through the firm's Australian agent. The manuscript of Jean Campbell's first novel, *Brass and Symbols*, was taken to England to place with a publisher by John Gorton, the future Australian Prime Minister, in the early thirties when he was on his way to study at Oxford. Campbell was Gorton's father's mistress. The novel was accepted by Hutchinson and published in 1933. Three more followed and in 1937 Hutchinson offered Campbell a £60 advance for three novels, but only *The Babe is Wise* (1939) appeared. She was one of many writers whose means of getting published was killed off by the war.[42]

Some of these Australian 'circulating library writers' were included in the Australian Authors' Week exhibition held at Australia House in London in early October 1931. Organised by the Australian Literature Society in Melbourne, approximately 1700 books were on display under various subject headings. Most of the titles were published in the preceding 40 years or so with the combined fiction, poetry, literature, and *belles lettres* categories accounting for more than half of the exhibited books.[43] The display was augmented by a large number of Australian books lent by the Royal Society of Literature.

In terms of royalties, until the late 1930s, according to Debra Adelaide,[44] Australian authors published in England still received what was known as the 'colonial royalty'. This was only half the normal royalty of 10 per cent. So Campbell (and the many others) would have only received a royalty of four-and-a-half pence for each copy of a novel selling in England at the standard 1930s price of 7s 6d. If their novel managed to sell 1000 copies, then their royalty return would be just under £19, the equivalent to about six weeks wages for someone on the basic wage in Australian in the 1930s.

Prolific Australian crime writers of the twenties and thirties included John G. Brandon (42 titles), Carlton Dawe (34 titles), James Francis Dwyer (7 titles), Arthur Gask (22 titles), Gavin Holt/Charles Rodda (25 titles), Paul McGuire (16 titles) and J.M. Walsh (43 titles). Of these, only Gask was based in Australia. Many of the novels of Brandon, Holt and Walsh were translated into various European languages while all bar Dawe also had American editions of many of their books. Brandon, Dwyer, and Walsh, and possibly others, also wrote prolifically for the magazine market, with Brandon, for example, having around 40 complete novels published as single issues of *Thriller Magazine: the magazine of a thousand thrills* and *Detective Weekly* over the decade

1929–1939. Of these 40, only about a third to half appeared in book form.[45] In addition, Brandon and another Australian writer based in England, R. Coutts Armour, were also two of the main authors of the famous Sexton Blake detective stories for older boys.

The dominant Australian romance writer of the same period was the prolific Maysie Greig (born Maysie Greig-Smith). Her first novel was published in London in 1926.[46] Writing under her own name and that of Jennifer Ames and other pseudonyms, she had published another 73 by the end of 1940 and by the time she died in 1971, her total output was a staggering 178 titles.[47] Other Australians writing romances in the twenties and thirties were Mary Gaunt (7 titles), Elizabeth Milton (6 titles) Mary Mitchell (10 titles including 3 crime) and Alice Grant Rosman (14 titles).

An English firm that did publish Australian writers independent of the circulating library market was Arthur Stockwell. Initially based in London, the firm moved to Ilfracombe in Devon in 1939.[48] Miller and Macartney list 34 books by Australian authors published by Stockwell between 1913 and 1950. Of these 18 are books of verse, 14 are fiction, one is a biography and the other a book of essays. The National Library of Australia holds a substantial number of books of fiction and verse by Australian authors published by Stockwell. Some of these have distinctly Australian titles such as Ruth Young's *Nancy Vane and Other Verse from Gippsland* (1933). None could be classed as books that would have been widely read let alone ever being profitable sellers. Why Stockwell published these Australian authors is a mystery. A recent inquiry to the firm elicited a courteous but not enlightening reply.[49] It is possible that they were acting, effectively, as a vanity publisher: offering to publish if the author contributed to the cost of publication or agreed to buy a number of copies. How they advertised in Australia and how they attracted Australian authors is unknown.

The majority of the novels published by Australian writers in London in the period 1900-1940 had little or no Australian content. This is especially so for the crime and romance novels. They were mainly written for an English audience and, for many of the authors actually living and working in England, by writers who, one suspects did not specifically see themselves as Australian writers, but simply as writers or journalists. There are, of course, notable exceptions: Henry Lawson's three collections of stories published in London – *The Country I Came From* (1901), *Joe Wilson and His Mates* (1901) and *Children of the Bush* (1902) – are quintessentially Australian. Katharine Susannah Prichard's *The Pioneers* (1915), written in London and joint winner of the 1914 Hodder and Stoughton £1000 novel prize, is a novel with a distinct Australian setting, as are the early works of Martin Boyd, particularly *The Montforts* (1928), winner of the inaugural Australian Literature Society Gold Medal. Henry Handel Richardson's trilogy, *The Fortunes of Richard Mahony* (1917, 1925, and 1929), is distinctly Australian, while Christina Stead's second novel, *Seven Poor Men of Sydney* (1934) is wholly set in Australia, as is John Harcourt's suppressed novel dealing with Western Australian politics and society, *Upsurge* (1934). Patrick White's first novel, *Happy Valley* (1939) is set in New South Wales. Expatriate Jack Lindsay wrote a children's novel on the Eureka Stockade published as *Rebels of the Goldfields* in 1936 and also worked in the 1930s on compiling an anthology of Australian poetry although the project was never finished, while the novels of Jean Campbell and Georgia Rivers referred to above are partly set in Melbourne or its suburbs, as is Capel Boake's *The Dark Thread* (1936).

AUSTRALIAN WRITERS IN LONDON

Henry Lawson concluded his 1899 essay 'Pursuing Literature in Australia' with the following:

> My advice to any young Australian writer whose talents have been recognized, would be to go steerage, stow away, swim, and seek London, Yankeeland, or Timbuktoo – rather than stay in Australia till his genius turned to gall or beer.[50]

In 1902, Louise Mack, in a letter from London published in the *Bulletin*, claimed that only six Australians had any reputation in London and they were all singers and actors. She went to say that no artists, writers or poets or musicians 'had lifted themselves above the middle rank of innumerable English men or women of like professions'.[51] Fifteen writers are included in Mrs Leonard Matters' *Australasians Who Count in London* (1913).[52] The number would have increased substantially if she had she compiled another such compendium on the eve of the Second World War.

An appendix given at the end of this chapter lists some 119 Australian writers, including Henry Lawson and Louise Mack, who did leave Australia and who were working in or were based in or who spent some time in London over the period 1900–1940. Some were established writers, many were aspiring to that classification. Others were journalists working in or seeking to make their mark in Fleet Street. Some were primarily academics, two – Arthur Lynch and R.L. Outhwaite – were MPs, Will Dyson was a cartoonist and artist, while Oscar Asche was an actor as was Mary Marlowe. All had something in common – other than being Australian – in that they had a work of creative writing published in England in the first 40 years of the twentieth century. Of these 119 Australians, it is estimated that 40 to 45 per cent returned to Australia either permanently or for an extended period (for example, Martin Boyd) while just over half are included in the *Australian Dictionary of Biography*.

Jack Lindsay in *Fanfrolico and After* (1962) gives a vivid portrait of his and P.R. Stephensen's literary and social activities in 1920s London. They were frequent drinkers at the Plough Inn in Museum Street and also the Fitzroy Tavern off Charlotte Street and took many visiting Australians to one or either of these pubs. Both were notable literary and bohemian haunts. Augustus John is alleged to have said: 'If you haven't visited the Fitzroy you haven't visited London'.[53]

Other Australians active in the London literary scene in the 1920s included W.J. Turner and Bertram Higgins. Turner was born in Melbourne in 1884 and educated at Scotch College.[54] He moved to England as a young man and made a name for himself as a poet and drama and music critic. Before his death in England in 1946, he had published 16 books of verse (2 appearing under the imprint of the Mandrake Press) and 6 dramas. Bertram Higgins (1901–74) was another Melburnian working in England. He studied in Oxford[55] and in the 1920s was assistant editor of the influential *Calendar of Modern Letters*,[56] the first film critic for the *Spectator* and a frequent reviewer. He returned to Australia in the 1930s. Fellow poet and student Roy Campbell described Higgins in his 1937 autobiography *Broken Record* as 'the most interesting of the poets at Oxford'[57] while critical comment quoted in the foreword and the introduction by A.R. Chisholm to his posthumous and only collection of published verse makes a strong claim for him as an important modernist poet.[58]

Anna Wickham was another respected poet of the period. Born Edith Harper in England in 1883, she came to Australia aged 7, living initially in Queensland and then Sydney.[59] She published two plays in Sydney under her birth name before returning to England in 1904 to pursue a career as a singer. Her pseudonym of Anna Wickham came from a memory of walking with her father in Wickham Terrace, Brisbane, when he made her promise that one day she would be a poet. She had two books of verse published by Harold Monroe's Poetry Bookshop and also wrote poetry and music under the name 'John Oland'. A collection of these was printed as single songs by the Women's Printing Society in 1911. She also contributed verse to various periodicals including the *The London Aphrodite*. An edition of her selected poems was published with a foreword by David Garnett in 1971 and Virago published *The Writings of Anna Wickham: Free Woman and Poet* in 1984.

CONCLUSION

Can we measure the contribution of the many Australians working and writing in England in the first four decades of the twentieth century? In one sense, their contribution was simply as writers and journalists working alongside and in competition with hundreds of other professional and aspiring writers rather than making or trying to promote their own Australianness or to create a distinct 'Australian' presence in London. Many like Katharine Susannah Prichard and Patrick White returned to Australia and became major international writers from an Australian base. Others like J. Murray Allison[60] and Max Rittenberg[61] stayed on in England and made important contributions to their respective fields of advertising and retailing and marketing.

Two, who probably made the most lasting contribution, were Jack Lindsay and Eric Partridge. Living mainly in the West Country, Lindsay published some 30 substantial books plus a considerable amount of journalism and criticism in the decade from 1931–1941. He also became a committed Marxist in the mid-thirties. After service in the British Army on the Home Front in the Second World War, he returned to full-time writing. His output over the next four-and-a-half decades until his death in 1990 is simply staggering. In all, he wrote some 150 books ranging from historical and contemporary novels to studies of the ancient world, translations of eastern European and Russian poetry and well-received biographies of noted artists such as Turner, Constable and Cezanne. He maintained an Australian interest by writing on Australian literature for *Meanjin* and *Overland*. Eric Partridge became a full-time writer in the early thirties focusing on the history and use of words, particularly slang and published numerous books on lexicographical subjects.

Output is a tangible way of measuring the impact of Australian writers and Australian books in London.[62] Readership and reception is another and the Australian authors whose main market was that of the circulating library is noted above. However, many of the readers would not have known they were reading a book by an Australian. But through their books and writings, their accents, their carousing in pubs and at parties, Australians in London over the period 1900 to 1940 had a presence and left their mark on the local literary scene. Arguably, the main difference between them and the later generation of expatriates[63] is that the former left Australia to further their careers while the latter left not only to further their careers but also to escape.

APPENDIX

AUSTRALIAN AUTHORS LIVING AND WRITING IN ENGLAND, 1900–1940

J. H. M. ABBOTT*
Arthur ADAMS*
Max AFFORD*
J. Murray ALLISON**
R. Coutts ARMOUR
Oscar ASCHE*
E. Rupert ATKINSON*
Ken ATTIWILL
Vere Latham BAILLIEU
William BAYLEBRIDGE*
Barbara BAYNTON*
Louis BECKE*
Dora BIRTLES
Guy BOOTHBY*
Martin BOYD*
John G. BRANDON
Hilda BRIDGES (?)
Roy BRIDGES*
Mary Grant BRUCE*
E. C. BULEY
Ada CAMBRIDGE*
Frances CAMPBELL
C. Haddon CHAMBERS*
C. H. CHOMLEY*
Chester COBB*
Dale COLLINS*
Alec COPPEL
Hugh CORLETTE
Florence Rose DARNEY
Carlton DAWE
Dulcie DEAMER*
Emily Elizabeth DICKINSON
Campbell DICKSON
Alfred DORRINGTON*
James Francis DWYER*
Peers ELLIOTT (?)
Velia ERCOLE [Margaret GREGORY]
Louis ESSON*
James Griffyth FAIRFAX
Mackenzie FAIRFAX
Dorota FLATAU

Hermoine FLATAU
Theodore FLATAU
Mary FORRESTER
Frank FOX*
Miles FRANKLIN*
Mary FULLERTON*
Mary GAUNT*
Maysie GREIG*
A. G. HALES*
Evelyn HENTY
Ada HOLMAN*
William Austin HORN*
Winifred JAMES*
Helen JEROME
Dora Egerton JONES
Carleton KEMP*
Vernon KNOWLES
G. B. LANCASTER*
Henry LAWSON*
Jack LINDSAY
Joan LINDSAY
Philip LINDSAY
Joice Nankivell LOCH
Sydney LOCH
Arthur LYNCH*
Louise MACK*
Dorothea MACKELLAR*
D. MANNERS-SUTTON* (ADB
    under Doris Gentile)
Frederick MANNING*
Arthur MAQUARIE
Mary MARLOWE*
Frances MCGUIRE
Paul MCGUIRE*
Norman MCKEOWN / Norman GILES
Ida MCLAREN
Jack MCLAREN*
Irene Rutherford MCLEOD
Janet MITCHELL*
Mary MITCHELL*
Tom Inglis MOORE*

Alan MOOREHEAD
Nina MURDOCH*
Kathleen O'BRIEN
R. L. OUTHWAITE
Nettie PALMER*
Vance PALMER*
Eric PARTRIDGE*
Frank PENN-SMITH
Brian PENTON*
Mrs Campbell PRAED*
Ambrose PRATT*
'John PRESLAND' [Gladys SKELTON]
Katharine Susannah PRICHARD*
Evadne PRICE [Helen Zenna SMITH]
Arthur J. REES
Rosemary REES
Peter RENWICK(?)
Henry Handel RICHARDSON*
Max RITTENBERG
Charles RODDA [Gavin HOLT]
Alice Grant ROSMAN*
Helen SIMPSON*
Mary SKINNER
Christina STEAD
P. R. STEPEHENSEN*
E. TAIT-REID
A. THOMAS-GORING
John THOMPSON
P Walker TAYLOR
Henry TIGHE
W. J. TURNER*
Alan VILLIERS
W S WALKER (COOEE)*
J. M. WALSH*
John Reay WATSON
Arthur Wesley WHEEN
Patrick WHITE
Anna WICKHAM
Dora WILCOX*
W. N. WILLIS*

*Australian Dictionary of Biography, **Gibbney and Smith, 1987
NB: Soldiers based in the UK during the First World War who had a book or verse published while in London are excluded, e.g. Oliver Hogue (Trooper Bluegum) as they were not really in the UK by choice.
Sources: Miller with Macartney, 1956; Arnold and Hay, 2001–2008; Arnold and Hay, 1995.

ENDNOTES

1. For example, see Lyons, 2001 and Johanson, 2000, chapter nine 'Statistics'. Johanson calculates that between 1841 and 1953, British publishers exported a total of 231,269 tons or 4,625,37 hundred-weight of books to Australia. Examples of books on visiting writers include Brissenden and Higham, 1961, and Harman, 1985.

2. For example, 100 copies of Arthur Jose's *The Growth of Empire* (1900) and 200 of Sarah Christie Boyd's *Causeries Familiars a Simple French Course* (1897) plus 40 additional copies for review were sent to Simpkin and Marshall.

3. Details of Angus and Robertson's London links taken from Allison, 1997, 74–75, 101–102.

4. Biographical details taken from Miller with Macartney, 1956, 323. See also Austlit 2008.

5. Biographical details from Miller with Macartney, 1956, 53–54; Bonnin, 1979.

6. See Rutledge, 1990.

7. The date of his departure is uncertain. Rutledge, 1990 suggests around 1910 but it was probably a year or so earlier. Whatever, he left for his own and arguably his country's good, making him 'a true patriot'.

8. Pearl, 1958, 190.

9. Willis, 1917, *Should Girls Be Told?*, Preface, vii. The book was later reissued by the Anglo-Eastern Publishing Company as part of its 'Social Science Series'.

10. Quoted in Rose, 1993, 114.

11. Knowing that this is the author's only title and the significance of the name 'Wentworth' in Australian history, I am assuming a pseudonymous work and that it is by Willis. Although undated, the British Library copy was received in May 1910, shortly after Willis arrived in London.

12. The 'Bree' and the 'Narran' are two rivers in northern New South Wales, in the area that Willis once held a seat in the New South Wales Parliament.

13. Rutledge, 1990 A view supported by Holden, 1950, in which he discusses Bree Narran, 1919, *Cora Pearl*, 'The lady of the pink eyes', London: Anglo-Eastern Publishing Co.

14. Biographical details from official sources and correspondence with and copies of letters supplied courtesy of family members, Willis Jnr's daughter, Magda, and grand daughter, Joanne Finnegan.

15. *The Times*, 2 February 1932 and 22 November 1932.

16. Undated press cuttings, copies supplied courtesy of family members.

17. Issued with early thirties reprints of the Bree Narran novels by the Anglo-Eastern Publishing Company. For details on the novels of Bree Narran and other works by W.N. Willis see Arnold and Hay, 2001–2008, 726–727.

18. See Arnold, 2009; Arnold, 2004, 65–74.

19. Lindsay, 1923, *Fauns and Ladies*.

20. Huxley, 1928, *Point Counter Point*. See 168 and 178. Although the parody of the Fanfrolico partners (Lindsay as Willie Weaver and Stephensen as Cuthbert Arkwright) is regularly attributed, for example, Munro, 1984, 64, and the character of Arkwright could be a somewhat harsh portrait of P.R. Stephensen, that of Weaver is nothing like Jack Lindsay.

21. Sagar and Boulton, 1993, 4584, 118–117; D.H. Lawrence to P.R. Stephensen, 2 January, 1929, 4584.

22. For an account of his time in London see Buckridge, 1994, ch. 5

23. Lindsay, 1962, *Fanfrolico and After*, 182n.

24. Lindsay, 1962, *Fanfrolico and After*, 182, 189.

25. Ransom, 1929, *Private Presses and Their Books*, 167.
26. Cave, 1971, 206.
27. Serle, 1988; Serle, 1987, Introduction.
28. See Partridge, 1930, *The First Three Years: An Account and a Bibliography of the Scholartis Press*; Partridge, 1937, Appendix, 'A bio-bibliographical note', 312–317; Fotheringham, 1972, 338–342.
29. Its last title was published in 1935 but its most active period was from 1927 to 1931.
30. See Munro, 1984, 84–87 for details on the publication of *The Paintings of D.H. Lawrence* and Chapter 6 for the subsequent history of the Mandrake Press.
31. See Carr, 1985 for details of all the Mandrake books published.
32. For an interesting assessment of this parody and the two others produced by Stephensen, see Doan, 2004.
33. Stephensen, 1928, *The Sink of Solitude*, no pagination.
34. Essays, books of criticism and anthologies listed by Miller with Macartney, 1956 are not included in the tabulations in the table, nor are children's books.
35. It can be argued whether or not these men are really Australian writers with only two – Boothby and Hales – being born in Australia and most of the others having only spent a few years here. Only the two Australia-born are included in the list of Australian writers working in London in the first four decades of the twentieth century given in the appendix to this chapter.
36. Reported in the *Argus* (Melbourne), 25 October 1933, 9.
37. Nettie Palmer, 'Some London libraries: a letter from Mrs. Palmer', *All About Books* (Melbourne), 12 August 1935, 127.
38. It is estimated that the rental libraries in the United Kingdom attached to the stores of Boots the chemist and the railway stalls of W.H. Smith numbered up to 10,000 while in 1935 the *Publisher's Weekly* estimated that there were 50,000 rental libraries in the United States compared to 10,000 bookstores. Figures from Rassuli and Hollander, 2001. For an account of the phenomenon in Australia, see Arnold, 2001.
39. Georgia Rivers. Pseudonym of Marjorie Clark (1897–1989). Several of her later unpublished novels are in the State Library of Victoria.
40. Arnold, 2007. The manuscript of one of her unpublished postwar novels is in the State Library of Victoria.
41. For a recent assessment of both, see De Lacy, 2009.
42. Arnold, 2007.
43. Australian Literature Society 1931. *Catalogue of Books Shown at Australia House, London*. Details from Australian Author's Week.
44. Adelaide, 2001.
45. *Thriller Magazine* and *Detective Weekly* details from collection formerly in the author's possession.
46. Greig, 1926, *Peggy of Beacon Hill*. A US edition had appeared two years earlier.
47. Rutledge, 1996.
48. Stockwell, 2008.
49. Email to the author from Peter Nicholas, Director, A.H. Stockwell Ltd, 1 January 2006.
50. *Bulletin*, January 1899. Reprinted in Kiernan, 1976, 225–227.
51. 'Gouli-Gouli' [Louise Mack], *Bulletin* 28 June,1902. Quoted Pesman, 1996, 49.
52. Matters, 1913, *Australasians Who Count in London, and Who Counts in Western Australia*.

53 See Fiber and Powell-Williams, 1995.
54 Biographical details from Miller with Macartney, 1956, 469–470.
55 See Higgins, 1969, 'Some autobiographical notes ('twenties Oxford and London, early 'thirties Melbourne)'.
56 Bradbury, 1961.
57 Quoted on the back of the dust wrapper of Higgins' posthumous collection of verse. Higgins, 1981.
58 Higgins, 1981.
59 Jones, 2003.
60 J. Murray Allison was born in Victoria in 1877 and died in London in 1929. After working on the *Argus* he left for England around 1905. He became involved in Fleet Street publishing in 1926 *First Essays on Advertising* London: Palmer, several books of verse and a novel. *The Times*, 10 June 1929. See Gibbney and Smith, 1987; Austlit 2008.
61 See Austlit, 2008.
62 See, for example, relevant entries in Arnold and Hay, 2001–2008.
63 See Alomes, 1999.

PRIMARY SOURCES

All About Books (Melbourne), 1935.
Argus (Melbourne), 1933.
Australian Literature Society. 1931. *Catalogue of Books Shown at Australia House, London, at an Exhibition Held Under the Auspices of the Literature Society of Australia* [Australian Literature Society] *from September 29th to October 5th, 1931*. London: Australian Literature Society.
The Bulletin (Sydney).
Greig, Maysie. 1926. *Peggy of Beacon Hill*. London: Jenkins.
Higgins, Bertram. 1969. 'Some autobiographical notes ('twenties Oxford and London, early 'thirties Melbourne)'. *Quadrant* 13 (6): 51–54.
Huxley, Aldous. 1928. *Point Counter Point*. London: Chatto and Windus.
Lindsay, Jack. 1923. *Fauns and Ladies*. Sydney: J.T. Kirtley.
Lindsay, Jack. 1962. *Fanfrolico and After*. London: Bodley Head.
Matters, Mrs Leonard. 1913. *Australasians Who Count in London, and Who Counts in Western Australia*. London: Truscott.
Partridge, Eric. 1930. *The First Three Years: An Account and a Bibliography of the Scholartis Press*. London: The Scholartis Press.
Partridge, Eric. 1937. *A Covey of Partridge*. London: Routledge.
Ransom, Will. 1929. *Private Presses and Their Books*. New York: Bowker.
Stephensen, P.R. 1928. *The Sink of Solitude*. London: Hermes Press.
The Times (London), 1929.
Willis, W.N. 1917. *Should Girls be Told?* London: Werner Laurie.

REFERENCES

Adelaide, Debra. 2001. 'How did authors make a living?' In *A History of the Book in Australia, 1891–1945: A National Culture in a Colonised Market*, edited by Lyons, Martyn; Arnold, John. St Lucia, Qld: University of Queensland Press.

Allison, Jennifer M.E. 1997. 'Angus and Robertson as publishers 1880–1900: A business history'. PhD thesis. Sydney: University of New South Wales.

Alomes, Stephen. 1999. *When London Calls: The Expatriation of Australian Creative Artists to Britain*. Melbourne: Cambridge University Press.

Arnold, John. 2001. 'The circulating library phenomenon'. In *A History of the Book in Australia, 1891–1945: A National Culture in a Colonised Market*, edited by Lyons, Martyn; Arnold, John. St Lucia, Qld: University of Queensland Press.

Arnold, John. 2004. 'Fanfrolico frolics', *Meanjin*, 63 (3): 65–74.

Arnold, John. 2007. 'Campbell, Jean May (McNeil) (1901–1984)'. *Australian Dictionary of Biography*. Vol. 17. Carlton, Vic.: Melbourne University Press.

Arnold, John. 2009. *The Fanfrolico Press: Satyrs, Fauns and Fine Books*. Pinner, Middlesex: Private Libraries Association.

Arnold, John; Hay, John, editors. 1995. *Bibliography of Australian Literature Project: List of Australian Writers, 1788–1992*. Clayton, Vic.: National Centre for Australian Studies, Monash University.

Arnold, John; Hay, John, editors. 2001–2008. *Bibliography of Australian literature*. Vols. 1–4. Kew, Vic.: Australian Scholarly Publishing (vol.1); St Lucia, Qld: University of Queensland Press (vols 2–4).

Auslit. 2008. 'The Australian Literature Resourse'. [Internet]. Accessed 21 November 2008. Available from: http://www.austlit.edu.au/.

Bonnin, Nancy. 1979. 'Baylebridge, William (1883–1942)'. *Australian Dictionary of Biography*. Vol. 7. Carlton, Vic.: Melbourne University Press.

Bradbury, Malcolm. 1961. 'The *Calendar of Modern Letters*: A review in retrospect'. *London Magazine* 1 (7): 37–47. Accessed 16 August 2008. Available from: http://www.poetrymagazines.org.uk/magazine/record.asp?id=10040.

Brissenden, Alan; Higham, Charles, editors. 1961. *They Came to Australia: An Anthology*. Melbourne: Cheshire.

Buckridge, Patrick. 1994. *The Scandalous Penton: A Biography of Brian Penton*. St Lucia, Qld: University of Queensland Press.

Carr, Reg, editor. 1985. *The Mandrake Press, 1929–1930: A Catalogue of an Exhibition, Cambridge University Library, September–November 1985*. Cambridge: Cambridge University Library.

Cave, Roderick. 1971. *The Private Press*. London: Faber and Faber.

De Lacy, Gavin. 2009. 'Three neglected women writers of the 30s: Jean Campbell, "Capel Boake" and "Georgia Rivers"'. *The La Trobe Journal* 83 (May): 27–40.

Doan, Laura. 2004. 'Sappho's apotheosis? Radclyffe Hall's queer kinship with the Watchdogs of the Lord'. *Sexuality & Culture* 8 (2): 80–106.

Fiber, Sally; Powell-Williams, Clive. 1995. *The Fitzroy: The Autobiography of a London Tavern*. Lewes, Sussex: Temple House Books.

Fotheringham, Richard. 1972. 'Expatriate publishing: Eric Partridge and the Scholartis Press'. *Meanjin* 31 (3): 338–342.

Gibbney, H.J.; Smith, Ann. 1987. *A Biographical Register 1788–1939: Notes from the Name Index of the Australian Dictionary of Biography*. Canberra: Australian Dictionary of Biography.

Harman, Kaye, editor. 1985. *Australia Brought to Book: Responses to Australia by Visiting Writers, 1836–1939*. Balgowlah, NSW: Boobook.

Higgins, Bertram. 1981. *The Haunted Rendezvous: Selected Poems*. Newcomb, Vic.: Alella Books.

Holden, Wilfred Herbert. 1950. *The Pearl from Plymouth, Eliza Emma Crouch Alias Coral Pearl with Notes on Some of Her Celebrated Contemporaries*. London: British Technical and General Press.

Johanson, Graeme. 2000. *Colonial Editions in Australia, 1843–1972*. Wellington, New Zealand: Elibank Press.

Jones, Jennifer Vaughan. 2003. *Anna Wickham: A Poet's Daring Life*. Lantham, Maryland: Madison Books.

Kiernan, Brian, editor. 1976. *Henry Lawson* (Portable Australian Authors). St Lucia, Qld: University of Queensland Press.

Lyons, Martyn. 2001. 'Britain's Largest Export Market'. In *A History of the Book in Australia, 1891–1945: A National Culture in a Colonised Market*, edited by Lyons, Martyn; Arnold, John. St Lucia, Qld: University of Queensland Press.

Miller, E. Morris, editor; (with Macartney, F.). 1956. *Australian Literature: A Bibliography to 1938 Extended to 1950*. Sydney: Angus and Robertson.

Munro, Craig. 1984. *Wild Man of Letters: The Story of P.R. Stephensen*. Carlton, Vic.: Melbourne University Press.

Pearl, Cyril. 1958. *Wild Men of Sydney*. London: Allen and Unwin.

Pesman, Ros. 1996. *Duty Free: Australian Women Abroad*. Melbourne: Oxford University Press.

Rassuli, Kathleen M; Hollander, Stanley C. 2001. 'Revolving not revolutionary books: The history of rental libraries until 1960'. *Journal of Macromarketing* 21 (2): 123–134.

Rose, June. 1993. *Marie Stopes and the Sexual Revolution*. London: Faber.

Rutledge, Martha. 1990. 'Willis, William Nicholas (1858–1922)'. *Australian Dictionary of Biography*. Vol. 12. Carlton, Vic.: Melbourne University Press.

Rutledge, Martha. 1996. 'Greig, Maysie Coucher (1901–1971)'. *Australian Dictionary of Biography*. Vol. 14. Carlton, Vic.: Melbourne University Press.

Sagar, Keith; Boulton, James, editors. 1993. *The Letters of D.H. Lawrence*. Vol. VII, Nov. 1928–Feb 1930. Cambridge: Cambridge University Press.

Serle, Geoffrey, editor. 1987. *Eric Partridge, Frank Honywood, Private: A Personal Record of the 1914–1918 War*. Carlton, Vic.: Melbourne University Press.

Serle, Geoffrey. 1988. 'Partridge, Eric Honeywood (1894–1979)'. *Australian Dictionary of Biography*. Vol.11. Melbourne: Melbourne University Press.

Stockwell, A.H. 'Welcome to Arthur H. Stockwell publishers'. [Internet]. Accessed 16 August 2008. Available from: www.ahstockwell.co.uk.

Cite this chapter as: Arnold, John. 2009. 'Australian books, publishers and writers in England, 1900–1940'. *Australians in Britain: The Twentieth-Century Experience*, edited by Bridge, Carl; Crawford, Robert; Dunstan, David. Melbourne: Monash University ePress. pp. 10.1 to 10.19. DOI: 10.2104/ab090010.

CHAPTER 11

AUSTRALIAN TOURISTS IN BRITAIN, 1900–2000

Richard White, *University of Sydney*
> Richard White teaches at the University of Sydney. His publications include Inventing Australia *and* On Holidays. Symbols of Australia, *co-edited with Melissa Harper, will appear in 2009. This article is based on research for an ARC project on Australian travel.*

> Tourists represent the largest Australian presence in Britain but also the most fleeting. After considering the particular definitional problems posed by Australian tourism in Britain, this chapter sketches three broad changes in that presence over the twentieth century: increasing democratisation as overseas tourism opened up to an increasing proportion of Australia's population; logistical changes brought about by plane travel to and car travel within Britain, and the shift from family to friends in providing accommodation; and finally, transformations in the cultural capital that the Australian tourist brought with them, reflecting the diminution of a specifically 'British' culture in Australian life.

Of all Australian experiences of Britain in the twentieth century, the tourist experience was the most frequent and the most fleeting. Being so common, it deserves notice, but it has been robbed of serious attention by the persistent notion that it is superficial. It is also a surprisingly difficult subject to research: the evidence of the tourist experience is often elusive, the traces both ubiquitous and hard to find, too easily descending into cliché, too often hidden in slide boxes under beds.

The tourist has always had a bad press. Ever since the word was invented at the end of the eighteenth century, tourists were, as James Buzard has shown, defined as superficial and blinkered, their experience ephemeral and pre-packaged.[1] In the conventional dichotomy of traveller and tourist, it was always the tourist who was the butt of the joke. We can recognise that dichotomy as an artefact of the democratisation and commercialisation of travel, a process whereby the figure of the traveller, defined by 'his' individuality, came to be valued and promoted over the conventionality of the mass: often female, often American, almost always further down the social scale, a precursor to the cultural distinctions drawn between the high and the popular. But even in acknowledging this dichotomy as a sham, we need to accept that tourists are by definition the most temporary of Australian visitors to Britain. They are too transitory to penetrate society in the way other individual Australians have,[2] and too few in number to have a distinctive mass impact; but as the largest Australian presence in Britain numerically, and in the very fact that they return to Australia, they arguably have more influence on popular Australian attitudes to Britain back home than does any other group.

Against conventional expectations of tourist behaviour, the Australian tourist in Britain poses particular problems of definition. Within the variety of Australian types in Britain that have attracted scholarly attention – migrants, expatriates, guest workers, sojourners, exiles, waifs, backpackers, professionals who are not exactly backpackers[3] – where do tourists fit?

Conventionally tourism is defined against two aspects of the everyday, the routines of work and the routines of home. As John Urry has put it, tourism is a leisure activity that is the 'opposite' of work and takes place away from home.[4] True, it has often been argued that while travel is supposed to be an escape from work and home, tourists persist in the routines of work and behave as the 'the relentless representative of home'.[5] Nevertheless, tourism is fundamentally positioned against work and home.

These are the points where definitions are muddied for so many Australian tourists in Britain, and for those who looked down on them. Take the interweaving of work and travel. Many Australians travel to Britain in order to work. For many occupations over much of the twentieth century, work in Britain was the logical extension of a career: Fleet Street for journalism, the West End for theatre, the City for finance, and so on. At the same time, many other Australians worked in Britain in order to travel. In the working holiday, the border between work and holiday is porous. Work in the working holiday became not merely the *means* to travel, a way of financing it, though that was crucial to the conception. In addition, the work component was often the key with which Australian travellers could penetrate 'back stage', to experience British society from the inside, rather than being merely the observers of the 'staged authenticity' of tourism.[6] So the irony was that working holiday-makers established their superiority to the mere tourist, not in their greater distance from the routines of work, but in their very emulation of those routines.

Just as being in Britain could be equated with being at work, it could also be equated with being at 'home'. The particular symbolic value that Britain acquired as 'Home' in Australia can be dated from the 1840s, when it began to acquire a capital letter and/or a set of inverted commas.[7] It is no coincidence that this was when the Victorian idealisation of home as the domestic sphere was taking hold, becoming sentimentalised as a refuge from a brutal world, a haven of culture and peace, and the domain of women.[8] While the idea of England as 'home' would be satirised by many Australians, a century later, in 1948, the Lord Mayor of Melbourne, Sir Raymond Connelly, could still claim that 'As long as members of the Empire refer to London as "coming home" the Empire is safe'.[9] Such claims did not survive much longer, although wishful thinking might have affected judgements on both sides of the political spectrum: the socialist Brian Fitzpatrick thought the habit of calling England 'home' died during the Second World War, while the conservative Frederic Eggleston still confidently asserted 'England is "Home"' in 1953.[10] But at least until the middle of the twentieth century, its definition remained problematic: how can someone be travelling when they have just arrived 'home'? When it came to Britain, the superior travellers were those who were, paradoxically, the most domesticated. Even for a later generation, as Clive James and Murray Sayle explained, Australians were not tourists in London because they *belonged* there.[11]

What this suggests is the impossibility of 'travel' as distinct from 'tourism' for Australians in Britain. In the conventional hierarchy the tourist is conventional, timid and clichéd, and the traveller is the individual adventurer who quests for the unexpected. Australians arrived armed with those hierarchies. In 1954 Lindsay Parker wrote on 'Tourist or traveller' for the *Sydney Morning Herald*, and produced this 'infallible formula' for distinguishing the various visitors:

I am a Traveller
You are a Tourist
He, She or It is a Tripper.
We are Travellers (be certain of your company)
You are an Organised Tour
They are ruining the place.[12]

But Britain was too well known: the chances of adventure and the unexpected were few and far between.

When writing about the experience, Australians *could* adopt the language of travellers – of adventure, exploration and discovery – but it was a personal, interior adventure, as Ros Pesman, Angela Woollacott and Graeme Davison, in his 'emancipatory tradition', have shown, often slipping into the language of discovery themselves.[13] Woollacott writes of Alice Grant Rosman's 'serialised adventures exploring London', and Nancy Phelan of Louise Mack, 'walking for miles [in London], exploring, discovering, astonished, enthralled to find so much unexpected beauty'.[14] Barbara Hanrahan even insisted that riding London buses and the tube was 'always an adventure'.[15] Australian women seemed particularly fond of the adventure narrative. Alternatively, the traveller-adventurer pose could be adopted ironically to point up the paradox, as in Randolph Bedford's *Explorations in Civilisation* of 1914.[16]

But when they wrote about the external place rather than the inner journey, when they produced travel writing rather than memoir or fiction, Australians were less likely to be able to sustain the idea that they were travellers rather than tourists. This posed a problem. As Patrick Holland and Graham Huggan suggest, most successful travel writing – despite its popularity – is anti-democratic; it reinforces the traveller–tourist distinction as a way of identifying and then pandering to a middle-class audience, and remains 'a refuge for complacent, even nostalgically retrograde, middle-class values'.[17] For Australians writing about their experience of Britain however, to make the claim that they were travellers rather than tourists would have strained the credulity of their readers.

The dilemma was perhaps most stark in Ethel Turner's travel book, *Ports and Happy Havens*.[18] Turner was born in Yorkshire, but was taken to Australia when she was 7 (she called Australia 'home'). On her first trip to England she disembarked at Marseilles and detailed her travels through Italy, Germany, Holland and Belgium, recognising herself as a 'devoted tourist' – the Dutch children in traditional dress and clogs already adopted poses and expected payment for photographs – but nevertheless offering perceptive judgements on foreign ways, and having adventures as good travellers should. She had dismissed the advice to 'get off the beaten track', saying that as an Australian she had to see the beaten track first, but she wrote of her travels as discovery. At Naples, 'our first of the old-world cities, we can plunge humbly enough into that, we crude, unhistoried Australians'.[19] Several times she played with a postmodern conceit that the view from the train was a tableau staged for tourists. Finally at Ostend, they crossed the channel to Dover: 'Who, with any of England's blood in them could any longer refuse to hear the call?'. Here, at what might have been the climax of her tour, the travel writing suddenly stopped: this 'shining interlude' in England found no expression in the published travel account, though her diary was packed with detail. It was as if she had been struck dumb. Her 15 weeks in England were dispensed with in 15 lines, and then, back in France, the thread of discovery and travel writing and ironic post-tourism was resumed.[20]

There is a curious sense of disempowerment here. Australians simply could not be travellers in Britain. They could merge in (or try to), or they could be tourists; they could engage in a journey of *self*-discovery, or be ironic about their colonial status; but they could never claim to discover anything new. Travel to Britain was the necessary validation of the known rather than the discovery of the unknown. Indeed, as I have suggested elsewhere, words simply failed them when confronted by the England they knew so well in their imaginations. The standard response was that England was 'beyond description'.[21]

Part of the problem was H.V. Morton and other English writers who embarked from the 1920s on their own search for England, and claimed to have found it. In 1927 Morton wrote his first travel book, *In Search of England*, which was he said 'my adventure …off the beaten track'.[22] Its phenomenal success reached throughout the empire. It had 26 reprints by 1939 and spawned another five 'Search' books on Britain, five guides to London and three to the Holy Land. He could be said, in the *Saturday Review*, to have 'the true spirit of the adventurer'.[23]

To judge from its ubiquity in second-hand bookshops, *In Search of England* was a big success in Australia, often given as a gift, perhaps to prospective tourists or more poignantly to armchair tourists who would never be able to go. Morton created an England that seeped into the very bones of those 'independent Australian-Britons' described by Keith Hancock three years later.[24] Part of Morton's mastery of the genre lay in his ability to politely eroticise his adventures, particularly his encounters with women, while keeping within quite respectable bounds. Though married, Morton was something of a sexual predator, keeping a list of more than 100 sexual conquests in his private papers, and his solo journeys in search of England were perfect opportunities for extending it.[25] In response, Australians writing their own accounts of time in England could only defer to the Englishman's superior knowledge – or superior powers of discovery – and adopt a cultural cringe. For tourists in Britain there was, in A.A. Phillips's phrase, a 'minatory Englishman' sitting in the back of their mind, and his name was H.V. Morton.[26]

My favourite example of this deference to the superior descriptive powers of others was Hudson Fysh, in England on business with Qantas in 1937. At his first contact with English nature up close in Kew Gardens, he was lost for words. He laboriously copied into his diary 16 lines from Halliday Sutherland about 'England! our England!' which described 'old English parks, having within themselves peace, security, and contentment everlasting. In those gardens of Eden the mind for a few moments may know a pantheistic calm in which conflict, sin and death are forgotten'. Fysh added the comment, 'Exactly the words I have been groping for except that I don't know what pantheistic means'.[27]

Morton and others put Australians in an awkward position; if, when writing about their travels in Britain, they were not describing a personal journey of adventure, then they could only write, often quite frankly, as tourists. I have argued elsewhere that Australian travel writing in the middle of the twentieth century saw the emergence of a genre that (unusually) could celebrate the tourist over the traveller. Frank Clune was a master of the tourist book: not a tourist guide, but a style of travel writing that positioned the tourist as hero. I am suggesting that, when it came to Britain, Australians had no other option.

Clune's own book on Britain, *Land of Hope and Glory* (1949), was a perfect example of the genre.[28] He was, he said, 'a typical Australian' on his first visit, at the age of 53, to the 'Old Dart', 'a "home" I had never seen' despite its overwhelming familiarity from a lifetime of 'schools, newspapers, books, plays, cinema, radio, political oratory'. He would write as a tourist, seeking out the familiar: he had 'only six weeks in which to capture the rapture' so it would be 'some high-pressure sightseeing to make even a nodding acquaintance'. The results were recorded in a substantial 150,000 words, 'as a glimpse, and not as a full picture'.[29] All tourists, as Jonathan Culler suggests, are 'interested in everything as a sign of itself'[30] but Clune went further, becoming devoted to the sign itself, quite literally. He was an avid connoisseur of the monument and the memorial, the tourist seduced by the signifier. The typical photograph in his many books is of a tourist sign or monument, often with Clune posing in front of it. In his first travel book, the first five pages contain the inscriptions copied from seven monuments.[31] He was shocked to learn that Londoners took 'very little interest in their abundant memorials of past days and bloody deeds', but found it 'enchanting to a visitor from the Antipodes to discover wreaths are still placed on King Charles the First's statue … London is full of historical vestiges like that'.[32] Mathew Trinca has argued for a peculiarly Australian emphasis on London's monumentality, with its imperial and bourgeois themes.[33] Clune himself happily combined imperial and bourgeois sympathies with more populist Irish-Australian ones, and his enthusiasm for monuments was also the enthusiasm of the tourist. 'Being only an Australian', he once suggested, perhaps inadvertently, 'I see and depict what average tourists see'.[34]

This definitional struggle seems to have been a constant in the Australian experience of Britain throughout the twentieth century, but there were also changes. I now turn to three significant – if rather obvious – transformations: shifts in who went, how they did it and what they took with them. The trajectories of these three shifts were uneven, and they interacted with the dramatic changes taking place in Britain at the time, but they led to very different Australian tourist experiences at the two ends of the twentieth century.

First was the democratisation of tourism. Prior to the First World War Australian tourists in Britain were secure in their exclusivity. It took a lot of money and – more importantly – a lot of time to make the journey. This 'travelling class' was not simply defined by wealth.[35] Angela Woollacott has pointed out that many not particularly well-to-do women managed to make it to London, but that did not mean everyone could go.[36] These women generally had considerable cultural capital and hopes of working as journalists or in the arts, hopes that were not always realistic and not always fulfilled. Again we see the working holiday undermining our ideas of the nature of tourism. These women were, as Ros Pesman put it, 'duty free' – in that they possessed time and freedom from ties that might bind.[37] Each individual setting off for London had to strike a balance in their economy of desire between the cultural capital driving them to go and the (fluctuating) material means necessary to get there. For the vast majority of Australians, the desire to go was not enough to overcome the hurdles; no matter how strong the desire, many simply lacked the cultural or financial capital, the freedom or perhaps the foolhardiness to go. Most Australians could not expect to travel, and certainly not as tourists.

All this changed suddenly in 1916, when tens of thousands of ordinary Australian men – 'six-bob-a-day tourists' – visited Britain on leave or for training on what many treated as a sort of packaged working holiday.[38] Mere presence in Britain was now robbed of any social exclusiveness. I suspect the result was that after the war, in the 1920s, Australian tourism to Britain moved towards a self-conscious search for high culture, where social distinctions could be marked out, rather than a simple reconnection with family and place – which, after all, the troops had indulged in just as effectively.

By the 1950s it seems the range of ordinary young Australians on working holidays was increasing, with rising prosperity in Australia relative to Britain: Barry Humphries' Debbie Thwaite and her 1960 flatmates – physiotherapist, hairdresser, typist, comptometrist, nurse, phys-ed instructress – were archetypes, 'a type of Australian girl I kept meeting during my early weeks in

London'.³⁹ But a rite of passage before 'settling down' still called for time and commitment. With the arrival of the jumbo jet the commitment in both time and money was dramatically reduced: the reduced commitment of time would prove far more significant than the cost savings.⁴⁰

For younger Australians it says much about the cultural meaning of Europe that the 'Grand Tour' – a serious commitment of time to travel in Britain and the Continent to expand one's intellectual and social horizons – continued so long after it had become practicable to visit Britain for an annual holiday from the security of a permanent job. With this antipodean Grand Tour, we are venturing beyond the mere tourist experience, and we can only speculate about how it has changed. Has time in Britain shifted from being a socially sanctioned educational experience to simply providing a reasonably safe test of individual character? Has Britain lost much of its glamour, as distinct perhaps from the Continent, which continues to offer cosmopolitan panache? For older Australians, we can be more confident that those who travelled to Britain as tourists found it easier by the end of the century than ever before: an obvious point, but of profound consequence in the Australian tourist experience.

One effect of the democratisation of tourism was the rapid retreat by the Australian government from providing facilities for Australians in Britain. When it opened in 1917, Australia House took over the role of the agents-general and the offices of the *British-Australasian* in providing facilities for tourists, whom they could be confident were respectably middle class. In the 1920s the official role of the High Commission was to 'wish all Australian visitors to regard Australia House as a corner of Australia in London, a rendezvous ... where they can meet each other, where they may recapture their touch with home'. It offered an enquiry counter, a bookstall, a reception room and a commodious library, where 'Australian visitors might find it convenient to rest ... a while and arrange to meet their friends' (see Chapter 6). In a curiously tortured mission statement for a tourist bureau, they promised that 'The officials in charge are in a position to furnish information of a nature that may be helpful to visitors'.⁴¹ Always criticised for catering excessively to the elite who could afford to travel, those facilities were progressively wound down from the 1950s, just as travel was being democratised. By 1987 Bernard Lyman was bemoaning the fact that 'Australia House ... is no longer the home from home for Australians it used to be'.⁴²

The second major shift was in how Australian tourists travelled. The move from ship to plane meant not only a saving in time and money, but also a loss of the less tangible benefits of the voyage. Andrew Hassam and Angela Woollacott have pointed to the importance of the six-week voyage as preparation for the ensuing experience of Britain, heightening anticipation, increasing knowledge, supplying a sense of modern technological competence, reinforcing a sense of empire with ports of call on the way, and establishing helpful (or unhelpful) contacts among fellow passengers.⁴³ Tourists at the end of the century were denied that experience. Andrew Taylor has suggested the rise of air travel produced a profound psychic shift: not he stresses from exile to mere tourism, but from unitary to pluralistic patterns of identification with Britain, turning a taste for the tragic irony of the expatriate predicament into comic irony.⁴⁴

Another shift concerned accommodation for tourists arriving in Britain. As the century wore on, family connections in Britain grew more tenuous, though they were being replenished by those of the migrant 'ten-pound Poms'. While changing communication technologies – phone and email adding to postal links – reinforced those links, increased residential mobility might well have been breaking them. If it was easier to keep in touch, it was also becoming easier to lose touch. For increasing numbers the possibility of staying with relatives in Britain was no longer available, though even at the end of the century one third of Australian visitors to Britain stayed with relatives, at least for a time.

But if convenient relatives were fewer, convenient friends had multiplied. Globalisation, mobility, communication technologies and the democratisation of tourism all contributed to a situation whereby more Australians knew more people in Britain (other Australian visitors as well as British residents) than ever before, and so the decline in the relatives was made up for by the rise of the friends. Indeed, it is quite possible that the proportion of Australians spending time in English homes, 'the extremely important VFR (visiting friends and relatives) market segment' as the industry puts it, has not changed significantly over the twentieth century.[45] Certainly, the possibility of staying with locals remains more common for Australians in Britain than anywhere else. However, two differences accompany this shift from family to friends. First, if that sort of accommodation gave the tourist a sense of getting 'back-stage', of 'going native', friends presumably introduced them to a somewhat different 'back-stage' area from that offered by family. Second, there was a reduction in surveillance: with friends there was possibly less need to be on one's best behaviour, perhaps less sense of being judged, certainly less chance of adverse gossip getting back home.

Perhaps the biggest change in the ways Australians were tourists in Britain was their increasing automobility over the century. Many – especially the young – continued to rely on public transport and package tours, but the emergence of the car (and the Kombi / camper van / motor home) as a technology of tourism had major implications for the experience: as others have pointed out, the mode of transport is crucial to an understanding of the experience of travel.[46] The car, Jonas Larsen suggested, replaces John Urry's 'tourist gaze' with the travel 'glance'.[47] But it is not simply a matter of speed and (by implication) superficiality.

The car allowed the tourist to penetrate a very different England to that of the conventional tourist relying on public transport routes or even on organised tours. Indeed this was the very England that H.V. Morton went in search of; and the crucial departure he made was to search for England by car, a modest Morris Cowley 'Bullnose' he named Maud.[48] Australians followed suit in their droves. This modern technology allowed a new way to deprecate modernity. As Morton bowled along English lanes, seeking out-of-the-way villages, he deplored indications of modernity seeping into the countryside – the cinema, the wireless, bobbed hair, tourists in char-à-bancs, the manufactured quaintness of Clovelly. He even regretted that the safety razor and modern dentistry had replaced idiosyncratic old faces, full of character, with standardised modern ones. He sang the praises of villages in which nothing at all happened, as he hurtled along in the supreme symbol of modern progress. He drove from one place where people do nothing to another, he alone doing everything.[49] He was the modern in search of the pre-modern, the sophisticate in search of the simple life – and the car made it possible. In his wake, the car gave other tourists access to Morton's England, the ability to penetrate an England previously inaccessible.

The *British-Australasian* began promoting drive tourism in Britain from 1911. By the 1920s Australia House's tourist guide was full of advertisements extolling motor travel, whether chauffeur driven, motor coach or self-drive. In 1924 Australian tourists were being told by Lamrock Ltd that 'No visitor can afford to miss the beauty spots of the British Isles. To obtain a true appreciation of these famous localities, it is necessary to approach them by road'. Ena Smith offered her services as 'an expert driver who knows the country intimately'. Godfrey Davis promised that the 'pleasures' of a visit to England were 'considerably enhanced' by their 'Modern Cars for Hire': 'you can explore the beauty of old England, with its highways and byways, old ruins, woodland dells and rolling moors'.[50] Wrights welcomed Australians to 'the Home of Our Race. The country and the villages in all their old-world charm are most appreciated when approached by road', and the Indian & Eastern Car Agency (later Overseas Cars Ltd) insisted that 'The best way to enjoy your Holiday and see this country is to get a car'.[51]

The convention that the modern car allowed for a unique entrée into Britain's 'old-world charm' would continue for the rest of the century. In 1953 Jessie Sisson produced a 6000-mile itinerary for the Bank of New South Wales Travel Service, designed especially for Australians and New Zealanders. She explained that 'To motor leisurely through England in the springtime … is indeed to touch the heights. Travel can offer nothing more satisfying'. But she also offered a warning: 'Unfortunately across the face of this fair and lovely land stretches a great belt of industrial and mining country, which is incredibly ugly'.[52] Those tourists staying with relatives may have found themselves in these ugly towns, but the car gave them access to Morton's England.

From the 1950s most guides pointed out the benefits of the self-drive holiday, and assumed it was the dominant Australian mode of tourism. They emphasised the independence it provided, and the merits of, as Bernard Lyman put it, 'meandering on country lanes'.[53] By 1964 Stuart Gore explained that self-drive tourism was so common as to be 'old hat', though he noted, with a corporate plug, that more rarefied forms of car travel were still available: 'It is a rare Avis Australis indeed who wants to be chauffeur-driven!'.[54]

The car provided an entirely different experience of tourism, kinaesthetically. As others have pointed out, the corporeality of the tourist experience has always been more than a 'gaze', and that of the drive-tourist was always more than the 'glance'.[55] The meandering was a physical sensation created by the car, as was the occupants' experience of driving on cobblestones, negotiating roundabouts and ring-roads and motorways (which many Australians met for the first time when driving in England), learning the frustrations of 'queues' in the countryside, and of very narrow streets and impossible parking. Above all the car distinguished the independent traveller from the crowd and from the pre-packaged. Self-drive tourists regard themselves as travellers rather than tourists even as the car's very modernity made them, in Morton's view, a mass scourge on the landscape.[56] Their discoveries could only be those sanctioned by the tourist industry: the 'discovery' of the quaint teashop, the picturesque out-of-the-way village or the B&B with edible bacon and eggs.

Finally, there is the dramatic shift in what tourists brought with them. There was, as Simon Sleight and David Dunstan make clear, a world of difference between the cultural capital of those catered to by the *British-Australasian* in 1901 and of those catered to by *TNT* in 2001 (see Chapters 6 and 14). In 2005 I was privileged to hear, in the Bloomsbury square outside our hotel window just after 4 a.m., a rendition of 'I am, you are, we are Australian': I cannot say if the performers were tourists, or travellers or conference delegates – or even Australians – but clearly they had access to a different culture from their counterparts in 1901. Not that 1901 tourists were incapable of larrikin behaviour, but the cultural wells they drew sustenance from were different.

This shift is only partly related to the democratisation of tourism, from a quite privileged cultural elite to a much broader spectrum of Australian society a century later. There is also the shift away from being 'jolly proud' to be British (as Noel McLachlan put it),[57] from a culture that was British by default, where in the Australian imagination Britain represented the norm and Australia the exception. We can question how far that culture extended outside a polite middle-class setting – in the dance halls and cinemas of the 1920s the empire had arguably already lost out to Americanisation. But certainly what Jim Davidson long ago called 'de-dominionisation' was well underway in the second half of the twentieth century.[58] We can plot the change in tourist guidebooks.

Through the twentieth century an increasing number of guides explicitly targeted Australian tourists. During the Great War, at least two guides for 'colonials' catered to the influx of troops on leave.[59] In the 1920s Australia House itself published a guide to London, regularly updating it. It was unashamedly touristy, promoting the popular illusion over any pedantic search for authenticity. Of the Old Curiosity Shop: 'Though some people affect to doubt the authenticity of the quaint little house ... millions of Londoners and visitors are quite content to regard it as the house of "Little Nell" ... and in any case, all tourists are satisfied to believe that it was so'. The 'affect' is interesting, implying that any anti-tourist doubt about the authenticity was itself an affectation, a spurious snobbery, standing for the ironic genuineness of the tourist position. Apart from giving directions to Australian war graves, there was no attempt to identify anything of particular Australian interest: London's significance lay in its being 'a city which enshrines and epitomises the history of our race ... the heart, the centre, the rallying point of the English-speaking world'.[60] There was a generic interest in – as Mathew Trinca says – London's imperial sights, an understanding of Britain's significance shared throughout the empire. Arthur Mason explained in the Australia House guide that when inevitably the visitor came upon 'this or that memorial of a name, or a place, or an event he has known of all his life', he will be 'reminded of ever memorable things'.[61] This was still the case in 1953, in Jessie Sisson's motoring guide: 'There is no country in the world so completely satisfying to tour as the British Isles', with its good roads, 'enchanting' scenery and 'magnificent' history. 'And, above all', she was able to add, 'it is *ours*. It is our heritage'.[62]

But as the notion of Britain as 'Home' was falling into disuse in the decades after 1945, there was a change in what guides thought worth noticing. Frank Clune's eccentric endpaper map of his 1949 'prowl' around Britain, which showed such sites as Keswick ('Poets and Rain'), Hull ('Bombed by Jerries') and Doncaster ('Puncture here'), also included three places with Australian connections: Donington ('Matthew Flinders born here'), Great Ayton ('Captain Cook's Birthplace') and Middlesborough ('Sydney Harbour Bridge – parts here'). In 1960, the New South Wales Government's London offices published *Australians in the British Isles*, a brochure listing 'memorials and places that may appeal especially to Australians'; most items related to explorers but it also included a plaque where Henry Handel Richardson lived, a notice of Dame Nellie Melba's participation in 'the first pre-announced broadcast public entertainment in the world' and the grave of Yemmerrawanyea, who died in London soon after arriving in England with Phillip in 1793.[63] Here in a small way we begin to see attention being given to places with specifically Australian connections, even if only through the prism of empire. In 1958 Stuart Gore published the punning title *Australians, go home!* with no special interest in Australian sites, but in1964, his *Going to Britain?* had an index entry 'Australian Interest' which listed connections to Cook, Bligh, Macquarie, Billy Hughes, Simpson (of the Donkey), Melba and sheep![64]

By the 1980s such guides were both more common and more insistent that they were presenting Britain to an audience with specifically Australian interests. Among their authors were some names familiar to historians: Philip Derriman, *An Australian's Guide to Britain*; Bernard Lyman (who would later write *Outback house*), *An Australian's Britain and Ireland*; Gillian and Ged Martin, *Waltzing Britannia: A guide to Britain for Australians*; John Laffin, *An Aussie guide to Britain*.[65] Their Australian entries became increasingly elaborate. Lyman, for example, directed readers to the remote farmhouse on Mull said to be haunted by an Aborigine murdered by a 'bushranger', though according to his researches it was unlikely a bushranger was involved.[66]

Increasingly the associations Australians could make with Britain were contracting. If in Clune's lifetime school and other cultural institutions had made Britain intensely familiar, by the end of the century those same media had made it strange.[67] While these later guides extended the range of sights of interest to Australian tourists, they still deferred to the metropolitan valuation of more 'British' sights, which remained what most Australian tourists visited Britain to see. But now they were likely to visit it not as 'ours', but in order to enjoy its foreignness, a familiar foreignness more easily equated with that of France or Italy.

ACKNOWLEDGEMENTS

I want to acknowledge my debt to work-in-progress on two PhDs, Olwen Pryke's on Australia House (since submitted), and Mathew Trinca's on Australian postwar tourism in Britain. Thanks also to Laina Hall, Caroline Ford, Simon Sleight, Emily Pollnitz and Alex Roberts.

ENDNOTES

[1] Buzard, 1993, 18.

[2] Norman Lebrecht suggested most of them were 'out of their depth' Norman Lebrecht, 'Why do so many Aussies run the show?' *Evening Standard* 6 July 2005. Thanks to Stuart Ward for this reference. See also Alomes, 1999.

[3] See chapters by Graeme Davison and Jim Davidson in this volume. Conradson and Latham, 2005.

[4] Urry, 2002, 2–3.

[5] Buzard, 1993, 8; Cohen and Taylor, 1976. 119–121.

[6] MacCannell, 1999, 98–99.

[7] See 'Home' in *Australian National Dictionary*; Bruce Moore kindly gave me access to the dictionary's surplus cards.

[8] Perhaps Ruskin's is the classic statement of the 'separate spheres'. Ruskin. 1865. *Sesame and Lilies*. See also Cott, 1977, 57ff; Davidoff and Hall, 2002, 180–181. Sir Henry Bishop's immensely popular 'Home sweet home' appeared in 1823 (not so long before his wife ran off with the celebrated harpist, Nicolas Bochsa, eventually to settle in Sydney).

[9] C.f. Francis Adams: 'Ten years ago England was spoken of affectionately as the Old country or Home. Now it is "home" or more sarcastically "'ome". The inverted commas make all the difference, and the dropped "h" contains a class contempt'. Adams, 1893, *The Australians: A Social Sketch*, 41.

[10] Fitzpatrick, 1956, 15.

11. Ford, 2000, 56; Eggleston, 1953, 6; cf. W.E.H. Stanner, who claimed that the habit 'seemed to be dying fast' Stanner, 1953, 8.
12. Lindsay Parker. 1954. 'Tourist or traveller'. *Sydney Morning Herald*, 6 November 1954, 7. Cited in Ford, 2000, 55; C.f. Evelyn Waugh's comment that 'The tourist is the other fellow', Waugh 1930, 44; Fussell, 1980, 45–50.
13. Pesman, 1996, 3; Woollacott, 2001, Graeme Davison chapter 14 in this volume.
14. Woollacott, 2001, 49–50.
15. Hanrahan, 1992, *Michael and Me and the Sun*, 34.
16. Randolph, 1914, *Explorations in Civilisation*. Bedford was drawing on *Bulletin* articles from 1901.
17. Holland and Huggan, 2000, viii.
18. Turner, 1911, *Ports and Happy Havens*.
19. Turner, 1911, *Ports and Happy Havens*, 171, 175, 73, 27, 268.
20. Turner, 1911, *Ports and Happy Havens*, 213, 162; Poole, 1979, *The Diaries of Ethel Turner*, 233–239.
21. White, 1986, 47–49.
22. Morton, 1927 [1939], *In Search of England*, 4. The book was based on his series of articles for the *Daily Express*, which followed a series on London.
23. Cited in review on the dust jacket of Morton, 1927 [1939], *In Search of England*. On Morton, see Bartholomew, 2004. Others writing in a similar vein included E.V. Lucas and the contributors to Macmillan's *Highways and Byways* series.
24. Hancock, 1930, 50.
25. Bartholomew, 2004, 24, 30.
26. Phillips, 1958, 94.
27. Undated diary entry [London, October 1937], Hudson Fysh, Diary, MS 2413, Box K21833, Mitchell Library, State Library of New South Wales. Halliday Sutherland was a population propagandist who had already written travel accounts of Scandinavia and would visit Australia in 1941, publishing Sutherland, Halliday, 1942, *Southward Journey*.
28. It was based on his trip in 1947. Clune, 1948, *High-Ho to London: Incidents and Interviews on a Leisurely Journey by Air from Australia to Britain*, vii.
29. Clune, 1949, *Land of Hope and Glory: An Australian Traveller's Impressions of Post-War Britain and Eire*, v–vi.
30. Culler, 1988, 164.
31. Clune. 1935. *Rolling Down the Lachlan*. 1–5; see also White, 1997, 95–96; Dixon, 2001, passim; Tebbutt, 1997, 53–64.
32. Clune, 1949, *Land of Hope and Glory: An Australian Traveller's Impressions of Post-War Britain and Eire*, 15.
33. Trinca, 2006, 8.
34. Clune, 1952, *Castles in Spain: A Flying Trip from Australia to Europe with Some Quixotical Peregrinations in the Iberian Peninsula in Quest of Facts*, 1–2.
35. White, 1986, 44.
36. Woollacott, 2001, 17.
37. Pesman, 1996.
38. White 1987, 63–77.

39 Humphries, 1981, *A Nice Night's Entertainment: Sketches and Monologues 1956–1981*, 44–47.
40 Taylor, 1992, 14–16.
41 *The Australians' Guide Book to London 1929*, 1929, 4, 3. Thanks to Olwen Pryke for information on Australia House.
42 Lyman, 1989, *An Australian's Britain and Ireland*, 61.
43 Woollacott, 2001, 19ff; Hassam, 2000, 4, 30–31.
44 Taylor, 1992, 20–21.
45 Hall, 1995, 12.
46 Hall, 1995, 12.
47 Larsen, 2001, 80–98.
48 Bartholomew, 2004, 92.
49 Morton, 1927 [1939], *In Search of England*, 114, 116.
50 *The Australians' Guide Book to London*, 1924, 17, 25, 41.
51 *The Australians' Guide Book to London*, 1925, 23; *The Australians' Guide Book to London*, 1924, 17, 25, 41; *The Australians' Guide Book to London 1929*, 1929, 49; *The Australians' Official Guide*, 1936, 47.
52 Sisson, 1953, *A Tour By Car Through England, Scotland & Wales*, 9–10.
53 Lyman, 1989. *An Australian's Britain and Ireland*, 22.
54 Gore, 1964, *Going to Britain?* 17–18.
55 Jokinen and Veijole, 1994, 126–127. For a response see Urry, 2002, 145–153.
56 Prideaux and Carson, 2003, 307–314; Yabsley, 2005.
57 Trinca, 2006, 26.
58 Davidson, 1979, Davidson, 2005.
59 Manders, 1917. *The Colonials' Guide to London*. Campbell, 1916, *The Overseas Soldier's Guide to London*. See also Gilbert, 1999, 279–297.
60 *The Australians' Guide Book to London 1929*, 1929, 33, 4, 19–20.
61 *The Australians' Guide Book to London 1929*, 1929, 4.
62 Sisson, 1953, *A Tour By Car Through England, Scotland & Wales*, 1.
63 NSW Government Offices, nd [1960], *Australians in the British Isles*, 1, 5–8.
64 Gore, 1964, *Going to Britain?*
65 Derriman, 1980; Lyman, 1989; Martin, 1989; Laffin, 1995.
66 Lyman, 1989, 175.
67 Clune, 1949, *Land of Hope and Glory: An Australian Traveller's Impressions of Post-War Britain and Eire*, v.

PRIMARY SOURCES

Adams, F.W.L. 1893. *The Australians: A Social Sketch*. London: T. Fisher Unwin.
The Australians' Guide Book to London. 1924. 3rd edn. London: Australia House.
The Australians' Guide Book to London. 1925. London: Australia House.

The Australians' Guide Book to London 1929. Issued under the Authority of the High Commissioner, Australia House, London. 1929. London: Australian Advertising Agency, Australia House.

The Australians' Official Guide. 1936. London: Australia House.

Bedford, Randolph. 1914. *Explorations in Civilisation*. Sydney: S. Day.

Caiger, George, editor. 1953. *The Australian Way of Life*. Melbourne: Heinemann.

Campbell, W.S. 1916. *The Overseas Soldier's Guide to London*. London: R.J. James.

Clune, Frank. 1935. *Rolling Down the Lachlan*. Sydney: Angus & Robertson.

Clune, Frank. 1948. *High-Ho to London: Incidents and Interviews on a Leisurely Journey by Air from Australia to Britain*. Sydney: Angus & Robertson.

Clune, Frank. 1949. *Land of Hope and Glory: An Australian Traveller's Impressions of Post-War Britain and Eire*. Sydney: Angus & Robertson.

Clune, Frank. 1952. *Castles in Spain: A Flying Trip From Australia to Europe With Some Quixotical Peregrinations in the Iberian Peninsula in Quest of Facts*. Sydney: Angus & Robertson.

Derriman, Philip. 1980. *An Australian's Guide to Britain*. St Leonards, New South Wales: Standard Publishing.

Eggleston, Frederic. 1953. 'The Australian Nation'. In *The Australian Way of Life*, edited by Caiger, George. London: Heinemann.

Fysh, Hudson. 1937. Diary, 1937. Sir Hudson Fysh papers, MS 2413, Box K21833, Mitchell Library: State Library of New South Wales.

Gore, Stuart. 1958. *Australians, Go Home!* London: Robert Hale.

Gore, Stuart. 1964. *Going to Britain?* Brisbane: Jacaranda Travel Guides.

Hancock, W.K. 1930. *Australia*. London: Ernest Benn.

Hanrahan, Barbara. 1992. *Michael and Me and the Sun*. St Lucia: University of Queensland Press.

Humphries, Barry. 1981. *A Nice Night's Entertainment: Sketches and Monologues 1956–1981*. Sydney: Currency Press.

Laffin, John. 1995. *An Aussie Guide to Britain*. Kenthurst, New South Wales: Kangaroo Press.

Lyman, Bernard. 1989. *An Australian's Britain and Ireland*. Sydney: Philip Campbell Publishing.

Manders, A. Staines. 1917. *The Colonials' Guide to London*. London: Fulton-Manders Publishing Co.

Martin, Gillian and Ged. 1989. *Waltzing Britannia: A Guide to Britain for Australians*. Sydney: Hale & Iremonger.

Morton, H.V. 1927 [1939]. *In Search of England*. London: Methuen.

NSW Government Offices. n.d. [1960]. *Australians in the British Isles*. London: New South Wales Government Offices.

Phillips, A.A. 1958. *The Australian Tradition*. Melbourne: Cheshire.

Poole, Philippa, editor. 1979. *The Diaries of Ethel Turner*. Sydney: Collins.

Ruskin, John. 1865. *Sesame and Lilies*. London: Smith, Elder & Co.

Sisson, Jessie. 1953. *A Tour By Car Through England, Scotland & Wales*. Sydney: Bank of New South Wales.

Stanner, W.E.H. 1953. 'The Australian way of life'. In *Taking Stock: Aspects of Mid-Century Life in Australia*, edited by Aughterson, W. V. Melbourne: Cheshire.

Sutherland, Halliday. 1942. *Southward Journey*. Melbourne: J. Jaboor.
Turner, Ethel. 1911. *Ports and Happy Havens*. London: Hodder and Stoughton.
Waugh, Evelyn. 1930. *Labels: A Mediterranean Journal*. London: Duckworth.

REFERENCES

Alomes, Stephen. 1999. *When London Calls: The Expatriation of Australian Creative Artists to Britain*. Melbourne: Cambridge University Press.
Bartholomew, Michael. 2004. *In Search of H. V. Morton*. London: Methuen.
Buzard, James. 1993. *The Beaten Track: European Tourism, Literature and the Ways to Culture, 1800–1918*. Oxford: Clarendon Press.
Cohen, Stanley; Taylor, Laurie. 1976. *Escape Attempts: The Theory and Practice of Resistance to Everyday Life*. London: Allen Lane.
Conradson, David; Latham, Alan. 2005. Professionals and backpackers in a global city. Unpublished paper.
Cott, Nancy. 1977. *The Bonds of Womanhood: 'Women's Sphere' in New England 1780–1835*. New Haven: Yale University Press.
Culler, Jonathan. 1988. *Framing the Sign: Criticism and its Institutions*. Oxford: Blackwell.
Davidoff, Leonore; Hall, Catherine. 2002. *Family Fortunes: Men and Women of the English Middle Class 1780–1850*. Revised edn. London: Routledge.
Davidson, Jim. 1979. 'The de-dominionisation of Australia'. *Meanjin*. 38 (2): 139–153.
Davidson, Jim. 2005. 'De-Dominionisation revisited'. *Australian Journal of Politics & history*. 51 (1): 108–113.
Dixon, Robert. 2001. *Prosthetic Gods: Travel, Representation and Colonial Governance*. St Lucia Qld: University of Queensland Press.
Fitzpatrick, Brian. 1956. *The Australian Commonwealth: A Picture of the Community 1901–55*. Melbourne: Cheshire.
Ford, Caroline. 2000. 'Antipodean exodus: Young Australians in London 1949–1980'. History IV thesis. Sydney: University of Sydney.
Fussell, Paul. 1980. *Abroad: British Literary Travelling Between the Wars*. New York: Oxford University Press.
Gilbert, David. 1999. '"London in all its Glory – or how to enjoy London": Guidebook representations of imperial London'. *Journal of Historical Geography* 25 (3): 279–297.
Hall, Colin Michael. 1995. *Introduction to Tourism in Australia: Impacts, Planning and Development*. 2nd edn. Melbourne: Longman Australia.
Hassam, Andrew. 2000. *Through Australian Eyes: Colonial Perceptions of Imperial Britain*. Carlton, Vic.: Melbourne University Press.
Holland, Patrick; Huggan, Graham. 2000. *Tourists With Typewriters: Critical Reflections on Contemporary Travel Writing*. Ann Arbor: University of Michigan Press.
Jokinen, Eeva; Veijole, Soile. 1994. 'The body in tourism'. *Theory Culture & Society* 11(3): 125-151
Lebrecht, Norman. 2005. 'Why do so many Aussies run the show?' *Evening Standard* (6 July).
Larsen, Jonas. 2001. 'Tourism mobilities and the travel glance: The experience of being on the move'. *Scandinavian Journal of Hospitality and Tourism* 1 (2): 80–98.
MacCannell, Dean. 1999. *The Tourist: A New Theory of the Leisure Class*. Berkeley: University of California Press.
Pesman, Ros. 1996. *Duty Free: Australian Women Abroad*. Melbourne: Oxford University Press.
Prideaux, B; Carson, D. 2003. 'A framework for an increasing understanding of self-drive tourism markets'. *Journal of Vacation Marketing* 9 (4): 307–313.
Tebbutt, John. 1997. 'Frank Clune: Modernity and popular national history'. *Australian Journal of Communication* 24(3): 53–64.

Taylor, Andrew. 1992. 'From sea to air: The impact of jet travel on Australia's "Australia"'. In *The Making of a Pluralist Australia 1950–1990: Selected Papers from the Inaugural EASA Conference, 1991*, edited by Senn, Werner; Capone, Giovanna. Bern: Peter Lang.

Trinca, Mathew. 2006. 'Reading the war in London'. Unpublished paper.

Urry, John. 2002. *The Tourist Gaze: Leisure and Travel in Contemporary Societies*, London: Sage.

White, Richard. 1986. 'Bluebells and fogtown: Australians' first impressions of England 1860–1940'. *Australian Cultural History* 5: 44–59.

White, Richard. 1987. 'The soldier as tourist: The Australian experience of the Great War'. *War & Society* 5 (1): 63–77

White, Richard. 1997. 'The retreat from adventure: Popular travel writing in the 1950s'. *Australian Historical Studies* 28 (109): 90–105.

Woollacott, Angela. 2001. *To Try Her Fortune in London: Australian Women, Colonialism, and Modernity*. New York: Oxford University Press.

Yabsley, Louise. 2005. 'I Still Call a Trailer Home: A History of Grey Nomads'. History IV thesis. Sydney: University of Sydney.

Cite this chapter as: White, Richard. 2009. 'Australian tourists in Britain, 1900–2000'. *Australians in Britain: The Twentieth-Century Experience*, edited by Bridge, Carl; Crawford, Robert; Dunstan, David. Melbourne: Monash University ePress. pp. 11.1 to 11.15. DOI: 10.2104/ab090011.

CHAPTER 12

PART OF THE PAGEANT
AUSTRALIAN TOURISTS IN POSTWAR LONDON

Mathew Trinca, National Museum of Australia
Mathew Trinca is the General Manager of Collections and Content at the National Museum of Australia, Canberra. Formerly a history curator at the Western Australian Museum, he has research interests in Australian cultural history and museology.

Australian travellers to London after the Second World War were fascinated by the bombed ruins and other traces of the city's wartime experiences. In their travel accounts, these visitors tended to extol the grit and resolve of Londoners during the Blitz and abstracted this to a broader conception of British virtue. The city became an emblem for all that they considered 'great' about Britain. This paper examines Australians' tourist impressions of postwar London and their views of two key celebrations – the Festival of Britain in 1951 and the coronation of Queen Elizabeth II in 1953.

The restoration of international travel and communications services with the rest of the world was a priority for the British Government after the Second World War. This sprang in part from the palpable need to re-assert Britain's traditional role as a centre of world trade. In particular, it was thought desirable that passenger services be resumed as quickly as possible to allow for the recovery of the foreign-currency-earning tourist industry. However, the speedy resumption of civilian services was also driven by a desire to recover the comforting forms and conventions of peacetime.

In the late 1940s, Australian tourists to Britain constructed a series of largely congratulatory narratives of a London unbowed by the war years. Their accounts focused on the survival of the city's landmarks, such as St Paul's, and the stoicism of its people. Yet there were tensions between these celebratory narratives and the visible evidence of hardships experienced by Londoners. The jagged, apocalyptic ruins of the East End did not lend themselves to easy or simplistic idealisations of the city and its people. Visitors from Australia, which had been largely insulated from the trials of total war, sometimes found the realities of postwar life in London different from the imagined victory. They were shocked by the destruction wrought by German bombs, by the interminable queues for basic foods and goods, and by the apparent dullness of Londoners' lives in the postwar austerity years that gripped the capital. Some were unconvinced that victory had been worth the cost. Bomb-battered residential quarters and careworn inhabitants signified the city's vulnerability and decline, as much as any ideal of British indefatigability and collective courage.

THE AFTERMATH OF WAR

Arriving in February 1946, the United Netherlands Navigation Company's *Oranjefontein* was the first all-civilian passenger ship to arrive at Southhampton from Australia after the war. Aboard were just 150 adventurous passengers.[1] Despite the easing of travel restrictions, there were still significant shortages of berths for several years. The Melbourne *Argus* warned prospective tourists that competition for passages to Britain would remain high throughout the year and into 1947.[2] Its predictions proved accurate, with 6,702 temporary journeys (regarded at that time as a journey of under a year's duration) from Australia to any destination overseas in 1946. This contrasted starkly with the interwar traffic, which hit a high point of 24,459 temporary departures in 1929.[3] The Travel Association of the United Kingdom, intent on re-priming the tourist trade, noted that the number of visitors to Britain from all Commonwealth countries in 1947 was still limited by the continuing lack of berths.[4] Currency restrictions and difficulties with food supplies also militated against a more pronounced rise in tourist traffic.[5] The high cost of fares dissuaded others.[6]

Notwithstanding a jump in costs, the frequency of services improved as the exigencies of the war years receded. Shipping companies sought to recommission vessels for civilian traffic as soon as they were returned by the military. Australia's postwar immigration drive added more vessels to the route. The liner *Orontes* – a troop transport during the war – returned to the Australia-Britain run in 1948, while newer, larger and faster vessels, such as the *Orcades*, were now being commissioned.[7] By mid-1949, more than 20 per cent of the total tonnage of passenger ships on the United Kingdom register had been committed to meeting the demand for berths to and from Australia, compared to about 13 per cent the previous year. While this increase was primarily driven by the need for Australian-bound migrant transports, it also ensured that there was a steadily increasing supply of berths for Australian travellers to Britain.[8]

By early 1950, all ships leaving Australia for British ports were heavily booked. Much of this travel boom was enabled by the rising levels of affluence, and was in keeping with the broader expansion in international travel and tourism. The postwar years were marked by the development of travel as a global leisure industry, within the broader thrust of a new consumerism that came to dominate life in affluent nations. Tourism became, as Gareth Shaw and Alan Williams argue, 'part of the major shift which occurred in consumption and in expectations regarding consumption'.[9]

Accounts of Australians who travelled to Britain focused on London's physical survival and the stoicism of its people. At the same time, at home and in the metropolitan centre of London there were Australian avowals of a secure sense of the British family of nations. London, the Imperial/Commonwealth capital, remained a key symbolic location in these narratives. Yet there were tensions between these celebratory narratives of the city and the hardships experienced by ordinary Londoners. Some texts included both these themes, but left the implicit conflicts unresolved. But there were others in which the contesting themes were reconciled by arguments for a broader conception of Britishness that drew from the periphery as much as the centre.

It was almost inconceivable that Australian visitors to Britain would not spend at least part of their time in London. A survey in 1958 found that 93 per cent of all Australians stayed for some time in the capital, and that the average duration of their stay was 81 nights.[10] For these visitors, like those before the war, London landmarks became basic elements in their tourist impressions of the country. At home they had been concerned, via press and radio reports, at the prospect of the destruction of the city's buildings and streets, as familiar to them as to any provincial Briton. An example was Qantas chief Hudson Fysh's broadcast to Australia from London via the BBC. Speaking in 1943, Fysh pointedly emphasised his expectation that listeners would have a 'natural' desire to see the city. He linked the capital's traditional attraction to Australians and the courage of Londoners at war:

> I am speaking to you from London, the London you knew and long to revisit,
> or the place you hope to see as a life's ambition – London, capital of Great

> Britain, the home of our grandfathers and grandmothers. It's bomb-scarred today, and as I wander through London's streets and watch the people's faces it is hard to imagine that these are the staunch front liners who took the shock of that great air blitz on Britain.[11]

Fysh's broadcast invoked a familial regard for the city, drawing on its established meaning as a spiritual and material home for Australians. But there was the added gravitas of the perilous moment, the threat of destruction, to heighten the emotional content of his words.

As a result of this and other reports like it, war became a presence in Australian imaginings of the city, with some enduring effects. Many tourists disembarking at Tilbury or Heathrow were intent on plotting their own maps of the city's wartime survival. In his early postwar account of Britain, *Land of Hope and Glory*, travel writer Frank Clune used the signs of war damage to confirm his arrival in London. From Heathrow, Clune drove into the West End, where he 'glimpsed many a crater-lake fringed with rubble detritus. So yes, I really am in London, said I'.[12] He rendered his view of war damage as accidental, implying that the destruction was on such a scale as to have been unavoidable – and so accenting the sense that bomb ruins were a key or defining element of the cityscape. Yet radio broadcaster Norman Banks, in London seven years after the war, did not leave his view of the destruction to chance; he actively sought out craters now overgrown with weeds and regarded them as a tourist sight. Banks was a self-confessed Anglophile, writing in *The World in My Diary* that he 'loved England and everything about it'. He admitted to searching with a friend for the 'badly bombed areas' of the East End and the pair did indeed find a razed half-mile stretch of land in the docklands area where 'not even a tall wall' was left standing. A shocked Banks wrote that the destruction was 'horrible to see'. But there was a clear implication that he was reassured at having seen it for himself. London's bomb damage had become an exotic element that confirmed the alterity of the location, and it carried the air of authenticity craved by tourists.[13]

Such interest in witnessing the legacy of war in London was not unexpected, nor was it singular. Some of the framers of Britain's postwar tourism policy correctly envisaged that tourists would be attracted – however morbid it might seem – by the prospect of seeing the damage firsthand. A 1944 report prepared for the Travel and Industrial Development Association of Great Britain and Ireland predicted a postwar tourism boom driven, in part at least, by this impulse.[14] People were 'hungry for travel after the isolation of the war years' and the prospect of seeing the effects of war would attract them to London, a subsequent report suggested.[15] With this in mind, tourist pamphlets and travel guides, which associated traditional images of London with valorisations of its people's doughty efforts during the hostilities, were produced in the late 1940s. The popular guide *Here's England*, published in 1951, described London as 'triumphant and lovely'. Its American authors clearly admired the city that had 'stood against the enemy, unbowed, unconquered and unafraid'.[16]

Would-be tourists were encouraged to gaze at the canyons cut through London by Axis bombs and connect these images with a broader celebration of the city's indefatigability and ultimate victory. Aside from iconographic force, this celebratory discourse helped distract attention from the very real shortcomings in service that visitors were likely to experience and that British authorities were eager to conceal.[17] The officially produced 80-page booklet *London, Past and Present* asked rhetorically:

> What, one wonders, would Queen Elizabeth, who sought to hold this giant in bonds, what would she think of the London of to-day? Perhaps, through the roar of London's teeming traffic and beneath the crumbled stones of London's war-time ruins, she would hear the firm beating of Britain's indomitable and unconquerable heart; perhaps in the London of to-day she would sense a spirit akin to her own, one that much experience has taught how to find the path to greatness through the troubled ways of adversity, how to face the future with confidence and calm.[18]

Facing this text was one of the most famous images of the war years – the cupola of St Paul's Cathedral soaring above the haze of smoke during the Blitz. This photograph, reproduced in newspapers around the world, including Australia, had become a symbol of the resilience and heart displayed by the British people. The text explicitly associated the nation's past glory, and one of its most iron-willed rulers, with the courage displayed by Londoners in the war years. It subverted the jarring effects on tourists of seeing destroyed buildings, by integrating these otherwise disturbing sights within a continuity of national greatness. And it urged visitors to see London as the heart of Britain and, by extension, of the empire.

Some visitors, like feminist and social activist Bessie Rischbieth, were impressed by the hopeful mood of postwar reconstruction in London, notwithstanding the material difficulties. Rischbieth had been in London during the Blitz and had broadcast on the BBC World Service extolling the British resolve. After the war, she returned as an observer to the first UN General Assembly in 1946. On this journey she applauded the policy changes that were remoulding Britain, and was buoyed by a faith in the city's future. In a notebook she used for speeches to Australian audiences after the trip, she reflected:

> I remained in London all through the blitz and in that time saw the Old Country pass through the greatest war in her history, and since hostillities [sic] ceased, a fundamental social revolution has taken place. But because of its evolutionary character, as a leading statesmen put it, *the people are hardly aware of* its deep seated nature.[19]

Rischbieth understood that the current conditions were less than comfortable for Londoners. Yet she failed to realise that many people were busy dealing with these daily imperatives and had little time to consider reconstruction plans or the breadth of the social change. To her, the accent on social planning and reform was inspirational. London promised so much, and not just for Britain. Rischbieth believed that what was taking place there would re-shape life beyond the seas as well. Much as it had always done, the city would provide the model for material and social change in the dominions, such as Australia and New Zealand. In this sense, the social activist Rischbieth was conventionally imperial:

> I feel strongly that there is a *much* closer bond between the Old Country and the Dominions as a result of the war. In fact I have seen this grow and if we want to preserve the British way of life this *bond* must be strengthened.[20]

Rischbieth linked her admiration for postwar change in London to the value of the Imperial/Commonwealth links between Australia and Britain. In her reading, this mood of reconstruction was a force that could lead to renewal of the broader imperial order. This was a vision of the city that was fundamentally restorative, particularly in terms of its meaning for Australians. For Rischbieth, the signs of postwar reconstruction in part substantiated her claim for a renovation of imperial loyalties.

The educationist Harold Wyndham, who became Director General of Education in New South Wales, was also struck by the possibilities of the postwar years. But his view was more qualified than Rischbieth's, and less optimistic. Wyndham had been dispatched to London to act as head of the Australian delegation to the new UNESCO in 1945. On his return to Australia, he recounted his travel experiences for a student journal at the Sydney Teachers' College. Wyndham made the customary, perhaps almost obligatory, associations between postwar London and Britain's inherent spirit and popular strength. Big Ben still 'welcomed visitors', and was 'the first of many reminders that there is much in England which is unchanged'. But then he noted, to a far greater degree than did Rischbieth, the character of the personal hardships felt by Londoners in the austerity years. Most men and women in the city looked, he wrote, 'threadbare and down at heel'. Even more disturbing was that '[p]ersonal life has assumed a dourness the effects of which are to be seen, in moments of exasperation, in outbursts of ill-temper and in a readiness to complain'.[21]

According to Wyndham, the city had undergone irrevocable change, and this meant that the old 'institutions and customs' would never be the same. But he guardedly welcomed the move to social planning and the new accent on education. London may have lost its former stature, yet Wyndham was hopeful that this destabilisation could have social benefits in the long term. His touristic view of the city was restrained and avoided the temptations of imperial triumphalism. Looking beyond the rhetoric of empire and victory in war, he reflected more deeply upon the city's fabric and circumstances. In Wyndham's account, London was portrayed as being in a liminal, changing state and its status as a symbol of imperial ascendancy was heavily proscribed.

The most striking problem for Londoners was the shortage of food. Rationing of foodstuffs continued to be severe long after the war's end and was only finally abolished in 1954. Such was the publicity surrounding Britain's plight that most Australian visitors were well prepared to 'discover' the shortage well before they left home. In 1948, two Country Women's Association members from Victoria travelled to London with the express intention of learning what it was like to live on these rations – no doubt to the disbelief of many of the city's permanent inhabitants.[22] Six years after the war's end, Kathleen Roberts, of Adelaide, could only describe the food as 'dreadful' when questioned by a magazine reporter.[23] Added to this were reports of Britain's embattled economic position, particularly during the currency crisis of 1949, which saw the pound devalue, and difficulties with supplies of energy, especially coal and petroleum.

Images of relative want in a dowdy, down-at-heel London provoked alternate readings that had little in common with celebratory narratives of the victorious city. They challenged the 'authorised' themes of imperial greatness and national ascendancy that surrounded key tourist sights.

Tourists approached life on the streets, and those iconic memorials and grand buildings connoted with imperialism, in very different ways. Alex Horne bluntly argued that the scarcity of food and clothing was a sign of decline:

> Although England won the war, her people have never been worse off for the bare necessities of life. They are being deprived of food to feed their late enemies, the Germans. The ration scale is about a third less than it was throughout the whole period of the war. In all the countries of the world I have visited since I left Australia, three months ago, England's food position is far and away the worst.[24]

Instead of attesting to the quality of British courage and valour, Horne found that Londoners were feeling that they had 'paid a staggering price for "winning the war"'.[25] Other visitors went further and questioned who had really won. John Barter, director of Wonderheat, from Melbourne, wrote, 'I am beginning to wonder if the patient forbearance of the English is a virtue or not. In Italy, a former enemy country, food is more plentiful and there is a greater variety of it even than in Australia'.[26] No wonder, as Harry Hopkins has pointed out, that the Dominions' immigration offices had little trouble finding potential migrants. In 1949, a Gallup poll showed that 42 per cent of London's population would emigrate if they could.[27]

Passages of Clune's *Land of Hope and Glory* reveal a similar cynicism amid the guide-book hyperbole. To be sure, Clune infused the book with the requisite elements of admiration for Londoners' phlegmatic wartime endurance. But there are also pointed statements striking at the myth of London as the triumphant centre, inspired by his own idiosyncratic view and the radical nationalism of his collaborator, P.R. Stephensen. London may have been the home of 'fairy-tales', but it was also in the hands of the 'money-changers' – the entire country suffering from a 'postwar anaemia'. He added that 'London seemed lousy with racketeering – (all quite legalized, no doubt) – and with "black-marketeering", the natural result of too many controls'.[28] Wyndham too might have hoped for better, but he also realised that despite the new 'social awareness', the 'blackmarket flourishes in the West End'.[29] Even the *Australian Women's Weekly* weighed in, telling its readers that a 'vast black market' was operated by Petticoat Lane traders.[30] The notion that London, the symbol of imperial rectitude and ascendancy, was actually riven by opportunistic racketeering made it difficult to idealise the city. After all, black-market trade hardly conformed to middle-class views of moral propriety and heroic nationalism.

POSTWAR RENEWAL

Despite the well of symbolism for London's resilience, spirit and courage, there was something sadly plaintive about the 'Britain Can Make It' exhibition in 1946. It was a well-patronised affair, with crowds of people crowded four to eight deep outside the Victoria and Albert Museum, and a queue stretching hundreds of yards along the road.[31] Intended as a demonstration of Britain's manufacturing capacity in peacetime, it also argued the nation's ability to survive and recover from the nadir of war. Yet this broader statement of national survival carried the implicit doubt that the country might not 'make it', despite the best intentions. The longed-for victory had delivered scant rewards. Food was still rationed, as were clothes and many other goods; currency problems weakened the once proud pound; and London was again plunged into darkness, though this time it was an energy crisis, not the German bombers responsible for the blackout.[32]

Towards the end of the 1940s, the quest for national renewal became bound to a more expansive exhibition program, one deliberately conceived as a postwar 'pick-me-up'. The Festival of Britain on the Thames's marshy South Bank was to be a physical demonstration of the nation's postwar recovery, while marking the centenary anniversary of the 1851 Great Exhibition. But whereas the Great Exhibition had been marked by high Victorian faith in Britain's imperial purview, the Festival of Britain was conceived as a popular celebration with an altogether more domestic ambition.[33] An official guide pronounced it an '[o]ccasion for a national spring-cleaning, for repointing and repainting the Town Hall, gilding the church clock, for planting window boxes, flower baskets and temporary gardens, for painting the street lamps, decorating the streets and floodlit buildings'.[34] The festival's Director General, Gerald Barry, described it as a 'tonic for the nation' filled with 'fun, fantasy and colour'. In temper, the festival consciously eschewed national boastfulness and hyperbole, in keeping with Britain's postwar retreat from empire. This was to be a people's festival, for the People's Peace.[35]

Despite conservative denouncements of its waste and irrelevance, the festival proved a popular success. More than eight million visitors went to the South Bank between May and September – and more again visited the segments that toured major British centres and seaports.[36] The British Travel and Holidays Association set up a register of 5,500 householders willing to offer 12,000 beds at bed-and-breakfast rates to the throng.[37] In June, the *Australia and New Zealand Weekly* reported that about 25,000 Australians were in England and that all shipping berths were booked out until September. By year's end, Australian departures to Britain had reached 24,074, up 15 per cent on the previous year.[38]

Australian tourists were delighted by the city's bright face: 'London is looking really lovely and festive', wrote one correspondent: 'Flags and bunting, flowers and decorations are everywhere'.[39] The city was throwing off the shackles of the dour austerity years, they thought. There were those, like Edward Trainor of Melbourne, who claimed to be in London expressly for the festival. 'Australians were very Empire minded', said Trainor, conjoining the festival to empire attachment.[40] The writer Charmian Clift was bewitched by the sheer exuberance of Australian talent in the capital for the festival year, as she remembered that 1951 also marked the 50th birthday of the Australian Commonwealth. Clift recalled the Australian designer Gordon Andrews working on Hugh Casson's architectural and design team for the festival – describing it airily as the 'futuristic complex over on the South Bank'.[41]

Casson's team had used the festival as an opportunity to introduce modernism to the British public. In design and planning, the Festival's impact would be felt in Britain for many years, though most of the buildings – save for the Royal Festival Hall – were demolished soon after.[42] The *Sydney Morning Herald's* London reporter expressed misgivings, feeling that it was 'too highbrow', with too much 'arty-craftiness'.[43] The design of the hall surprised Australian visitors accustomed to received images of London's imperial monuments and tradition. Under the headline 'An Aussie Looks at the Festival', a correspondent to the *Australia and New Zealand Weekly* wrote, 'I found myself feeling surprised at the modernity of it all! I suppose one gets used to thinking of England's "show places" as bearing the marks of antiquity, and to suddenly enter, as it were, a new world, rather took my breath away'. But when the royal party arrived, the symbolism of the moment fell into place: 'Then suddenly the empty boxes were filled with a sparkling, glittering array of Royalty. It seemed that the whole side of the auditorium had been transformed into a storybook scene'.[44]

For these Australian visitors, the festival represented an equivocal success. It looked to a new future – marked by the hovering aluminium 'exclamation mark' of the Skylon, a vertical structure supported above ground by cables – rather than to the glorious past with which many tourists sought to connect themselves. While acknowledging the festival's achievements, there was little opportunity for Australians to relate emotionally to an event that so determinedly located British experience within the British Isles. The Festival of Britain's vision of British identity was restrained and modest compared to that of the Great Exhibition a century before.

It was easier for Australian travellers to locate London's postwar renewal in the coronation celebrations held two years later. Here was the city performing its past as empire capital, while the nation celebrated the accession of its young queen and a new 'Elizabethan age'. The celebrations symbolically restored London's imperial salience, with an exotic pageant drawing talent from the 'old Empire', now becoming the new 'Commonwealth'. It was heavy with appeal to tradition, which Australians recognised from the well-established lexicon of the city's traditional meaning and significance. Hamish Mathams's book *Crowns over England* opened with this description of the 1937 coronation of George VI:

> From the frozen wastes of Hudson Bay, from the blistering plains of Africa; from the wildest outposts of the Rocky Mountains, from the tangled swamps of Indian jungle, from the farthest corners of the earth, without regard to creed or caste or colour, the children of the British Empire are coming to see their king.[45]

Australians, though absent from this catalogue of British dependencies, heard its call. On George's death in 1952, interest in Elizabeth's coronation immediately grew.[46] Australians had been promised a royal tour by their king in 1949, but illness prevented it. Now, an opportunity to see the crowning of the new queen stirred the interest of would-be visitors. Alive to the moment, the Menzies Government undertook intricate negotiations with Britain over Australia's representation at the celebrations, securing its place in the official proceedings and a seat allocation for its citizens.[47] Duly, the aircraft carrier *Sydney* was dispatched to the Coronation Spithead Review of 220 ships.[48] A week before Coronation Day, Australian soldiers mounted guard at Buckingham Palace, the first in a series of duties undertaken by troops from Commonwealth countries.[49] A delegation of key figures in the Australian Government and Opposition was among the official guests.

Australian visitors faced stiff competition for seats on the processional route from Buckingham Palace to Westminster Abbey. The government was given a quota of 200 guests for the coronation ceremony in the abbey, and 7,000 seats on the route, later increased by another 1,200. The seats were secured by ballot, and then sold at official rates of between £3 10s and £5 10s.[50] By October 1952 the Melbourne *Herald* reported that 27,000 applications for seats had already been received at Australia House. Americans, the *Herald* further claimed, were willing to pay up to £100 for a spot.[51] Unsurprisingly, there was a flourishing trade in blackmarket tickets.

Among those lucky enough to snare tickets was 22-year-old Anne King. Not even the rain that fell sporadically through the day could diminish her excitement. King swelled with pride at the Australian presence on a shared British stage. In a letter home, she wrote:

> It really was the most magnificent procession you could possibly imagine … I've never felt the wonderful feeling – don't know what it was sort of excited, patriotic in excess awe and oh everything! When the Diggers marched by we nearly wept and Bob Menzies – Gee how we cheered and clapped him and he was nearly falling out of his coach with excitement when he saw all the Aussies screaming 'coo-ee-e' to him.

King's response exemplified an ability to move seamlessly between pride in Australianness and enduring loyalty to Britain, inspired in this case by royal pageant. As the procession moved past, she caught sight first of Churchill and then of the new queen:

> Winston was wonderful – imagine *seeing* him the old darling. Then right down the road we saw the great Golden Coach – very high almost seemed to be touching the trees and just swaying a bit – it looked like fairyland. I've never known anything like it and don't ever expect to again … Look I just can't tell you how I felt but I do know I'll be saying 'God Save the Queen' and realizing now just how very much I mean it.[52]

For Alice Nettleton, too, the long wait made the occasion all the more dreamlike, especially after waking at 3.30 a.m. to be there in time. She was entranced by the exotica of the Commonwealth dignitaries, who included the Queen of Tonga in an open buggy. But when the gold coach came into view, 'we could see the Queen and the Duke of Edinburgh so well. Drawn by marvellous grey horses, all exactly matching, it was indeed as though a fair-tale had come true'.[53]

If the Festival of Britain was a moment of national renewal, largely transacted at a domestic level for the people of the British Isles, the coronation reaffirmed London's capacity to represent a broader British ideal. In this sense, Australian tourists regarded the coronation as a moment when the capital shrugged off the war years, in a way quite unlike that of the festival two years earlier. Australia's first female member of federal parliament, Dame Enid Lyons, likened Coronation England to 'the Phoenix rising from the ashes of destruction'.[54] Mrs F.O. Jackman, of Adelaide, said that she felt 'Londoners wanted something like the Coronation to raise their spirits; it has had a remarkable effect'.[55]

These rhetorical flourishes made a conscious connection between London and the monarchical pageant and performance at the heart of empire. By describing the city's postwar recovery at this moment, visitors such as Lyons and Jackman revealed its enduring meaning as an imperial home and wellspring of a shared British identity. The new queen was the 'glue' that would bind the Commonwealth, in this Menzian vision, inspiring allegiance among its varied members.[56] Sitting in the transept of the abbey during the coronation, writer Gwen Meredith felt a wave of emotion for this Commonwealth ideal:

> Here we were all joined together, welded, as it were, by the strength of our mutual feelings, and I felt quite certain that those feelings were not limited to

those in the Abbey ... I thought that all over the Commonwealth, the Queen's people were held together in a moment of silence and strong emotional unity.[57]

Elizabeth's coronation encouraged a recommittal to the idea of a shared heritage and common tradition for Meredith, without displacing her sense of Australianness. These dual loyalties underpinned the popular reaction to the royal tour of Australia the following year. The couple's travels across Australia, Peter Spearritt has argued, excited a 'strange mixture of obeisance to the throne and nationalistic fervour'.[58]

CONCLUSION

Reflecting on London and its recent history allowed postwar visitors to connect the city to established discourses of empire. As a result, and despite the irony that Britain was then moving to dismantle much of its architecture of empire, London was re-centred in an imperial frame defined by its strategic capability in war and the ultimate Allied victory. The associated symbols of fortitude, resilience and victory that recurred in these travel accounts also reiterated an idealised vision of the British national character. These two readings – of London as the heart of empire *and* as the pre-eminent symbol of Britishness – were both essentially triumphal. The tropes had a shared semiology and their narration was often entwined. As Australians reflected upon London's wartime valour they often accented the notion of a shared British nationality, rather than a subordinate position in an imperial world order. Australian travellers looked on the doughty inhabitants of the metropolis scarred by bombs and claimed, as Noel McLachlan has noted, that they were 'jolly proud' to be British.[59] This was, after all, an era in which the assertion of Britishness was broadly expressed in Australia. A 1947 Gallup opinion poll found that 65 per cent of Australians wanted to retain British citizenship, compared to 28 per cent who wished to affirm a separate and wholly distinct Australian nationality.[60]

Australian visitors saw both the festival and the coronation as emblematic moments of London's renewal. But their responses to these events revealed contrasting impressions of the city's recovery. The Festival of Britain, a child of Britain's technocrats, envisaged the city as a modern capital and expressed this sense through modernist architecture and design. The festival also represented a more inward-looking, circumscribed national frame, in keeping with a refiguring of Britain's political stature and declining influence beyond its borders. Australian travellers to Britain in the nineteenth century had often remarked on London's character as a modern metropolis; but they were as often critical of its perceived 'new fangledness', as Andrew Hassam has noted.[61] In a sense, the modernist promise of the festival was more fully realised in the next decade, and impressed upon the minds of a new generation of Australians who flocked to the Swinging London of Carnaby Street, drug happenings and the Beatles.

The coronation exerted a broader claim, invoking a store of feeling for the Royal family across the Empire/Commonwealth. In itself, this kind of royal pageant was an essentially modern creation that had been forged by imperial necessity in the nineteenth century. But the cunning of such 'invented tradition' is that it dissembles as organic custom, as Eric Hobsbawm and Terence Ranger have shown.[62] Elizabeth's coronation reprised a glorious past, invoking a sense of the capital as an enduring imperial centre that drew provincial supplicants, among them Australians, to itself. The celebration was a performance of pan-British identity to which many Australians could respond and in which they could see themselves. It was in some senses a more palatable image of London's renewal of prestige and purpose after the constraints of war and the austerity years.

ENDNOTES

1. *British Australian, New Zealand and Pacific Weekly*, 16 February 1946, 9.
2. *Argus*, Weekend Magazine, 23 March 1946, 12.
3. These figures are for 'temporary' departures (i.e. for trips of less than one year's duration) by Australian residents for all overseas destinations. 'Table No.23-Migration: Classification of Persons who Arrived or Departed, Australia', Commonwealth Bureau of Census and Statistics, npd., *Demography 1946, Bulletin No.64*, 27; 'Table No.14m.-Migration-Age of Persons who Arrived in or Departed from Australia-Year 1929', Commonwealth Bureau of Census and Statistics, *Australian Demography, Bulletin No.47: Survey of Australian Population and Vital Statistics 1933 and Previous Years*, npd., 21.
4. Travel Association of the United Kingdom of Great Britain and Northern Ireland, Tourist Division of the British Tourist and Holidays Board, *Twentieth Annual Report*, 1948, 2.
5. 'Australian tourists are waiting to travel', *British Australasian*, 8 February 1947, 5.
6. 'Australian tourists are waiting to travel', *British Australasian*, 8 February 1947, 5. Before the war, a return trip from Australia to Britain cost about A£100. Yet in 1946, shipping companies offered limited berths at more than A£130 one way.
7. In January 1949 the *Orcades* berthed at Fremantle after a voyage of 22 days, 1 hour and 50 minutes, and at Melbourne after 26 days, both records. 'Impressive new Orcades', *Australia and New Zealand Weekly*, 17 December 1948, ii.
8. In 1946, Australia accounted for 14 per cent of British passenger ship tonnage, in 1947 12 per cent, in 1948 13 per cent and in 1950 20.5 per cent. *Australia and New Zealand Weekly*, 22 July 1949, 8.
9. Shaw and Williams, 1994, 8. See also Olszewska and Roberts, 1989.
10. *Australian and New Zealand Visitors to Britain*, British Travel and Holidays Association, London, 1959, 15, table 12.
11. Fysh, 1943. 'Topical Talk'.
12. Clune, 1949, *Land of Hope and Glory: An Australian Traveller's Impressions of Post-War Britain and Eire*, 1.
13. Banks, 1953, *The World in My Diary: From Melbourne to Helsinki for the Olympic Games*.35, 129. See MacCannell, 1976,101–107; Urry, 2002, pp. 8–11.
14. Pinney, 1944, *Britain – Destination of Tourists?*, 37.
15. British Tourist and Holidays Board, 1949, *Come to Britain*, 6.
16. McKenney; Bransten, 1951, *Here's England: A Highly Informal Guide*.
17. See Travel Association of Great Britain and Ireland, *Eighteenth Annual Report*, 1946, 5.
18. *London, Past and Present*, 1948, 10.
19. B. Rischbieth, '1946 – Experiences Abroad', Rischbieth Papers, National Library of Australia, MS2004/2/3, 1.
20. B. Rischbieth, '1946 – Experiences Abroad', Rischbieth Papers, National Library of Australia, MS2004/2/3, 1.

21. H. Wyndham, 'Article for Drylight, 1946: Magazine of the Students of the Sydney Teachers' College', Papers, Mitchell Library, MS5089/12, 11.
22. *British Australasian*, 9 July 1948, 2.
23. *Australia and New Zealand Weekly*, 25 August 1951, 8.
24. Horne, 1947, *I See the World*, 40.
25. Horne, 1947, *I See the World*, 34.
26. *Australia and New Zealand Weekly*, 12 August 1949, 12.
27. Hopkins, 1963, 91.
28. Clune, 1949, *Land of Hope and Glory*, 3, 40, 38.
29. Wyndham, 'Article for Drylight', 11.
30. *Australian Women's Weekly*, 8 February 1947, 15.
31. Mills, 1946-1947, 'Letter Home', 594–595.
32. See, Morgan, 1990, 68–77.
33. Conekin, 2003, 26–33.
34. Quoted in Gardiner, 1999, 45.
35. Morgan, 1990.
36. Nicholson, 1999.
37. British Travel and Holidays Association, 1951, *Bulletin of Information*, 10.
38. This total includes figures for Australian residents departing Australia for Britain temporarily and permanently. 'Table No.30-Overseas Migration: Country of Embarkation of Persons who Arrived, and Country of Disembarkation of Persons who Departed, Australia, 1951', Commonwealth Bureau of Census and Statistics, *Demography 1951: Bulletin No. 69*, npd, p.30.
39. *Australia and New Zealand Weekly*, 12 May, 1953, 2.
40. *Australia and New Zealand Weekly*, 24 October 1953, l5.
41. Clift, 1989 (1970), 'News of Earls Court – 15 Years Ago', 54.
42. Museum of London, 2008, <http://www.museumoflondon.org.uk/archive/exhibits/festival/tangible.htm>, accessed 28 October 2008.
43. *Sydney Morning Herald*, 18 September 1951, 2.
44. *Australia and New Zealand Weekly*, 12 May 1951, 2.
45. Mathams, 1937, *Crowns over England*, 5.
46. Letter from Thomas White to R.G. Menzies, 13 February 1952, National Archives of Australia, M2576/1,111.
47. See correspondence in National Archives of Australia, M2576/1,111.
48. *Australia and New Zealand Weekly*, 20 June 1953, 1.
49. *Australia and New Zealand Weekly*, 23 May 1953, 3.
50. Australian High Commission, London, cablegram to PM's Department, 1 August 1952, National Archives of Australia, A462/8, 821/1/46. External Affairs Cablegram from PM's Department to Australian High Commission, London, 30 April 1953, and official form issued by the Australian High Commission, London, NAA A462/4, 821/1/23.
51. *Herald*, 5 October 1952.

52. Letter, 'Coronation Day', 2 June 1953, Anne King Letters, Saloway Family Papers, 1856–1974, National Library of Australia, MS6442/2.
53. Nettleton, 1956, *Two Eyes and a Passport*, 72–74.
54. *Australia and New Zealand Weekly*, 20 June 1953, 16.
55. *Australia and New Zealand Weekly*, 8 August 1953, 15.
56. Brett, 1992, 145–150.
57. Meredith; Harrison, 1955, *Inns and Outs*,127.
58. Spearritt, 1988, 76.
59. McLachlan, 1989, 272.
60. Australian Gallup Polls, nos. 470–7, November–December 1947.
61. Hassam, 2000, 130–133.
62. Hobsbawm and Ranger, 1983.

PRIMARY SOURCES

Argus, 1946.
Australia and New Zealand Weekly, 1949, 1953.
Australian Women's Weekly, 1947.
Australian Bureau of Statistics, 'Overseas migration for quarter and year ended December 1948'.
Australian Gallup Polls, 1947.
Australian High Commission. Correspondence files, multiple number series, fourth system, Canberra, National Archives of Australia, A462.
Banks, Norman. 1953. *The World in My Diary: From Melbourne to Helsinki for the Olympic Games*. Melbourne: William Heinemann.
British Australian, New Zealand and Pacific Weekly, 1946–1948.
British Tourist and Holidays Board. 1949. *Come to Britain*. London. (January).
British Travel and Holidays Association. 1951. *Bulletin of Information*. (8) (May).
Clift, Charmian. 1989 (1970). 'News of Earls Court – 15 Years Ago'. In *The World of Charmian Clift*, by Clift, Charmian. Sydney: Collins.
Clune, Frank. 1949. *Land of Hope and Glory: An Australian Traveller's Impressions of Post-War Britain and Eire*. Sydney, Angus and Robertson.
Commonwealth Bureau of Census and Statistics. *Australian Demography, Bulletin No.47: Survey of Australian Population and Vital Statistics 1933 and Previous Years*. npd. Canberra: Commonwealth Government Printer.
Commonwealth Bureau of Census and Statistics, npd. *Demography 1946, Bulletin No.64*, Canberra: Commonwealth Government Printer.
Commonwealth Bureau of Census and Statistics. npd. *Demography 1951: Bulletin No.69*. Canberra: Commonwealth Government Printer.
Folders of papers maintained by Robert Gordon Menzies as Prime Minister. Canberra: National Archives of Australia, M2576.
Fysh, H. 1943. 'Topical Talk'. BBC London Pacific Service broadcast, 9 August 1943, typescript, Mitchell Library, State Library of New South Wales, MSS 2413, K21848.
Herald (Melbourne).

Horne, Alex S. 1947. *I See the World ...* Prospect, SA: Self-published.
London, Past and Present. 1948. London: Travel Association, Tourist Division of the British Tourist and Holidays Board.
Mathams, Hamish. 1937. *Crowns over England*. London: Reservations Ltd.
McKenney, R.; Bransten, R. 1951. *Here's England: A Highly Informal Guide*. London: Rupert Hart-Davis.
Meredith, Gwen; Harrison, Ainsworth. 1955. *Inns and Outs*. Sydney: Angus and Robertson.
Mills, K. 1946–1947. 'Letter home'. *The English Speaking World* 29 (1).
Nettleton, Alice. 1956. *Two Eyes and a Passport*. Sydney: John Andrew and Co.
Pinney, R.G. 1944. *Britain – Destination of Tourists?*. London: Travel and Industrial Development Association of Great Britain and Ireland.
Travel Association of Great Britain and Ireland, *Annual Report*, 1946–1948.
Letter from Thomas White to R.G. Menzies, 13 February 1952, Canberra, National Archives of Australia, M2576/1,111.
Rischbieth Papers. Canberra, National Library of Australia, MS2004/2/3.
Saloway Family Papers, 1856–1974, Canberra, National Library of Australia, MS6442/2.
Wyndham, Harold S., Papers, 1890–1988, Mitchell Library, State Library of New South Wales, MS5089.

REFERENCES

Brett, Judith. 1992. *Robert Menzies' Forgotten People*. Sydney: Pan Macmillan.
Conekin, Becky. 2003. *The Autobiography of a Nation: The 1951 Festival of Britain*. Manchester: Manchester University Press.
Gardiner, Juliet. 1999. *From the Bomb to the Beatles*. London: Collins and Brown.
Hassam, Andrew. 2000. *Through Australian Eyes: Colonial Perceptions of Imperial Britain*. Carlton, Vic.: Melbourne University Press.
Hobsbawm, Eric; Ranger, Terence. 1983, editors. *The Invention of Tradition*. Cambridge: Cambridge University Press.
Hopkins, Harry. 1963. *The New Look: A Social History of the Forties and Fifties in Britain*. London: Secker and Warburg.
MacCannell, Dean. 1976. *The Tourist: A New Theory of the Leisure Class*. London: Macmillan Press.
McLachlan, Noel. 1989. *Waiting for the Revolution: A History of Australian Nationalism*. Ringwood, Vic.: Penguin.
Kenneth. 1990. *The People's Peace: British History 1945–1990*. Oxford: Oxford University Press.
Museum of London. 2008. 'Outliving the Festival – Festival of Britain'. [Internet]. Accessed 28 October 2008. Available from: http://www.museumoflondon.org.uk/archive/exhibits/festival/tangible.htm.
Nicholson, Adam. 1999. *Regeneration: The Story of the Dome*. London: HarperCollins.
Olszewska, A.; Roberts, K., editors. *Leisure and Lifestyle: A Comparative Analysis of Free Time*. London: Sage.
Shaw, Gareth; Williams, Allan M. 1994. *Critical Issues in Tourism: A Geographical Perspective*. Oxford: Blackwell.

Spearritt, Peter. 1988. 'Royal progress: The Queen and her Australian subjects'. In *Australian Cultural History*, edited by Goldberg, S.L.; Smith, F.B. Melbourne: Cambridge University Press.

Urry, John. 2002. *The Tourist Gaze: Leisure and Travel in Contemporary Societies*, 2nd edn., London: Sage.

Cite this chapter as: Trinca, Mathew. 2009. 'Part of the pageant: Australian tourists in postwar London'. *Australians in Britain: The Twentieth-Century Experience*, edited by Bridge, Carl; Crawford, Robert; Dunstan, David. Melbourne: Monash University ePress. pp. 12.1 to 12.15. DOI: 10.2104/ab090012.

AUSTRALIAN ARTISTS IN LONDON
THE EARLY 1960s

Simon Pierse, Aberystwyth University
Simon Pierse is a lecturer at Aberystwyth University. His research interests are in postwar Australian painting and British perceptions of Australian art, identity and landscape.

During the early 1960s, an expatriate community of Australian artists lived and exhibited in London. They formed a loose-knit group of friends and associates centred on the Highgate/Hampstead and Ladbroke Grove districts of London. During a period that saw Australian contemporary painting reach its height of popularity in Britain, artists mingled with a varied mix of London society, meeting at parties, drinking with fellow artists in pubs and receiving invitations to aristocratic soirees in Mayfair. Bryan Robertson championed Australian art at the Whitechapel Gallery, whilst Sir Kenneth Clark offered hospitality to artists at his home at Saltwood Castle. Arthur Boyd and Sidney Nolan chose to remain in London but by the mid 1960s many artists began to return home to further their careers in Australia.

By the end of the 1950s a number of travel scholarships such as the Helena Rubinstein travelling scholarship and that offered by the Italian Government in conjunction with the Flotto Lauro and Lloyd Triestino shipping companies and Dante Alighieri Society were offering substantial sums of money as bursaries to young Australian artists, encouraging them to live and work for a time in Europe. In 1959, when Lawrence Daws went to London from Rome for a six-month stay at the end of his Italian Government Flotta Lauro Dante Alighieri Society scholarship, he had a first class ticket home under the terms of the award. 'I don't know whether I had any real intention of settling up in London permanently at that time', he recalled in an interview given in 1965, 'but I moved there and settled down and started painting a bit'.[1] Charles Blackman won the third Helena Rubinstein travelling scholarship in August 1960. At the time he was living with his wife in an old coach house in Melbourne and working very hard to try and save a hundred pounds.[2] Barbara Blackman remembers that they had no particular desire to go to England and were quite happy with their lives in Australia. Financial success came quite suddenly with a sell-out exhibition at Brisbane's Johnstone Gallery in June 1960 that made approximately £4500 plus £1000 from the scholarship and a further £1000 from the sale of the winning painting. In accepting the Helena Rubinstein award, the Blackmans had to agree to return to live and work in Australia and before leaving they bought a house in St Lucia, Brisbane.[3] They set out for London in early January 1961 with more cash than they needed, intending to take over the house that Arthur and Yvonne Boyd were renting in Highgate. On the afternoon of their arrival Arthur took Charles to see the Vermeer painting at Kenwood, a short walk from his home in Hampstead Lane. The Boyds had decided not to leave but to stay on in London and the Blackmans stayed with them for a short time before finding their own rented accommodation in nearby Jackson's Lane.[4]

Neither Daws nor Blackman, both of whom would become long-term expatriate Australians living and working in London, felt any great imperative to escape from Australia – for either financial or for cultural reasons. But once in London, they it found it a stimulating place to be – a city quite changed from the dreary postwar austerity that earlier expatriate artists had experienced in the late 1940s. Daws remembers his arrival in London in 1959 as 'a late, Indian summer, really hot, everyone in shirt sleeves, windows were open and there was a popular Cliff Richard's song *Living Doll* pouring out everywhere'.[5] Charles Blackman recalls that Britain was recovering from the war and had begun to look outwards on the world. It was an exciting time of *That Was the Week that Was*, David Frost, and the Profumo scandal:[6] 'The English were coming out of their chrysalis with their own painters and getting recognition for them and also introducing into England via the Tate Art Gallery American abstract expressionism. Big shows were being mounted which had never been mounted before'.[7]

London and Paris were still the most important international centres of contemporary art; commercial galleries regularly put on exhibitions of the latest work of the world's leading artists, and it was often possible to meet the great and the good at private views. Picasso, Magritte and Chagall lived in the south of France, but Francis Bacon, Victor Pasmore and Graham Sutherland could be seen at exhibition previews or in the galleries of Bond Street and Cork Street. Australian art was on the rise too, and following the success of Sidney Nolan at the Whitechapel Gallery in 1957, the presence of Australian artists began to be felt more strongly in London through the growing number of group and solo exhibitions that were held during the early 1960s. Roy de Maistre, a longstanding resident of London, usually attended the openings and took a fatherly interest in the younger painters.

While there was a growing market for Australian painting, there were no guarantees of success, however, particularly if an artist's work did not fit what was generally perceived to be the 'Australian school'. Much, too, depended on an artist's ability to understand and engage with a complex social hierarchy. The conservative art establishment in Australia, an under-developed Australian art market, and the desire to see great artworks in the galleries of Europe at first hand were all major factors in sending young artists to live and work overseas in the early 1950s. But now it was more the sense that 'things were happening' in London. Nolan's rapid rise to financial success and recognition in London was noted with some envy by artists of his generation in Australia. But Nolan had benefited greatly from the influence of Sir Kenneth Clark, and for other Australian artists who had left home to pursue their careers in London, things were not always so easy. Nolan's friend and contemporary Albert Tucker, whose first experience of London in 1947-8 had been one of poverty and rejection, wrote a cautionary letter from Rome to Yvonne and Arthur Boyd in an effort to dissuade them from leaving Australia:

> Prices in London are about the same as in Australia, but if I know the fish-souled English at all, they will reject Arthur's painting on sight. They like these sterile, tidy abstracts or milk and piddle landscapes. In France or Italy, prices are a quarter to one fifth Australian. Also the social and cultural life in Europe is incredibly tricky and complex – and corrupt. In many ways Australia is a haven of sanity and civilization by comparison. But then perhaps I've been here too long.
>
> And if you plan to settle in London and work for a living I feel like advising you not to come. … You would enjoy the first few weeks of course, novelty etc. But after one winter there – and it's mostly winter – with cold gloom and dirt, and a pompous, insular, unapproachable people who look on Australians as second grade Englishmen, you would start thinking in terms of flight; but

with a family you would be trapped and might take years to get back – and see very little of Europe in the process.[8]

Tucker predicted that Europe would be 'obstinately blind' to Boyd's painting and believed that 'he would have to strike very freakish circumstances indeed to make any worthwhile sales'. Tucker's pessimistic predictions proved to be wildly inaccurate. With sponsorship from the Australian Galleries in Melbourne, offering Boyd £20 a week for six months in return for an agreed number of paintings, plus money for their fares from the sale of a block of land, the Boyds set sail, on the *Iberia*, arriving on a chilly December day in 1959 with return tickets and no fixed plans to stay. For the first six weeks they lodged in Hampstead with a friend from Melbourne, the philosopher Brian O'Shaughnessy and his family (brother of actor and director Peter O'Shaughnessy), before finding a large old Victorian house to rent at 13 Hampstead Lane, Highgate. The property would become the Boyds' permanent London home and is still lived in by their son Jamie.[9]

Figure 13.1 Charles Blackman, Arthur Boyd and Barbara Blackman at the opening of Recent Australian Painting, 2 June 1961. Hanging on the wall behind them are two of Blackman's paintings: 'Reflections' and 'Dreaming in the Street' alongside John Coburn's 'High Noon'.
Source: Photographer unknown. Whitechapel Gallery Archive.

Not long after his arrival, Arthur Boyd achieved success with his first solo London exhibition at the Zwemmer Gallery in August 1960. Bryan Robertson, who saw Boyd's work at the gallery, offered him a one-show at the Whitechapel Gallery on the spot, and with proceeds from the sale of paintings at Zwemmer's, at relatively high prices of around £200, Boyd was soon able to buy the house that he had once rented. For a while he drove around in an old Rolls Royce with a squashed Nescafe tin instead of the silver lady on the bonnet, acquired from fellow Australian Geoffrey Dutton in exchange for a decorated ceramic tile.[10] But the Boyds never forgot earlier hard times and were always willing to offer a bed or at least a space on the floor to friends and fellow artists from Australia.

EXPATRIATE SOCIAL CIRCLES IN LONDON

The Australian quality of 'mateship'– the offer of a place to 'doss' and casual hospitality – could help to ease an Australian artist into life in England.[11] There was mateship not only in the sense that expatriate Australians tended to stick together in loose-knit groups, meeting at parties, in favourite pubs or at the theatre as well as the regular exhibition openings at London galleries, but contacts could also be made and introductions given. The British social and cultural scene could be tricky, but for the artist with the right timing, temperament and, above all else, the right kind of work, rapid success was indeed possible. Sculptor Steve Walker slept on a mattress for two weeks on the kitchen floor at Brett Whiteley's house in Ladbroke Grove whilst organizing a show at the Drian Gallery in Marble Arch.[12] Walker subsequently introduced Whiteley to Lilian Somerville, a leading figure in the British Council. Arthur Boyd introduced Brett Whiteley to Lawrence Daws in 1961, taking him in a taxi to a studio above the ABC bakery in Hampstead High Street where Daws was working on a series of paintings relating to early experiences of the outback.[13] Daws remembers a taxi drawing up and looking down from the first floor studio to see:

> this young, red-headed Groucho Marx leap out and help Arthur out. Arthur was blustering away, quite offended that this young turk had helped him out of the cab as though he was an old man … he was only forty or so at the time and Brett was about twenty. It was like a young walrus testing the strength of the old one.[14]

Charles Blackman and his family found a furnished house to rent off the Archway Road in Jackson's Lane, Highgate, an area of London where there were already a number of Australians living who were involved in the creative arts. Barbara Blackman described their first London home:

> … a proper house, as read about in books, with solid walls, carpets and indoor lavatory – indeed two of them. It spiraled up through five levels to the attics, one a children's room to kneel upon window seats and look down to the road far below and ours where a bright alcove contained a dressing table easily converted to a writing desk, and a view on a clear day to the dome of St Paul's.[15]

Al Alvarez would later write of the Blackman's home as 'the pungent – or punchy – centre of the Australian exiles'.[16] It was the focus for a bohemian Australian enclave in North London where a number of artists who had known each other at a distance in Australia all lived in the same vicinity at one time. The Blackmans' house became the meeting point, not only for Australian artists living in other parts of London, but also for expatriate Australians working in the broader field of the arts, such as Barry Humphries and his friend and collaborator Peter O'Shaughnessy. The Highgate habit was to gather on a Sunday evening at the local pub, Barbara Blackman recalls: 'Aussies passing through London and our circle of English friends would drink in the Rose and Crown and then repair to our house for a supper of soup and cheese'.[17]

Barbara Blackman remembers that 'We saw much of one another after that in those five years in London when our lives seemed to flow close together, to intertwine and follow common currents. There seemed to be endless parties, most of them at our house'.[18] Among their expatriate artist associates were Brett Whiteley and Mick Johnson who were living at Ladbroke Grove, Arthur and Yvonne Boyd, John and Mary Perceval, Sidney Nolan, Lawrence Daws, and Len French, who arrived in London with his family in 1962 to stay at the Blackmans' home following a period spent on the Greek island of Samos.[19] Others 'passing through' from abroad included Laurence Hope, Jean Bellette and Paul Haefliger and Lynn and Fred Williams.[20] There were also reunions with old friends from Australia: Charles Osborne, now co-editor of *London Magazine*, Jean Langley Sinclair, the cartoonist Bill Sewell, illustrator Virginia Smith from Blackman's early days as a copy boy for the Sydney *Sun*, and jeweller Rod Edwards. As Charles Blackman relates, 'my contemporaries in London were more or less the same that they were in Australia, except that I probably saw them more often, in London'.[21]

Ladbroke Grove, not far from Portobello Road in west London is still a racially mixed area famous for its Saturday market, but in the early 1960s it was arty and slightly on the edge. Peter Blake, Derek Boshier, Pauline Boty and Clive Godwin, Robyn Denny, Michael English, William Green and Ian Stephenson all lived or had studios within a mile radius of 'the Grove' which was also within easy walking distance of the Royal College of Art. Brett Whiteley and Mick Johnson, who lived at 129 – or what the Blackmans dubbed 'one two many' – Ladbroke Grove, would drink just across the road at The Elgin, a public house frequented by David Hockney, Joe Tilson and other young British artists. At other times Daws and Whiteley would join a group of Australians to see a play at the Royal Court Theatre in Sloane Square and to drink together afterwards at a pub in Chelsea, not far from Bryan Robertson's house in Draycott Avenue.

Barbara Blackman admitted that she was part of a formidable gang who did not have proper good manners. On one occasion they were all thrown out of the pub because of their rowdy behaviour. About seven or eight had pulled tables together and were ordering scotch eggs and drinking beer in pint pots. 'We would be talking and the noise would be incredible', Daws recalls. 'Barbara reached across for something and four or five of these big things smashed to the floor'.

> ... there were a couple of sweet old guys on the next table getting a bit harassed by this sort of going on. One of them said: "Could you quieten down a bit?" And Brett, quick as a flash, said: "Just keep your dinner down, Daphne." And the other guy said: "He called you Daphne!" ... With the broken glass we did get thrown out once because of that.[22]

Alannah Coleman, Australian artist and private art dealer based in London, was also central to the expatriate circle of artists living in London in the early 1960s. A stylish blonde, Coleman had been among other things a model and circus performer in her early life. Her glamorous looks were matched with a feisty entrepreneurial spirit that helped her make her way in business. She loved Siamese cats and Barbara Blackman described her as like a Siamese cat herself: 'She slinks about in Royal circles, she is smelling out the buyer, she will purr up to him and whispers the right names'.[23] Coleman had studied art at the National Gallery School in Melbourne where she had known Nolan and Tucker, but had later fled Australia in 1950 to get away from a murderous lover who had killed her favourite Siamese.

Since living in London she had become well known to dealers and auction houses as the resident expert on Australian contemporary painting. In the domestic setting of her gallery flat in Putney, Coleman promoted the work of long-term expatriate artists Louis James, Oliffe Richmond, Tony Underhill and, later, Arthur Boyd, with whom she cherished lifelong friendships. She set up her gallery one windy evening in 1959 with the help and encouragement of artist friends, cooking a huge pot of spaghetti for them as they arrived, bringing paintings and bottles of wine. A large canvas on the roof of Tony Underhill's car nearly took off in a gust of wind as he drove over Putney Bridge to deliver it to her flat. Paintings were installed the same evening and the Alannah Coleman Gallery was in business the next day.[24]

Alannah Coleman was to be seen at all the private views in town (once she attended no fewer than 10 in one evening) where she made many of her business contacts and was also able to keep an eye on young Australian newcomers such as Vernon Treweeke, Peter Upward and William Delafield Cook, whose paintings she subsequently sold for a modest commission. She invited clients to her home to view work, and arranged visits to artists' studios, always pressing for a sale and sometimes even accompanying the buyer home to advise on hanging. She would hold three–day parties over consecutive evenings where clients and artists could meet each other and to which the press was invited. At one particularly formal occasion, Brett Whiteley turned up, elegantly dressed in a white boiler suit.[25]

Sidney Nolan lived with his wife Cynthia in a large house overlooking the Thames in Putney, just around the corner from Alannah Coleman but at some distance from other Australian artists in the Highgate/Hampstead area of North London. Coleman had known Nolan from her art school days in Melbourne and had once owned an early Nolan (*Bondi Beach*, 1947), which she took with her on the boat to England. Nolan was now too successful to involve himself with the Alannah Coleman Gallery, although he would sometimes contribute paintings to her selling exhibitions. The Nolans placed themselves on the periphery of both the long-term expatriates and younger Australian artists associated with Coleman's gallery. They now moved in rather different and more elevated art and literary circles. Amongst their friends were Sir Kenneth and Jane Clark, the composer Benjamin Britten and the writers Robert Melville and Alan Moorehead.

The Nolans were often away from London, although Sidney continued to see Arthur Boyd for gallery visits and lunch every Thursday when they were both in town.[26] Between 1961 and 1963 they spent periods of time in Paris, Egypt, Africa and Greece, travelling first class and staying at the best hotels. In 1958 Nolan was awarded a two-year Commonwealth Fund Harkness Fellowship to the United States 'to record the American scene'. Travelling extensively throughout America during this period, Cynthia would later write about their experiences in *Open Negative*.[27]

When in London she spent many hours in her Thames-side garden, tending the flowers beds and climbing roses[28] and enjoying the anonymity that expatriate life in London could offer, where everyone was very busy, had their own lives and would see each other a few times each year.[29]

Performer and artist Barry Humphries was also part of the expatriate London circle and a friend of Boyd, Nolan and Charles and Barbara Blackman. The Blackmans met Humphries and his second wife Rosalind at a party at 27a Jackson's Lane about a year or so after their arrival, and when they moved into a larger house in Southwood Lane, just up the road in Highgate village, the Humphries moved into their old house. When not understudying the role of Fagin in *Oliver!* Barry Humphries took centre stage at parties, conspicuous as 'the only man present in a Turnbull & Asser shirt, antique Chavet tie, pin-stripe double-breasted Savile Row suit, Lobb shoes, black fedora and a monocle'.[30] He moved within a broad circle of friends and acquaintances that included both renowned literary figures such as the English poet John Betjeman and down at heel Australian artist Francis Lymburner, whom he first met at a party in 1961.

After the Humphries moved from Jackson's Lane to a small basement flat in Notting Hill Gate, Lymburner stayed with them for nearly a year. Humphries admitted that 'we found ourselves falling for Francis's hard luck story and offering him our spare bedroom for a few nights. It seemed he had been living rather grandly in other people's guest rooms for some time but that he was otherwise homeless'. Although Lymburner was included in the 1961 show *Recent Australian Painting*, he was more commonly grouped with Donald Friend, Justin O'Brien and other members of the now unfashionable Sydney 'charm school'. Whilst the prices of Nolan and Boyd rocketed, Lymburner was unable to afford paint and made drawings instead, frequenting a coffee lounge called *The Palette* in nearby Queensway, where a 'nude model posed on a dingy rostrum for the clientele of "artists" ... invariably a group of seedy middle-aged men in raincoats who pretended to sketch with their free hands'. Humphries recalled:

> When I met him in London he was bewildered and mildly amused, rather than embittered by his spectacular fall from fashion. Nolan was extolled everywhere, Arthur Boyd was beginning his international career, Blackman was exhibiting in Bond Street, but Lymburner remained on the periphery, a languid dandified figure in a black velvet jacket, a jaunty red neckerchief and always a cigarette and a glass of wine. If you did not know he was an artist you would have taken him for an attractive, if slightly down-at-heel *flaneur*.[31]

Having lived in London since 1952, Lymburner had witnessed the arrival of Nolan and Boyd and their rapid rise to success with some ambivalence. He thought Boyd's success was well deserved[32] but was perplexed about Nolan's work: 'I went to Sidney Nolan's opening the other night and Princess Margaret was there so one can take it he's really arrived. I can't quite make up my mind about his paintings, when they are good they are very good and when they are bad they are awful'.[33] Lymburner lived in the hope that figuration would eventually triumph over abstraction, sensing a big swing against it in London in 1962.[34] The same year he wrote: 'The big excitement in London just now is the Kokoschka show at the Tate. It fills seven rooms and is very exciting. It also helps to drive the nail into the coffin of abstract art – which is all very helpful to me'.[35]

Following the Australian exhibitions at the Whitechapel there was some resurgence of interest in Lymburner's work and he held an exhibition at the Qantas Gallery in Piccadilly. 'My plans for my show with Qantas are going well in spite of the paralysing cold', he wrote in the freezing January of 1963. 'John [Douglas] Pringle has agreed to open it, and there is a great deal of interest in Aust[ralian] art as the big show is on at the Tate. They had a rather splendid reception there the other night'.[36] Sir John Rothenstein visited and praised Lymburner's exhibition, and a short film on the artist and his work appeared on BBC television.[37] Being a non-commercial gallery, Qantas did not take any commission, which suited Lymburner's circumstances well since throughout most of the 1960s he was perpetually hard up, and at times was reduced to holding drinks parties at which he would sell his drawings to friends and acquaintances. Brett Whiteley, who would occasionally drink with him at Ladbroke Grove, or dine with him at an Italian Trattoria,[38] attended one of Lymburner's 'rough Spanish red & drawings on the wall' nights when he sold about £70 worth of 'pretty crummy work'.[39]

Pub drinking was central to the Australian social scene in London as indeed it was to 1960s artistic life in general. Imported Australian wine was expensive and available only at the Australian Wine Centre in Soho. Barry Humphries discovered that the cheap Algerian wine that he was serving to his friends could be made more appetizing by mulling it with spices and brandy, the only drawback being that it turned the teeth black. At the Whitechapel Gallery, Bryan Robertson would lay on stylish and generous hospitality at parties after the exhibition openings, when big scotches and gins and tonic were handed around on trays. They were popular occasions for some of the younger Australian artists when free drinks would be knocked back before heading off to a favourite pub or an arranged meeting point. Photographer Axel Poignant documented exhibition openings and the lives of the Australian artists in London, visiting their studios and photographing their paintings. With his wife Roslyn, he occasionally entertained with dinner parties at their home at 19a Oakcroft Road, in the South London suburb of Blackheath. Brett Whiteley wrote of one occasion: 'it was all Scandinavian food with special drinks and special songs before the drinks: then down the hatch with the Swedish fire water and everyone smiling their eyes burning with tears and Axel bullshitting on in the background about what this all meant'.[40]

Despite the strong sense of identity that Australian painting benefited from in London during the early 1960s, expatriate artists were influenced by the British artists around them, both through friendship, and the exhibitions that took place in the London commercial galleries of Cork Street and Bond Street. Charles Blackman got to know Adrian Heath, Prunella Clough, Keith Vaughan and Michael Ayrton through Bryan Robertson, who showed their work at the Whitechapel, whilst Brett Whiteley was for a while strongly under the influence of Roger Hilton and William Scott. They also met socially: Scott was frequently at the exhibition openings, whilst Hilton and Whiteley became regular drinking companions at Ladbroke Grove. Whiteley's combative manner – especially in regard to art – meant that he would sometimes gang up with Hilton to 'put the word' on somebody, Daws recalls. Joe Tilson, who had a studio off Holland Park, not far from Ladbroke Grove, was another British artist whom Daws and Whiteley would see informally, and Peter Phillips, John Hoyland, Lucian Freud, Bridget Riley, Phillip King and Patrick Procktor were amongst other British artists that Brett and Wendy Whiteley met either at exhibition openings, or socially. Regular invitations to openings at Marlborough Fine Art came through Tony Reichardt, whilst Ann Forsdyke, assistant director at the Whitechapel Gallery, sent out private view cards to Australian artists with a friendly note of invitation. At the Marlborough Gallery Daws and Whiteley occasionally met Francis Bacon – another great influence on Whiteley, who adopted his style of heavy gilt framing behind glass and made a series of portrait drawings of Bacon between 1964 and 1965.

The early 1960s saw the opening of the new Commonwealth Institute in High Street Kensington and a renewed interest in art from the Commonwealth. Australian artists benefited considerably from exhibitions such as Commonwealth Art Today and the Queen, the Duke of Edinburgh, Princess Margaret and the Queen Mother were all buyers of contemporary Australian painting. But the cosmopolitan nature of London and the sheer diversity of artwork being created and exhibited could also be bewildering, as Charles Blackman related:

> One of the funny things about living in Australia as against living in Europe [London] is you more or less know where everything is coming from; you get few actual shocks, once you become familiar with the painters who are working around you. But living in a big metropolis you have some bloke, perhaps from Greece, you've never even heard of, pops up with a full-blown job – it's a sort of shock to the system, and sometimes it's quite difficult to relate yourself to it, it seems all a bit unreal. I found that a very exciting aspect of looking at things.[41]

In addition to the overlapping social circles in which expatriate Australian artists moved, centring on parties and various pubs in Highgate, Ladbroke Grove and Chelsea, they sometimes received invitations to grander affairs. These included occasional lunches arranged by Jane and Kenneth Clark and held in a private room at the Eastern Dining Room of Liverpool Street Station, to which all expatriate Australian artists would be invited, along with Bryan Robertson and other guests.[42] Artists from Britain and abroad intermingled at dinner parties given by Hans and Elsbeth Juda, and by Lilian Somerville of the British Council. To Whiteley, Somerville was 'the most important woman in the art world in England'. He first met her in 1961 when she took him out to lunch with fellow Australian Steve Walker, and wrote excitedly to his mother about the woman 'who was on the selection committee for all the Biennales' and who had 'made Moore the name he is … Next minute there's an invitation for this very exclusive party so here goes!'

The evening went well, with guests including British artists Merlyn Evans (who represented Britain at the 1960 Venice Biennale), Victor Pasmore, and sculptor Kenneth Armitage. It was at this party that Whiteley met Scottish painter William Scott for the first time – finding him 'completely inarticulate, half my size but quite mighty as expected'. Whiteley thought Eduardo Paolozzi (also represented at the Venice Biennale) 'a complete egotist with a bilious Oxford voice' whom no one seemed to like, while Australian expatriate Frank Hodgkinson was merely condescending, treating Whiteley 'like the young student from Orstralia'. Arthur Boyd was also there along with three critics, two poets, a composer from New Zealand and a young painter whose drunkenness ruined his chance of getting anywhere.[43] The party went on until the early hours with 'heavy aesthetic' discussions at four in the morning. Pasmore and Evans remained the perfect English intellectuals throughout, constructing sentences 'of almost eighteenth century complexity without pausing to take breath'.[44]

RELENTLESSLY MEETING THE ENGLISH

Already a close friend of Sidney Nolan, Sir Kenneth Clark took a special interest in the younger Australian artists to whom he was often introduced by Bryan Robertson.[45] Attracted by what he perceived as Australian directness and honesty, Clark encouraged their company and he became especially friendly with Charles Blackman, whom he first met at the opening of the Whitechapel show in June 1961. They immediately got on well together and subsequently Barbara and Charles Blackman were invited with Bryan Robertson to lunch with the Clarks at Saltwood Castle, in opulent surroundings that included a butler, and separate lavatories for men and women, hung with paintings by Renoir and Seurat. Clark's informality impressed Barbara Blackman: 'He was regal, knowledgeable. He had every reason to be haughty but he wasn't. His way of handling things was wonderful'.[46] After lunch, Clark personally drove the Blackmans to the station and waited with them for their train back to London.

As their friendship grew, Clark invited the Blackmans to leave London to live in one of the cottages on the Saltwood estate, suggesting that it might be good for the children. 'Clark was magnanimous to make the offer, Barbara Blackman relates, 'but we couldn't have handled living at Saltwood ... Charles didn't like the countryside ... he was afraid of a falling leaf'.[47] Charles Blackman admired Clark's intellect and recalled a lunch at Saltwood with Sidney Nolan and others when the subject of Velasquez's *Las Meninas* was raised in conversation. Blackman pronounced it a 'shithouse painting', as knives and forks clattered to the table and his wife kicked him under the tablecloth. About an hour or so later Blackman was admiring Clark's Turner painting and Clark remarked: 'You Australians have a problem inasmuch as you've never had the experience of the Renaissance. ... You've also never had a lot of other problems because you haven't had that'.[48]

It has been claimed that Clark had 'a special category reserved for Australians, who were expected to break all rules and conventions'.[49] Sometimes Sidney Nolan, who was a regular weekend guest at Saltwood, would try making deliberately contentious statements about modern art in an attempt to goad Clark into a response, but always without success. Clark, who felt that Australians were 'the only truly democratic and non-hypocritical people of the world' and not suited to what passed in British circles as 'sophistication',[50] was never dismissive and always helpful, saying: 'Let Sidney have his say, after all, he's an Australian'.[51] Nolan, on his part found Clark's upper-class diffidence and restraint frustrating on occasions. He once questioned an unchanging custom at Saltwood, which was for Nolan and Clark to breakfast together in silence over the Sunday papers and received a rebuff from Clark that 'we'll just have to continue as we are'.

Barbara Blackman summed up the 1960s expatriate circle as 'a pretty raucous lot to break on the English scene. If we went to parties, we spoke more loudly and we would talk across the room [whereas] English people don't'. She describes how Australians would spurn the sofa and sit on the floor to have their cup of tea – 'probably we'd have our ashtray on the chair. It was very "bush"'.[52] Such informality was no bar to mixing in the highest social circles, however. Australian artists could meet Princess Margaret on the gallery circuit, where on one occasion, while pregnant, she walked barefoot around the Whitechapel Gallery. Princess Margaret and Lord Snowdon invited the Whiteleys to Kensington Palace, while Charles and Barbara Blackman had their own friends among members of the British aristocracy. They would visit Penelope

Mountbatten, who had stayed with the Bell family in Australia. They also knew Fiona Campbell, a cousin of the Queen, who had an apartment in Mayfair, furnished with Royal crested furniture. The Blackmans would arrive for drinks in their ordinary clothes and mix with British aristocracy, but when their welcome had been worn out, the butler approached, offering to call a taxi. Once they took the Bryonic and abrasive John Perceval who caused a minor stir by dismissing the Turner paintings in the Campbells' flat as fakes. The British aristocracy was dreadful to one another at these parties, Blackman recalls. 'As soon as one went home they would pull them to pieces. We were so nervous we stayed right until the end'.[53] A few upper-class habits rubbed off on the Australians. Barbara Blackman took to smoking Ariston Muratti oval cigarettes with gold tips that had 'as smoked by aristocracy and royalty' embossed on their grey and purple box, and Arthur Boyd adopted a British telephone manner, answering calls with: 'Boyd of Highgate'.

Australian artists enjoyed a degree of immunity from the British structures of class in London society. They received invitations to upper-class parties because their presence acted as a social catalyst, diffusing the stiffness of such occasions and perhaps also helping to distract fellow guests from self-destructive snobbery and bitchiness. However, the Australians were more than simply an amusement for aristocracy. While they were in a social position roughly equivalent to British working class or, as one expatriate artist put it, 'like the Scots or the Irish ... outside the pale, but rather charming in an odd sort of way',[54] a certain degree of waywardness and unconventionality was accepted simply because they were artists. Added to this was their status as rough-diamond 'colonials' who were expected to break all rules and conventions. As part of a broader picture of changing attitudes towards the Commonwealth, a directness and simplicity of approach was indulged – even welcomed – from the people of Britain's former colonies. In the early years of Empire, Britain had exported its language, legal system, customs and infrastructure to dominions around the world. Now, as part of the shift away from Empire towards Commonwealth, Britain was looking towards its former colonies for new vigour and a fresh approach. While it could be argued that this was only colonialism in another guise, there is no doubt that Clark and many others like him, inured to the duplicity and snobbery of British society, welcomed the directness of the Australians like a breath of fresh air.

Bryan Robertson was another key figure in bringing Australian artists together and in strengthening friendships, both in his curation of the Whitechapel show of Australian contemporary painting and through parties and Sunday lunches at his home. He was also central to the promotion of the 'Australian school' of painting in London through his writings for the *London Magazine* and elsewhere. A number of other influential literary figures in London shared an enthusiasm for Australian art, notably Al Alvarez, the Australian author and poet Charles Osborne, who worked with John Lehmann and later Alan Ross on the *London Magazine*, and John Douglas Pringle who had previously been editor of the *Sydney Morning Herald* before returning to London as editor of the *Observer*. Tom Rosenthal, who worked for Thames and Hudson, wrote for *The Listener* and owned works by Boyd and Nolan, and Dennis Duerden, art critic for *Arts Review* were also influential supporters of Australian art.

Robert Hughes, who had collaborated with Robertson on the *Recent Australian Painting* exhibition catalogue, arrived in London just at the time when Australian art had reached its zenith of hype and popularity. As Clive James, an old friend from student days in Sydney observed, Hughes was 'already halfway way to everywhere'. Whereas James had arrived in London during a cold January in 1962 with 'nothing to declare at customs except goose-pimples under my white nylon drip-dry shirt',[55] Hughes was living near Piccadilly Circus in a suite of rooms at the Albany where neighbours included the novelist Graham Greene. Well off and well connected, Hughes seemed to know everybody.[56] James accompanied Robert Hughes on a visit to the Colony Room in Soho (renowned drinking club and favourite watering hole of Francis Bacon, Lucian Freud and Bruce Bernard), where James met and immediately fell foul of Colin McInnes – another long-term expatriate. With Clark and Robertson, McInnes had extolled the work of Nolan in a recently published Thames and Hudson monograph – cynically dubbed 'Three Authors in search of a Painter' for its verbose style.

Robertson's close circle of artist friends included Prunella Clough, Bridget Riley, Keith Vaughan, Patrick Procktor, Roy de Maistre and Lawrence Daws. At the time of Daws' return to London in early 1961 Robertson was already putting the Whitechapel exhibition together. 'He heard about me and he wanted to see me and he came round', Daws recalled … 'Later I also went and saw him in Draycott Gardens [sic] and he worked out a couple of paintings he wanted in the show'.[57] Robertson regularly visited Australian artists' studios to see what was being produced or to select paintings for exhibition. His visit to Brett Whiteley's Ladbroke Grove studio proved a *eureka* moment for Robertson; a high point in his curatorial life and a breakthrough for Whiteley. Elsewhere artists did their best to put on an impressive show, knowing that Robertson's influence could be crucial to success in London. When Robertson went to Arthur Boyd's house at 13 Hampstead Lane to choose paintings for a retrospective exhibition at the Whitechapel Gallery, he was shown into a room that had been cleared and the curtains drawn to shut out the daylight. A chair and table with a whisky bottle on it had been placed at one end to put him at his ease, while paintings were brought out one by one, lit by a studio light 'against a backdrop of red velvet curtains'.

MOVING UP AND MOVING IN

The prosperity that many Australian artists achieved in London in the early to mid-years of the 1960s often meant a move to properties in more expensive and centrally located parts of London. Lawrence Daws, whilst keeping his studio over the ABC bread shop in Hampstead High Street, moved into Brett Whiteley's old residence at 129 Ladbroke Grove where Mick Johnson was still living upstairs on the second floor. The Blackmans moved to a second-floor flat in Hanover Gate Mansions, a massive block of apartments just off Regent's Park, where Yoko Ono had previously lived with her first husband. It had a large studio that Charles furnished with curtains of canvas off-cuts and carpeted with masonite paintings. Three apartments in the same block were occupied at various times by Australian artists. Leonard Hessing shared with Colin Lanceley, who was visited on one occasion by the surrealist painter Joan Miró. The sculptor Roger Klippel, painter John Olsen and the art critic Robert Hughes all stayed at Hanover Gate Mansions during periods spent in London during the 1960s.

Despite financial success that saw the price of his paintings rise almost weekly during the early 1960s, Arthur Boyd chose to stay in Highgate and the area became a focal point for other members of Boyd's extended family – such as his sister Mary, who settled there with her husband the painter John Perceval and their four children in 1963.[58] Brother David and his wife Hermia also returned to London with their three daughters in 1962 and lived for a time in the Priors apartment building on the edge of Hampstead Heath, before buying their own house in Islington. Son Jamie described how the three-floor Victorian town house on Hampstead Lane became 'a powerhouse, a factory, a place for generating art',[59] with work gradually filling the whole house. Brenda Niall, the Boyd family biographer, describes the ground-floor sitting-room as being 'always under threat, and whenever a buyer came there would be frantic tidying-up so that paintings could be seen to advantage'. The basement was used for the storage of paintings and materials where there was a 'fortune's worth' of dry colour in ten-gallon drums of dry colour, copper sheets, rolls of canvas and framed and unframed paintings 'against every wall'.[60] The whole of the ground floor was taken over as studio space. The front room (or 'tidy room' as it was known) had a white carpet which was covered in sheeting and reserved as a clean space whilst the 'splashy stuff' went on in the adjoining back room:

> everything would be splattered with paint, including Arthur's gramophone … and the postcards he put up to look at. … He put up two 1000-watt bulbs in the studio so that he could keep painting through the dark London afternoons, when daylight failed early. Often he would paint till midnight or later: he would have to be called to his meals or he would forget them.[61]

Brett Whiteley, married to Wendy at Chelsea Registry Office in 1962, moved to an imposing studio in Melbury Road near Holland Park, where Sidney Nolan, keeping his visits a secret from Cynthia, frequently came to keep an eye on what his young rival was painting. The split-level, garden pavilion had once been owned by Pre-Raphaelite William Holman Hunt, and the great oak that grew in front of it, under which the artist had played with his children, was now the place where Whiteley and his friends would gather for drinks. Clive James, previously living in a basement in Tufnell Park, moved subsequently to a top-floor flat of the house in Melbury Road, which held a large contingent of Australian expatriates. He observed Whiteley's rapid success with some envy, whilst enjoying his expensive cigars and imported Australian beer. One night James joined a circle of 'murmuring people in fancy dress, passing, after one dainty puff each, an oddly defeated-looking roll-your-own cigarette around in a circle' that he sucked 'to a stub in two jumbo drags'.[62]

In his memoirs, under the pseudonym 'Delish', James describes Wendy Whiteley as a 'seraphically lovely van Eyck angel in jeans and T-shirt' with 'a hard business brain' who 'could spot anyone who would waste her husband's time a mile off … she had a clock running somewhere in the background and always made sure he was dead on time for dinner with Sir Kenneth Clark'. The 'golden-haired' Whiteley, 'rugby-nosed and as restless as a surfer on a wet day … chose a theme, painted every possible variation on it, and then sold his sketchbooks and preliminary drawings along with the pictures'.[63] Whiteley's ability to work quickly was a factor in his rapid rise to success, mirroring that of Nolan in some respects, although evidently the two artists viewed each other rather differently. While they appeared to rub along together as friends, Whiteley privately satirised Nolan's prolixity and mechanistic approach, whereas Nolan admired Whiteley's natural talent, counselling him to 'Just build your world regularly and shove it out regularly. It all belongs to you just as much as your fingers and toes'.[64]

CONCLUSION

For Australian artists in London, the early 1960s was both a beginning and an end: a prelude to the 'Swinging 60s' and also the end of a brief postwar period of colonial expatriation for artists who had still sought international status and recognition in the 'mother country'. Emphasizing the ephemeral and artificial nature of the cultural 'colony' of Australians in London, Alomes has compared it to an artificial plant or fragile pot plant. It was, he contends, 'a post-colonial aberration, engendered by the meeting of the last post-imperial waves with the emerging era of international travel and global diversity'.[65] A changing cultural scene, increased prosperity and an unprecedented boom in the art market back in Australia, made returning home an enticing prospect for long-term expatriate artists, whilst increased air travel made it possible. As the 1960s progressed, expatriate Australians working in the broader field of the creative arts returned to an 'Australia in which the people felt more in touch with the land and its history than the derivative English "cultural pattern" they had left'.[66]

Cultural displacement, it has been argued, can be a spur to creativity, but for many of those in London in the early 1960s, expatriation was not an aim in itself, but rather 'the route to continued work at one's profession'.[67] Charles Blackman would later describe himself as an Australian 'isolated' in Britain,[68] whilst Francis Lymburner, who returned to Sydney in 1964, continued to feel an outsider in both countries. The artist Tony Underhill, who lived in London until his death in 1977, described Australian identity as something not rooted to place, but carried internally. Louis James, for whom a 15-year period spent in London had felt like 'being in a dream', continued to feel pangs of 'homesickness' for England several years after returning to Australia. Others, like Lawrence Daws, were content to live between two countries for a period of time, whilst Sidney Nolan achieved international fame, becoming, at the same time, an artist who never quite belonged to either country. Family ties were often a factor that either led to permanent roots being put down in Britain, or to the eventual return to Australia. The fact that Arthur Boyd's children and later, grandchildren would grow up in England has been given as one of the reasons that the artist chose to remain there (along with Boyd's fear of flying) that made the means of return slow and sporadic. There was no sudden end to the presence of Australian artists in London, and just as Charles Blackman, Brett Whiteley and others returned home in the mid 1960s, so more young Australian artists such as Colin Lanceley, Michael Ramsden, Philippe Mora, and others took their place. Arthur Boyd and Sidney Nolan, affluent and comfortable in the British art world, remained to paint Australia from afar, where the peculiarly lyrical and literary qualities of their work continued to appeal to the sensibilities of the British art market.

ACKNOWLEDGMENTS

I would like to acknowledge all those who generously gave of their time to talk to me about expatriate life in London: To Barbara Blackman, Edit and Lawrence Daws, Guy Warren, and Beryl Whiteley, who all agreed to be interviewed, sharing much useful information and greatly adding to my understanding of the period. I also wish to thank Christine France and David Rainey for introductions given in Australia, and Professor Carl Bridge for much enthusiastic support in Britain. Steven Miller of the Art Gallery of New South Wales, and Janeen Haythornwhaite and

Nayia Yiakoumaki of the Whitechapel Gallery have all offered generous support with archive research. Lastly, I am very grateful to Traudi Allen, not only for a memorable lunch, but also for introducing me to David Dunstan, resulting in this collaboration.

ENDNOTES

1. Lawrence Daws interviewed by Hal Missingham, 1965.
2. Barbara Blackman interviewed by the author, 2006.
3. Shapcott, 1967, 52.
4. Barbara Blackman interviewed by the author, 2006. See also Shapcott, 1967, 52.
5. Weston, 1982, 39.
6. Charles Blackman interviewed by Thomas Shapcott in 1987; Shapcott, 1989, 2–3.
7. Charles Blackman interviewed by Thomas Shapcott in 1987; Shapcott, 1989, 2–3.
8. Niall, 2002, 319–320.
9. Niall, 2002, 326–327.
10. Niall, 2002, 332.
11. Alomes, 1999, 80.
12. Brett Whiteley, letter to his mother, dated 'Thursday', Sydney, Art Gallery of New South Wales, FA 759.994 W594 4.
13. Lawrence Daws interviewed by Hal Missingham, 1965.
14. Lawrence Daws interviewed by the author, 2005.
15. Blackman, 1997, 231.
16. Al Alvarez, 'The Paintings of Charles Blackman: The Substance of Dreams', *Studio International*, September 1965. Quoted in Shapcott, 1967, 67.
17. Blackman, 1997, 264.
18. Blackman, 1997, 258.
19. Shapcott, 1989, 4.
20. Moore, 1993, 21.
21. Shapcott, 1967, 67.
22. Lawrence Daws interviewed by the author, 2005.
23. Cosgrove, 2007, 82.
24. Alannah Coleman interviewed by Wendy Bradley, 1988.
25. Alannah Coleman interviewed by Wendy Bradley, 1986.
26. Bungey, 2007, 500. See also Adams, 1987, 168.
27. Nolan, 1967.
28. Adams, 1987, 167.
29. Adams, 1987, 129.
30. James, 1985, 295.
31. Kolenberg and Pearce et.al., 1992, 17.
32. Lymburner to Teddy Krips, London, 28 June 1962, Francis Lymburner papers, Sydney, Art Gallery, MS1999.11 (personal correspondence box 4).

33. Lymburner to Krips, London, 7 May 1963, Francis Lymburner papers, Sydney, Art Gallery, MS1999.11 (personal correspondence box 4).
34. Lymburner to Krips, London, 28 June 1962. Francis Lymburner papers, Sydney, Art Gallery, MS1999.11 (personal correspondence box 4).
35. Lymburner to Krips, London, 29 September 1962. Francis Lymburner papers, Sydney, Art Gallery, MS1999.11 (personal correspondence box 4).
36. Lymburner to Krips, London, 25 January 1963. Francis Lymburner papers, Francis Lymburner papers, Sydney, Art Gallery, MS1999.11 (personal correspondence box 4).
37. 'The artist at work: Francis Lymburner explains his ideas', *Town and Around*, BBC TV, 21 February 1963, interview conducted by Richard Baker.
38. Whiteley to his mother, January 6 [1961]. Letter on *Ram Hotel, Newark, Notts.* headed notepaper, Sydney, Art Gallery of New South Wales, FA 759.994 W594 4.
39. Ibid.
40. Whiteley to his mother, London, 4 December 1960, Sydney, Art Gallery of New South Wales, FA 759.994 W594 4.
41. Charles Blackman interviewed by Thomas Shapcott, 1987, 67–68.
42. Lawrence Daws interviewed by the author, 2005.
43. Whiteley to his mother, January 6 [1961], Sydney, Art Gallery of New South Wales, FA 759.994 W594 4.
44. Whiteley to his mother, January 6 [1961], Sydney, Art Gallery of New South Wales, FA 759.994 W594 4.
45. The phrase 'relentlessly meeting the English' is taken from Blackman, 1997, 257–258.
46. Barbara Blackman interviewed by the author, 2006.
47. Barbara Blackman interviewed by the author, 2006.
48. Shapcott, 1989, 4.
49. Adams, 1987, 148–49.
50. Clark, 1977, 150.
51. Adams, 1987, 148.
52. Barbara Blackman interviewed by the author, 2006.
53. Barbara Blackman interviewed by the author, 2006.
54. Guy Warren interviewed by the author, 2007. Guy Warren (b.1921) was an expatriate artist based in London in the 1950s. He returned to Australia in 1959.
55. James, 1985, 179.
56. James, 1985, xi.
57. Lawrence Daws interviewed by the author, 2005.
58. Niall, 2002, 327.
59. Niall, 2002, 328.
60. Niall, 2002, 329–330.
61. Niall, 2002, 328–329.
62. James, 1985, 304.
63. James, 1985, 299–300.
64. Nolan to Whiteley, 'Antarctica', 24 January 1964, AGNSW (FA 759.994 W594 4).

65 Alomes, 1999, 264.
66 Alomes, 1999, 253.
67 Alomes, 1999, 261.
68 Shapcott, 1989, 4.

PRIMARY SOURCES

Barbara Blackman interviewed by the author, 1 December 2006, Canberra.
Charles Blackman interviewed by Thomas Shapcott, 1987.
Alannah Coleman interviewed by Wendy Bradley, October 1986, London.
Alannah Coleman interviewed by Wendy Bradley, September 1988, London.
Francis Lymburner papers, Sydney, Art Gallery of New South Wales, MS1999.11.
Lawrence Daws interviewed by Hal Missingham, 21 September 1965, London, Hazel de Berg tapes, Canberra, National Library of Australia, ORAL DeB 107.
Lawrence Daws interviewed by the author, 6 December 2005, Beerwah.
Guy Warren interviewed by the author, 4 November 2007, Sydney.
Brett Whiteley, folder of photocopied correspondence, Sydney, Art Gallery of New South Wales, FA 759.994 W594 4.

REFERENCES

Adams, Brian. 1987. *Sidney Nolan, Such is Life, A Biography*. Hawthorn, Vic.: Century Hutchinson.
Alomes, Stephen. 1999. *When London Calls: The Expatriation of Australian Creative Artists to Britain*. Cambridge: Cambridge University Press.
Blackman, Barbara. 1997. *Glass After Glass: Autobiographical Reflections*, Ringwood, Vic.: Viking/Penguin Books.
Bungey, Darleen. 2007. *Arthur Boyd : A Life*. Crows Nest, NSW: Allen & Unwin.
Cosgrove, Bryony, editor. 2007. *Portrait of a Friendship; The Letters of Barbara Blackman and Judith Wright 1950–2000*. Carlton, Vic.: The Miegunyah Press.
Clark, Kenneth. 1977. *The Other Half, a Self-Portrait*. London and New York: Harper and Row, Publishers.
James, Clive. 1985. *Falling Towards England*. London: Jonathan Cape.
Kolenberg, Hendrik; Pearce, Barry. 1992. *Francis Lymburner 1916–1972: Retrospective*. Sydney: Art Gallery of New South Wales.
Moore, Felicity St John, editor. 1993. *Schoolgirls and Angels, a Retrospective Exhibition of Paintings and Drawings by Charles Blackman*. Melbourne: National Gallery of Victoria.
Niall, Brenda. 2002. *The Boyds: A Family Biography*. Carlton, Vic.: Melbourne University Press.
Nolan, Cynthia. 1967. *Open Negative: An American Memoir*. London, Melbourne: Macmillan.
Shapcott, Thomas. 1967. *Artists in Queensland: Focus on Charles Blackman*, St. Lucia, Qld: University of Queensland Press.
Shapcott, Thomas. 1989. *The Art of Charles Blackman*. London: André Deutsch.
Weston, Neville. 1982. *Lawrence Daws*. Frenchs Forest, NSW and Wellington, New Zealand: A.H. & A.W. Reed Pty. Ltd.

Cite this chapter as: Pierse, Simon. 2009. 'Australian artists in London: The early 1960s'. *Australians in Britain: The Twentieth-Century Experience*, edited by Bridge, Carl; Crawford, Robert; Dunstan, David. Melbourne: Monash University ePress. pp. 13.1 to 13.17. DOI: 10.2104/ab090013.

TOURISTS, EXPATS AND INVISIBLE IMMIGRANTS
BEING AUSTRALIAN IN ENGLAND IN THE 1960s AND 70s

Graeme Davison, Monash University
> *Graeme Davison has written widely on Australian history, where his publications include* The Rise and Fall of Marvellous Melbourne *(1978 and 2004),* Car Wars *(2004) and, as co-editor,* The Oxford Companion to Australian History. *He is a Sir John Monash Distinguished Professor at Monash University.*

> Images of the Australian presence in Britain have long been dominated by the self-justifying narratives of the Expatriates. But literary intellectuals are less representative of the general experience than the thousands of working holiday-makers who arrived during the 1960s and 70s. These young, usually female, teachers, nurses and office-workers were sometimes sojourners, returning to Australia after a year or two, but others stayed on and merged with the British mainstream. Their letters and diaries constitute a valuable unexploited source on the Australian diaspora. This chapter examines the letters of two Australian women, one a sojourner, and the other an 'invisible immigrant'.

Looming in the path of the student of the Australian diaspora is the large and now familiar figure, the Expatriate. For half a century, we have been amused and occasionally outraged by the gang of self-conscious, articulate writers, artists, entertainers and academics whose self-justifying narratives largely define what it means to be an Australian in England.[1] It is hardly surprising that historians have been drawn so strongly to figures like Clive James, Barry Humphries, Germaine Greer, Rolf Harris and Peter Conrad, who have made careers simultaneously performing and ridiculing a standard repertoire of Australian characters for an English public happy to have their stereotypes of Australia confirmed. The expatriates, however, have been at most a subsection of a much larger population of Australians in Britain. For most of the twentieth century, the Australian diaspora has been more female than male, and has found employment in a wide range of occupations, professional and manual, including teaching and nursing, office work, and domestic labour as well as the 'cultural industries' such as academia, broadcasting and entertainment. While the largest single concentration of Australians in London, from the 1920s onwards, was in the boarding houses and bed-sits of Kensington and Earl's Court, many others consciously avoided Kangaroo Valley and merged with the English mainstream, where their Australianness nevertheless remained an important part of their experience and identity.

Expatriatism was a stance characteristic of the generation of Australians who came to England during the 1950s and 1960s, often in self-conscious revolt against the strictures of suburban Australia, and who encountered an England still struggling with the legacy an imperial past. Their ambivalent relationships with both countries derived from the conflicts inherent in the transformation of each. Before the Second World War, only a minority of Australians, mostly members of an Anglophile upper middle class, could afford to make the voyage to England. By the 1960s rising affluence in Australia, and a fall in the relative cost of passages, as Italian and Greek cruise liners joined the P&O steamers on the Australian route, began to broaden the social mix of travellers making their way from Australia to England. Living in London, often as a base for a backpacking or Kombi-van tour of the Continent, was becoming a popular, if not yet obligatory, rite of passage for young Australians. The lines of camper-vans parked along the Strand, as one cohort of young Australians sold their temporary homes on to the next, was perhaps the most conspicuous advertisement of the Australian presence in London during these years. As the flow of Australians enlarged, so, we might hypothesise, did the tensions of expatriatism begin to abate. By the 1970s, with the advent of air travel and the beginning of the steep drop in telephone costs, the communication gap between England and Australia had begun to close.

Living in England, especially in London, has become firmly inscribed in Australian consciousness as a rite of passage, and a gateway to personal liberation. In her perceptive book *To seek her fortune in London*, Angela Woollacott has examined the personal testimony of the generations of middle-class Australian women who made the epic voyage to London between the 1870s and the Second World War. 'Women's travelling', she writes, 'was an assertion of independence, a bid for self-discovery, and escape from domestic gender constraints'. London was a symbol of success. 'Going to London', she continues, 'was a way for an Australian woman to express and act on her ambition: to advance her education or skills, to absorb the latest styles, genres, research, or techniques, to study under the most renowned practitioners, to gain access to the most renowned publishing houses – or simply get a job'.[2] Some Australian women, she observes in passing, found employment in music halls or choruses, the food service industry, teaching, nursing, and other less glamorous areas. For such women, she suggests, the romance, the distance, and the promise of adventure of the metropolis were what mattered. Woollacott's study draws heavily on the memoirs and other published writings of the social and literary elite, sources arguably more heavily influenced by the wisdom of hindsight and the self-justifying narratives of expatriatism than the family letters of their humbler sisters, the nurses, teachers and office-workers who, from the 1960s onward, constituted the majority of the Australian diaspora.

This chapter offers a commentary on the ways in which Woollacott's narrative of female liberation was played out in the lives of two young women who made the great voyage to London in the 1960s and early 1970s. In the age before cheap telephone calls and the internet, the process of writing letters and diaries was an integral part of the travel experience: a means, not only of communicating the events and scenes of the trip to the writer's family and friends, but of defining its significance for the writer herself. Often, no doubt, they were subject to a degree of self-censorship: not everything that the young travellers were experiencing was considered fit for the eyes of parents, siblings or the wider circle of readers among whom they were often passed around, but they are often as revealing in their silences and understatements as in their more self-conscious reflections. It is likely that many thousands of such European travel diaries and blue airmail letters now reside, neatly bundled and numbered, in cupboards and garages across Australia. A researcher appealing to readers of the *Australian Women's Weekly* to contribute such documents would probably have to cope with an avalanche of blue paper. The following narratives are the product of a first unsystematic dip into this deep well of youthful experience, disclosed through the private correspondence of two such travellers. It makes no claim to representativeness – Alison Griffiths and Helen Davison were not self-conscious feminists – but their personal testimony does suggest how some of Angela Woollacott's themes played out in the lives of women for whom the quest for personal ambition and self-discovery were pursued on more limited terms. Both were schoolteachers, one secondary, one primary; one from Sydney, one from Melbourne; one a sojourner, returning to Australia after about eighteen months of working holidays, the other, as it turned out, a long-term resident of the United Kingdom who has never, however, surrendered her Australian passport or identity.³

*   *   *

Alison Griffiths was nearly 24 when she set out in January 1964 in company with her cousin Elizabeth G. and her friend Sue J. on the maiden voyage of the *Marconi*, an Italian migrant ship that doubled as cruise liner for young Australians heading for Europe on the return journey. Elizabeth, who came from Melbourne, was also a teacher, while Sue, a nurse, came from Sydney. Alison had grown up in Gordon, on Sydney's North Shore, and was educated at the Presbyterian Ladies' College before completing an Arts degree at Sydney University. She had taught, not altogether happily, at Ravenswood School for Girls before deciding to join her friends on an overseas trip to Europe. Her father, a former missionary in the Solomon Islands, was now the Sydney-based secretary of the interdenominational mission, and Alison's horizons were broadened, geographically if not socially, by the almost constant flow of returning missionaries and Solomon Islanders passing through the family's house at Gordon. Her mother Margaret, a lively well-read Sydney Science graduate, had herself travelled to England in the 1920s, to study at a missionary training college, and Alison's home letters were written primarily for her, often describing places that her mother had visited over 30 years earlier. In the dying days of empire, England, for all three girls, remained a kind of spiritual Home where bonds of family and emotional attachment were still strong. Each had British aunts, cousins, second-cousins or family friends to whom they could look for hospitality during their visit.

When the *Marconi* docked in Genoa, at the end of its voyage, three travellers took the train across the snow-clad Alps, only to arrive at Calais in the midst of a wild storm.

> There [Alison related] we lugged our baggage on to 'Cote d'Azur', a French ferry, & soon saw the coast of France disappear into the haze on the horizon. Then we forgot all emotional association with past, present and future, & just endured the next hour and half. It was a rotten crossing, the first time in 12,000 miles I've really felt at sea. I lost track of the others (but Libbie felt pretty crook, I believe). I just staggered around the deck … wiping the saltwater off my glasses … Then – the white cliffs of Dover! through the sea mist. Soon we were on shore again, with a comfortable English bobby on the wharf, & people speaking English, & £.s.d. etc.! Gee we all felt pro-English! Customs was no problem at all – we must have looked painfully honest, – then we were in the train, with two other NZ boys, Ian and Murray there too – 'and the sun shone and the water had abated' (?) and the birds sang.

Like Noah's passage through the flood, the three young Australians' stormy channel crossing had brought them safely Home.

A few days later they were excitedly walking the streets of London. 'We're very happy here: today we went into town – on a 97 horsepower scarlet painted London omnibus – and watched fascinated – like being in a book – we each fixed up finance and mailing addresses with our respective banks. Gee, it was strange to be in Piccadilly Circus, & Victoria Station, and Berkely [sic] Square'. The sensation of 'being in a book', of experiencing a world previously only known indirectly through print, pictures, family recollections or the gramophone records of Flanders and Swann, would gradually dim, though never quite disappear, as the day-to-day realities of life in London sank in. A few days later Alison reported: 'This afternoon we all went to the Tate Gallery, it was absolutely <u>marvellous</u> to <u>see</u> the real paintings, to walk up close and <u>see</u> the brushstrokes in a Van Gogh, a Turner, a Monet, then step back and explore the whole painting, the <u>original</u>!' When expatriates dismissed Australians as 'second-hand Europeans', they drew in part upon precisely this sense of being detached by distance from the original sources of their civilisation: a European trip was a deeper draught from wells they had already tapped at home.

The cultural splendour of London could sometimes overawe the young Australians, though never repress their glee. 'We went into the West End again today, & wandered round … it was fun – we must have looked patently new to London, brown faces, broad smiles as we looked eagerly all around us, "beaut" and other idioms besprinkling our conversation. We blew around London like three hayseeds'. The winter landscape, so different from Sydney's, was a special delight. After an expedition to Kew Gardens Alison wrote, lyrically, to her mother:

> I see what you mean, Mum, about the trees, leaflessly stark and beaut: like the great veins branching into the finest twisting arteries, etched against the sky so clearly and finely … In the Gardens themselves, we saw crocuses – deep blue & yellow – bursting open amongst the grass, and beautiful snowdrops too. And we saw ducks and swans and moorhens on the lakes, & the gleaming Thames, and great droopy trees on the wide grassy patches. All very peaceful. And you can imagine how we felt on entering the great greenhouses: it was the smell, the moist, warm tang of the bush, unmistakeable, which first impinged on our senses, & then we saw crimson bottlebrush & golden wattle, & gum trees – bless them! – and lovely-scented brown boronia.

This picture of a winter English landscape, shared through memory with her mother, yet mixed with her own present memories of an Australian landscape suddenly evoked by the nostalgic aroma of eucalyptus in an English greenhouse, is expressive of the kind of double-vision characteristic of an Anglo-Australian sensibility.

Two of the three friends, Alison and Elizabeth, took up residence in a tiny third-floor flat with a low sloping roof in Roehampton, arranged on their behalf by Sue's parents, who were renting an apartment nearby. (Sue's father, a teacher at a Sydney private school, was on a year's leave, teaching in London). The flatmates' day-to-day experience of London was defined, physically, by the unfamiliar exigencies of the coin-in-slot gas-meter, the communal bathroom, heavy overcoats and boots, the hot-water bottle and the Laundromat. By travelling and flatting together, sharing cooking and cleaning, Alison and Elizabeth had entered an arrangement similar to those made by many other young Australian women living in London. By pooling their finances they were also able to smooth out some of the economic ups and downs of short-term employment. In the eyes of their parents, no doubt, the arrangement also offered a degree of protection, or mutual chaperonage, not available to those travelling alone.

London was a magnet, but it was just as important as a base from which the Australians could reach the even more magnetic cities of Paris, Rome, Athens and Florence. Both Alison and Elizabeth spoke serviceable French and had taken Italian lessons on the *Marconi*. Their university studies had given them some familiarity with European art and history and they had already acquired an interest in French and Italian cooking. About five of the eighteen months they spent abroad was spent on the Continent, most of it in southern Europe. In order to save the funds for these expeditions, they were obliged to live frugally in London, making only occasional visits to theatre and opera, looking out for free concerts, exhibitions and museums.

In search of homeland company or flatmates, many Australians gravitated to the traditional centre of the expatriate Australian community in Kensington and Earl's Court. Alison and Elizabeth were wary of its reputation.

> Uncle David is quite right: Earl's Court still is full of Australians, too full. They call it Kangaroo Valley; Aussies are renowned – or notorious – for their wild parties. We had resolved that Earl's Court was the one place in London where we definitely did <u>not</u> want to flat. Also, it's not an awfully nice area, very cosmopolitan.

After returning from their second trip to the Continent, they spent several anxious days as winter approached searching for a new home, before finding a pleasant flat on a monthly tenancy near Gloucester Road.

> The flat we now have is better than either of the others. a) we won't be tied for 6-9 months b) we won't be tossed out after 2 months <u>and</u> it is at Gloucester Road near the Tube, which is on <u>three</u> lines, the Circle Line, the Piccadilly Line & the District Line (direct to Surrey for supply teaching) – & yet within walking distance of Harrods and other Knightsbridge shops, the Albert Hall (concerts), the Victoria and Albert Museum & Kensington Gardens. We are also only about 10 minutes walk from the Presbyterian Church we attended last Sunday and liked.

Like other young Australians, Alison and her friends had come in search of new experiences – of lands, peoples, cultures and experiences different from their own – although, as her letters make plain, the itinerary they followed was shaped in accordance with their own tastes and standards.

Within England, their circle of acquaintance extended upward, from their own solid middle class, via their English cousins, into the lower rungs of the English gentry and downwards into the working class whose children they encountered, day by day, as supply teachers in government and Catholic parish schools. Back home they had taught only in private schools; now they were suddenly plunged into London's blackboard jungle. 'The children are rather tough, but we are glad of the experience', Elizabeth admitted after a few weeks at the Gainsborough School for Girls. Alison approached her temporary job at St Edward the Confessor School, a Catholic secondary school in Richmond, with a 'what-the heck feeling', a combination of economic pragmatism and almost anthropological curiosity. 'Sue and Libbie are desperately trying to prevent my landslide crash into a London semi-cockney accent, into which I lapse unconsciously at the slightest provocation. "Goo'ness", says Libbie, "that Customs man has no consonants at all. We must get Alison out of here quick."'

During weekends and school holidays they sometimes stayed as house-guests of their English friends and relations. Aware of the reputation of Australians for 'botting' on their English relatives, they usually waited politely to be asked. Some of their hosts had themselves been born in Australia, or had lived there, and were eager to return the hospitality they had enjoyed in Sydney or Melbourne. Yet there was always an element of uncertainty in these encounters: the nuances of upper-class manners and English under-statement, the subtle gradations of class and status, often left the young Australians uncertain of exactly where they stood. It was a fascinating, but often perplexing, experience.

Alison describes these visits in loving detail, recording every detail of the furnishings of their hosts' houses, the food they ate, and the landscape through which they rambled and cycled. For young women of their class and background, life in the English country house was a kind of finishing school, an opportunity to observe and emulate a way of life they found fascinating. 'We had deliciously English roast beef – hot on Sat, cold on Sunday: a most delicate delicious flavour', Alison reported after a weekend visit to Reigate to stay with her sister-in-law's aunt and uncle, the Storrs, whose butcher, she explained, maintained that Australian beef 'has to walk too far!' In the spring, just before they departed for France and Italy, all three stayed for several weeks with Sue's parents at their house in Pewsey Vale, where they heard their first cuckoo, hunted for old books and prints in nearby Marlborough, and cycled across the Wiltshire countryside.

Perhaps the most memorable of these encounters, however, was a visit to the home of Elizabeth's mother's distant cousin, Bertine ('Babs') Hay. 'Mrs Hay is awfully nice, she really is a pet', Alison enthused. Back in the 1920s Bertine Hay had swum in London's literary world, becoming one of the city's first independent woman publishers. Now, a widow still young at heart, she was the very model of an unconventional English gentlewoman while her home, Stoke Hill Farm, a seventeenth century farm house, left all three girls almost speechless in admiration.

> Mrs Hay's house is just perfect, there's no other word for it: everything is unobtrusively and exactly right [Alison wrote]. There's a wonderful view, as the house is set on the side of a hill, & half a cyclorama of lovely valley extends to the horizon, with trees and daffodils in the foreground … There's a most wonderfully thatched barn, and a grove of young beeches, & we picked our first primroses there! … Inside there are little beautiful antique pieces such as paperweights, & china & a beautiful old hearth, & terracotta tiles, & one room was once a barn, & has the hayloft still there, with clean whitened boards. But it's indescribable really, I just sat there almost open-mouthed, it was all so beautifully right.

The ideal of femininity represented by Bertine Hay and Stoke Hill Farm was a subtle blend of the modern and the antique, of personal independence lived, however, within a traditional rural way of life. To the young Australians it may have suggested some of the possibilities of personal fulfilment and aesthetic expression to be found within a conservative social and moral order. Personal emancipation and modernism, in its aesthetic forms, were perhaps only accidental allies. Many young Australians arrived in England not to discover the new, but to revere the antique.

Cultural historians look back on the 1960s as the period of notable innovation when 'swinging London' became synonymous with bold experiments in drama, film, political satire and popular music. It was the era of the Rolling Stones, *Private Eye*, the plays of John Osborne, Harold Pinter, Peter Shaffer and Joe Orton. However, it was Olivier's *Othello* and the comic songs of Flanders and Swann, not the plays of Britain's Angry Young Men, that drew Alison and her friends to the West End. Even the mild satire of 'Beyond the Fringe' Alison found 'hammy' and unconvincing.

Yet it would be wrong to conclude that London had left the visitors unchanged. The three friends would eventually return to Australia, but, along with their Kodachrome memories of a wider world, would come subtle changes in taste and outlook, a new measure of personal independence, wider social and cultural sympathies and the satisfaction of having contemplated life-choices different from those they ultimately settled for.

By November, with the two trips to the Continent behind them, and another winter coming on, Alison's thoughts were tending homeward. Less than a year after their departure she felt 'more than a year older in experience', although, oddly, much 'younger than Miss Griffiths of Ravenswood'. Over the year, she noticed, her attitude to the idea of returning had fluctuated:

> It's funny, Mum, but in the past few weeks I seem to have gone further: right at the start of travelling I was sort of homesick. Then for a long time I had a kind of anti-homesickness, a claustrophobic trapped feeling that, in a way, I couldn't go home because a fledgling can't fly away then go back to the old nest, as it were. I felt I'd 'burnt my boats'. Now I seem to have got beyond that again, and am content with the idea of going home.

Yet while she was now happy to come home, 'I don't quite see myself fitting into the same old niche anymore'. She would not go back to teaching at Ravenswood and gave notice that things would have to change at home too. In London, she explained, she had been able 'to be completely myself & do this unencumbered by conflicting loyalties, & with no-one around to keep my conscience for me. There are some things [she confessed] I've felt pretty strongly about for a long time which have crystallised while I have been away. In particular I have for many years felt troubled by the "double life" I've had at home regarding what I feel perfectly happy for me to do (eg go to theatres) and what visiting missionaries etc disagree with'. If she now decided to stay at home, she would have to be free to come and go and to invite her own friends. 'I've never been very emphatically certain about the rights and wrongs, the "black & white" of issues. It seems though that what could be wrong for one could be right for another, & we are not to judge'.

Alison acted on her decision to go back to living with her parents in Sydney, where she researched and wrote a book about the story of the mission she had viewed earlier with such ambivalence. After her mother's death she moved to Melbourne, where her love of teaching and writing fostered a satisfying career, and where her father joined her for the last 13 years of his life. London, perhaps, had brought no sharp break in the outward pattern of her life, but it had given her the time and space to consider its direction as well as the courage to renegotiate the relationship with her family. Some of this might have occurred, perhaps, if she had been living somewhere else in Australia, but England had also furnished models of a different kind of life, the possibility of becoming what she modestly called 'a normal, cultivated, educated person'.

*   *   *

Helen Davison was nearly 28 when she arrived in London, along with her friend Helen J ('Flo' as she was usually called by her friends), in the winter of 1971. Since graduation from the Melbourne Teachers' College, she had spent several years as an infant teacher in Victorian schools, mainly in the country, before moving back to Melbourne where she taught in working-class Broadmeadows. Helen and Flo had grown up in the bosom of the North Essendon Methodist Church, and most of their social life occurred within its fellowship. Helen was a warm-hearted, sociable young woman, close to her family but with a lively interest in other cultures that had led her, again under Methodist auspices, to spend her summer holidays as a volunteer on the Aboriginal mission at Yirrkala and to visit the Methodist community at Vatakoula in Fiji. (Long afterwards, Helen continued to sign off her letters home with the Fijian salutation 'Loloma'). Helen's father had been born in England and emigrated to Australia as an infant; she had introductions to one or two of his relatives in the Midlands, but the links were now slender, and she could not draw upon the close network of hospitality enjoyed by Alison and her friends.

In London, the two friends gravitated, through their Essendon friends John and Sue S, to the Methodist Church in Finchley. Through a local agent, they found accommodation nearby, 'a bedsitting room with a kitchen in the corner ... very clean and quite reasonable £ 7-7-0'. They visited Australia House to register their names and address and the nearby London branch of the State Savings Bank to establish a bank account. Afterwards, they wandered down Fleet Street towards St Paul's, visited Samuel Johnson's house and explored churches in search of brasses for the brass-rubbing expeditions that would become one of their favourite activities in the coming months. It was still midwinter, the trees in Hyde Park looked 'rather dainty' without their leaves and there was the occasional sprinkle of snow. They had applied for jobs soon after their arrival, Helen as a supply teacher, Flo as a typist. In the meantime they occupied their days as tourists, beginning in London but venturing further into the countryside, to St Albans and then to York and Scotland, as spring approached. 'I have picked my first wild primroses and forget-me-nots, heard the first cuckoo, eaten roast beef and yorkshire pudding, played darts in a little pub, seen deer running wild across the moors and done other Englishy things that are not as noteworthy as these' she reported in April. 'Englishy' was code for the idealised landscape of thatched cottages, country gardens, cream teas and long summer evenings that Helen and her mother had shared since childhood, when Beatrix Potter and A.A. Milne had been among their favourite bedtime reading. 'I would love you all to be here to see how "Englishy" England is', she enthused after another expedition.

Not everything English was 'Englishy', of course, and Helen was soon noting other less advertised differences from her homeland:

> [Countryside] It's not like our country of course. You can always see buildings and are never more than a few miles from houses and shops.

> [Dress] We don't find English girls as neatly dressed as girls at home. They dress for comfort ... with boots, heavy coats, often hats.

> [Refrigerators]: They don't seem to worry about them here.

[Pubs] People go to pubs here to drink, eat, talk and be entertained ... not loud, boozy, unrefined hotels like they are at home.

[Dogs] London people are very 'dog'. They take them into shops, trains, homes – everywhere.

[Beaches] The people on the beach were not dressed like beach-lovers at home. Lots of people don't go onto the beach but sit on deckchairs or on the lawns and paths ... They all seem a bit quiet and with no energy but I suppose they are enjoying themselves.

By April Helen had found a job teaching at a primary school nearby, and, momentously, a new boyfriend. Barry Hobbs, a secondary teacher from Bristol, was also working in London and attending the Finchley Methodist Church. Over the following weeks, their outings to the theatre and cinema and car trips into the countryside – to the New Forest, Barry's old university town, Southampton, to Lymington, and eventually to Bristol to stay with his parents – began to dominate Helen's weekly narratives, inspiring growing speculation among her family at home. By July, as the summer break approached, and she planned a five week camping trip to Spain and Morocco, the implications of the continued friendship began to occupy her thoughts. She pondered whether the time was approaching to break off the friendship, but by October, when she returned from the trip, it was still going strong.

It was only as Helen and Barry began to contemplate marriage that the working tourist began the long, and sometimes difficult, transformation into an expatriate. Barry's parents, for whom London, let alone Melbourne, was a world away, reacted to the news of their engagement with shocked disbelief. Eventually the decision was made: after their marriage in England, they would come out to Australia for two years, so that Barry could get to know Australia and Helen's family, before returning to live permanently in England. They married in 1972 and spent two happy years working and saving in Melbourne before flying back to England, as promised, in April 1974.

The England to which they returned was a gloomier country than the one they had left. Reeling under the combined effects of inflation, unemployment, petrol shortages, strikes and civil strife in Ireland, the government of Edward Heath, returned without a clear majority in the March elections, was vainly trying to stitch together a coalition with the Ulster Unionists. At Heathrow they met their Australian friends, John and Sue, now longer-term residents in England, before driving west to Bristol. It was a chilly morning at the beginning of spring and Helen scanned the countryside, alert for reassuring signs of growth and regeneration. 'The daffodils and narcissi are all out – also tulips, hyacinths and other bulbs. The trees are beginning to shoot & the blossoms are out. I expect too [that] the little country lanes with tall hedges along each side have little thatched cottages along the way. But it's very cold 10 [degrees] last night when we arrived and fog along the motorway. The sun came out this afternoon and everything looked cheerful'. Determined not to add to the heartache of separation, Helen's letters adopted a tone of defiant cheerfulness. Being back in England felt somehow strange and familiar, not unlike the feeling she had when she first left home to teach in the country.

I think I must think I'm in Bendigo for the week and will see you all again soon because we have settled in quite well really. We still miss you but there has been so much to do and think about that we have been kept busy. I suppose it will all hit us when we have somewhere to live by ourselves and can't just 'pop in' to see you. Everything and everyone is [sic] just the same as when we left and in many ways it seems as though we've never left. That's how it will be when we're with you again.

'When we're with you again' – in 1974, with oil prices rising and an English pound at only A$1.50, the prospect of reunion must have seemed a long way off. In the meantime there were the challenges of finding jobs and a home. After a trip to London to visit their Australian friends John and Sue, they returned a little disappointed. 'We would love to be near them but housing is so expensive we feel we may never get out of London as when they get teachers they don't want to loose [sic] them. Also the countryside is so pretty'. The prettiness of the countryside was one of the consolations for a life that sometimes seemed more confined than the one she had left. They concentrated their search further west, in Wiltshire, closer, but not too close, to Barry's hometown of Bristol. Aware of the pecking order among English schools, Barry was hoping for a post in a good grammar or direct grant school where he could teach A-level Physics. For several anxious weeks they lived in a miserable bed and breakfast near Andover, as Barry taught supply in a local grammar school and attended interviews for a permanent job in the new school year. 'We are still without anywhere to live or a job for September', Helen reported early in June. 'We get a bit depressed about it but don't stay that way for too long'. Two weeks later Barry was offered a job, teaching A-levels, at a good secondary modern in Salisbury. Without local qualifications and scant experience in English schools, Helen found the search even more difficult. 'I don't think they like Australians', she mused after two unsuccessful interviews, 'or rather they don't think that I've had enough experience in English schools. It's a bit disappointing as I really need to work if we're to buy a house and I don't think we can rent'. Supply teaching, a boon to the working holiday-maker, living for the day, seemed less attractive to a young couple wanting to settle down.

In the face of English indifference, Helen retained a proud, almost defiant, sense of the superiority of everything Australian. She was amused when colleagues at Barry's school invited them to what she considered a 'funny' barbecue. The evening was cold, even for an English summer, and chicken was the only meat on the griddle. 'I kept rubbishing it and comparing it to an Australian barbecue' she reported. A few weeks later they invited Barry's family to a barbecue of their own. 'They came about 5 and we had a big table with lots of salad, bread, etc and B[arry] and his Dad barbecued about 5 lb of sausages. I think everyone enjoyed it. We used our little barbecue from Australia. Some of the people [she exclaimed] had never been to a barbecue before'. The 'funny' barbecue was not the only sign she noticed of English backwardness.

It was hard to feel at home when they had still to find a place to live. Houses in Salisbury were almost as expensive as London, and with petrol prices rising almost daily, it was costly to commute. Eventually they made an offer on a new house in Warminster, a pleasant market town on the edge of Salisbury Plain. 'We want to give our house an Australian name', Helen decided. 'I wonder what Merrimbula means. What about other Australian names? We will have plenty of room for visitors if we get this house!!!' Already she was anticipating the moment when she would welcome her Australian family, especially her parents who had never visited England. 'There will be lots of little jobs that you would excel at Dad!' In October they moved in. With Barry away for most the day and no job of her own as yet, Helen was left to while away the days alone, 'the real little housewife', as she glumly described herself. 'I hope you are all well', she wrote a few weeks later. 'We think and talk of you often and feel quite close. We have hung our Australian painting in the lounge … Must choose a name soon. Lyn and Bruce suggested Gunnedah'. Responding to the hint, Helen's mother sent a book of Aboriginal place names and their meanings. 'We have had a bit of a look at the aboriginal book', Helen wrote a month or so later. 'We are rather keen on 'Karingal' ['Happy Home'] at the moment but will have another look before we decide'. Karingal, in fact, it would be. Soon they had planted an Australian snow gum in the garden. Later in the winter their first Australian guests, Helen's cousin and her new husband, arrived. 'We never expected Jo and Paul to come. I wonder who'll stay with us next? Perhaps we should have called the house "Australia House"'.

Over the following months and years, as she settled into the routines of everyday life, Helen's sense of dislocation eased. Soon she would find a regular teaching job, and later she would become mother to two girls. In the mid-1970s her parents would make a single memorable visit, long enough for her father to do some odd jobs and see the young couple in their new home. In the mid-1980s the twin horrors of Chernobyl and Mrs Thatcher prompted them to try settling in Australia, but, after a few months living on the outskirts of a Victorian country town, they decided to return to England. They live now on the Surrey-Hampshire border only a few minutes' drive from the village from which Helen's mother's English forebears had migrated to Australian in the 1840s. In the eyes of her Australian family Helen has gradually become more English, her accent, even some of her attitudes, subtly changing with the years. Life at its best is now 'brilliant' or 'smashing' rather than 'beaut'. Yet in her own eyes Australia remains Home and she has transmitted her love of the land of her birth to her English daughters, who have now travelled the Australian Outback more extensively than their Australian-born cousins. Cheap airfares have enabled the Hobbs family to visit Australia regularly, and over the years the house in Ash has indeed become 'Australia House' for dozens of Helen's relatives visiting the United Kingdom. The emails now flow back and forth so quickly that one might almost imagine that the old barriers of time and distance had dissolved. Yet these changes have possibly only accentuated the ambiguous status of being an Australian in England.

* * *

In a celebrated passage of his seminal book *Australia* (1930), Keith Hancock, speaking for his own generation of 'independent Australian Britons', protested that it was 'not impossible for Australians, nourished by a glorious literature, and haunted by old memories, to be in love with two soils'.[4] The literature, by implication, was English literature, although the land could be Australian bush as well as English countryside.

Well into the twentieth century, there would be many Australians, like Alison Griffiths, with close family and personal links with Britain, who would have felt similarly. As tourists in London, 'being in a book', they could dwell imaginatively, and for a season, on two soils. By the end of the century, however, as Britain entered the European Community, and a multi-cultural Australia sought new friends in the United States and Asia, this sentimental bond was gradually weakening.

It was much easier, now, for expatriate Australians to travel back and forth between England and Australia, even to live, alternately, on two soils, but it was becoming harder, as the cultural foundations of Anglo-Australia crumbled, to imagine both lands as one's own. For those, like Helen Hobbs, who chose to live permanently as Australians in Britain, the issues of personal and group identity were often complex and hard to resolve. Though she has lived in Britain for 30 years, she is still regarded by her friends, and indeed regards herself, as Australian. In their recent study of postwar English emigrants to Australia, *Ten Pound Poms*, Jim Hammerton and Al Thomson chart the dimensions of personal and group identity among immigrants who, because they spoke English and seemed to share many Australian traits, were often 'invisible' as immigrants to other Australians.[5] Some long-term Australian residents of Britain, they acknowledge, experienced a similar dilemma. In the twilight of empire, they had still enjoyed (if that is the word) the definite, if subordinate, status of 'colonials'. But in the shadow of its passing many Australians simply felt displaced and unrecognised: neither colonials nor expatriates, they had become invisible immigrants.

ENDNOTES

[1] Alomes, 1999; Britain, 1997.

[2] Woollacott, 2001.

[3] These letters belong to members of the author's immediate or extended family. I am grateful to Alison Griffiths and Helen Hobbs for their permission to read and quote from them. They remain, however, in private hands and closed to other researchers.

[4] Hancock, 1930.

[5] Hammerton and Thomson 2005, 10–11.

REFERENCES

Alomes, Stephen. 1999. *When London Calls: The Expatriation of Australian Creative Artists to Britain.* Cambridge: Cambridge University Press.

Britain, Ian. 1997. *Once an Australian: Journeys with Barry Humphries, Clive James, Germaine Greer and Robert Hughes.* Melbourne: Oxford University Press.

Hancock, W.K. 1930. *Australia.* London: Ernest Benn.

Hammerton, A. James; Thomson, Alistair. 2005. *Ten Pound Poms: Australia's Invisible Immigrants.* Manchester: Manchester University Press.

Woollacott, Angela. 2001. *To Try Her Fortune in London: Australian Women, Colonialism and Modernity.* New York, Oxford: Oxford University Press.

Cite this chapter as: Davison, Graeme. 2009. 'Tourists, expats and invisible immigrants: Being Australian in England in the 1960s and 70s'. *Australians in Britain: The Twentieth-Century Experience*, edited by Bridge, Carl; Crawford, Robert; Dunstan, David. Melbourne: Monash University ePress. pp. 14.1 to 14.12. DOI: 10.2104/ab090014.

CHAPTER 15

'WE CAME ON A HOLIDAY LIKE YOU'
THE AUSTRALIAN COMMUNITY PRESS IN LONDON IN THE 1970s AND 80s

David Dunstan, Monash University

> David Dunstan is Deputy Director and Senior Lecturer with the National Centre for Australian Studies and a member of the Tourism Research Unit at Monash University. He was one of the organisers of the 2005 Symposium on Australians in Britain jointly organised by the National Centre and the Menzies Centre for Australian Studies, King's College London.

> The Australian community press in London was reborn in the 1970s through catering to the needs of a new generation of mobile and youthful travellers. Australians were given the opportunity by cheap air travel to undertake in unprecedented numbers extended work and travel experiences in Europe in the 1970s and 80s. Mobile and wealthy through casual and temporary labour, both skilled and unskilled, the Australian immigrant community became well defined as part of a geographic enclave and the city's extensive cultural mosaic. This essay explores the development of the Australian community press and associated industries in these years and expressions of travel and tourism, popular culture, work and leisure.

The Australian community in London revealed itself materially in the late 1960s in the informal 'van mart' on Saturday mornings where Volkswagen Kombi vans lined up outside Australia House on the Strand. These practical box-like vehicles were the preferred means of transport for group campers travelling around Europe. The passing on of the van to the next group of itinerants was a ritual conducted by home-goers or movers-on from the Grand Working Holiday tour of Europe. This period of sojourning, as one participant, Bill James, reflected, had become 'an essential finishing school before any thought was given to taking up a 'real job' and a 'real life' at home'.[1] But when it was over the van had to go. The barter transfer was conducted under the benign and at first protective aegis of the Commonwealth government's great edifice. The civic authorities proved tolerant initially but a change in traffic regulations forced the van mart to relocate. It moved to less visible and certainly less symbolic locations on the south bank of the Thames, first at Doon Street, near Waterloo Station, and then in nearby Belvedere Road until, in 1987, it was closed altogether as a traffic hazard.[2] It moved finally to a parking lot near Old Street before fizzling out in the early 1990s. What had begun as a casual meeting place for buyers and sellers had grown to something much more demanding, with anything between 30 and 100 vans (at the height of the selling season) parked in the streets.

The fate and memory of the van mart would be of little consequence, other than for its nostalgic appeal for those involved, were it not indicative of the changing character of the population overall. Australians in the 1970s and 1980s were among the most visible of London's new immigrant groups. As late as the 1960s Australian sojourners to the UK generally travelled by boat and were still a curiosity. But their numbers were steadily increasing and by 1968 there were some 250,000 short-term (less than a year) and around 50,000 long-term Australian departures abroad; most were destined for the UK. This was a big increase on the 30,000 short-term and 20,000 long-term departures of 1950. By 1975, as Stephen Alomes observes, the 'baby boom' generation born since 1945 had arrived, causing a further increase in short-term (900,000) and long-term (66,000) departures.[3]

This growth was aided considerably by the benefits of mass jet travel. The world's first commercially successful jet airliner, the Boeing 707 and later its successor, the larger 747, was transforming the journey from Australia to the UK. In 1971 Qantas, introduced its 747Bs on the so-called Kangaroo Route, to Singapore and thence to London. Prices were cut to chase volume and to beat off competition from charter interlopers. An 'excursion fare' of A$700 and a one-way fare of A$420 reversed a steady decline in traffic. From 1972, 747 flights increased from three to five a week and a reduction in stops brought the flight time to Europe to under 25 hours. These were peak years for the arrival of young Australians in London. In 1971–72 the Kangaroo Route alone carried 40,000 passengers and in the year ending March 1975 the total increased more than six-fold to 255,000.[4]

Britain had become easier to get to but it was also easier to return home from, thus creating a more transient Australian community in London and softening any dramatic increase in numbers overall. The frequency of journeys induced other changes. One was a greater turnover in Kombi vans, and hence the van mart. Another was enhanced self-consciousness among the expatriate Australian community. Greater mobility generated more of a herd mentality among travellers, with the need or inevitability of blending in not so great. Although the census figures reveal otherwise it seemed the Australian presence was disproportionately metropolitan, with London the great base camp. Living in and near places like Earl's Court (Kangaroo Valley) meant being part of a semi-permanent enclave characterised by Australian and other transients. It was to this group that a revived immigrant press catered.

THE REBIRTH OF THE AUSTRALIAN IMMIGRANT PRESS

As late as the early 1980s the Australian expatriate community in London still operated in advance of the communications revolution and the instant data resources we now take for granted. The last journal catering to Australians in London was the *British Australasian*, which survived in attenuated form as the *Australia and New Zealand Weekly* until 1969. From that time until 1973 there was nothing.[5] But there was still a need for information, to find jobs and housing for example, and for the advertisement and sale of facilities serving the travelling expatriate community. The informal exchange and information networks that existed lacked sophistication and direct appeal to Australian newcomers.

For many newcomers, London was a lonely place. Australia House had long been a symbol and a practical refuge. Arriving in 1972, Colin Speairs would queue there to read the Australian newspapers, many of them up to six weeks old, with news that was stale even by the standards of the day. A journalist himself, Speairs had followed a classic career path from country regional, then suburban, through to metropolitan newspapers. He spent six years with the Melbourne *Age* prior to taking off to see London and then the world. It occurred to him that there had to be an opening for a publication that would cater to Australians in London, of whom the Victorian Agent-General had told him there were in excess of 100,000 – quite enough for a good-sized Australian country or suburban newspaper.[6] Speairs had taken six months leave of absence from his Australian employers but was to remain in London ten years and to lay the foundations of a revived immigrant press that survives to this day. A check of likely advertisers revealed that travel companies and camping suppliers would support such a venture. The Europe travel market, after all, was extensively patronised by Australians. Through his knowledge of Australian community newspapers Speairs knew this publication had to be distributed free. A dummy was produced over three months from rented rooms in Knightsbridge. Speairs's landlord was Iraq-born businessman Ibrahim Razuki, who had fled Iraq after the Baath Party came to power in 1963. Razuki had established himself in the London property market and was enthusiastic and open to new commercial opportunities. In April 1973 he agreed to back Speairs's newspaper, now entitled the *Australian Express*. Within a few weeks it had changed its name to the *Australasian Express*, hoping to appeal also to the smaller but evident cohort of New Zealanders.

Notice boards for accommodation and jobs, and advertisements in community newspapers were important for this highly mobile community. There was a frequent need to shift goods quickly. With the five-year working visa (on which many Australians arrived in the 1970s) one could get entrenched, building up a stock of linen, furniture, chairs, refrigerators and the like. More rapid departures, coupled with new arrivals, meant that Australians were already extensive users of free publications driven by advertising. As the name implies, *Exchange and Mart* was one local publication given over to the sale and exchange of goods. *Loot* was another, popular for the sale of second-hand goods and still going. While such publications had very practical and straightforward purposes, they had no particular identification with Australians. But it soon became apparent to commercially minded souls that for a distinct class of people, who were now staying for shorter periods, had immediate needs for travel and work, and were turning over their personal belongings more quickly, such identification would bear fruit. Australians had enjoyed publications of their own in the past and there was an apparent need for them still.

Figure 15.1 *Australasian Express* editor Colin Speairs hand delivering copies of his newspaper to young Australian in London c.1974.
Source: Courtesy Colin Speairs.

The intention was to put London's expatriate Australian community on a pedestal. The paper was a 16-page tabloid, originally a fortnightly. The free graphic layout that web-offset production permitted had revolutionised community newspapers in both Britain and Australia. The *Australasian Express* had something of the youthful appeal and layout – but not the politics – of university newspapers of the period. It advanced quickly to weekly status with a circulation of 45,000, and within a year it had successfully defined the market. Speairs worked as managing editor, employing an editor, Jonathan King, and an advertising manager. The paper carried feature articles, a mix of Australian news and sport, two pages of photographs of 'Australians in London' and advertisements for European travel, employment, accommodation and entertainment, with as many as ten pages of classifieds.[7] In its reporting and self-promotion *Australasian Express* pandered to Australian sentiment and humour. A steady diet of Australian girls in bikinis near water, and job and travel advertisements deliberately targeted the expatriate community. Profile features on successful or visiting Australians in London were a mainstay – these included film-maker Bruce Beresford, director of *The Adventures of Barry McKenzie*, Nicholas Whitlam, 27, son of the Australian prime minister, who is 'forging a career in high finance'; and Erin Stratton, 29, 'mother' in charge of 230 'bunnies' at the Playboy Club in Park Lane, but originally from Hillston, a small town in outback New South Wales.[8]

Generations of Australians had considered the return 'home' to Britain a rite of passage, or even a permanent right given the extremities of success or failure. Many, no doubt, had put such aspirations on hold, or abandoned them altogether, due to Depression, war or family constraints. Buoyed up by postwar affluence and untouched by the horrors of war or deprivation, a new generation of Australians, still supported by ancient aspirations, family connections and friends, now made their way back. Australia may have been changing but it was still anglo-centric.[9] That London was a destination for so many youthful travellers was a comfort to worried parents.

We can characterise these youthful sojourners under various headings: immigrant worker-sojourners, adventurer backpackers, drifters, independent travellers and aspiring professionals. The tags are by no means exhaustive, for they often overlapped as individuals matured, progressed or simply changed status. Like Alomes's better-known and more individualised creative artists and name journalists, they were not so much pushed as called.[10] London, heart of empire and monarchy, great centre of culture, trade, communications and commerce, was the source of siren images, both written and visual, peddled in the Australian media. The scars of the Blitz and Old World decay may have abounded in London's sprawling form but from the 1960s it was minted newly trendy and celebrated as a centre of youth culture. Britain's world-beating rock and roll band, the Beatles, may have come from Liverpool, but London was the first citadel they captured and the appeal of the clean-cut Beatles to Australian audiences was seen in their sell-out 1964 tour.[11] Australia's affluent youth of the 1960s and 1970s were eager consumers of the new cultural cargo seen in the circulation from one teenager-filled house to another of magazines – *Rolling Stone* from the United States, *New Musical Express (NME)* from Britain and local variants like *Go-Set* in Melbourne – and the proliferation of import record shops in the major cities and copy-cat bands in the suburbs. But as with the Beatles, the baby-boomers changed from neat conformity to lifestyle experimentation and even more provocative adaptations. Dour necessity, and parental and other tiresome forms of authority in Australia, gave the overseas jaunt a particular appeal.

London presented no language barrier, an important consideration for mainly mono-lingual youngsters venturing abroad for the first time. London offered jobs and accommodation and sympathetic support networks, for even the ingenuous young. Barry McKenzie was Aussie ingenuous-ness incarnate. First brought to life as a comic-strip character drawn by London born but New Zealand raised Nicholas Garland in the satirical publication *Private Eye*, McKenzie was built on enduring popular stereotypes.[12] Garland approached *Private Eye* in 1964 with a cartoon-strip idea for a naive strong-jawed young northerner newly arrived in London. The editor, Richard Ingrams, liked the idea but wanted the central character be an Australian, not an Englishman, and expatriate Australian actor Barry Humphries to provide the story-line. The name was taken from Humphries's own and that of Graham 'Garth' McKenzie, the burly Australian cricketer of the period. The over-sized jaw belonged to the popular American backwoodsman cartoon character, Desperate Dan, while the double-breasted suit, striped tie and wide-brimmed hat came courtesy of ANZAC ex-servicemen seen by Garland marching down Whitehall in a Remembrance Day parade.[13]

The comic strip ceased in 1974, but 'Bazza' endured in comic books (banned in Australia) and two films, and in popular association among young sojourners in London to this day. Interestingly, Humphries's equivalent female character, Debbie Thwaites, never achieved the same success, notwithstanding the large numbers of young women who entered Britain in these years. McKenzie was not alone. *Australasian Express* maintained separate columns for males and females under the pseudonyms and caricatured images of Prue and Bruce.[14] Such images resonated, as they still do. Reflecting on his first sojourn in 1972, the playwright David Williamson said, 'I felt my Australianness was bizarre, that my accent was … an embarrassment, that people would think I behaved like Barry McKenzie, all the things that Australians do find when they travel, I felt then'.[15] Up until at least the mid-1980s it was not fashionable in London to be seen to be Australian. This is reflected in the testimony of individuals who had stayed from the earlier decade and in defensive and self-parodying images in the community press.

COMINGS AND GOINGS

There is safety in numbers but a nation of barely ten million, far removed on the other side of the globe could scarcely swamp Britain with adventurous youth. Besides, Australia was evolving its own imperative of progressive cultural development with the promise of the Whitlam Government.[16] Officials at Australia House urged the youthful adventurers to go back home, citing Britain's perennial power crises, petrol shortages and appalling weather as reasons for doing so.[17] The *Australasian Express* meanwhile reported the observation of Bernard Marks from the Alfred Marks employment agency that, despite the current economic crises, demand for temporary employees in London would remain strong; the figures defied the usual downward winter trend, with a quarter of a million unfilled vacancies for office staff in London and even greater demand for nurses, catering staff and agricultural labourers.[18] There were clear signs of an enduring and growing demand for labour that would continue to suit sojourner travellers. Many had good reasons for returning home. But for every Australian inspired by a sense of national responsibility or desiring a more settled life, there was another whose decision was made by the British authorities.

In the late 1970s things became tougher for longer term itinerants in Britain. But still the stream continued to flow the other way, with each new landing at Heathrow from the now fully extended services run by British Airways and Qantas bringing visitors on one-way tickets. My journalist cousin Marsha went over on a five-year working visa in 1973, landed a job (as she admits, 'through complete nepotism') and stayed.[19] The rules, however, were tightened the year that she arrived. It was fine for a while, but she and others soon found themselves embroiled with the Home Office. They consequently became 'walking encyclopedias of information on the Immigration Act'.[20] A good job or a boyfriend, for example, provided a moral case to stay longer. One's determination was certainly a factor. The British were, admittedly, generous by comparison with the United States, where the elusive 'green card' permitting a visitor to work was not so easily obtained. The years passed and by 1980 Marsha had obtained her 'residency'. But along with many of her friends she had been made acutely aware that if she left the country she would have to apply for another visa, which she might not get. Trips back home to Australia, even to Europe, were postponed. It was a form of gentle harassment, or prompting. The less resolute simply packed their bags and returned. Australia was still a pretty good place. People knew when it was time to go and take one's London memories and European travel stories back home, perhaps sowing seeds of desire in a younger sister, brother or cousin, or even children, to make the trip.[21]

Things got tougher again in the 1980s when the Working Holiday visa was cut from five years to two, resulting in a much shorter stay. London, however, maintained its insatiable appetite for human fodder, and this was being met. But as far as Australians were concerned, they were welcome to visit, even to work, but not to stay. These years were not particularly happy ones for the host society, with successive Labour governments progressive and well-meaning but out of touch with emerging international and economic trends. Stodgily socialist in politics and dourly conservative in its social habits, Britain was saddled with tensions that beggared resolution. There was civil war in Northern Ireland and the ever-present threat of bombing terror from the IRA, trouble with racial minorities at home and an obstructive trade union movement. Britain was not the international power it had been. Formal relations with the old dominions, including Australia and Australians, were growing more distant. Britain, having joined the European Union in 1973, was now more conscious of being part of Europe. It was becoming inevitable that all visitors and potential immigrants would be treated equally, and a more sensitive consciousness of issues of race was being adopted across the board – something for visiting white Australians to take note of.

The election of a Conservative government in 1979 marked a tougher new Britain, with Prime Minister Margaret Thatcher confronting the miners at home and Argentina in the Falkland Islands. Economically, the UK began to focus on commerce rather than industry, with coal mines closing and banks expanding. While this meant unemployment and decline in the industrial north, the south benefited and employment opportunities improved in London, which remained the entertainment and financial capital. These trends benefited migrants aged between 25 and 30, whose average wage levels were higher than those of their English contemporaries. The resultant boom in financial markets careered across industry, with almost every business that supported financial traders benefiting – travel agencies, bars, and restaurants that catered for long lunches. The expansion of newly deregulated financial markets created work opportunities for skilled Australians, with the pattern mirroring the expatriation of creative artists of years gone by.

For many young Australians this new and buoyant London offered ready and easily accessible employment that would fund their lust for travel. The new travellers' high levels of education meant that many who were attracted by the cheap travel opportunities in Europe, as well as those just escaping overseas, fell into better career opportunities than they might have back home. Most sought work to supplement the meagre and fast-disappearing funds they brought with them. For in London, and particularly central London, living was expensive and pressures on desirable facilities available for transients were constantly at a premium.

As the economic welcome was being extended conditions were being made tougher. The expulsion of the Kombi van mart from its Eden on the Strand would be just another sign. The message was mixed: economic opportunity with political difficulty; the welcoming hand now but in due course the reflexive boot. This was confirmed by further changes to the immigration laws. The British Nationality Act 1981 abolished the status of Commonwealth citizens, enabling them to be classified as British subjects without the benefits of citizenship. Changes to the Immigration Act 1988 increased from one to four years the qualifying requirement for Commonwealth citizens with British parents or male grandparents to gain British citizenship. And so from the mid-1980s Australians who had been around a while were being forced out and those coming in were staying for shorter periods. Conditions for working visitors to London – many of them Australians – remained good. But the expatriate community was now even less permanent in character and increasingly affected by the youth travel market. There was a correspondingly greater need for agency and the exchange of information. If anything, the Australian community in London was becoming more obvious, not just because of its increased numbers but also because of its volatility. London's appeal as a convenient and friendly stopover point was underscored by a perceived 'lack of welcome' from other countries, in Asia and Europe especially. French nuclear testing in the Pacific inflamed relations and, following the Rainbow Warrior incident in 1987, Australians and New Zealanders were not welcome in France.

A TALE OF TWO MASTHEADS

By 1977 *Australasian Express* had a competitor in the *London Australasian Magazine* (later *London Alternative Magazine* or simply *LAM*). Started by Rick Leeming and George McCarthy as a monthly magazine, it moved to a fortnightly and then a weekly format. Another point of the consumer media compass was (and remains) *Time Out*, established in 1968 by entrepreneur Tim Elliott. This weekly magazine listing of events, including films, music, exhibitions and fashion, was already a London institution. The difference between it, the weekly newspaper supplements and free lifestyle and 'what's on' publications was *Time Out*'s low price and relative freedom from dependence on advertising.[22] By 1979 *LAM* was providing serious competition to *Australasian Express*. In addition to hitting the streets a day before its rival, the magazine also had a longer shelf-life. When *Australasian Express* went to Thursday publication, *LAM* responded by going to Tuesdays. *LAM*, now styled 'London's alternative magazine' and incorporating the *Australasian News and Post*, was an A5-sized magazine of 70 pages devoted to 'lifestyle' consumer information and travel and with heavy advertising and 'advertorial' reflecting its status as free from 24 pick-up points.[23] It covered Events (with a strong emphasis on film) and Travel (features on the Royal Opera House, visiting Jordan in the Middle East and skiing in Eastern Europe), with three pages on sport and an equivalent number on Australian news. The news was a random collection of stories with Australian tags pulled off the wire services. The sport, mainly Australian cricket and rugby, was of the same character.

Editorial staff came and went, often working as a prelude to the Continental tour and a return home. Graeme Johnston edited *Australasian Express* in 1980–81. The 30-year-old *Sun News-Pictorial* staffer in Melbourne had responded to an advertisement placed by the Razukis, and taken his wife and young family over. He continued working for the newspaper informally as a columnist on his return to Australia.[24] When *Australasian Express* ceased publication in a bankrupt state in September 1983, it appeared that it had lost the commercial war. But ten days later Ibrahim Razuki's sons, Ghadir and Ali, started *The News and Travel* (*TNT*) as a magazine of 48 pages, accepting the *LAM* format and the increased costs of magazine production. *TNT* mirrored closely *Australasian Express*, *LAM* and other equivalent publications in style and content, and was still a give-away.[25] It was produced in a single office at 52 Earl's Court Road in the run-down heart of Kangaroo Valley. It remained there for 15 years before two residential properties were converted into four offices in nearby Child's Place. The move reflected the publication's growing revenue and expanding size.

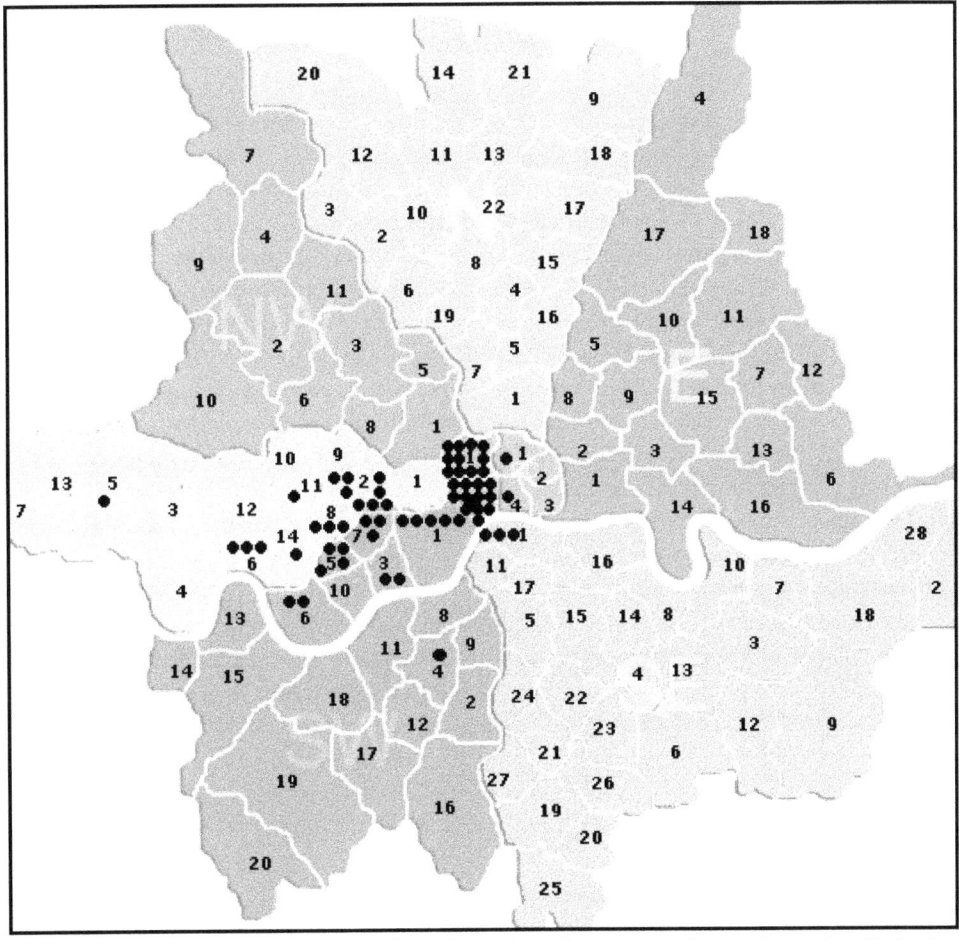

Figure 15.2 Distribution points for *TNT* showing a distinct preference for London's central and inner west as key drop-off points for the free magazine targeted at Australians.
Source: *TNT*, 15 April 1986.

With Australian, New Zealand, Canadian and United States flags on the cover, the new magazine now pitched to a variety of immigrant communities. Canada and the United States were soon dropped, on the grounds that the United States was 'all over the news' in any case and that while Canadians were in London in big numbers, they were not 'surface travellers' like the Australians and New Zealanders (according to Ghadir Razuki, the magazine simply 'couldn't define their patterns'). As with *Australasian Express* the new publication was 'a subbing medium' with copy purchased from Rupert Murdoch's News Limited. Each week's edition featured a selection of stories, including sport, from the different Australian states and a mix of articles on travel, entertainments and Australians in London. There were also many advertisements, both classified and feature. Providing an estimated 90 per cent of the revenue, advertising was the fuel that kept the magazine going. Ghadir Razuki claims that its B4 format was a crucial move in the commercial war with its competitor, as was its move to a Monday distribution drop in 1986. Not only was *TNT* the first out in the new week, its Sunday copy deadline meant that it could be first with Australian weekend sport. By 1984 the orientation was almost exclusively Australian. New Zealanders complained, but news of the 'three sheep go missing' variety from that part of the world (or Australia for matter) was not a big draw card.[26]

Neither *LAM* nor *TNT* featured outstanding journalism. But they were driven by youthful energy, blessed with advertising resources and they had an audience. Both picked up on Australian leads of all kinds. *LAM*'s 4 January 1983 edition features the then youthful federal treasurer, John Howard, sporting a brightly coloured paisley tie. Both mainstream Australian political parties had active groups in London, and with an election approaching Howard would have been well aware of the potential absentee vote. The business driver of *LAM* was its advertisements. By targeting Australians it was tapping a niche market. *LAM* thus courted the returning-home market with three pages of freight advertisements every week. Three pages of job advertisements targeted Australians at the opposite end of their trip, and in its edition of 8 February 1983 they are indexed into the following categories: accountancy, bar and catering, computers, hotel staff, industrial, nurses, secretarial and miscellaneous – the latter includes a position for someone to drive the truck delivering the magazine. Crude Australian signifiers were commonplace in the images and text, with kangaroos and koalas being particularly popular – we are only 'a hop, skip and a jump away'. The ANZAC Nursing Service unequivocally tied its colours to the mast while the Nightingale Nurses Bureau adopts a sympathetic tone: 'We came on a holiday like you so understand your needs'.[27]

Incredibly for such a successful enterprise *LAM* magazine, in its farewell to editor Jeff Hayward, announced a move away from targeting Australians. Hayward was credited with having guided *LAM* editorially 'through its climb from an Australian publication to London's free weekly entertainment guide'. The new editor was Donald McLeod, formerly a journalist in New Zealand and writer for *Time Out*.[28] Soon afterwards, in 1985, Leeming and McCarthy sold out to a consortium of businessmen and *LAM*'s editorial management continued its tilt at the British *Time Out* market. Stories of a left-wing nature (such as ones against fox hunting) that had often been published by *LAM* had little appeal to Australian itinerant travellers, in the opinion of Ghadir Razuki. This, he felt, gave *TNT* its advantage. Over the same period *TNT*, by contrast, cleaved towards its Australian audience. By 1988, after about a year of falling advertising revenue, *LAM* ceased publication, leaving *TNT* with a virtual monopoly. *Southern Cross*, started by an ex-*TNT* staffer in 1988, lasted as an independent publication until 1991, when TNT purchased it from the liquidators and kept it as a secondary publication. About this time *TNT* began to carry some South African news. Mandela's release in 1990, Apartheid's progressive demise, and South Africa's return to the Commonwealth meant that South African numbers in London were growing and that South African subjects had now gained in respectability – not that *TNT* saw itself as a political organ at any stage.[29]

'STRANDED ... SO FAR FROM HOME'

The cover of *TNT* from 26 November 1985 features a cartoon of the Hoodoo Gurus, a leading Australian rock band. Described as 'protopunk', the Perth-based band was touring the UK to promote an album. Their gig at the Kings Head hotel in Fulham was well reported in *TNT*. Not surprisingly, the hotel was a prolific advertiser, with its 'Comedian – Gentlemen's Entertainment' and Thames River cruises and as home to the Colonials Rugby League Club.[30] A 'yuppie' pub these days, it still plays Australian Rules football on the big screen. *TNT* pages evince considerable competition for the patronage of visiting Australians, with the Drifters Club in Bayswater offering 60p drinks all night and wet T-shirt contests. Removed from parental and other restraints the young itinerants could play up. Among 1980s venues catering for Australians, The Church on Sunday became notorious for its wet T-shirt and wet-jock competitions, and strippers, attracting patrons by word of mouth. Punk rock, a modish expression of disaffection in these times, included in its canon of performers an Australian band, the Saints, who had had a hit with their single 'I'm Stranded' even before they had arrived. Their music was better appreciated in London than Brisbane, which had spawned them.[31] Like the wandering youth themselves, bands and performers simply ended up in London, and then they worked the pubs. David McComb from The Triffids thus recalled, 'once we'd left Perth, we'd left home. We basically figured we were traveling from then on. There was no distinction as to how far we could go from home, including overseas'.[32]

Punk rock was already, in 1985, on the way out. Pub-based band music was more enduring and an identity-link for Australians abroad. The bands that obtained regular gigs and followers, and the magazines that helped promote them, reflect the mélange of self-consciousness of a mobile community of young transient workers and experiential travellers. Other graduates from the Australian pub circuit extended their appeal beyond the expatriate community. When *TNT* columnist Susan Muranti claimed half the audience at the band's Albert Hall concert on 24 June 1986 were Australian, INXS lead singer Michael Hutchence replied mockingly that he doubted there were 4000 Australian 16- or 17-year-olds in London.[33] At the other end of the spectrum, venerable Aussie rocker of the 1950s, Johnny Devlin, was playing to considerably smaller audiences in London pubs.[34] Music and pub advertisements were a feature of *TNT* pages, but the freebie Aussie mag could hardly claim the youthful audience or myth-making impact of the regular music press.[35] It sponsored a sense of community in other ways. Following a tradition begun by *Australasian Express*, *TNT* ran advertiser-sponsored barbecues on Australia Day and at Christmas that attracted, on occasion, more than 2000 people.[36]

TNT's editor in 1985 was Sonia McLeod. With the cover message 'Focus on London, Australian News & Sport, Accommodation, Jobs', it now boasted fourteen named staff, with specialist writers handling news, sport and music, and two advertising representatives. Sixty-two distribution points (including Australia House) were listed, with locations in the city, inner west, north and south predominating and individual spots as far afield as Ealing and Clapham. There were 11 in WC1 (including the West End), 13 in WC2 (the Strand) and 8 in W2 (Bayswater). Within a year McLeod had resigned to holiday in Cyprus.[37] The new editor, Ross Stokes, 28, had been a journalist with the Western Mail Group of newspapers in Western Australia. Copy included 'the news from home' and speculations on the emerging *zeitgeist* of Australia in the 1980s. In April the subject was the new breed of ANZACs, 'the children of peace and prosperity', and the new Australian entrepreneurs – Rupert Murdoch, Alan Bond, Robert Holmes à Court and John Elliott, who have made their mark with 'an astonishing degree of shrewdness and success that observers have been left wondering just which unheard of Antipodean is going to surprise them next'.[38]

The magazine expanded to include a jocular editorial, the Bull Sheet. Driven by advertising – increasingly by classified advertising – *TNT*'s journalistic method remains clear: identify wherever possible with a perceived Australian audience, or create one. A hardy perennial was a 'vox pop' asking visiting Australians what they thought of the English summer. Jeanie Hope from Melbourne offers 'pathetic … depressing and miserable' while two travellers from Brisbane – ten and five months respectively in London – consider they hadn't experienced it yet, but might have 'missed it last Monday'. A 'whingeing Aussie' tone emerges: 'with its mass unemployment … lack of national morale and comparatively low standards of living, Britain is a perfect example of everything Australia, supposedly, is not'.[39] To the question 'Why come in the first place?' come the answers, it 'still is the world's entertainment capital' and 'it's the cheapest European or English speaking place of any distance for Australians to fly to'.[40] For the impending Bicentennial celebrations, a front-page feature is the re-enactment of the arrival of the First Fleet planned by Jonathan King, popular historian and journalist – and former editor of *Australasian Express*.[41] The magazine also ran a 'get-in-touch' cum dalliance or lonely hearts column, but it disappeared following a spate of spurious entries.[42]

Not all the news was good. In July 1986 *TNT* readers are informed that the Australian dollar has fallen to a mere 42.7 pence in the pound – sobering news for those newcomers still living off their savings from home.[43] Fortunately, regular advertisers continue to offer work, including some, like grape picking in Burgundy, that appeals to the adventurous.[44] Closer to home Stuart's Personnel offers 'immediate registration' for labourers, tradesmen and semi-skilled construction workers, and vacancies for warehouse porters, electricians and visiting accountants.[45] The facts of life are dealt with in occasional articles: Australians and New Zealanders are entitled to a two-year working-holiday visa, if under the age of 27. This can be obtained in one's country of origin or at the Home Office's vast tower block, the aptly named Lunar House at Croydon in the 'outer reaches of London beyond the underground system': 'There's an interview hall where several hundred people may be waiting – you take a ticket and take your turn. If you arrive after 10.30 a.m. you probably won't be seen that day'.[46]

Outstay your welcome and you could face deportation and removal. At the very least you will receive a 'terse and rude letter' with dates filled in and fines and imprisonment threatened. *TNT* also reports what officials cannot say: that such orders are still practised mainly against Black and Asian people, not white former 'Colonials'.[47] As for employment, secretaries and nurses will find little difficulty getting a job. Pub work is acceptable but represents extremely long hours at comparatively poor pay, even with live-in arrangements. This is also the case with nanny work, while shop assistant jobs are plentiful though moderately paid.[48] Flat hunting in

London is described as 'really fierce', with readers advised to allow a whole week to look for shares and 'bed-sits', and two weeks to find decent semi-permanent and self-contained accommodation – 'so don't just pound the pavements hoping to find a place by the end of the day'. For those without hospitable friends or family, B&Bs provide a short-term solution:

> B+B's are good for short term stays. They're found in areas like Earl's Court or, more centrally, in W2 (Bayswater, Paddington, Notting Hill Gate, Queensway for as little as £6.00 a night or £38 a week. They provide some comforts – a kitchen, TV and lounger for guests. For a longish stay try a bedsit £30 pounds a week single, £45 double, a studio self-contained with kitchen and bathroom, and from £60 a 1–2 bedroom flat. – Don't rely on the adverts in the dailies. You have to be fast on your feet when the [free] newspapers come out.[49]

Apart from park benches (not a good idea in winter) there are the youth hostels. Holland House in Kensington was temporary home to 69,500 visitors in 1983, with over a third being 'Antipodeans'. New readers are also warned: 'at Victoria Station, touts, paid one pound for every customer they ensnare hustle with predatory zeal'.[50]

DO POMMIE AGENCIES MAKE YOU ANGRY?

Once settled, travel became an option. If it is all too much, readers are advised to 'just take a holiday'. Reaching Spain is easy – 'find your way to Victoria Station, board a Paris train, cross Paris by Metro and take a Southbound train to Madrid'. *Australasian Express*, *LAM* and *TNT* were all contemporaneous with the remarkable growth of travel companies and individuals, including Graham 'Screw' Turner whose Top Deck adventure tour business with double-decker buses evolved into a multi-million dollar enterprise, Flight Centre, in 1981. Top Deck Travel started when Turner, a veterinary surgeon on a locum in Yorkshire in 1973, spotted a double-decker bus fitted out for camping tours. He brought it to London and recruited a party to travel overland in it to Morocco.[51] Already, the options for travellers were abundant, according to Bill James:

> You bought a VW Kombivan, a hand-me-down from a home-going Aussie, at the car yard disguised on the Strand outside Australia House or you joined one of the dozens of cheap tour operators based in London catering for the colonial market. Autotours, Protea, Pacesetters, Penn, Transit, Contiki, Vikings, NAT, CCT, Sundowners … You could walk down Earl's Court Road at any time of the day or night and see them loading or unloading their punters.[52]

Contiki Tours was founded by New Zealander John Anderson in the 1960s, but by the 1980s was identified with young Australians. Trailfinders was founded by ex-SAS officer Mike Gooley in 1970. Most of these travel companies advertised in *TNT* and the magazine responded in kind. Cover stories between 1983 and 1985 featured travel activities on the Nile, the Trans-Siberian railway, Kathmandu, Jamaica, Turkey, Brazil, Paris, British festivals, Russian air travel, Eastern Europe and Spain.[53] But the appeal to readers would have been the ads. They urge readers to 'Take a Break' across the English Channel with the Travel Young organisation – Paris accommodation, return and breakfast for £47, Amsterdam for £47 and Brussels for £53. Travel reports provide further impetus for those with itchy feet. An unnamed staff writer 'peeps behind the iron curtain' to examine not social conditions under communism but skiing in Yugoslavia, Romania and Bulgaria. *Après-ski* in Yugoslavia, *TNT* readers are assured, won't break the bank. Romania is labelled 'a cheapie's paradise' and visitors are urged to take low denominations 'or you won't spend it all', but 'just don't expect European standards'.[54]

TNT endorsed tours for established European 'highlights' include youth daredevil and indulgence favourites, the Pamplona bull run and the Munich Oktoberfest. Turning to the business pages we find three pages of advertising for baggage and transport companies, including the Australian Forwarding Agency – 'Trippers Get that Load off Your Back – the ANZ Excess Baggage Company and the Austral Shipping and Packing Limited', 'From a "Jumbo" Trunk to a complete "Mousehold"'. There is the International and Student Moving Company Ltd – auto experts who will ship your Rolls-Royce or Mercedes and have facilities for 'the smaller car'. This edition has three pages of travel advertisements and four pages of jobs.[55] The ANZAC Nursing Service wants 'hard-working girls, preferably drivers', while Broadbent, Lemon and Company (computer programmer recruiters) ask 'Do Pommie agencies make you so angry you could throw the phone down? … Then why not come over to Quattro and join our friendly team of Aussies and Kiwis?'. Travelmood offers return flights to Sydney and Melbourne for £630, hoping to catch the Christmas return-home market. Barry Humphries's satirical creation, Sir Les Patterson, and the comic actor, Paul Hogan – signifiers to an Australian audience both – make it clear to newcomers that they are in demand. A leering Sir Les, 'Australian cultural attaché to the Court of St James', informs readers in a large advertisement that 'you'll be right with Quattro Industrial and Catering Staff'.[56]

Like latter-day *padrones*, the labour bosses of former times who waited on the New York wharves for the immigrant ships, these larger-than-life images of Australian identity abroad lured young travellers to the temping agencies. Sir Les Patterson's brief was expanded in a double-page colour advertisement for British Telecom – he spends 'a lot of time on the blower and occasionally calls the wife'.[57] Even mainstream companies could see the point of niche marketing, the targeting of a specific group of free-spending itinerants. Bligh Appointments urges 'Downunders' to 'Unite and Join Us on Top of the World' while Alexis Temps Personnel promises 'No Convict Jokes Allowed'. Bligh Appointments, a leading recruitment agency, covered 'secretarial, accountancy, industrial, nannies and mother's helps'. The firm, which still survives, was founded in 1974 by two Australian friends in London. The late Dick McMahon, who was already with an employment agency, joined with John Brauer, a temporary accountant, to broker temporary employment for Australians to British firms. The survival at sea after the mutiny on HMS *Bounty* of namesake William Bligh seemed an appropriate metaphor. Initially they advertised in the *Australasian Express*, but John Brauer recalls that this was hardly necessary to reach Australians: 'We knew where they all were, in Earl's Court and in Fulham. We could just go to the pubs and flats'. The 1970s were 'golden years' for the business when it had minimal competition and a well-defined community of Australians upon which to draw. The company's big break was the exploration and development of North Sea oil, with a number of large off-shore construction companies drawing on its services for labour.[58] The records of these employment agencies could tell us much about the work undertaken by travelling Australians, and young women in particular.

FROM COMMUNITY PRESS TO BIG BUSINESS

By the mid 1990s the Razuki brothers had triumphed over their competition and *TNT* enjoyed a virtual monopoly. They sold the magazine in 2000 when they were faced with uncertainties born of the challenge of the World Wide Web and the extensive investment in new printing technology required to give them full colour throughout. *TNT* now has a bevy of internet-based competitors providing services that were formerly the preserve of print-only publications.[59] The magazine now has an excellent website.[60] Its new owner is the Guardian Group, whose chairman, Bob Phillis, takes the publication very seriously.[61] What chairman of a newspaper group would not take such a well-established money-spinner seriously? Although clearly identified with the Australian community in London in the 1980s and 1990s, *TNT* these days embraces a wide range of entertainment and travel activities, reflecting the growing sophistication of the London audience and the continuing example of rivals like *Time Out*. Now targeting New Zealanders and South Africans as well as Australians, it is billed as 'the bible for Aussie, Kiwi and South African travellers in the UK' – indeed, the whole of the young independent traveller movement into London.

The magazine is still free, and a self-avowed resource for the backpacker and itinerant travelling community. It is a substantial publication and reflects higher standards of journalism and production. It is a big business. The print-run in 2007 was 70,000 a week, with over 700 distribution points and 100 per cent take up, which is why it is not littered everywhere like the free evening papers for tube and bus travellers. Each copy is thought to pass through many hands, with total readership estimated by the publisher at 294,000, or four people for each copy.[62] Copies are placed in special red bins at strategic locations throughout London by 10 a.m. on Mondays, and most are gone by 5 p.m. Still principally about jobs, accommodation, travel and lifestyle and consumer wants, it remains heavy with advertising. In the modern marketing-driven manner, the company is obsessed with its audience and undertakes considerable market research. It is not big on corporate memory or retaining editorial staff. According to Business Manager Mark Goddard in 2005, *TNT* likes to see (and accepts) staff moving on to ensure that the 'voice of the newcomer' is privileged.[63] For this reason *TNT* still uses 'unfamiliar' expressions and prioritises 'Austral English' rather than 'English English'.

Although the market has widened, the 'former colonial' category of young visitor-immigrant still includes a strong leavening of Australians, whom TNT estimates make up 46 per cent of its readership.[64] This number was given a boost when Australian university students were able to defer their enrolments. Australians who have right of entry by virtue of holding a recognised passport of another EU country have swelled the numbers beyond those in official statistics. But the biggest transformation has been in the economic 'placing' of many of the new itinerants. There are now more of them working in London under the Highly Skilled Migrant Program, which privileges youth, educational attainments and proven earning capacity.[65] Of the Australians, in particular, Lynette Eyb, editor of *TNT*, said in 2005, 'They're not just pulling pints anymore … you've still got backpackers who are planning to stay 12 months or so but you're now getting an increasing number who have come here looking for high-end jobs in professional areas'.[66]

CONCLUSION

Great cities are magnets, to young people especially, and they make their contributions in return by driving economic growth and shaping cultural and social agendas. London has long been host to generations of migrants from its extended hinterland – Irish, Scots, Midlanders and Welsh, not to mention whole communities of Jews, Pakistanis, Indians, West Indians and Turks. It was perhaps inevitable that London would host large numbers of expatriate Australians and, indeed, they were a presence well before the dawn of cheap air travel in the early 1970s.

The phenomenon has since become so much a part of contemporary experience that it is often taken for granted. But it was in the 1970s and 1980s that the Australian population in London began to represent the cultural mobility made possible by cheap travel, and to cater to London's enduring and expanding appetite for temporary casual and temporary labour, both skilled and unskilled. In these years Australians became well defined, not just as part of a geographic enclave, but also as a visible part of the city's cultural mosaic, as one of the most distinctive immigrant groups. The experience of travelling Australians was of moving from relatively free, informal and makeshift ways of doing things to more regulated, commercialised and ritualised activity. The duration of stay was in many instances dampened by the host community's increasing restrictions, but many still went home of their own volition. In any case, enhanced mobility was becoming the defining experience of the Australian community in London. The ephemeral community press began to cater specifically to the sojourners' needs and in so doing became a historical record of those associated industries that advertised so heavily in its pages.

ACKNOWLEDGEMENTS

The author acknowledges his sources of family and friends in London, in particular Marsha Dunstan, Sam Dunstan and Dylan Nichols. Also Ghadir Razuki, Graeme Johnston and Colin Speairs. Thanks to Carl Bridge who had the original idea and John Nieuwenhuysen of the Institute for Global Movements at Monash University. Glenn Calderwood and Robert Crawford assisted with research. The resources of the Menzies Centre for Australian Studies, the British Library newspaper collection at Colindale and the National Library of Australia in Canberra were invaluable.

ENDNOTES

1. James, 1999, 35.
2. *TNT*, 4 May 1987, 21; 25 May 1987. A new commercial venue was found in Islington.
3. Alomes, 1999, 167–168.
4. Stackhouse, 1995, 152–153, 155.
5. The National Library of Australia catalogue lists *The British Australasian* as the publisher of the *Australia and New Zealand Weekly* with its last holding 24 December 1969.
6. Personal communication, Colin Speairs, 2007.
7. *Australasian Express*, 13 July 1977.
8. *Australasian Express*, 15 November 1973; 29 November 1973; 10 January 1974.
9. Horne, 1980, 4–6.

10. Alomes, 1999.
11. See Moore, 2005, 58–71.
12. See the films *The Adventures of Barry McKenzie* (1972) *Barry McKenzie Holds His Own* (1974); the cover of Nichols, 2007 has a latter-day 'hayseed' Barry McKenzie character complete with contemporary suit but cork hat and a confused expression in an inner-city London location.
13. 'Nicholas Garland – The Birth of Bazza', *Spectator,* 29 October, 1988, 33–34.
14. *Australasian Express*, 20 September 1973.
15. *TNT,* 20 May 1986.
16. See Horne, 1980.
17. Australia House information officer, Mr Peter Kay. Quoted in *Australasian Express*, 10 January 1974, 3.
18. *Australasian Express*, 10 January 1974, 3.
19. Personal communication, Marsha Dunstan, 2005.
20. Immigration Act (UK), 1973; Marsha Dunstan, personal communication, 2005.
21. For example, Dylan Nichols, whose mother preceded him, see Nichols, 2007, 3.
22. Wikipedia, 2007.
23. See *LAM,* 4 January 1983.
24. Personal Communication, Graeme Johnston, 2007.
25. The first copy of *TNT* held in the British Library newspaper collection at Colindale (UK) is 26 Nov 1985 (the company have earlier editions but their ephemeral nature has made them rare). The National Library of Australia is the only Australian public repository.
26. Ghadir Razuki, personal communication, 2007.
27. *LAM,* 8–14 February 1983, 41.
28. *LAM,* 1–7 February 1983.
29. Ghadir Razuki, personal communication, 2007.
30. *TNT,* 18 March 1988, 4.
31. Strongman, Parker and O'Shea, 2007, 186–187.
32. Quoted in Walker, 1996,113.
33. *TNT,* 8 July 1986, 149.
34. *TNT,* 20 May 1986, 168.
35. *NME* (New Musical Express), *MM* (Melody Maker), *Smash Hits* or the new style and music fusion magazine of the period, *The Face*.
36. For example, 'The Great Colonial Reunion' planned for 24 March, 1974, with Max Merritt and the Meteors, *Australasian Express*, 7 March 1974; 'Australia Day Party', *TNT,* 17 January 1984, 20 April 1987; *TNT,* 22 June 1987, 4, 30; Ghadir Razuki, personal communication, 2007.
37. *TNT,* 15 April 1986.
38. *TNT,* 22 April 1986, 4.
39. *TNT,* 19 August 1986.
40. *TNT,* 1 February 1988.
41. *TNT,* 1 July 1986, 24.
42. Personal communications, Dylan Nichols; Personal communication, Ghadir Razuki, 2007.

43. *TNT*, 8 July 1986, 5.
44. *TNT*, 5 August 1986.
45. Abacus Recruitment, *TNT*, 8 July 1986, 47; *TNT*, 24 June 1986, 46.
46. 'Waiting for the knock on the door', *TNT*, 30 October 1984.
47. 'Waiting for the knock on the door', *TNT*, 30 October 1984.
48. 'Stretching the Pennies', *TNT*, 23 October 1983, 23–24
49. 'Flat Hunting … Know the Facts', *TNT*, 18 March 1988, 16–17.
50. 'Hostels', *TNT*, 27 November 1984, 22–23.
51. See James 1999; Sammartino 2007, 175–194.
52. James 1999, 35.
53. *TNT*, 22 February, 8 March, 18 October, 25 October 1983; 17 January, 26 February, 19 March, 10 April, 25 June, 27 November 1984.
54. *TNT*, 26 November 1985, 28.
55. *TNT*, 26 November 1985.
56. *TNT*, 26 November 1985.
57. *TNT*, 17 June 1986.
58. Personal communication, John Brauer, 2007; Bligh, 2007. See also *TNT*, 19 March 1988, 63.
59. Such as *eBay*, *My Space* and *Gum Tree* <www.gumtree.co.uk>.
60. TNT Online, 2008.
61. Personal communication, Mark Goddard, 2005.
62. TNT Online, 2008, <http://tntonline.co.uk/advertise/>.
63. Personal communication, Mark Goddard.
64. TNT Online, 2008, <http://tntonline.co.uk/advertise/>.
65. See TNT Online, 2008, <http://tntonline.co.uk/movingtolondon/default.aspx>.
66. Quoted 'Home and away' by Annabel Crabb, *Herald-Sun* (Melbourne), 6 March 2005.

REFERENCES

Alomes, Stephen. 1999. *When London Calls: The Expatriation of Australian Creative Artists to Britain.* Melbourne: Cambridge University Press.

Burrell, Ian, 'Tony Elliott: Time Lord'. 2006. [Internet]. Released online 20 June 2006. Accessed 20 October 2008. Available from: http://www.independent.co.uk/news/media/tony-elliott-time-lord-405472.html.

Blight Recruitment. 'Welcome to Bligh'. [Internet]. Accessed 17 August 2007. Available from: http://www.bligh.co.uk/

James, Bill. 1999. *Top Deck Daze: Adventures on the Frog and Toad.* Avalon, NSW: Halbrooks Publishing.

Horne, Donald. 1980. *Time of Hope: Australia 1966–72.* Sydney: Angus & Robertson.

Moore, Keith. 2005. 'Beatlemania: the Beatles in Melbourne, 1964'. In *Go! Melbourne in the Sixties*, edited by Seamus O'Hanlon and Tanja Luckins. Melbourne: Circa (Melbourne Publishers Group).

Nichols, Dylan. 2007. *What are You Doing Here? The Question of Australians in London.* Brighton, UK: Pen Press Publishers Ltd.

Sammartino, André. 2007. 'Retail'. In *The Internationalisation Strategies of Small-Country Firms: The Australian Experience of Globalisation*, edited by Dick, H.; Merrett, D. Cheltenham, UK: Edward Elgar.

Stackhouse, John. 1995. *From the Dawn of Aviation: The Qantas Story 1920–1995*. Sydney: Focus Publishing Pty Ltd.
Strongman, Phil; Parker, Alan; O'Shea, Mick. *Pretty Vacant: A History of Punk*. London: Orion Books.
Walker, Clinton. 1996. *Stranded: The Secret History of Australian Independent Music 1977–1991*. Sydney: Macmillan.
Wikipedia. 2007. 'Time Out'. [Internet]. Accessed 17 August 2007. Available from: http://en.wikipedia.org/wiki/Time_Out.

Cite this chapter as: Dunstan, David. 2009. '"We came on a holiday like you": The Australian community press in London in the 1970s and 80s'. *Australians in Britain: The Twentieth-Century Experience*, edited by Bridge, Carl; Crawford, Robert; Dunstan, David. Melbourne: Monash University ePress. pp. 15.1 to 15.18. DOI: 10.2104/ab090015.

CHAPTER 16

GOING 'OS' FOR THE 'OE'
AUSSIES, KIWIS, AND SAFFAS IN CONTEMPORARY LONDON

Robert Crawford, University of Technology, Sydney
> Robert Crawford is a Senior Lecturer in Public Communication at the University of Technology, Sydney. He is the author of But Wait There's More... A History of Australian Advertising, 1900–2000 (2008). As the MSA Research Fellow at Menzies Centre for Australian Studies, King's College London, and Monash University, he recently completed a study of South Africans in contemporary Britain.

Australians in London have popularly been identified as young travellers who spend their time in London either in front of or behind the bar. While some continue to live up to this Bazza McKenzie inspired image, an increasing proportion of Australians in London are more likely to be found in the offices of a multinational bank. This study examines these changes and contextualises these developments alongside those occurring among New Zealanders and South Africans. While the professionalisation of Australians in London has meant that they are interacting with the city in a different way, there are nevertheless certain aspects that have remained the same.

In the early 1990s, the Australian journalist Mike Carlton moved to London with his young family. Writing of his experiences in the British capital for the *Age* in 1993, he recalled that the locals' attitudes towards Australians and Australia were changing: 'The Brits no longer expect drooling Ockers to appear through an upstairs window in a hat hung with corks, to roger their daughters and to pocket the cutlery. The short explanation is that we all grew up'.[1] For Carlton, it was the illustrious careers of Germaine Greer, Clive James and Barry Humphries that signified this coming of age. Significantly, he made no mention of the thousands of young Australians who were then trying to launch their careers in the British capital. Another article that appeared in the *Age* just months after Carlton's partially accounts for this silence: 'Every year, many young Australians see out winter in the Northern Hemisphere from behind London's public bars, hoarding away their pounds and their dreams of travel in sunnier days ahead'.[2] It seems that Carlton felt that young Australians in London did not matter – they were only there for a good time and a short time.

While this story had certainly been a reality for a large number of Australians in London, migration patterns over the course of the 1990s indicate that it was already well on the way to becoming an anachronistic stereotype at the beginning of the new millennium. Within a decade, the maturation that Carlton noted among expatriate celebrities was becoming endemic within the broader Australian community. A 2004 article in the *Sydney Magazine* thus observed that 'today, you're just as likely to see Australians at the top levels of art and commerce as you are pulling beers in a pub or nannying'.[3] In short, Australians in London were becoming more professional, more likely to stay beyond the two-year working visa, and more integrated into the British community.

Most surveys of the contemporary Australian experience of living in London have been undertaken by journalists in London either writing home or writing for the local expatriate community via such publications as *TNT Magazine*. Recent books such as David O'Reilly's *Britain's global Australians* and Dylan Nichols's *What are you doing here?* have similarly given anecdotal accounts of this experience. While surveys by Stephen Alomes, Ian Britain and Angela Woollacott have provided an informative context for understanding the Australian experience in London, they nevertheless leave the contemporary situation unexamined.[4]

The dearth of scholarly investigation into the lives and experiences of Australians living in London in the more recent period has also been noted by New Zealand scholars who, in stark contrast, have shown a more active interest in the stories of their nation's expatriates. Their interest might be attributed to certain differences between the Australian experience of going OS (overseas) and the New Zealand experience of gaining the OE (overseas experience). For New Zealanders, the OE is regarded as a cultural institution that ranks with leaving school, obtaining a degree and getting married – failure to undertake such a journey is considered unusual and 'almost requires justification'.[5] While Australians also celebrate OS travel as a rite of passage, there appears to be little social or cultural pressure on them to do it – a situation that might account for the paucity of Australian research on the topic.

Such differences should not detract from the unique insights to be gained from examining the Australian experiences in relation to the extensive work on New Zealanders. Indeed, the New Zealand scholars' methods as well as their findings are used as a template for this study. The trends and developments among London's South Africans also offer interesting perspectives. Although there is virtually no scholarly research on the South African experience of contemporary London, the anecdotal material and statistical data pertaining to them are useful for this study. By comparing and contrasting the demography and experiences of Australians living in London with those of their antipodean counterparts, this chapter seeks to identify the changing patterns and trends during the 1990s and 2000s and to develop an understanding of the ways that they affected the contemporary Australian experience of London.

LIVING IN LONDON

The 2001 Population Census of Great Britain counted 106,404 Australia-born individuals in the UK (see Figure 16.1). This number is somewhat conservative as it fails to recognise the presence of Australians who were not born in Australia. Almost one quarter of all Australians were born overseas, and they and their direct descendants are entitled to dual citizenship. Approximately 4.4 million Australians can therefore enter the UK on non-Australian passports.[6] Significantly, an estimated 1.5 million Australians hold British passports.[7] These Britain-born Australians are therefore absent from the British census data. Whereas estimates based on the data collected by the Department of Foreign Affairs and Trade place the number of Australians in the UK and Ireland at somewhere between 183,000 and 220,000, Graeme Hugo's demographic research places it in the area of 300,000.[8]

In terms of Australia's antipodean counterparts, Figure 16.1 shows 57,916 New Zealand-born individuals living in the UK in 2001. This also is a conservative figure that fails to recognise the estimated 400,000 New Zealanders who are British passport holders or, indeed, those who hold other passports. More liberal estimates contend that the number of New Zealanders in the UK is between 150,000 and 200,000.[9] The number of South African-born individuals is listed at 140,201, which is also a conservative figure. While one journalist courageously claimed that there were 1.4 million South Africans in the UK, a more plausible upper estimate (based on the trends identified for Australians and New Zealanders) is 550,000.[10]

The immigration patterns in Figures 16.1 and 16.2 provide an interesting overview of the Australian, New Zealand and South African trends. While the Australian and New Zealand patterns prior to 1991 are quite similar (with New Zealanders arriving at a slightly faster rate), the 1990s saw Australia-born individuals arriving in the UK in greater numbers and at a higher rate than their trans-Tasman counterparts.

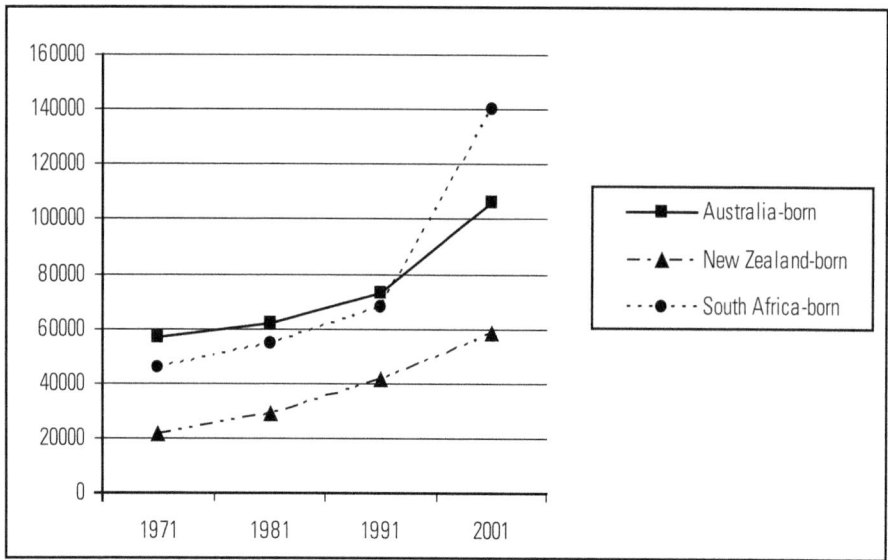

Figure 16.1 Antipodes-born in the UK
Source: *UK Population Census*, 1971, 1981, 1991, 2001

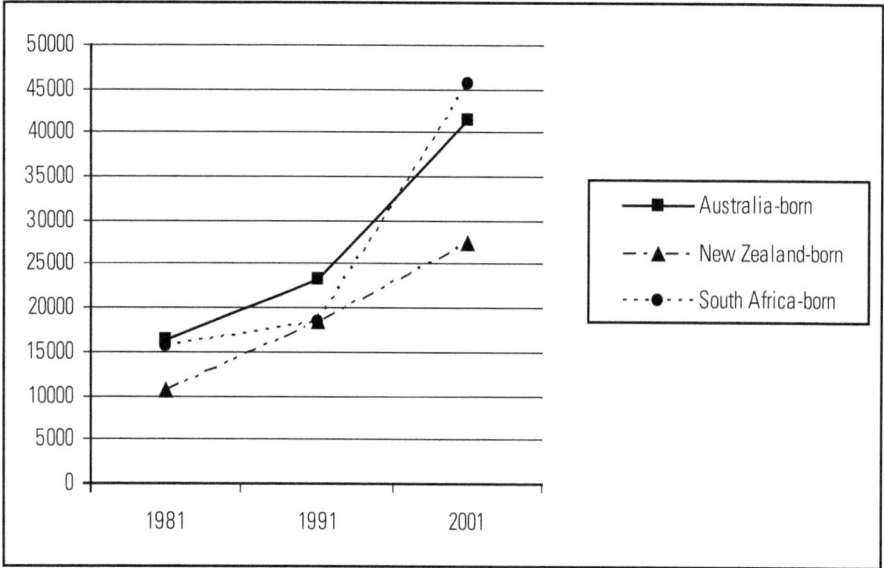

Figure 16.2 Antipodes-born in London
Source: Population Census of Great Britain, 1981, 1991, 2001

Economic factors appear to have played an important role in this trend. In the early 1990s Australia's economy was still struggling with recession while the New Zealand economy was stable. As Australia's economy improved in the late 1990s, the number of Australians in the UK was bolstered by a growing number of professionals (particularly in the areas of IT, banking and accountancy) hoping to cash in on the international economic boom.[11] It seems that New Zealand professionals in these industries were significantly fewer in number; they were also more likely to travel to Australia than to the UK to advance their careers. In addition, the speedier return of migrants under the two-year working-holiday visa may have concealed the number of professional New Zealanders in the UK – their growth may have covered any decline in the number of non-professionals. In the Australian situation, the influx of professionals displaced rather than replaced their non-professional compatriots. Economic factors were no less important for South Africans. In addition to the pull factors that appealed to Australians, for them there were significant push factors. Economic and social instability in the post-Apartheid 1990s, coupled with South Africa's re-entry into the Commonwealth, served to produce a massive upswing in the number of South Africans in the UK and in the rate at which they were arriving.

In terms of the percentage of expatriates living in London, the Australian pattern displays greater similarities to the South African. Between 1991 and 2001, the percentage of Australians living in the capital rose from 32 to 39 per cent and the percentage of South Africans from 27 to 33 per cent. This drift towards London suggests that Australians and South Africans are increasingly drawn to the UK for its economic and professional opportunities. The New Zealand figures differ markedly in concentration and rate of growth. During the same decade, the percentage of New Zealanders living in London remained relatively steady, climbing only marginally from 45 to 47 per cent. However, the opportunities that London offers to professionals cannot account for the concentration of New Zealanders in London. For them, it seems that London's size, location and cosmopolitanism, as well as the existing Kiwi friendship networks, all function as powerful pulling factors.[12]

The bare statistics coupled with anecdotal evidence suggest that similar factors determine a specific type of antipodean migrant. Their age is prescribed by British visa regulations on the one hand and personal responsibilities on the other. These factors similarly determine their socio-economic status. While the two-year working-holiday visa was open to all Australians, New Zealanders and South Africans under 28, longer visas or work permits are available only to skilled migrants working in priority professions.[13] Interestingly, the gender division is not uniform. Statistics for working-holiday makers admitted to the UK in 1999 reveal that 58 per cent of Australian applicants were female, a figure consistent with historical trends. In contrast, 52 per cent of South African applicants were male while New Zealand applicants were almost evenly spread, with just under 51 per cent being female.[14] It is perhaps unsurprising, then, that the 'typical Australian living in Britain' in 2005 was described as 'in her 20s, working as a professional and earning the equivalent of $50,000 to $150,000 a year'.[15] Overwhelmingly, she was likely to be white. Data from the 2001 Population Census of Great Britain reveals that of the 70,634 Oceania-born individuals living in London, 94 per cent (66,612) identified themselves as being white. Without separate racial categories for Aborigines, Maoris or Pacific Islanders, this figure might have been artificially boosted. A further 1455 (2 per cent) identified themselves as being racially Chinese or East/South-East Asian.

Research on the ethnic and socio-economic composition of New Zealanders on their OE provides useful insights into the Australian experience. New Zealanders in the British capital are not only overwhelmingly young, they also tend to be 'wealthier and more visibly "white" and middle-class than the population of New Zealand in general'.[16] Only a minority of New Zealanders on their OE are employed in manual occupations.[17] This socio-economic barrier also accounts for the 'whiteness' of New Zealanders in the UK. Claudia Bell observes that members of New Zealand's Maori and Pacific Islander communities, who constitute some 20 per cent of the national population, are significantly less likely to embark on an OE than their Pakeha counterparts. In addition to their lower socio-economic status, these New Zealanders do not readily identify with this 'cultural rite', and 'religious ties and family expectations generally have priority over that personal development that is central to the Pakeha OE'.[18] Any temporary or long-term emigration will be towards Australia rather than the UK.

The South African situation appears to conform strongly to the Australasian pattern. Of the 45,507 South African-born people living in London, 87 per cent (39,630) identified themselves as being white – a figure that is massively disproportionate to the Rainbow Nation's actual racial composition, where whites currently constitute 10 per cent of the population. The historical correlation between race and socio-economic status in South Africa suggests that the majority of these South Africans are likely to have come from middle-class backgrounds.

Covering just under 40 per cent of the Australian-born population in London, Table 16.1 reveals the five most popular districts in London for Australians. These figures underscore the similarities between Australians and New Zealanders. Following in the footsteps of previous generations, Australians have continued to cluster in the west, although gentrification has shifted Kangaroo Valley further west. While the influx of Australian professionals and gold collar migrants does not appear to be borne out in these statistics, Brigid Delaney writes that this statistical 'absence' actually underscores contemporary migration patterns:

> Upper-class expats try to blend in with Londoners, living in hot 'hoods such as Islington, Clerkenwell or Hackney. Time and money is spent in gastro pubs and on weekends in the English countryside … Working-class expats develop intense patriotism, spending their time in Australian-themed pubs such as the Walkabout and the Church. They live in Earls Court, Shepherds Bush or Acton, dossing in rooms that often have two or three others sleeping in them.[19]

The consistency of the New Zealand statistics across the two periods conforms to the overall rate of growth of New Zealanders in London illustrated by Figure 16.2. Australians appear to have followed their Kiwi counterparts to Wandsworth. South Africans have also followed this charge to Wandsworth, albeit at a higher rate. However, in contrast to the Australian and New Zealand trends, the top five locations for South Africans have changed. Putney and Wimbledon, for example, replaced suburbs in the inner west. Such changes are not simply the result of the enormous influx of South Africans into the UK in the post-Apartheid era; they also indicate a different type of immigrant with different motivations and interests. While Australians, New Zealanders and South Africans have congregated in slightly different suburbs, their concentration in the city's west and south-west underscores their socio-economic status. In addition to providing access to a ready network of friends and compatriots, these comfortable leafy suburbs also have good connections to underground railway stations, facilitating work in central areas of the city.

Australian-born	1991	2001	% change
Camden	1,495	2,641	77
Hammersmith & Fulham	1,617	3,459	114
Kensington & Chelsea	2,262	2,889	28
Wandsworth	1,643	3,488	112
Westminster	1,977	3,236	64
Total	8,994	15,713	75
New Zealand-born			
Brent	1,188	1,996	68
Camden	1,250	1,657	33
Ealing	1,223	2,064	69
Hammersmith & Fulham	1,221	2,098	72
Wandsworth	1,337	2,126	59
Total	6,219	9,941	60
South African-born			
Barnet	1,611	3,144	95
Camden	1,562	2,324	49
Ealing	581	2,148	270
Kensington & Chelsea	1,138	1,695	49
Merton	565	3,041	438
Wandsworth	985	4,671	374
Westminster	1,237	1,738	41
Total	7,679	18,761	144

Table 16.1 The Top Five Districts for Antipodeans in London
Source: Population Census of Great Britain, 1991, 2001

LONDON CALLING

London has a long history of attracting young immigrants hoping to expand their horizons. As the political, financial and cultural centre of the British Empire, it offered unique opportunities that were otherwise unavailable in the far-flung colonies of Australia, New Zealand, and South Africa. For Australian women in particular, the UK and especially London have long offered an opportunity for self-actualisation that was unavailable at home.[20] While the empire has long disappeared, the appeal of the British capital to those from former colonies has not diminished. As Figure 16.2 illustrates, neither the growing sense of national identity within these former dominions, nor their dislocation from the empire have halted the number of young antipodeans moving to London – their number has, in fact, accelerated.

In Australia, New Zealand and South Africa, distance and mobility are important themes in the conceptualisation of national identity. As distant colonial outposts, such concerns would inevitably impact on the way that these settler societies viewed themselves and their relationship with their British 'home'. The popular success of Geoffrey Blainey's *The Tyranny of Distance* as both an account of the impact of distance in Australian history and as a shorthand expression for it suggests that Australians remain anxious about their place in the world. David Conradson and Alan Latham similarly contend that migration from the former dominions to London, particularly of New Zealanders, must be understood within its historical context: 'The OE as a distinctive and recognisable style of mobility needs to be seen in the context of … broader cultural formations; it can reasonably be interpreted as a contemporary articulation of … long-standing practices of movement'.[21] For New Zealanders, notions of personal autonomy, resourcefulness and adventure associated with mobility have become key components of their national identity. '[D]ue in part to our isolation, we are *travellers*', assert Barbara Myers and Kerr Inkson; 'We do more travelling than anyone'.[22] The South African experience of mobility highlights the centrality of race – the opportunity to travel cannot be separated from it. Being white, notes Richard Dyer, functions as a 'passport of privilege'.[23]

Common cultural, historical and linguistic bonds have made the UK the primary destination for young Australians, New Zealanders and South Africans wanting to experience life abroad. While the practice of travelling to Britain to expand one's horizons has long been commonplace in Australia and New Zealand, South Africa's withdrawal from the Commonwealth in 1961 effectively denied ready access to life in Britain. This changed in 1994 when South Africa returned to the Commonwealth. Strong familial and ethnic connections in each country reinforce Britain's popularity. In addition to working-holiday visas, descendents of British migrants can obtain ancestral visas, while those whose ancestors came from other European Union states could also take advantage of ready access to the UK.

In an article that appeared in *LAM: London's Australasian Magazine* in Australia's bicentenary year, Susan Pfisterer outlined why she decided to set out for London:

> I wasn't satisfied with Sydney but I didn't expect London to make me feel any better. I was travelling to meet an obligation to myself. An immature attitude in a way. And after four years at university the prospect of a fulltime job with only four weeks holiday was terrifying … Finally it all became too boring and I bought my ticket to London. Choice of destination was simple. Where else in the world could I go with a one-way ticket and very little money?[24]

The letters accompanying Pfisterer's article similarly cited opportunities to see the world and to experience a different lifestyle as the main reasons for moving to London.[25]

Almost 20 years later, *TNT Magazine* identified a clear division between the traditional 'working class expats' and the professional 'upper class expats'. 'Are Australians in London a patriotic melting pot of snobs and yobs, split according to class?' it asked, before profiling two Australians at different ends of the spectrum.[26] While London's drawcards remained the same for both sides, the cost of living, strict visa regulations and the recent influx of non-professionals from Eastern Europe all made it harder for the non-professional working-holiday maker to live the lifestyle that previous generations had enjoyed. In contrast, professional Australians working in finance or law faced a market where demand exceeded supply. Moreover, they enjoy an admirable reputation. 'Professional Australians have the best reputation for hardworking values and the best reputation for attitude. They have a real can-do attitude', explained the head of a London-based recruitment agency.[27]

The importance that Australians and South Africans in the 1990s placed on the economic and professional advantages of moving to London does not appear to have been shared to the same degree by New Zealanders. For many New Zealanders, the financial benefits of the OE were more easily accessed by traversing the Tasman; Australian wages were higher, the cost of travel was lower, and no visa was required. It was the UK's access to the broader world that led the more adventurous New Zealanders to relocate themselves on the other side of the globe. In her survey on their return, Jacqueline Lidgard observes that unlike the New Zealanders travelling to Australia for their OE, those who moved to the UK were primarily motivated to travel.[28]

Standing as a gateway to Europe, North Africa, the Middle East and North America, the UK and especially London provide an ideal base for anyone hoping to see the world. London's status as a world city is no less appealing. Its buzz, opportunities and cosmopolitanism are all attractions that in themselves serve to distract most New Zealanders on their OE from focusing too heavily on their professional careers.[29] Conradson and Latham found that most New Zealanders on their OE 'tend' their career while in London rather than actively pursue it. For these migrants, the experiences gained from being overseas concern personal development rather than professional advancement.[30] Obviously, this emphasis on personal development was not shared by the smaller number of gold-collar migrants whose decision to leave New Zealand for London was primarily motivated by economic opportunities.[31]

Unlike their New Zealand counterparts, Australians and South Africans do not have ready access to a larger and more prosperous neighbour on their doorstep. While the United States might meet these criteria, visa requirements (though recently relaxed for Australians) serve as a barrier to any large-scale influx of these young immigrants. It is the UK, and specifically London, that offers them the most accessible opportunities for professional development. Travel, however, remains an important, albeit interconnected, factor; a London base effectively overcomes the tyranny of distance, while a job earning British pounds overcomes the financial barriers. This is not to say that Australians and South Africans do not consider their time abroad as an opportunity for personal development. Australian Dylan Nichols observes in a personal account that London functions as a 'finishing school' where 'people go ... to become more worldly; to gain an appreciation of what is around them and what is important to them'.[32] Personal development therefore remains an important component of the Australian and South African overseas sojourn but it does not appear to have the same dominant resonance as it does for New Zealanders on their OE.

(RE)CREATING ANOTHER HOME

Australians and New Zealanders arriving in the UK throughout the 1990s and 2000s had ready access to an established expatriate community that could offer them a helping hand and emotional support. It was not long before the new generation of South African migrants established their own community and support mechanisms. Although these communities are united by links to their respective homelands, they have nevertheless developed their own distinct culture – one that is not necessarily representative of their actual home. Recounting his first experience as an 'Aussie expat' in London, Nichols was perplexed by the paradoxes he encountered:

> my first night was spent at The Slug and Lettuce in Fulham where I was fed 'Snakebites' ... and was amazed at the number of Australians present and the constant stream of Australian pop music played ... It seemed to me like I was taking part in some 'Australian' demonstration that was being used to show aliens our way of life, which really wasn't accurate at all, but did somehow reflect the 'Australian in London' spirit my countrymen were trying to live up to. Apparently mine was not an isolated experience, as soon after I read about another expat who had been taken to an Aussie pub on his first night and he was introduced to the same ritual.[33]

Adherence to these rituals does not appear to be absolute. Speaking to *TNT Magazine*, Blake Penson, a technical architect, revealed that the changing demographic of the Australians in London has had an impact on the ways in which such rituals were performed:

> I don't try to be Aussie and walk around barefoot on the streets, pouring snakebites over my blue wife-beater singlet just to prove to people around me how Aussie I am ... I used to be like that when I first arrived, it's like the induction period of living in London where proceedings are kicked off in your nearest Walkabout [pub]. But over time you grow up, respect the country you're in and try to slot into society a little more.[34]

Nichols, an IT professional, likewise moved on from his initiation. When he returned to the Slug and Lettuce some three years later, it was still full of antipodeans – albeit of the Afrikaans-speaking variety.

In her examination of the sense of home among New Zealanders in London, Janine Wiles develops a useful means for understanding all three antipodean communities by arguing that these young immigrants 'do not simply arrive in London with an intact, static identity and they do not create a new set of migrant identities'.[35] Their identity is instead somewhere between the two. New Zealanders establish a new identity for themselves by plugging into an established set of networks linking the city's New Zealanders. Such networks and the discourse surrounding them help prescribe what it means to be a New Zealander (or Australian or South African) living in London. While the class division emerging in the Australian community might prescribe different images of the Australian in London, this process of identity formation nevertheless remains. Moreover, as Brad West observes, such rituals provide a means by which the uninitiated and the old hand are able to establish or reaffirm their connection.[36]

Formal organisations have traditionally provided an opportunity for Australians to socialise with their compatriots. The Britain-Australia Society has performed this function since 1971. Today's members tend to be over 40 and are a combination of British-based Australians and Britons who have an active interest in Australia. As the number of Australians in London expanded in the 1990s, the organisations and groups for Australians duly diversified. Established in 1990, the British Australian Rules Football League and the location of its six teams (North London Lions, Putney Magpies, Sussex Swans, Wandsworth Demons, West London Wildcats and Wimbledon Hawks) are illustrative of the number of Australians in Britain as well as the areas most populated by them. In addition to sporting clubs, they have established various professional clubs and associations.

While these bodies united Australians working in a specific sport or profession, more recent organisations serving London's Australians have become more diverse in their membership. Created by expatriates, Advance arrived in London in 2006 with the aim of establishing 'a dynamic and diverse global community of Australian professionals overseas committed to advancing Australia'.[37] Underscoring the increasingly professional status of Australians in contemporary London, Advance's London branch currently boasts 2100 members from a diverse range of professions. The development of New Zealand organisations closely follows the Australian pattern, whereby the number and diversity of organisations reflect the changing nature of the local New Zealand community. A similar pattern can be discerned in relation to South Africans, however the massive influx of migrants since 1994 has inevitably spawned professional and cultural organisations at an accelerated rate (including a South African Evangelical Church for English and Afrikaans-speaking South Africans).[38]

National days, such as Australia Day and Anzac Day, provide an opportunity for the broader Australian population in London to engage in a range of formal, semi-formal and casual events celebrating their Australian heritage. While the High Commission and the Britain-Australia Society organise formal Australia Day functions, a significantly larger number of the younger Australians celebrate their national day at various bars and clubs across the city. As Nichols notes, such events are a curious ritual that simultaneously links contemporary Australians to their predecessors and to their imagined homeland:

> Australia Day … is celebrated with perhaps more gusto by expatriates in London than it is in Australia … Far from being exclusive, the Australia Day celebrations are extremely inclusive with all non-Australians invited, although at their peril … decades-old pop songs … are replayed on Australia Day ad-nauseum [sic], which makes for a slightly unnerving time when added to incredibly drunk/homesick and boastful young Australians.[39]

Outwardly, Anzac Day is regarded as a more solemn occasion. The growing interest shown by young Australians during the 1990s was also reflected in the UK. In 1992, *TNT Magazine*'s coverage of the event amounted to a single paragraph outlining the ceremonial arrangements at Gallipoli. Only two sentences were devoted to the official events in London.[40] In terms of unofficial events, the magazine carried a full-page advertisement for an Anzac Party at the Hippodrome nightclub in Leicester Square, as well as a couple of smaller advertisements for events organised by specific pubs. By 1997, a significant change had occurred. *TNT Magazine*'s cover carried the headline 'the creators of the ANZAC legend were the men themselves'. Inside, it ran a two-page feature article on the Anzac spirit and a half-page article on the TNT Anzac Day Ball. Another half-page article discussed the events taking place across London:

> However, this weekend is the one time of the year when Antipodeans all over London stop in their tracks and drink to the heroic ANZAC troops who sadly lost their lives fighting for their country … From Acton to Willesden, Ealing to Earls Court, travellers and permanent residents raised a glass on one of the most moving days in the Antipodean calendar.[41]

Where these glasses were to be raised reveals the growing division among the city's Australians. TNT's Anzac Day Ball, for example, advertised itself as 'The most prestigious Australasian event in London's social calendar ... Champagne reception, wine, sumptuous food in luxurious surroundings, entertainment spanning four decades of music ... string quartet'; tickets began at £56. At the other end of the spectrum, the Walkabout advertised its 'TNT ANZAC DAY BASH'. For £3 punters were treated to '3 BANDS FROM 6PM', with expatriate Australian and BBC radio star Jonathan Coleman acting as the evening's MC.[42]

The traditional experience of the working-holiday maker was that informal links were the primary means to connect with compatriots in London. Informal links, of course, provide vital emotional support to all migrants, antipodean or otherwise. Such network patterns as those identified by Conradson and Latham among New Zealanders provide an insight into the broader antipodean experience. They found 'the remarkable centrality of *friendship* networks' to be distinctive among New Zealanders in London, and to have a significant impact on patterns of mobility.[43] Such networks, they argue, have a bearing on the decision to undertake the OE in the UK in the first place and affect subsequent decisions, including where to live, the 'must see' travel destinations and, ultimately, when to return to New Zealand. The strength of these friendship networks might also provide a partial explanation of why New Zealanders, proportionately to their home population, are more significant than their Australian and South African counterparts in London.

For those Australians, New Zealanders and South Africans who are homesick or want to socialise with 'their own', there are various antipodean-themed pubs that offer them a taste of home. The first Walkabout bar opened in London in 1994, just as the number of Australians arriving in the UK was taking off. Despite their Australian theme, this chain of bars features the motto, 'the awesome spirit of the Southern Hemisphere', indicating that it does not consider its clientele to be exclusively Australian. Indeed, the dispersal of Walkabouts across London and the rest of the UK demonstrates that most of their clients are British. The Walkabouts have been adopted by New Zealanders and, to a lesser degree, South Africans (who are also targeted by South African-themed bars).

In Janine Wiles's survey of New Zealanders in London, one respondent explained the appeal of the Walkabout: 'I quite like going to the New Zealand / Aussie pubs because I like the atmosphere. Everybody's there doing the same things you are and everybody's got something in common'. While various others were repelled by the hackneyed images of 'home' and the patrons' willingness to live up to stereotypes, Wiles observes that such venues perform an important role in cultivating identity in the city – whether it is the proud Kiwi living it up in Pommieland or the New Zealander whose rejection of this image illustrates his or her worldliness.[44] West's interviews with Australians in London's Walkabouts reveal a similar relationship, whereby 'young Australian working holidaymakers are typically critical of the projections of Australia in these places yet the venues can simultaneously prompt meaningful reflection upon their national identity'.[45] Presumably, a similar dichotomy informs the relationship that South Africans have with such venues.

The internet has further facilitated the connections between all antipodeans in London and the UK, those living elsewhere across the globe, and those who remain back at home. The gumtree.com website, for example, began as social place for Australians to locate accommodation, work, and other necessities for living in London – it has since become a key portal for all migrants in the capital. In terms of linking Australians with home, newspapers and radio stations are accessible online, while YouTube enables expatriates to watch recent Australian television clips. In addition to the old telephone, sojourners are able to make contact with friends at home via email, Skype, and social networking sites such as Facebook and MySpace. In short, the developments in communication technology since the 1990s have meant that the recent generation of travellers are less isolated than their forebears.[46] Australians in London can remain up to date with the latest developments at home – from national politics to family gossip.

The communications revolution has caused a significant recasting by newspapers aimed at London's antipodean communities. Although such publications as *TNT Magazine*, *In London* and the *Australian Times* continue to publish news stories and sporting results from Australia, their feature articles are aimed at local readers and help to reinforce a sense of what it is to be an Australian in London (subject, of course, to the demography of their particular audience). Significantly, they simultaneously seek to cultivate an image of the Antipodean in London – in order to maximise their niche readerships. *TNT Magazine* and *In London* are also aimed at New Zealanders and South Africans, while the *Australian Times* differs from its stable mates, the *New Zealand Times* and the *South African*, only in terms of news stories from home and sporting results.[47]

While these publications are homogenising their respective audiences, the internet is being used by various organisations and individuals to ensure that global Australians do not become too globalised and therefore lost to home. The Southern Cross Group, for example, was founded in 2000 in Brussels by a group of Australians who felt that there was 'a need for an advocacy organisation which could actively focus on and work for changes to law and policy that negatively impacted or disadvantaged those in the Diaspora'.[48] The New Zealand Edge website performs a similar function for New Zealand's international diaspora.[49] Wiles suggests that such sites are both a reaction to fears of the 'brain drain' and a deliberate articulation of an idea of community among a disparate group of New Zealanders (and Australians).[50] Similar websites link South Africa's diasporas with home. However, these appear to lack the popularity of the Homecoming Revolution website, which is a fundamentally different response to the nation's brain drain. Rather than encouraging expatriates to remain connected with their homeland, the website actively encourages South Africans abroad to return home.

RETURNING HOME

Sooner or later, the decision as to whether or not to return confronts each Australian. For some, the decision is straightforward: an expired visa, frustration with London, and the desire to return to friends have triggered it. Graeme Hugo found that some 90 per cent of his respondents had returned because of lifestyle while 76 per cent had cited family. Various others remain less sure – at least in the short term. Many of the young professionals who emigrated to the UK to advance their careers face an unclear future. Hugo's findings indicate that only 15 per cent of Australians returned for work-related reasons, suggesting that many in the new generation of professional migrants are likely to stay abroad longer.[51] This is not to say that they will necessarily remain in London. For many, the return trip home might well consist of working in their company's branches in New York, Hong Kong or Singapore. In his contribution to a collection of stories by expatriate Australians, management consultant Robert Miller expresses such uncertainties in a conversation with a fellow Australian:

> 'It's frightening how fast it goes. The time I mean,' I said to her.
>
> 'I know. A lot of my friends say that the longer you stay, the more stressful the whole idea of going home is'.
>
> 'I can believe it. Even though it's only been three years for me, it makes you think how long you will actually stay. I want to have some kind of plan for the future. Right now I want to buy a place, but it's hard to know where to buy when you have no idea where you will be in two years'.[52]

This last point is pertinent. While the average stay for Australians in the UK is currently estimated to be 2.2 years, research reveals that age has a negative correlation with return.[53]

New Zealanders and South Africans display marked differences to the Australian pattern. While Richard Bedford and Jacqueline Lidgard have argued that New Zealand's immigration and emigration statistics do not point to the crisis that many New Zealanders have claimed, they note that there remains a real concern about the slow rate at which New Zealanders are returning home.[54] The primary concern is with Australia, as Britain's visa regulations effectively limit the time that young New Zealanders spend in the UK. The authors of the *New Zealand Talent Initiative* survey thus observe: 'New Zealand is losing people across all skill levels at an ever-increasing rate, much of it to Australia. Of most concern, is the accelerating loss of highly skilled people'.[55] Concerns about the brain drain have been more strident in South Africa, whose talented young people are much less likely to return than are Australians or New Zealanders.

The situation of Australians who have returned from an extended period overseas remains under-examined. Here again, research on the New Zealand experience can be used, and it reveals that homecoming is a mixed experience. Many individuals return to the city or region they left, underscoring the emotional pull of family and friends. They often take up work in a similar field and not infrequently with the same company (often in an elevated position). Others draw on their OE to begin a new career or to undertake further study.[56] However, the return home can prove to be a difficult period. Individuals who had been pushed home by visa regulations are often frustrated by being forced to give up the hectic, globe-trotting lifestyle that they had enjoyed in London.[57] For others, disillusionment sets in when it becomes apparent that the idealised image of home that they had patriotically clung to while overseas has failed to materialise.[58] A bout of unemployment similarly punctures such dreams, as does the realisation that friends no longer share the same interests or outlook on life.[59] In an online forum discussing Australians abroad, one person revealed that:

> I found Employers did not understand what I do. Revenue Assurance is not well known in Australia which is 10 years behind Europe in some business practices. I also found that Medicare designated me a non-person until I could prove I intended to stay in Australia. I was told conflicting answers from 3 different employees. Without this 'proof' I had to wait 6 months for access to the system – whilst my private fund for some reason was happy to cover me

from the date of return. No consistency. Makes you wonder at times why return?[60]

Unable to remain at home or abroad, many become 'boomerang' migrants, continually travelling between their two worlds. As the job market becomes increasingly globalised, it is likely that the number of professional Australians falling into this category will continue to grow.

At the beginning of the twenty-first century, young Australians continue to respond to London's call. Given that they are likely to be republicans and grew up in an Australia that embraced multiculturalism, the appeal of London seems almost anachronistic. Yet the number of Australians heading to the British capital has grown rather than declined. The appeal of London has also evolved, and its primary lure is now more likely to be financial than cultural. Moving to London, then, has increasingly become a career decision rather than the fulfilment of a cultural rite. This shift has been influenced by developments in the global job market as well as alterations to British visa regulations. London has opened its door to young professionals while making it harder for non-professionals to remain, and while non-professional Australians have been disadvantaged by these changes, their professional compatriots have profited handsomely. It remains to be seen whether this emphasis on professionals will alter the gender ratio of Australians migrating to the UK.

As Australians in London have become more professional, their actions and attitudes have also changed. Despite the ongoing popularity of the city's west, an increasing number have moved out into other areas in order to escape the Kangaroo Valley ghetto. Formal and informal networks ensure that their connections with fellow Australians are not entirely lost, and these networks are indicative of a new Australian Londoner – evident in an ambiguous attitude towards the Walkabout pubs and the socio-economic stratification of Anzac Day ceremonies. These trends have prompted the Fairfax press's European correspondent, James Button, to comment that this new generation of Australians is 'a far cry from the "Bazza McKenzie" and backpacking image of Australians in London'.[61] Pronouncements of backpacking Bazza's death might, however, be somewhat premature. While community rituals may not be practised with the same gusto as before, the new generation of Australian Londoners nevertheless maintains them. Hyper-Australianness still flourishes on national days and at the Walkabout, while travel remains an integral part of the London experience (even if it is to more exotic or exclusive destinations). It seems that Bazza isn't dead; he's just become middle class.

ENDNOTES

1. *Age*, 20 February 1993, Saturday Extra, 3.
2. *Age*, 23 May 1993, 13.
3. *Sydney Magazine*, 24 November 2004, p. 64.
4. Alomes, 1999; Britain, 1997; Woollacott, 2001.
5. Bell, 2002, 44–45.
6. Millbank, 2000.
7. UK Trade and Investment. 2008. 'Facts and Stats'.

8. See Fullilove and Flutter, 2004,15; 'Southern Cross Group. 2008. 'Estimated Number of Australians Living Overseas'; Graeme Hugo's chapter in this volume.
9. Walrond, 2007.
10. 'Home, Sweet Home – For Some', *The Economist*, 11 August 2005. [Internet]. Accesed 10 March 2008. Available from: <http://www.economist.com/world/africa/displayStory.cfm?story_id=4277319>
11. *Sydney Morning Herald*, 18 March 2000, employment section, 1.
12. Conradson and Latham, 2007, 251–252.
13. In November 2008 the working-holiday scheme was restricted to those Commonwealth countries with reciprocal schemes. Unlike Australia and New Zealand, South Africa did not initiate a reciprocal scheme and young South Africans are no longer eligible for this visa.
14. Dobson, Koser, Mclauchlan and Salt, 2001, 249.
15. *Age*, 30 September 2005, 1.
16. Wiles, 2008, 120.
17. Inkson and Myers, 2003, 174.
18. Bell, 2002, 155.
19. *Sydney Morning Herald*, 13 July 2007, 15.
20. Warner-Smith, 2005, 66.
21. Conradson and Latham, 2005a, 299.
22. Myers and Inkson, 2003, 3.
23. Dyer, 1997, 44.
24. *LAM: London's Australasian Magazine*, no. 500, 19 March 1988, 31.
25. *LAM: London's Australasian Magazine*, no. 500, 19 March 1988, 31.
26. *TNT Magazine*, no. 1252, 28 August 2007, 12.
27. *Sydney Morning Herald*, 18 March 2000, employment section, p. 1.
28. Lidgard, 1994, 8.
29. Conradson and Latham, 2007, 237.
30. Conradson and Latham, 2007, 234.
31. Conradson and Latham, 2005b, 166.
32. Nichols, 2007, 190.
33. Nichols, 2007, 144–5.
34. *TNT Magazine*, no. 1252, 28 August 2007, 13.
35. Wiles, 2008, 117.
36. West, 2006, 147.
37. Advance, 2008, 'What is Advance?'.
38. Die Suid-Afrikaanse Evangeliese Kerk, 2008.
39. Nichols, 2007, 156.
40. *TNT Magazine*, no. 451, 20 April 1992, 5, 23.
41. *TNT Magazine*, no. 712, 21 April 1997, 11.
42. *TNT Magazine*, no. 712, 21 April 1997, 10, 29.
43. Conradson and Latham, 2005a, 294.

44 Wiles, 2008, 125, 126.
45 West, 2006, 142.
46 Markwell and Stolk, 2005, 88.
47 The *South African* newspaper should not be confused with the now defunct *SA Times* newspaper, which had a different publisher.
48 Southern Cross Group, 2008, 'Who we are'.
49 New Zealand Edge, 2008, 'About'.
50 Wiles, 2008, 126.
51 See Graeme Hugo's chapter in this volume.
52 Miller, 2003, 146.
53 Fullilove and Flutter, 2004, 20.
54 Bedford, 2002, 311; Lidgard, 2002, 326.
55 L.E.K. Consulting, 2001, 19.
56 Myers and Inkson, 2003, 7; Walter, 2008.
57 Hotton, 2006.
58 Wiles, 2008, 134.
59 Hotton, 2006.
60 Radar, 2005, Comment posted by J to 'Do you cringe when you run into Aussies abroad? Or is it a relief to hear a familiar accent'.
61 *Age*, 30 September 2005, 1.

PRIMARY SOURCES

Advance. 2008. 'What Is Advance?' [Internet]. Accessed 12 March 2008. Available from: http://www.advance.org/en/cms/?16.

Age (Melbourne), 1993, 2005.

Die Suid-Afrikaanse Evangeliese Kerk. 2008. 'Die Suid-Afrikaanse Evangeliese Kerk'. [Internet]. Accessed 12 March 2008. Available from: http://www.saek.org.uk/saek/index.php.

Economist, 2005.

LAM: London's Australasian Magazine, 1988.

New Zealand Edge. 2008. 'About'. [Internet]. Accessed 14 January 2008. Available from: http://www.nzedge.com.

Radar Blog. 2005. Comment posted by J to 'Do You Cringe when You Run into Aussies Abroad? Or Is It a Relief to Hear a Familiar Accent'. 30 November 2005. Accessed 12 March 2008. Available from: http://blogs.smh.com.au/radar/archives/2005/11/post_37.html?page=fullpage.

Southern Cross Group. 2008. 'Estimated Number of Australians Living Overseas'. [Internet]. Accessed 10 March 2008. Available from: http://www.southern-cross-group.org/archives/Statistics/Numbers_of_Australians_Overseas_in_2000_by_Region_14_April_2001.pdf.

Southern Cross Group. 2008. 'Who we are'. [Internet]. Accessed 12 March 2008. Available from: http://www.southern-cross-group.org/general/whoarewe.html.

Sydney Magazine, 2004.

Sydney Morning Herald, 2000.
TNT Magazine, 2007.
UK Trade and Investment. 2008. 'Facts and Stats'. [Internet]. Accessed 10 March 2008. Available from: http://uktradeinvest.britaus.net/news/newsdefault.asp?id=298.

REFERENCES

Alomes, Stephen. 1999. *When London Calls: The Expatriation of Australian Creative Artists to Britain*. Cambridge: Cambridge University Press.

Bedford, Richard. 2002. '2001: Reflections on the spatial odysseys of New Zealanders'. In *2001 Geography a Spatial Odyssey: Proceedings of the Third Joint Conference of the New Zealand Geographical Society and the Institute of Australian Geographers*, edited by Holland, Peter; Stephenson, Fiona; Wearing, Alexander. New Zealand Geographical Society Conference Series No.21. Hamilton: New Zealand Geographical Society.

Bell, Claudia. 2002. 'The big "OE": Young New Zealand travellers as secular pilgrims'. *Tourist Studies* 2 (2): 143–158.

Britain, Ian. 1997. *Once an Australian: Journeys with Barry Humphries, Clive James, Germaine Greer and Robert Hughes*. Melbourne: Oxford University Press.

Conradson, David; Latham, Alan. 2005. 'Friendship, networks and transnationality in a world city: Antipodean transmigrants in London'. *Journal of Ethnic and Migration Studies* 31 (2): 287–305.

Conradson, David; Latham, Alan. 2005. 'Escalator London?: A case study of New Zealand tertiary educated migrants in a global city'. *Journal of Contemporary European Studies* 13 (2): 159–172.

Conradson, David; Latham, Alan. 2007. 'The affective possibilities of London: Antipodean transnationals and the overseas experience'. *Mobilities* 2 (2): 231–254.

Dobson, Janet; Koser, Khalid; Mclauchlan, Gail; Salt, John. 2001. *International Migration and the United Kingdom: Recent Patterns and Trends*. Research, Development and Statistics Directorate. Occasional Paper. No. 75.

Dyer, Richard. 1997. *White: Essays on Race and Culture*. London: Routledge.

Fullilove, Michael; Flutter, Chloe. 2004. *Diaspora: The World Wide Web of Australians*. Lowy Institute Paper. No. 4. Sydney: Lowy Institute for International Policy.

Hotton, Mark. 2006. 'Culture shock: The challenges of heading home'. 8 December 2006. Accessed 25 February 2008. Available from: http://www.nznewsuk.co.uk/news/?ID=4947.

Inkson, Kerr; Myers, Barbara. 2003. 'The big OE: Self-directed travel and career development'. *Career Development International* 8 (4): 170–181.

L.E.K. Consulting. 2001. *New Zealand Talent Initiative: Strategies for Building a Talented Nation*. Auckland, L.E.K. Consulting.

Lidgard, Jacqueline M. 1994. 'Return migration of New Zealanders: A profile of 1990 returnees'. *New Zealand Journal of Geography* (97): 3–13.

Jacqueline Lidgard. 2002. 'Time to celebrate international brain exchange: New Zealanders still come home'. In *2001 Geography a Spatial Odyssey: Proceedings of the Third Joint Conference of the New Zealand Geographical Society and the Institute of Australian Geographers*, edited by Holland, Peter; Stephenson, Fiona; Wearing, Alexander. New Zealand Geographical Society Conference Series No.21. Hamilton: New Zealand Geographical Society.

Markwell, Kevin; Stolk, Paul. 2005. 'Travelling the electronic superhighway: Independent travel and the internet'. In *Down the Road: Exploring Backpacker and Independent Travel*, edited by West, Brad. Perth: API Network.

Millbank, Adrienne. 2000. 'Dual Citizenship in Australia'. *Current Issues Brief* (5) 2000–2001. [Internet]. Accessed 10 March 2008. Available from: http://www.aph.gov.au/library/pubs/CIB/2000-01/01cib05.htm.

Miller, Robert. 2003. 'Just a while longer'. In *Australian Expats: Stories from Abroad*, edited by Havenhand Bryan; McGregor, Anne. Newcastle: Global Exchange.

Myers, Barbara; Inkson, Kerr. 2003. 'The big OE: How it works and what it can do for New Zealand'. *Business Review* 5 (1): 44–54.

Nichols, Dylan. 2007. *What Are You Doing Here? The Question of Australians in London*. Brighton, UK: Pen Press Publishers Ltd.

Walrond, Carl. 2007. 'Kiwis Overseas'. *Te Ara: The Encyclopedia of New Zealand*. Updated 21 September 2007. Accessed 18 February 2008. Available from: http://www.TeAra.govt.nz/NewZealanders/NewZealandPeoples/KiwisOverseas/en .

Walter, Naomi. 2006. 'Returning Home from the OE'. Paper presented at the Tourism & Hospitality Research Conference, University of Otago – December 2006. [Internet]. Accessed 18 February 2008. Available from: http://www.nzedge.com/features/repatriating_nz.htm.

Warner-Smith, Penny. 2005. 'Dollybirds of passage: The rise and rise of the independent woman traveller'. In *Down the Road: Exploring Backpacker and Independent Travel*, edited by West, Brad. Perth: API Network.

West, Brad. 2006. 'Consuming national themed environments abroad: Australian working holidaymakers and symbolic national identity in "Aussie" theme pubs'. *Tourist Studies* 6 (2): 139–155.

Wiles, Janine. 2008. 'Sense of home in a transnational social space: New Zealanders in London'. *Global Networks* 8 (1): 116–137.

Woollacott, Angela. 2001. *To Try Her Fortune in London: Australian Women, Colonialism and Modernity*. New York, Oxford: Oxford University Press.

Cite this chapter as: Crawford, Robert. 2009. 'Going "OS" for the "OE": Aussies, Kiwis, and Saffas in contemporary London'. *Australians in Britain: The Twentieth-Century Experience*, edited by Bridge, Carl; Crawford, Robert; Dunstan, David. Melbourne: Monash University ePress. pp. 16.1 to 16.18. DOI: 10.2104/ab090016.

Lightning Source UK Ltd.
Milton Keynes UK
UKHW051314030220
358072UK00004B/247